DEBBIE

DEBBIE

My Life

DEBBIE REYNOLDS

with David Patrick Columbia

SIDGWICK & JACKSON
LONDON

First published in Great Britain in 1989 by Sidgwick & Jackson Limited
1 Tavistock Chambers, Bloomsbury Way, London WC1A 2SG

First published in the United States of America in 1988 by William Morrow and Company, Inc.

Grateful acknowledgment is made for permission to use the following:

"All I Do Is Dream of You" by Nacio Herb Brown and Arthur Freed. © 1934, renewed 1962, Metro-Goldwyn-Mayer, Inc. Rights throughout the world controlled by Robbins Music Corp. Assigned to SBK Catalogue Partnership. All rights administered by SBK Robbins Catalogue, Inc. International copyright secured. Made in U.S.A. All rights reserved. Used by permission.
    "I Wanna Be Loved by You" by Herb Stothart, Harry Ruby, and Bert Kalmar. © 1928, Warner Bros. Inc. (renewed). All rights reserved. Used by permission.
    "Straighten Up and Fly Right" by Nat "King" Cole and Irving Mills. © 1944 by American Academy of Music, Inc. Copyright renewed. All rights reserved. Used by permission.

Grateful acknowledgment is made for the use of the following photographs:

Bernie Abramson: 38, 39 • AP/Wide World: 32, 43, 56 • Zinn Arthur: 40 • John Ascuaga's Nugget: 59 • Bob Beerman: 10 • Columbia Pictures Corporation: 55 • Nate Cutler: 67 • Desert Sea News Bureau: 21 • John Engstead: 45, 47, 53 • Hyman Fink: 14 • Friedman Abeles: 64 • Loew's: • 35 © 1956 Loew's Incorporated • 44 © 1959 Loew's Incorporated and Arcola Pictures Corp. • 12 © 1951 Loew's Incorporated • 17, 19 © 1952 Loew's Incorporated • Ren. 1979 Metro-Goldwyn-Mayer Inc. • 8 © 1950 Loew's Incorporated • Ren. 1977 Metro-Goldwyn-Mayer Inc. • 9 © 1950 Loew's Incorporated • Ren. 1977 Metro-Goldwyn-Mayer Inc. • Lou Jacobs, Jr.: 42 • Metro-Goldwyn-Mayer: • 49 © 1962 Metro-Goldwyn-Mayer Inc. and Cinerama, Inc. • 60 © 1966 Metro-Goldwyn-Mayer Inc. • 50, 51, 52 © 1964 Metro-Goldwyn-Mayer Inc. and Marteen Productions, Inc.: 13, 16, 18 • Sue Mueller: 61, 62 • G. B. Poletto: 41 • Phil Roach: 58 • Phil Stern: 24 • Universal: 36 Copyright © by Universal Pictures, A division of Universal City Studios, Inc. Courtesy of MCA Publishing rights, a Division of MCA Inc. • Warner Brothers: 6, 7, 54 • Will Weissberg: 43

ISBN 0 283 99829 6

Printed in Great Britain by Mackays of Chatham PLC
for Sidgwick & Jackson Limited

For Lillian Burns Sidney

My brilliant friend, mentor, and second mother without whose efforts and encouragement this book never would have been written

ACKNOWLEDGMENTS

I WISH TO THANK Solly Baiano, Phyllis Berkett, Margie Duncan, Camille Fielding, Curtis Harrington, Jeanette Johnson, Lori Nelson, Bill Orr, Rudy Render, Bob Sidney, and my mother, Maxene Reynolds, for the recollections and memories that assisted us in putting together this book.

I would also like to thank my editor, Lisa Drew, and my literary agent, Charles Hunt, for their constant enthusiasm for this project.

Throughout what has now become a long career, there have been many wonderful people who have been so helpful to me, giving so generously and lovingly of their time and their talents. Many are acknowledged within the following pages, including Jerry Wunderlich, Abe Marks, Sandy and Tex Avchen, and my former mother-in-law, the late Rose Karl, who taught me what the word *mitzvah*, "good deed," meant. One who is not mentioned but to whom I shall always be grateful for his friendship is Mr. Louis E. Wolfson.

I would like to thank my mother for her eternal patience with her headstrong daughter, and my brother, Bill, for his quiet strength and unquestioning loyalty throughout our lives.

I would also like to acknowledge my children, Todd and Carrie Fisher, who have always been a source of joy in my life, and who love me, try hard not to judge me, always support my many activities, and (thank God) have yet to ask me to cook them a meal.

DEBBIE

CHAPTER 1

FOR A MOVIE STAR, ultimately there really is no such thing as Hollywood. It's a name, and it's a map. It's not an industry. It's a very fickle business where you're here today and gone tomorrow. After one hell of a ride.

I was a child with a different destiny, at least different from the rest of the Reynoldses and the Harmans. When someone asks me if my dreams have been realized, I always answer yes. But it would be closer to the truth to say I started without any. Dreams I never dreamed were laid at my feet. A life in the Movies.

Mine is a reluctant talent. I have tremendous energy, tremendous stamina, and the ability to work very, very hard; that's how I see myself. Do as you're told and compete to win. That's me.

Fortunately, I was given a talent. I don't know how I got it; it certainly didn't run in the family.

When Sophie Rosenstein, the acting coach at Warner Brothers, told me back in 1948 that I had great potential as a "comedienne," I didn't even know what the word meant. I never looked at myself; I didn't know that was me. Life, however, presented others who did know. They pushed me out there in the right directions. Jack Warner; Lillian Burns Sidney, my acting coach at MGM; Louis B. Mayer, who created the greatest studio star system in the history of Hollywood. Even Gene Kelly, who pushed with a vengeance. They planted the seed; the world discovers you and then you become what they saw.

I never thought I was beautiful. I wasn't. Cute, yes; attractive, yes. I didn't think I was an ugly dog either. When my first husband left me for Elizabeth Taylor and I was feeling like a complete failure, I did have the sense to look in the mirror and think: "This is not a bag of bones." Besides, no woman living was as beautiful as Elizabeth.

Some people think I'm tough. They've written it and they've said it to my face. If a man's smart because he's a good businessman, then you can call me tough. You have to be—man or woman—in order to make

11

a living in show business year after year for forty years. Besides, I don't care so much about words anymore. I am thicker skinned than when I started. It's something you learn to be.

I was born on April Fool's Day, 1932, in El Paso, Texas. Maxene and Ray Reynolds's second kid. Daddy was twenty-six and Mother was twenty. My father wanted to name me Maxie Pearl, after my grandmothers. They'd named my brother, Billy, after his grandfathers William and Owen, so why not? Mother put her foot down, however. They fought for a week and finally came up with Mary Frances—Francis being my father's middle name and Mary the name of my mother's sister. Mother called me Mary or Frannie or Mary Frances, and most everyone else in the family called me Sis.

Texas 1932 was big oil, big ranches, and the Great Depression. They took me home from the hospital to two tiny rooms with a screened-in porch behind a filling station on a long, not very lovely boulevard of mostly boarded-up windows.

Just about everyone was broke, and people did anything to get food on the table. Our kitchen was a hot plate, and the bathroom where Mother bathed us (Billy came eighteen months before) was the station's rest room. That was a luxury. A lot of people didn't even have indoor plumbing.

My father was always in old clothes, gray or navy, blackened forever by the stains of oil and grease. Everybody smelled of it. Mother pumped gas and washed windshields. My father, who was a mechanic by trade, fixed the tires and the cars. All that for the combined astronomical salary of one dollar a day—and the "living" quarters, of course.

The dirt and the tumbleweed blew all day. Canvas flaps covering the windows and door shielded us from the wind and kept in the heat. We sweltered all night out there on top of the hill, in the company of the scorpions, the vinegaroons and the occasional rattlesnake. Vinegaroons, in case you don't know, are like tarantulas, except when you kill one it smells like vinegar. Things could have been worse, and eventually they were.

Business was so bad the gas station's owner had to let my parents go. Daddy got a job fixing broken-down houses for some enterprising landlord. In exchange, we got to live in each house until the place was ready for someone who had real money to pay. One place had no walls or ceilings when Daddy first went to work on it, and we lived in the cellar, which had a dirt floor.

Mother took in washing—which she did piece by piece with a bar of soap, a washboard, and a galvanized tub full of hot water she'd heated on the stove while Billy and I played in the mud around her feet. When she thinks back on those days, Mother recalls that we were "middle class," but one step lower and we would have been sleeping in the Rio Grande.

Then Daddy went to work for Mr. Roosevelt's WPA for a couple of dollars a day. This was prosperity. We moved into a little house on a dirt road called Magnolia Street. When it rained, the street became a river of mud, full of litter and broken bottles. The neighbors were all Mexicans except one black family, who had the best-kept-up place on the block.

My father was a good man, a man of few words, fair and honest, although not demonstrative. He never kissed me, but he also never beat me. He was quiet and rocklike, but gentle. Anything Daddy said went. However, I learned very early—by the time I was three or four years old—that I could usually get around my father by making him laugh. I'd jump up on his lap or tickle his knee; or make a face, or mimic somebody, or hug him. Sometimes if I diverted him enough I might even get away without doing what he asked.

From the WPA my father went back to his old job on the railroad. Several months later he was laid off again. No job, no food, no roof. We moved in with my mother's family, Grandma and Grandpa Harman and their four boys on Wyoming Street.

It was a small, white clapboard house with a front porch. A front porch to me meant moving up in the world. Ten people shared one bathroom! That really bothered me, especially the boys' spraying all over the walls and the seat—something I always hated and was forever cleaning up.

It wasn't much but there was a backyard—dirt, no grass—surrounded by an old, unpainted picket fence that kept in the chickens. The next-door neighbor threw everything she didn't want out the back door—water, trash, garbage, everything. Every time you heard the bang and the clatter of her screen door flying open, you knew trash was being airmailed.

Living with the grandparents was physically uncomfortable. No one had any space or privacy, or their own bed. My mother, being the eldest child, had helped raise her brothers, so she was more like a mother to them than a sister. She got out of the house by marrying my father when she was only sixteen. But not very long after, she wound up back in the same house.

We were not unhappy, however. The family always sat down to eat together in the kitchen. Grandpa Harman said the prayer, or assigned somebody to do it. We ate mostly beans, rabbit that the men shot themselves, and enchiladas. On weekends we'd have eggs, fresh from the chickens in the backyard.

The chickens, which seemed about my size, used to chase me around, pecking at my legs. One day my grandmother came out and grabbed one, rescuing me. Or so I thought. Holding it up in the air, the poor, helpless bird clucking and glurking and gasping, Grandma wrung its neck. Quick and simple.

"*Grandma!!*" I cried. "What are you doin'?!"

Then this little woman, just four feet ten, as placid as can be, took a hatchet in her other hand, placed the chicken on a tree stump, and POW! with one chop, its head flew off. I jumped a mile in shock, my stomach turned over. I threw up and flew into the house.

It was a quiet world out there after the sun went down. There was no radio; and no movies. They were forbidden. There was no bedtime storytelling or reading.

The big thing in the Harman family was church. They were Baptist Nazarenes, about as fundamentalist as you could get in south Texas. Grandpa, besides being a railroad man, was a lay preacher. He went around visiting the neighbors, reading the Bible and preaching the tenets. There were a lot of rules. Besides the "Thou Shalt Nots" of the Ten Commandments, for the Nazarenes there were also: no drinking, no smoking, no partying, no gambling, no movies, and no dancing. No nothing.

Once when Mother was fourteen, without telling her parents, she entered a Charleston contest and won. She never said a word about it afterward, but it was written up in the local newspaper and Grandma Harman saw it. Those dancing legs were given a harsh and painful walloping.

We were never out of church. On Wednesday night there was prayer meeting, prayer suppers on Fridays, and something else on Saturday. You spent God's day in church. I loved going because it was like a party—large groups of people. Jesus was Christmas and Christmas was church. We had no lights, no tree, and never enough money for presents anyway.

My grandfather made life fun for me. I was born on his fortieth birthday and I was adored. He was a very strong man, very handsome, wide in the shoulders, with a big predominant nose, and very loving. He had wonderfully large hands and fingers that I used to hold on to all the time. He would embrace me and make me feel very warm and sheltered.

My grandma made me feel the same way. She was very plump. I could never get my arms about her but her bosom and girth were so warm and marvelous. They were both very affectionate. My mother hugged a lot but Daddy never did. Grandpa insisted; he loved it.

When he came home from work, he'd set me on his lap and tell stories. Not a man of travel or booklearning, mostly he told me about his day, or the disciples and Jesus. On Sunday he'd take me to church with him. We'd walk down the aisle together to put pennies in the basket while the whole congregation watched—this tiny little girl so proud to be at his side. Sometimes he'd place me up on the altar and I'd sing a little song he'd taught me.

> "This little light of mine;
> I'm gonna let it shine;
> Let it shine, let it shine, let it shine."

I'd have my grandpa, my grandma, my mother, and half the church in tears; such a darling child! My first audience. I loved it!

Mother was also big on revival meetings and the evangelists who were always traveling through El Paso. They were something right out of *Elmer Gantry*, although I don't recall any of the preachers looking as good as Burt Lancaster. She went to every meeting, or so it seemed. From the time I was able to walk, I had to go too. They pitched big circus tents with the sides strung up, filled with wooden benches and with sawdust on the floor.

Some man in his shirt sleeves would stand up on a platform raving, waving his arms, screaming and yelling that everyone was going to hell and damnation. It all meant you'd die and go to hell—a place where people burned forever! That scared me to death.

When they were finished with the hellfire shouting, and had everyone jumping out of their skins with fear, they'd have some music and ask for money. The music wasn't wonderful, but it was a relief.

I didn't realize until I was much older that for Mother it was her only escape from a life of struggle and drudgery. Despite all the taboos that were part of the religion, at least it provided a social life.

My father wasn't much help either. He went to church until the preacher told him he couldn't play baseball on Sunday because it was God's day.

This was a problem because Daddy *loved* baseball. It was his only escape. He was also a great player. You had to practically kill him to beat him. Other players would cleat him and even sometimes take out knives, threatening to fight. No way was he going to give any of that up. So he cut out the churchgoing. He never discussed it again. My brother never had to go either because he played baseball too.

CHAPTER 2

THOSE EARLY YEARS in Texas, it was just me and the boys. But I myself, as a girl, was very much an outsider. I was, in my mind, definitely different. Billy could stay home on Sunday, read the comics, and be with Daddy and the boys. Frannie had to be with Mommy. I always resented that. Why couldn't I be a boy too? Maybe Daddy would like me better. He never gave me the time he gave Billy.

It seemed to me that I was always very small.

Everyone and everything seemed bigger, like the rolling tumbleweed always chasing me down in the wind. I'd keep trying to jump over it but a strong gust would roll it up behind me, its sharp bare briars pricking my legs.

I was a friendly child, but alone, without playmates. The boys always excluded me because I was the girl. Why? I wanted to know, chasing after them, constantly punching, and vying to belong.

I did everything in my power to overcome their prejudice. In my mind I was a boy. I wore the boys' hand-me-downs, pants, shoes; everything. I was tough. I could run fast. I could do anything they could do. Except be a boy. It didn't seem fair.

If they paid any attention to me, it was as a pack, always running after me. Eight boys: my brother, a little more than a year older than I; an uncle a year younger; my uncle Wally who was two years older than my brother; another uncle two years older than he; and another two years older than that; plus three cousins—ages seven through eleven—and me the five-year-old, tiny really, constantly faced off against the big guys.

They'd trip me, push me, twist my arms, pull my legs, pull my hair, jump on me—anything to get rid of me. Once they dug a hole and started to bury me. My uncle Owen had the presence of mind to pull me out before I was completely covered.

I never said a word about it to anyone. My mother never knew. I didn't want to be any more ostracized than I was. I did have a temper from an early age and that helped me to survive the boys. Whenever I'd had enough of them, I would wait for the moment—even if it took two weeks—when Grandpa Harman was around, and then I'd retaliate. I'd push one of them, or trip him, or pull his hair, or slam him in the back of the head with a two-by-four, if it was available (and I could lift it). Then I'd run right over to Grandpa's loving arms. Grandpa would never let *anyone* lay a hand on me.

The boys would never complain for fear I'd tell on them. They'd just wait and get back at me later when no one was around. It was a no-win situation for me.

I swore like crazy. Cussing we called it. Uncle Owen taught me every word he had learned in the Coast Guard. One day my mother was having a group of the church ladies over for a quilting bee. My uncle had just spent two hours on the back porch instructing me. When he finished, I marched into the living room with the ladies sitting all around and very innocently said: "Goddamnit, Mommy, some-a-bitch and shit." Mother almost passed out, while my uncle stood outside under the window nearly apoplectic from laughter.

There were no little girls but only boys in the neighborhood, besides those in my own family. One afternoon, passing a neighbor's garage, I heard some boys inside giggling. I peeked through the doorway but couldn't see anything.

"Hey, Frannie!" one of them called. I pushed the big, squeaky door open enough to squeeze through. It was suddenly quiet as if no one were there. I couldn't see anyone.

Giggles. "Fran-neeee!"

"Where are you?"

More giggles. "Oh, Fran-neee!"

I was giggling too. My curiosity led me toward the dark, and BOO! out they jumped, two boys twice my size, attacking me, tickling me around my waist and under my arms, their hands on my legs, tugging at my dress.

I screeched and jumped back, striking out at them. At first I thought it was a joke—two boys trying to wrestle me. Until I was cornered.

"What're you doin' here, Frannie?" one of them asked menacingly.

"You called me," I answered.

"I didn't call nobody," the other boy said. "You call Frannie?" he asked his friend.

"Uh-uh, not me," said the first boy.

"Your ma know where you are, Frannie?" the other boy asked, as if I had done something wrong.

"No."

"You wanna play a game, Frannie?"

"Yes," I answered hesitantly, a little uneasy at the sound of his question.

Then he grabbed the hem of my dress and tried to pull it over my head. I screamed in defiance.

"You wanna take off your dress, Frannie? Come on, we're gonna help her take her dress off."

The two of them started pulling at it. I kicked and thrashed and yelled at them to stop, my tiny fists punching when I could get a hand free. Before I knew it I was on the ground underneath the two boys, screaming my lungs out, kicking and squirming.

"HEY, WHAT'S GOING ON HERE?!" It was my brother's voice. The boys jumped up as if struck by lightning.

"Frannie was pickin' a fight," one of them said, moving carefully toward the garage door until he disappeared down the alley.

Billy looked at me as if I was hopeless.

"Com'on," he said, exasperated and disgusted, "get up and get on home."

Billy dragged me back to the house, covered with dirt as I was, shaking and frightened. Something was wrong but I didn't know what it was. Furthermore, my brother wasn't mad at the boys. He was mad at me, as if the whole thing had been my fault.

Sometimes my solitary explorations had their rewards. Up the street from us in an adobe cottage lived an old Indian lady who wore her gray hair in a long braid. She was exotic and unusual, an adventure to visit. I'd just go knock on the door, and she'd invite me in.

"Come in, Mary Frances," she'd say, and I would. "And have a cookie?" And I would. Then she'd go into her closet. Standing on a chair to reach the top shelf, she'd bring down a neatly stacked pile of Indian shawls. She'd unfold each piece carefully and hold it up for me to admire and touch. Then she'd pick out several for me to try on; to feel what it was like to be a real Indian woman. It was my idea of an Indian ritual and I loved it.

I don't think my mother ever knew of my visits to the Indian lady, just as she never knew about most of my daily travels. I was a little girl in a neighborhood. I was six. Everybody knew who everybody was, but they didn't always know what everybody was doing.

Two teenage boys lived next door to the Indian lady. One day the two boys, driving a car, stopped and asked if I wanted to go for a ride. Are you kidding?! Go for a drive in a car? I gladly got in.

We were riding along and the boy not driving asked me if I wanted a piece of gum. Gum *too*?! Gum was a big treat, second only to riding in a car.

I took the piece of gum and began to chew. Then the boy said that he would hold my gum for me for a minute because he wanted me to "kiss *this*." "This" was a tall thing sticking up out of his pants. I'm sure, as a child, I'd seen my brother and even my uncles without clothes, but "this" was something I'd never seen before.

"Here," he said, "lick it."

I looked at it for a minute, probably wondering why anyone would want to lick that.

"Go ahead, Frannie, lick it. It won't hurt. You'll like it."

So I did. He told me to.

They drove me around for awhile and then took me home. When I got out of the car, he gave me my gum back. I was never frightened. I didn't even think enough of it to tell my mother.

A few months later I overheard my mother talking with a friend about a little girl from a couple streets over who had disappeared. She was about my age. When they finally found her, she had been taken to Juarez by an older boy. The boy's father found them. He was so angry with his son, he took him out to the desert, castrated him, and left him to die. "The law will never fix you, but I will," he was supposed to have said to his boy.

I didn't know what my mother was talking about, obviously, but I knew the boy. He was the same one I'd gone with for a ride in the car.

"Oh, Mommy, that's the boy who had me kiss his thing," I volunteered.

"He had you WHAT, Mary Frances?!" I could tell from her face something was wrong. I told her what had happened in the car that day.

Mother became hysterical. Something about my story was Very Bad, the kind of bad those preachers in the tents yelled about. *He* was the bad one, the boy; not me. But why, I never knew. It was just bad, very very bad. Bad enough that the boy had been left to die—and burn in hell forever.

My mother is a very emotional woman. She can keep much of it to herself for long stretches. She didn't spank me on a regular basis, for example. But when she did, it was sudden and unexpected.

Often I would anger my mother without meaning to. One day I was in the bedroom with her when from out of nowhere she hit me so hard I was knocked across the room and against the wall. I remember being on the floor looking up at her, wondering what I had done.

Mother always said she thought I had the energy of twins. She felt I got out of control. I was precocious in that I picked things up quickly and would say what I felt. I was always the clown. It must have seemed relentless to her at times.

I was obedient, but also the kind of kid who would react if I felt she was unjustified. She still tells the story of one day when she didn't want me playing with the boys. I thought she was unfair and let her know. She was so outraged by my reaction that she locked me in her closet. A few minutes later she heard me calling for a glass of water.

"Whatta you want a glass of water for?" she wanted to know.

"Because I've spit on your dresses, I've spit on your coat, I've spit on your shoes; and I've run out of spit!!"

Now that, she thought, was very funny.

I'm sure it was one of those times when she felt she couldn't take any more of me. After all, she was almost a baby herself. At times she needed to strike out at that feeling of not being able to cope, and so I caught it. I was too much then and I'm too much now.

CHAPTER 3

By THE LATE 1930s the country was beginning to come out of the Depression. The railroad offered Daddy a steady job as a carpenter if he wanted to transfer west. A lot more work was opening up in California. There was nothing in Texas so he took it.

The pay wasn't much, at least not enough to take a family along. My mother, my brother, and I stayed behind for almost a year with Grandma and Grandpa.

In order to send money home to us and feed himself, Daddy slept every night in MacArthur Park in downtown Los Angeles, his only clothes the ones on his back. Every night he'd place his one blanket under a tree or on a bench and that was home. Finally he and Mother saved enough for us to move too. I am still in awe of his sacrifice, although I know for my daddy, there was never any question of what he had to do, or how he had to do it.

Mother, Billy, and I left Texas the day before Christmas in 1939. It was dismal, cold, and gray in El Paso. Grandpa and Grandma Harman took us to the station, where we were catching the Southern Pacific. For a child of seven, it was an exciting trip. The railroad had allotted us a boxcar to move our furniture. A boxcar is big enough to hold a houseful and we had hardly a roomful, so there was enough space for our old Model A Ford. Everybody hugged and kissed good-bye. Grandma cried and Mother cried and we were off.

Daddy was waiting for us at the station in Alhambra. We stepped out of that tired, musty railroad car into a fantastic sunny California afternoon. Right away the dry air felt so different. The sky was blue and crystal clear. It was the first time in my life I noticed the color of everything around me. I could smell the perfume of flowers. It was like Dorothy landing in Oz, like nothing I could have ever imagined.

Daddy had got us rooms in a motel until he could find us a house. There were not a lot of places available for a young family on our budget. Daddy went around to dozens of places. Nobody wanted kids. Finally, he found one in the hills south of Glendale. As usual, the landlady asked if he had kids.

"Yep," he replied, "boy and a girl. Ages seven and nine."

"Well, whatta you going to do about them?" she wanted to know, implying that she didn't allow children.

"I'm gonna take 'em out and drown 'em in the Los Angeles River tonight and come back tomorrow." That was my father—ask a silly question and just wait. She must have had the same sense of humor: We moved in the next day.

After more than a year, Daddy had saved enough to buy a lot for a house. Every Sunday we'd get into the Model A and drive all over Los Angeles looking.

My parents finally found what they were looking for in the San Fernando Valley: 1034 Evergreen in Burbank. There were four other houses on the street. At the end of the block were a grocery store and a drugstore. That was the neighborhood. There were more stores up the hill in downtown Burbank, but you had to take two buses to get there.

The Warner Brothers Studios were only a couple of blocks away, although I had no idea what movie studios were. I had never seen a movie in my life. Movies, according to the Church of the Nazarene, were for sinners only.

The Valley in those days was one great big expanse of mainly unoccupied land. It was surrounded by majestic mountains, snowcapped and green in the winter and spring, purple and brown in the summer and autumn. The air was thick with the fragrance of orange and grapefruit blossoms. It was like paradise. There were farms—many of which were owned by Japanese-Americans and referred to as Japanese farms—walnut groves and citrus groves, ranches, horses, and empty land. After that was desert; sand. It was incredible.

But then everything was all so much nicer than El Paso. There were cleaner, prettier avenues with beautiful flowers and shrubbery. In nearby Toluca Lake, where Bob Hope and Bing Crosby lived, were lovely big houses with perfectly manicured lawns. I had no idea people lived so luxuriously.

Daddy paid $250 for the lot on Evergreen. With a $4,000 loan from the FHA, my parents built a small, simple house with three bedrooms, a bathroom, a living room, and a kitchen. Daddy did all the finishing, including the wiring and the plumbing and of course the painting.

We had no furniture when we moved in, except for beds. On weekends, I'd go with my father, who loved junkyards, combing them for bits and pieces to furnish the house.

We never shopped in stores. We never had two of anything either. Flatware, plates, glasses, pots, pans, chairs—nothing matched. We took what we needed.

We actually had less than everybody else around us. I was aware of it. My mother was aware of it. But it was still more than we'd had before. We always had food. Now we had a house too.

The world had changed for me. I was aware that my girlfriends had nicer shoes and clothes, and more of them. In Texas nobody had anything. I had a shirt, a pair of pants, a skirt, and a pair of penny loafers from the Salvation Army. I went to school every day in a pair of pants and a shirt. Mother washed my things every night so that my clothes were always clean.

At Christmastime in Burbank, there was still no tree. Daddy would cut a piece off somebody's hedge and bring it home. The neighbor would come home and find a gaping hole in his shrubbery.

There were no gifts, because there was no money. Instead we made something. On my brother's birthday, Mother made him a lemon meringue pie. One birthday my mother gave me a can of black pitted olives. They were so special, such a delicacy. Every birthday and holiday I would write a poem for my parents about how much I loved them. We had each other.

The biggest thrill about our new home was having my own room. It had a door and it was mine. I could *close* it. It was a very small bedroom with a very tiny closet, maybe three feet wide.

We still had only one bathroom but this time for four people instead of ten. Whatever we had to go without, it didn't matter. In three short years my father had gone from being jobless to owning his own little castle and I was very proud of him. Coming to California had changed everything.

There was so much more food than I'd ever seen in Texas. The Concord grape farms were only a couple of blocks away. The workers would give my brother and me buckets of grapes and Mother would make jellies and jams. From another farm we'd get all the carrots we wanted. Our own backyard, once farmland too, had asparagus that grew wild by the bushel every year.

In El Paso my life had been bounded by the family. But in Burbank, it opened up to include the neighborhood. Suddenly there were lots of kids to play with, boys *and* girls. There was no TV of course; there was radio. We played outside in the yards and in the streets. People went bowling. That was a *huge* step!

On Sundays after church we went to North Hollywood Park for a picnic. That was our entertainment. We played baseball. The women would do their little chores—fix the food, clean up, sit around and talk and knit. Often they'd work on quilts, or little squares of embroidery. To this day, when I drive by parks, I'm reminded of those times.

The first time a friend drove us to the beach and I saw the ocean I was awestruck. I loved the beach. I loved swimming.

Daddy took us camping a lot. My brother and I joined the Scouting program. Billy could do everything including starting a fire by rubbing two sticks together. He won every award in the Boy Scouts, so I had to win every award in the Girl Scouts. I won forty-two out of one hundred Girl Scout merit badges. I really loved Scouting. I loved hiking. I loved the games. I could compete and win. I could excel. I could learn everything a boy could.

The year I finished the sixth grade I went to Girl Scout camp, Camp Condor, up in Taft. There was no money for me to go, so I sold Girl Scout cookies to earn it. You got a penny a box. I couldn't sell just a few boxes, I had to sell a bakery, more Girl Scout cookies than were ever sold by one person. Even then I couldn't really earn enough to pay the tuition, so my mother went as a counselor, for which she was paid thirty dollars and part of my fee.

The Girl Scout experience had a very positive effect on me: It taught me leadership, and I learned to love the out-of-doors. I met girlfriends from other schools.

I was the bugler at camp and every morning I'd get up and play reveille. I was also the entertainer. This was something that developed quite unconsciously.

When I was ten years old, my mother decided to let me go to the movies. All my friends went and I wanted to go too. As religious as Mother was, she realized that a movie on Saturday afternoons wasn't going to bring about my downfall and ruination. I loved musicals and comedies and their stars—Judy Garland, Fred Astaire, Gene Kelly, Betty Grable, June Haver, Betty Hutton. Garland was a great singer and actress, a wonderful everything. But Betty Hutton was it for me.

The first time I saw her I was no more than ten or eleven. It was in a picture where she sang a song, "My Rocking Horse Ran Away." She appeared on the screen, the music started, and with this tremendous energy she filled that dark movie house and tore the place apart. Just seeing her had this enormous freeing effect on me. I totally related. I could be that person, I'd think to myself. I could be her.

She was the girl who was not accepted. She was rowdy; the girl who was always chasing after the boys and could never catch them. Of course, at that time in my life I was chasing after the boys, catching them, and beating them up.

There would always be a scene in the movie where she'd sing a love song, soft and misty-eyed, with that smoky voice; the teenage tomboy becomes a woman. I wanted to be just like Betty Hutton. She had a personality. She was crazy and different. She didn't have a great voice like Garland or a figure like Grable or a face like Rita Hayworth. But that was part of it. I never thought of myself as actually being someone up on the screen. I was thinking more in terms of daily life. Betty Hutton was very, very funny. I got my way, I was accepted, by being funny. She was like everything I thought I could be.

From an early age, from the time I used to sit on my grandpa's knee, I was a mimic. No one else in the family did that. They laughed when I did, however, and I must have noticed. In Girl Scouts we always put on shows and Frannie always did impersonations. I used to copy Red Skelton. He did a bit about a lady driver in a too-tight girdle. He had a routine that he did on the radio and, then in the movie *Ziegfeld Follies*, called "Guzzler's Gin," where the announcer does a commercial for gin and accidentally gets drunk demonstrating the product. I learned every word of it. I'd practice at home in front of the mirror and then I'd perform it.

There was a comedienne, Beatrice Kay, known as the "Broadway Hillbilly," who did a routine to the song "I'm Only a Bird in a Gilded Cage." I got an old bird cage in some junkyard, cut the bottom out, painted it, put it over my head, strapped it to my chin, and wore a straitjacket. I'd do an entire routine, lip-synching to her record. I'd do an impression to a Spike Jones record. And of course, I'd do Betty Hutton.

People who knew me would ask me to do these little performances for other organizations like the Boy Scouts and Job's Daughters, or even just for a group of friends. I never thought of it as entertaining because I didn't dance or sing. I didn't think of myself a person who could dance or sing. I was just this nutty kid.

If you ever meet anybody who's a comic, they'll tell you they acted that way in school to be accepted. I was embarrassed by how I looked, that I had no clothes. When I was a teenager, the rage among the girls was cashmere sweaters. When I was cold, I wore the gray sweatshirt I'd bought at the Salvation Army for twelve cents; I'd embroidered "Frannie" on the front of it. Instead of cashmere, I wore a comic routine. I was being Betty Hutton. She was my mentor.

*   *   *

But meanwhile, when Frannie Reynolds, age eleven in Burbank, was not being Betty Hutton, she still wanted to play baseball with the boys. As usual, they didn't want me. This remained a very difficult matter for me to accept. I felt I should at least be allowed in the game. I was as good as any of them, if not better. But they just didn't want me around because I was a girl. Still. Yet. Thank God.

However, the girl was not only rejected, she was also taunted.

"Hey, Frannie, you can't get on the team!"

"Yes, I can."

"Oh, no, you ca-*ah*-n't. You can't be a part of the game."

"Yes, I can . . ."

"No, you can't," and then someone would give me a shove and that was that. Sock 'em, stomp 'em, grab their heads and bang 'em against the ground. I had to win somehow. I was the only girl like that. Everybody knew about it. Don't mess with Frannie. If you do, it's a fight. So the boys would do it on purpose. They'd stand together in a corner. One would say to another, "Go ahead, push her." And he would.

They couldn't believe it. One boy I had a fight with, Gene Post, to this day claims he's bald because I pulled his hair out in a fight. I won a lot of fights. I'm sure I lost some too. The battle was usually stopped by a teacher. Three guys would be pummeling me on the ground, and because I was so small, the teacher would worry about me.

"Okay, who started it?" the teacher would ask.

It was always one of the boys, but they'd never admit it. One of them teased me and I wouldn't take it.

I would also swear any boy under the table. I was sitting on the bench in the principal's office every other day. The bench was mine. "Where's Frannie?" In the principal's office. They'd call my mother down to the school.

"Did you know that Mary Frances swore?"

"Yes," she'd answer, "but what did they do to her?"

They'd usually start it. I'd always finish it. Sometimes I'm sure I started it. I must have wanted the attention. I wanted to be in a world that didn't accept me.

But the fights didn't help because obviously the boys got a charge out of seeing what this four-feet eight-inch, sixty-five-pound kid would do if provoked. One boy named Jimmy never let up. He was always teasing, picking on me.

One day he annoyed me so much I went home that afternoon and collected a jar full of worms. I had to get them one by one, out of the ground. One whole jar. You can imagine how long that takes. I didn't care; I had a plan.

The next day in school, I sought out my adversary. When I found him, I poured the jar of wet, squiggly worms all over him. I figured that should give him a couple of good nightmares. I was sent to the principal's office for that, of course.

Except for these skirmishes with the boys, my progress reports had only one complaint: "Talks too much."

It was the attention that I wanted; I knew that. I'd do anything to get a laugh. I never minded making a fool of myself. Once I climbed the school flagpole and wouldn't come down. Don't ask me why; I just did. Doing it was what was important to me. I played the French horn in the school band and of course had a band uniform. I bought it on time with money I'd earned myself. It was the best clothing I had. I'd wear it to school at least twice a week, walking through the hallways from class to class with my uniform hat on backward.

All of this "behavior" mortified my brother, who was the big baseball star in school and a very popular fellow.

"Is Frannie Reynolds your sister?" someone would ask.

"Uh-uh." Billy, like my father, is a man of few words.

"You sure she isn't your sister? She says she is."

"Uh-uh, I don't have a sister." It was too embarrassing for him.

One teacher who had no complaints was Miss Rutledge, my physical-education teacher. Florence Rutledge was tall and skinny, rawboned and serious. She was a positive and strong influence because she gave me time, time, time. My friend Jeanette Johnson and I loved sports. We were a pair and we had the real tiger instinct to win. Jeanette was tall and fast and I was short and faster. We'd play speedball and win every game. I could do anything gymnastically—the bar work, the rings; triple flips, back flips, and front flips.

I was captain of the basketball team. I was so small I could practically run under the players' legs to make it to the basket. I'd play so hard that I would faint at the end of the game. Turn purple and pass out so they'd have to revive me. But we won, so I didn't care. I only knew one way of approaching life even then: the need to win; to avoid defeat.

I knew that Miss Rutledge really cared about my progress. She encouraged me in every sport. I was finally accepted for what I was or what I could be: a great athlete.

Because of Miss Rutledge, I decided that I would one day become a gym teacher. I would go to college, get a degree, teach phys. ed., get a good job and be independent. I could do what I loved and help others. Someday a Miss Reynolds could instill confidence in a young child the way Miss Rutledge did in me.

CHAPTER 4

APPROACHING MY TEENAGE YEARS I still felt the boys had the better deal. They had freedom. They got to hitchhike. They got to stay out overnight. They got to do everything I wanted to do. Girls had to be home. Their mothers worried.

Girls were always told they were going to have "something" happen to them. It meant you were growing up to be a woman. Totally in the dark about all this, I'd think, I don't even want to be a girl; why do I want to be a woman?

I wasn't prepared for my menstrual period. I was eleven years old and at Girl Scout camp. I thought I was dying. I hated everything about it, which I'm sure every girl does. I hated it so much I never told my mother.

Although the area of sex and physical intimacy was completely avoided, Mother and I were very close as I was growing up. She would come into my bedroom every night, give me a hug and tuck me in. Just about everything I thought about I discussed with her, although I never told her if anything bothered me.

She would confide in me at times. Mother frequently felt lonely. My father worked all day and came home every night to his baseball games or his repair work in the garage. For years she'd ask him to take her to a square dance, or maybe a movie, but he never would. Never.

They had separate interests and she was stuck. I always felt so bad although there was nothing I could really do. I often felt her hurt when I saw my friends' parents do things together. Daddy couldn't have cared less. He loved her in his own way.

But that was the way he was. I loved him. But my mother was unhappy. I felt that I was all she had. When Eddie Fisher proposed, and I knew I was going to accept, the first thing I asked him was if my mother could move in with us if she wanted to. I was so afraid that she'd be miserably lonely with me gone from the house.

My mother and father were mismatched. Yet he could be contradictory. When they were first married, Mother had gotten a job in a department store in El Paso. Despite the hard times, and the scarcity of jobs, my father would take off from his to go see what Mother was doing in that store. He showed strong signs of jealousy.

Mother had a very full figure and beautiful legs. Men did look at her. My father didn't like that. He wanted her in the house and that was that. He provided the roof, the food, the bed and was as loyal and loving as he could express.

Mother thought that she was getting married to a friend. She thought marriage meant kissing and being with someone you loved. A reasonable expectation for a sixteen-year-old who knew *nothing* of sex. After their wedding, when my father presented her with, shall we say, a sexual moment, she almost fainted. He had to draw her a picture every day for three weeks about life and love and lovemaking.

So for her, life began rather traumatically in the matter of sexual knowledge.

I discovered as a very young child that there were two distinct sides to my parents' relationship. In the day-to-day, Mother was always the talkative, even outspoken one. Daddy said what he had to say and that was it. However, about once a month, after the lights went out and the house was quiet, there were disagreements. I became aware of it because my room was next to theirs.

I would be lying there in my bed, under the covers. All of a sudden, my mild-mannered father's voice would come like a jolt out of the darkness. The tone of his voice frightened me. Mother would say very little, but sometimes she would cry.

Their argument was always about "that thing." The issue was "making love." But why, I wondered in eternal confusion, were they fighting over "love"? What kind of "love"?

I was stuck in the middle of an argument and didn't know what the point was. I never would have asked. I never would have dared. I kept very still and listened, wishing they wouldn't fight; wishing that he wouldn't yell, that she wouldn't cry. I'd muffle my own tears with my pillow so that they would never know I heard.

I grew up thinking that sex and "making love" and "that thing" were all disgusting. It was obvious. The only lovemaking that I knew about was what I saw in the movies. Namely, kissing. Judy Garland kissing Gene Kelly. Van Johnson kissing June Allyson. It wasn't like today, where you go to a movie and you actually see pornography. If it had been, I wouldn't have been allowed to go.

My girlfriends knew as little as I did. No one I knew had sex—

intercourse, or even petting. No one. "Necking" was about as much as we got into discussing sex. We even had a group called the Non-Neckers Club. It was all a joke; nervous maybe, but safe.

Needless to say, I was very self-conscious about it. Sex? Necking? On a date? What *if* some boy tried to kiss me? What would I do? I could deck him, I knew that much.

When I was about thirteen I went to baby-sit one night for a couple who lived down the street and arrived a few minutes early. They were in their living room. The wife was sitting in her husband's lap kissing him, and he was fondling her breasts. I was shocked. I was fascinated. I had never seen such a thing. I had never seen my parents show physical affection with each other; I had never even heard my father *express* any affection. If I said, "I love you, Daddy," he'd say, "Ditto." I never heard him say the words "I love you" to another human being until I was fifty years old and he was seventy-seven. I had been talking to him on the phone and just as I was about to hang up, I said, "I love you, Daddy." He said, "I love you too." I almost dropped the phone. But when I was a child, we never got past "ditto."

I never understood, until I was much older, the complexities of their relationship. When she was a young woman, sex to my mother meant mainly—and logically—the risk of pregnancy. She had almost died giving birth to me. She was told she should never have another child.

Yet my mother adored my father, and he, in his way, adored her. That I never doubted. But underneath, the problem became a very tight, bitter memory of lost emotions never discussed.

With the coming of the Second World War, Burbank went from being a sleepy little town into a small city. The local Japanese-Americans were taken from their homes and farms and put in a concentration camp with barbed wire around it over in Griffith Park. Their houses and farms were taken from them. All of a sudden huge developments of tract houses were put up in their place, for all the new workers at Lockheed. People came from all over America to work and they stayed.

We had a blackout every night. All white light bulbs were replaced with yellow. Sheets and blankets covered the windows. We'd use candles and flashlights. Big troop caravans would go through the city. Huge spotlights would fill the sky searching for Japanese warplanes. At Lockheed Airport, they had a gauzelike material stretched over blocks and blocks of airfield. It was camouflage, we were told. We had to be ready because everyone thought we were going to be invaded. It was scary for a ten-year-old.

It was war. Over the radio we listened to President Roosevelt's talks. In school we had to learn the names of all the great world figures, like Winston Churchill. All the men who were eligible went off to fight. All the women went to work in the factories.

At school, in church, in the Scouts, we had paper drives. Papers, papers, papers. We collected bottles, got the deposits, and turned the money over to the War Relief. Mother worked for the Red Cross. My father was ineligible for active duty because all railroad workers were considered a necessity to national security. He worked long, extra hours.

Then they started bringing home the dead and burying them over on Sawtelle and Wilshire in Westwood. My mother lost Uncle Patrick in Saipan.

My brother was the star in the family. I was the second born. I was the girl. Therefore I was always number two. Billy was tutored and groomed to be a baseball star. When he was seventeen, four baseball clubs came to see him play in high-school games.

Frannie was just there. I was being raised, but not groomed. Any dreams and hopes that Daddy might have had were pinned to my brother. My father had a direction for his son. I was his daughter. Sis. Skinny. No talent. Cute and funny. That's all.

I accepted his attitude. My parents were always right. Yes, sir. Yes, ma'am. I believed it. I had every reason to: I couldn't get on the ball team and I wasn't good at anything a boy does. I didn't realize that I could be good at being a woman. It never occurred to me.

I was a joiner. I joined all the clubs. I played basketball, volleyball, baseball, and speedball. I belonged to the A Cappella Choir, besides the school band. I was a baton twirler and a cheerleader. I went out for all the dramatic-club plays but never got picked. I ended up backstage as the thunder or the lightning.

I didn't have a perception of myself. When I reached my teens, I wished that boys would like me and ask me out. Meanwhile, I was still tackling them, knocking them over, and throwing cusswords at them. Besides, I'd tell myself: If someone did ask me out, I couldn't go because I didn't have the clothes.

Nevertheless, I got attention and it certainly seems as if that was what I was after. Every year I'd win the contest in the school paper for Most Personality. Not the Most Popular or Most Beautiful. It was, I can see now, my way of competing with my brother.

I felt left out. I felt I deserved to have what the other girls had but I didn't know how to make things better. All I could do was make faces and do impressions. I could get the laughs. After the football games, everyone went over to Bob's Big Boy, where carhops in uniforms served Cokes, hamburgers, and french fries. A lot of girls had dates after the game at Bob's Big Boy. I was not one of those girls, although, being in the band, I went there on the bus, or with my girlfriends, Jeanette, Diane, and Barbara. There was one boy on the football team I really liked. His name was Marty Steele, and he was short and stocky with blond hair. The only way I could have had a date with Tex would have been for me to ask him. That was something nobody did. So I decided to give a big party after the game for the football boys at my house. Jeanette and I asked everyone.

Mother prepared a ham and made potato salad. Jeanette and I hurried back to the house right after the game. We were the first to get there. Everything was ready. Jeanette, my mother, and I sat and waited. And waited. After more than an hour, when nobody had shown up, I realized nobody was *going* to show up.

After Jeanette left, I went to my room, where I could close the door and cry by myself.

My mother would say to me: "Don't be one of the sheep; be the head of the flock. Be different." She would sympathize, yet she didn't seem to understand that I *was* different, oddly enough.

There was one football player who had sort of a liking for me. He took me out once to an early movie. During the picture, he put his arm around me and tried to hug me. I shoved him and smacked him in the face. That's not the way to get a favorable reputation with the boys. But anything physical frightened me.

My friend Leon Tyler and I used to go dancing every Friday night. We did everything: the lindy, the jitterbug, and the foxtrot. The two of us won a lot of contests. Leon taught me to touch dance. I didn't want to do anything where the two bodies got close.

"You can't dance if you won't dance close, Frannie," he finally said to me. "That's the point of the dance . . . to touch, to move together." He kept after me until I tried it. It was very difficult. I was just very nervous about being physically close. I would break out in a cold sweat. I felt very awkward and ill at ease. Learning to do it was a real breakthrough.

There was a tall, nice-looking boy a half year ahead of me, Jerry Odens, who asked to take me to a Scout Jamboree. I was almost sixteen. I said yes but when it came time to go, I was a wreck. We had to drive to the event. I was so nervous about being alone with him in the car that I could barely swallow. It also happened that I had to go to the bathroom. But I didn't want to say anything about it because *that* was too personal to talk about with a boy. By the time we arrived at the Jamboree, I was ready to burst.

We got out of the car and I said, very nonchalantly: "Oh, I wonder if there's a powder room nearby," which must have sounded odd considering we were out in the middle of the desert without a single permanent building to be seen for miles.

At the same event, a little later, I was dying of thirst, but I didn't dare tell Jerry. Somehow the idea of making reference to anything physical made me feel shy.

Everything I worried about was silly, but nothing is silly to a teenager. I worried that all men were going to be aggressive and I wouldn't know how to handle it. I knew I couldn't go through my life decking every man who came near me. But that was the only solution I knew. I didn't want *anything* to start. I didn't want to know about it. I didn't want to discuss it.

One afternoon Mother sat me down with the intention of telling me what a man looked like. I knew she was trying to tell me about sex and intercourse. But I had already heard about that from sitting on the other side of closed doors.

"So don't *ever*," she continued, "ever let a man get too close to you because it can make you pregnant. You can't ever have any kind of sexual activity. Not even petting. If a boy wants to kiss you, he can kiss you through the screen door. You want to make sure you're a virgin when you're married."

"Yes, ma'am."

Jerry Odens never made a move. He was simply sweet and dear, as if he understood my predicament. He was the first boy I ever felt safe with.

The great thing to me about being a teenager was that I could work and earn money. I baby-sat. Thirty-five cents an hour. One woman paid me fifty cents an hour because she had an infant and I had to do more. I'd clean houses, clean out garbage buckets. I washed cars and for a short while worked in Newberry's, blowing up balloons. I loved to paint fences and mow lawns. I would do anything. Anyone could make money if they wanted to be a laborer.

When I was fifteen, I'd saved up enough to buy a bathing suit. I decided I was going to have a really good one—a Jantzen.

When I told my parents one night at the dinner table that I was going to buy it, Daddy said, "No!"

"But why?" I asked, confused and disappointed.

"Because I can't afford to buy you a bathing suit. If you're going to live in this house, you're going to have to live with what I can afford. You live beyond me and you can leave."

Period.

It was one of the few times I went against his orders. I bought the bathing suit anyway. I used it so much I wore a hole in it the first year.

CHAPTER 5

ONE MAY DAY in 1948, my friend Norma Harris and I were walking down Magnolia Boulevard when we saw a little handbill advertising the Miss Burbank contest that was being sponsored by Lockheed Aircraft. Every girl who entered, it said, no matter what, received a blouse and a scarf. All you had to do was enter and they gave you a scarf and a blouse?! The only requirement was that the girls had to be sixteen or over. I made it by a month! We hurried right over to the Recreation Hall to sign up.

It seemed like half the girls in my class were there registering—the pretty half, that is. After all, it was a beauty contest. But that didn't matter to me. I didn't tell anybody, but I never dreamed of going through with it. I was not exactly a member of the glamour department; I didn't even wear lipstick. What did matter was getting the white silk sports blouse and a green scarf.

Plus we were all going to be taken someplace for a free lunch! A party!

My mother thought we were crazy when we told her.

"Miss *Burbank*?!" She couldn't believe there was such a thing.

The night of the contest, we were sitting at the dinner table when Mother brought it up. I thought she'd forgotten.

"What time you supposed to be down at the auditorium, Mary Frances?"

"Oh, I'm not going till about eight-thirty."

"What? Isn't that starting a little late?"

"Well, it doesn't matter for me because I'm not going to be in it," I answered blithely.

"What? How come?"

"Well, because . . . I'm not going to go enter some *beauty* contest! I'm not that dumb."

"You were dumb enough to sign up and collect the free blouse and scarf and the lunch!" she reminded me reproachfully.

My father said, "Sis is going to be in a beauty contest? You kiddin' around?" he asked Mother. He wasn't putting me down. He just saw it as another one of my jokes.

"I don't know, but she signed up to be in it."

"Oh, Mother, Daddy's right," I said. "It's silly for me to do that. For one thing, it's wasting their time."

"That's not the point, Mary Frances."

But then my father said, "Oh, no, you don't. You gave your word. Anytime a Reynolds gives his word, he keeps it."

"Well, I can't go. I got a hole in my bathing suit."

"Well, I'll sew up the hole in your bathing suit," Mother said, "but you're gonna go."

So that was it. Yes, sir. Yes, ma'am.

I called Jerry Odens and told him what my parents had said. He agreed.

I couldn't believe it.

I had to show some talent in the contest, but what? I could play "Pomp and Circumstance" on the French horn. But in a beauty contest? I could do a jitterbug, but not without a partner. I couldn't sing; I couldn't dance. I could do an impersonation the way I did for the Scouts. An impersonation was it. Jerry took charge of the record player and record.

Jerry said I had to wear high-heeled shoes. It's a good thing he thought of it. I never would have. I didn't have a pair. Who had high heels? Jeanette, Diane, Barbara; none of them did. We were going to be gym teachers! Finally I thought of Patsy Hockensmith. She always had beautiful clothes. I knew she must have a pair, and I was right.

I put my hair up in bobby pins. Mother darned up the hole in my Jantzen, and Jerry came by with a box of chocolates for me.

We got to the auditorium as they were giving out last-minute instructions. There were going to be three categories: Talent, Beauty, and Personality. We would be interviewed, do a couple of turns in our bathing suits, and then our little routines. This was all going to be judged by a distinguished panel of three people: two men who were talent scouts from a couple of the movie studios, and a lady casting agent.

All I could think of was how was I going to pull off hiding the patched-up hole in the back of my bathing suit. Every time I turned they were going to see it. Unless I could remember to swing my left arm back behind me every time I did a turn, covering that spot.

Out in front the auditorium was filling up. Grandma and Grandpa Harman were up from Texas visiting. They came with my mother.

Daddy stayed home. My girlfriends were all there. Billy and a bunch of his friends came to stand in the back and get a good laugh out of Sis in a beauty contest.

First came the Beauty Parade. I went through my turns backstage, rehearsing how I was going to hide the bathing-suit hole. But the real problem was the shoes. Patsy Hockensmith's heels were a size four with what seemed like four-inch heels. I'm a size two. It was the first time in my life I'd ever had a pair on. My heel came up only to her arch. I stuffed Kleenex in the toes and discovered that if I lifted the shoe just enough, I could slide my feet most of the way.

Then I heard them announce me.

"Miss Mary Frances Reynolds."

I took three steps out onto the stage. The sliding worked but the shoes made a loud cloppety sound as the heels slid on and off my feet. All that was on my mind was not tripping or losing my balance. Forget the patch on my bathing suit. My legs were so wobbly, they must have looked as if they were going to come loose. Then, after each girl had paraded around, the emcee asked us one by one why we wanted to be "Miss Burbank."

"I don't want to be," I answered.

That got quite a few laughs, especially from some of the boys up in the back of the auditorium.

The emcee looked at me, confused.

"I'm here because I know I won't win," I said, almost blasé. There was more twittering from the seats. "I'm just here because I live in Burbank." I shrugged.

Everyone thought that was hysterical. Well, it was true, wasn't it?

Then came the talent. There were girls with beautiful voices; one girl played the harp. Another did a tap dance. Another acted out a scene from *Little Women*. I stood back in the wings watching. Each girl was better than the last.

I came out lugging my record player, balancing precariously on Patsy Hockensmith's high heels. I almost fell over with my backside to the audience as I placed the record player on the floor. There was a big laugh out front. I realized they thought I had planned it. So I turned around and said, "I'm wearing heels for the first time in my life and they're killing me. May I take them off?"

They loved it! They started clapping and shouting, yelling "Yes!" at me. It was just like the Girl Scouts for this natural-born ham. I went into my Betty Hutton routine in comfort, performing "I'm a Square in the Social Circle."

When I finished they hooted and stomped. I packed up my things and left the stage, barefooted, high heels balanced on top of the record player.

I was walking out the stage door with my things when the man from the Chamber of Commerce stopped me.

"Where you going, Mary Frances?"

"Home," I answered.

"Oh, you gotta stay till it's over," he said. "Those are the rules."

After the girls were finished, we all waited in the back.

The man from the Chamber of Commerce repeated the categories. Beauty, Talent, and Personality. The winner of the Beauty was . . . Juanita Castelo, a beautiful Spanish girl. A big round of applause. Then the winner of the talent was . . . the girl who played the harp. More applause. Then I heard him shout: "MARY FRANCES REYNOLDS!" and a big war whoop went up from the audience.

What? I thought. *What?!*

Then someone pushed me out onstage. Jerry Odens was going wild, shouting his excitement. My girlfriends were cheering and crying. My brother was shocked.

In the pictures that were taken that night, my mouth is hanging open and I've got a dazed stare on my face. The winner? Of a beauty contest?

Which was what my father thought when we got home and told him.

"Well, wasn't there anybody else in the contest?" he asked.

We all thought that was very funny. Daddy was as shocked as I was when he realized it was true.

I was to reign as Queen of Burbank for two weeks. There would be parades and festivities for me to take part in. I'd won a robe-and-pajama set, a string of pearls, and a trip for two to New York, all expenses paid.

CHAPTER 6

THE NEXT NIGHT at dinner, Daddy, in his matter-of-fact, poker-faced way, buttering his bread, announced, "Well, I got a call from the Warner Brothers Studio today, Sis."

"Oh, really, Daddy?"

"A real gentleman named Solly Baiano. Says they want to put you in a screen test. You know what that is?"

"I think so." Up until then, I'm sure my father had no idea. He'd never been to a movie in his life.

"They're going to put you in front of a movie camera and find out if you can be in the movies," he continued, putting a forkful of mashed potatoes in his mouth.

"They want *Mary Frances* to be in the movies?!" Mother was astounded. "She's just a kid. What's she gonna do in the movies?"

"Don't ask me," Daddy shrugged. "First they make her Miss Burbank, now they wanna put her in the movies. Must be somethin' there, Sis," he said with a big grin on his face. I loved it when my father smiled at me.

". . . *The Burbank Chamber of Commerce was running a beauty contest and they asked me to be one of the judges. That night it was me, Al Trescone, who was the talent scout from MGM, and Ruth Birch, an independent, who were the judges.*

"We were sitting at a table right next to the orchestra pit, watching all the girls come out. I noticed this one little girl standing in the wings. Every time one of them came out, she'd be jumping up and down, clapping for them. I nudged Al. 'That kid has some personality,' I says. Thirty-two girls later, she comes out—carrying this Victrola. Puts it down, winds it up, and did a thing of Betty Hutton. She just killed the people. She was just herself.

"Al says to me, 'I want to see her.'

"I says, 'Yeah, I'm with you. This is such an extraordinary person.'

"We flipped a coin over who would interview her first. I won. I says, 'I know we might be able to sell her to Jack [Warner] if I can get her to do a test.'

"Al says, 'If you do, I'd like to see the test and see her afterwards.'

"Then we did a little test. She had no inhibitions at all. Completely natural. Sparkling. She was very young. Sixteen.

"One day I was playing tennis with Warner. I says, 'Did you see that test of Mary Frances?'

"He said, 'How old is she?' I told him. 'Sixteen years old?!' He said, 'Don't make tests of any more ingenues. We don't want ingenues. We can only use 'em in certain spots.'

"'But, Jack,' I says, 'she's such a personality. I don't see very many like this.'

"So he calls me in the next day. He'd seen the test. He says, 'How much?'

"I says, 'Anything you want to give her.'

"He says, 'Fifty bucks a week.'

"I said, 'Fifty bucks?! Jack, there's a Guild here.' He told me to sign her.

"After we signed her I called Al Trescone right away and I said, 'Al, we're signing this little girl, Mary Frances.' . . ."

—SOLLY BAIANO
Bel Air, California
August 1986

During his long career Solly "discovered" many of today's film legends. He found a teenage Judy Turner—working as a sales clerk in a Los Angeles lingerie shop, contrary to popular legend—took her to the studio, tested her, and renamed her after his daughter Lonnie. (Lana made that into Lana.) Solly loved the picture business.

Warner Brothers Studios looked like a pastel-colored fortress to a teenage kid riding by on her bicycle. It looks much the same today, except it now shares the lot with Columbia Pictures. Pale-pink walls and a big gate with a guard. It was only a few blocks from our house on Evergreen, but a million miles from our lives.

I wanted to see behind those walls. "That's Warner Brothers," people would say in hushed, reverent tones. I had gone by it hundreds of times. No one real was allowed in. It was movie stars only. Bogart,

Cagney, Bette Davis, Errol Flynn were inside. It was another world, and I was going to see it.

The following Sunday after Solly's call, Mother, Grandma and Grandpa, and I went, as usual, to church. After the service, as we were leaving, one of the deacons asked Mother if he could have a word with her.

Deacon Turnbill and his wife were a graying, middle-aged couple, very straitlaced, who often held Bible readings in their home. Mr. Turnbill also happened to work in the post office at one of the studios. He was the only person Mother knew who ever went near a movie studio.

"He heard about Mary Frances's interview at Warner Brothers," Mother reported. "He says if Mary Frances goes into motion pictures, she'll be damned."

"Damned? But I haven't done anything."

"He said it would be going against the principles of the church."

"But I'm just a kid," I protested.

"Oh, he said some terrible things. He said it was a regular Sodom and Gomorrah behind those walls. Everybody in the movie business is either a wanton woman or a pimp, take your pick!"

Grandpa laughed. "I don't see little Mary Frances becoming anybody's wanton woman."

Did he mean *wanting*, as in wanting a glass of milk? I had never heard that word before. Wantin'? What would I be wantin'?

The whole thing sounded absurd to me. Deacon Turnbill and his wife were always holier than thou. Besides, it wasn't as if Warner Brothers had even signed me. They just wanted to interview me. Meanwhile, I could see he put the scare into my mother.

She was mad but he'd got to her. The deacon did, after all, work in a studio post office. He knew nothing about show business, but we didn't know that. He was the expert.

I knew she was also annoyed by the whole idea. She thought it was ridiculous. The studio people were wasting their time. What were they going to do with a kid who played the French horn and beat up the boys who made her cry? Why bother? And not least of all, why bother my mother, who had better things to do with her time.

That afternoon when my father came in from the ball game, Mother told him about the deacon. I sat outside the kitchen door and listened. "Maybe you better go over and have a look first," he told Mother.

The next morning Mother called Solly Baiano at Warners and went over that afternoon.

She came home unperturbed and looking quite calm. According to Mother, there wasn't a naked person around.

"They're just people like you and me," she told Daddy when he came home from work. "They got carpenters there, and electricians, people working cameras. Those people aren't having orgies. They don't have time even if they wanted to, they're so busy working."

Frannie was permitted to be in the movies. Provided the movies wanted her.

I wanted to look nice for my interview. The first thing I did was to go out and buy a dress at Lerner's. It was gray with a purple sash. It cost eleven dollars and didn't fit—in those days they didn't make junior sizes. Mother did some alterations, which didn't help much. But I thought I was hot stuff. I loved that dress.

I rode my bike down to the studio for my appointment with Solly Baiano. He met me at the gate. Behind those walls a lovely, fascinating world instantly opened up.

There were so many people. It was like an anthill of activity.

Solly took me up to meet the studio acting coach, Sophie Rosenstein. Sophie was a very tiny lady, even smaller than I—four feet ten, with a very plain face and a big nose. She wore an elegantly tailored suit and I soon learned that she was a beautiful woman inside. She was chic and gracious, wise and patient. She was obviously very attractive—Gig Young later married her. Years later when she died of cancer, every actor who had ever worked with her turned out for the funeral. She was beloved.

I was very impressed with Sophie. I had never met a woman with such self-confidence and presence; a professional woman.

In her office was a small stage where the actors would do their scenes. She had a class full of stars who were studying with her at the time including Alexis Smith, Virginia Mayo, and Doris Day.

Sophie asked me a few questions about myself and then gave me a scene to learn. I took the scene home to memorize and went back to the Studio the following Monday.

". . . *We had several people read that day. Then out comes this little girl. She's got another little girl with her. She reads a scene from* One Sunday Afternoon, *which we made as* Strawberry Blonde *with Cagney and Hayworth. It was a cute period scene, innocent and perky for those times. She was cute as a bug's ear. When she was finished, she said, 'I have a record, a song that I'd like to sing, uh, mouth for you.' So she did this Betty Hutton number—'Murder He Says.' It was one of those ener-*

*getic bombshell, rowdy numbers. Then I said, 'Uh, Mary Frances, why
don't you sing it yourself? Forget the record.' Well, she didn't know
about that. So I said, 'Go ahead, it's a hot little song; you can sing it.'
She sang it. She had so much spunk and spirit. The talent was just
there.*

*"We all decided we should do something about her. Somewhere along
the line Solly mentioned Al Trescone from Metro and the thing about
flipping the coin. So I said, let's get an agreement today. We had standard forms for these things. Since Mary Frances was a minor and
couldn't sign her own contract, Sophie called her mother to see if she
could come in and sign it. She said, 'Well, my hair is in curlers.' She got
there about an hour later and we drew up an option test. . . ."*

—WILLIAM ORR
*Former Warner Brothers Executive
Beverly Hills, 1986*

Sophie introduced me to Alice Kelley, the girl I'd be reading the
scene with. She was my age but tall and beautiful—dark-haired and
olive-skinned, with big dimples and huge brown eyes. But what I was
doing there, that was the question.

We read the scene in Sophie's office first. Alice did a very straight
reading. I, of course, had no idea what a scene was, so I played it for
laughs. When we finished, Sophie gave me some direction on how to
read it, and I knew her way was absolutely right.

The following Saturday we did the scene for Solly, Sophie, and Bill
Orr, who was one of the studio executives and Mr. Warner's son-in-law.
I was the funny one and Alice was the beautiful friend. After the scene,
I did a Betty Hutton record, as Solly had told me to.

Then Bill Orr asked me to sing it without the record, which caught
me off-guard. I did it anyway, a cappella. They liked that too. Then
they called Mother.

As soon as Mother signed, they did the test. It was very much like
the way they do a video today. They sat me down in front of a camera
and asked me simple questions about myself.

It was mid-June. School was letting out in a week. Mother and I
were going to New York on the trip I'd won. Otherwise, I was thinking
about how I was going to earn money over the summer.

Solly Baiano called a few days later. I was in my bedroom when I
heard Mother answer the phone.

"Oh, hello, Mr. Baiano."

My ears perked up. I quietly inched my way into the living room, curious, watching Mother on the phone.

"Well, why would you want to put my daughter under contract?" she was asking.

I couldn't believe what I was hearing: They were actually going to do it?

"But what do you mean you find her talented?" Mother continued. "She doesn't sing, you know. She doesn't dance."

Mother would have made a great agent. Instead of being thrilled and curling my hair and rushing me right over there, she was busy talking them out of it.

"I'll have to talk it over with my husband and call you back," she said into the phone. "All right, good-bye."

Mother put down the phone and stood there, just looking at me dumbfounded, as if I were someone she had never seen before.

She didn't seem very excited. As soon as Daddy came in the kitchen door, she told him. "They want to sign Mary Frances over at Warner Brothers."

"They want to sign her? What for?"

"Well, how should I know?" Mother replied.

Daddy put down his lunch pail and went into the bathroom to wash up.

Mother spoke up so he could hear her. "I suppose it can't hurt her to have a few dancing lessons. I don't know about the dramatic lessons—she's dramatic enough as it is," Mother cracked.

"If you don't think it'll do her any harm, it's all right with me."

Then Mother said, "Well, you know they're going to pay her sixty-five dollars a week."

My father appeared in the doorway, drying his hands with the wash towel. He looked at Mother like she was crazy. "What for?"

This was also the first I was hearing about it.

"To study," Mother answered. "And maybe use her in a picture."

"Why would they want to pay her to teach her what they're hiring her to do?" Daddy looked confused about the whole thing. "Sounds a little nuts to me."

The next week the studio publicity department put my picture in the paper.

MARY FRANCES REYNOLDS OF 1034 EVERGREEN STREET, MISS BURBANK OF 1948, HAS BEEN SIGNED BY WARNER BROTHERS TO A SEVEN-YEAR CONTRACT.

It was big news for a Miss Burbank to be signed on as a movie starlet. If it could happen to me, that meant it could happen to anyone. Frannie Reynolds? The one who wore her band uniform and the hat on backward, who decked the boys and was at every baseball game? Never pretty, feminine, or glamorous, signed to be in the movies? My father wasn't the only one saying "They gotta be nuts." It was a joke.

Except to Deacon Turnbill. He hit the ceiling. He couldn't wait until the next Sunday at church. He said he was definitely going to have to bring this up before the board of deacons. They were going to have to seriously consider excommunicating Mother and me. Little Frannie, gone astray, would be burning in hell, over at Warner Brothers. He wasn't kidding.

Mother wasn't intimidated. It just made her more angry.

Eventually there was an exodus of the Reynoldses and the Harmans from the church.

I'm not going to blame the Nazarenes. They have changed over the years. I was invited to speak at the Nazarene church in Las Vegas about twenty years later. I took Little Richard with me. I always loved Little Richard, and he happened to be playing one of the cabaret rooms in Vegas. The minister was a little upset, but they had a big turnout, mostly younger people. Little Richard sang his songs and the church really rocked that day.

I signed a standard seven-year contract with Warner Brothers, with an option and a raise every six months. At the end of seven years I would be earning $350 a week. It was more money than I could imagine. My father, after working for thirty years, was then bringing home less than $200 a month.

The Coogan Law required that 20 percent of a minor's salary had to be automatically put away until the person was twenty-one. But Daddy insisted I put it all away. He had no intention of using any of my money and no intention of letting me use it either. If he couldn't buy it, I couldn't have it, no matter how much I was making.

I figured out that eventually, if I saved all the money I made over those seven years, I could pay for my college education and buy Daddy a car and Mother a new stove. But that would be years.

Mother and I took our very first plane ride on our trip to New York. We went to the top of the Empire State Building and the Statue of Liberty. We rode the Staten Island Ferry, saw the Rockettes dance at Radio City Music Hall, and walked our feet off. We took every sightseeing bus ride available.

We returned to California exhausted. The next day I got up at 6:30, had breakfast while Mother made a sandwich for my lunch, got on my bike, and rode over to Warner Brothers. Smitty, the guard at the gate, who was soon to become a good friend, gave me instructions to get to the schoolhouse where Miss Horne would be waiting for me.

Wait a minute. The schoolhouse? Miss Horne? No one had said anything about school three hours a day for however long I was under contract. What was wrong with Burbank High during the school year? I didn't like the sound of this.

The schoolhouse was on the other side of the lot near the gym. Inside the small, one-story building was Miss Lois Horne, standing in a typical schoolroom with the blackboard and the desks. She was a tall, thin, formidable woman with gray hair pulled back in a bun.

And she knew everything I didn't.

The child-labor laws were very strict, which was one reason a studio like Warners wasn't enthusiastic about signing up talent who were un-derage. The law required not only a school but a social worker or a parent to be with the child, like a duenna or a governess, at all times. Mother wasn't about to take that job, so Lois Horne doubled as social worker.

The child actor was also not allowed to work more than three hours a day. The studio got around that by putting a schoolroom on the set and keeping track of the minutes on camera.

It turned out that Alice Kelley and I were the only juveniles un-der contract to the studio. Other than that, she and I had nothing in common.

School really was private tutoring. Three hours of books. No re-cess, no sports, no fun, just studying. There was no one there for me to entertain. I had to mind my manners. Lois Horne knew I was bored being alone, but she had no say. Her job was to teach. That was the law.

After school, I'd explore. The lot was a very busy, small commu-nity, like a wonderland to me. Streets of houses, city streets, western streets where they shot the cowboy pictures, African villages. I was al-lowed to go into wardrobe and look at all the fabulous clothes. I met other actors and actresses. If I wanted to, I ate in the commissary. It was the first time I saw knives and forks that matched. I made friends with the carpenters and the electricians.

Jimmy Cagney was the biggest star on the lot. He had his own "bun-galow," an enormous eleven-room house that had originally been built for Marion Davies on the MGM lot in Culver City by William Randolph Hearst. When Marion and Hearst left MGM and went to Warners, they had the whole thing moved over the hill to Burbank. Cagney had two brothers who ran everything for him. No other actor had a setup like that. Doris Day and Virginia Mayo were the biggest female stars then. Bette Davis had left the studio but had come back to make a picture.

Besides school, I also had a drama class with Sophie Rosenstein, and a ballet class, which I hated.

Whenever I had the chance, I would go to the gym. Mushy Callahan, who had been the Middleweight Boxing Champion of the World, had been hired to run it. Cagney, Dennis Morgan, Gordon MacRae, George Raft, and Humphrey Bogart all worked out at the gym.

I watched Kirk Douglas training with Mushy for *The Champion*. I'd sit in the back so Douglas wouldn't notice me. One day he stopped what he was doing.

"What's that kid doing here?" I heard him ask Mushy. "Get her out of here."

I left. But I went back. Mushy knew that I often had nothing else to do. I always wanted him to practice basketball with me.

I was all over the place and no one knew my name. During lunch I'd sit and eat my sandwich by the tennis court and watch Mr. Warner play tennis with Bill Orr or Solly. That's how Mr. Warner probably got to know me. He'd call me "the kid" too.

Everyone called me Kid, and the kid was bored stiff.

CHAPTER 7

". . . Jack had always been a hard man to persuade. We'd said, this is a most talented little girl, Chief. We gotta grab her—Metro wants her. They got Elizabeth Taylor and this one and that one—because Metro would carry people longer than other studios. Warners, if they weren't working, they weren't necessary. Metro would hand-polish and clean up and fix a young person they thought was going to be a star, and move them into something.

"So we signed her. But now the thing was what to do with her. I got Ray Heindorf, who was our musical director, one day when he had an orchestra for something. I said I've got this little girl I want to come down and sing a song. I forgot what she sang. But she sang well enough for me to say she can be in musicals. But they didn't come up that much.

"Next we thought she needed a cute name. It so happened that Delmer Daves, a writer/producer who was working for Warners, had just become the father of a baby girl. He came into my office passing out cigars one afternoon when we were thinking about names. I congratulated him and asked what he'd named the baby. He said, 'Debbie.' I said, 'You mean Deborah?' He said, 'No, Debbie.' And when he left, I said to myself, we'll change Mary Frances's name to Debbie. . . ."

—WILLIAM ORR

ONE DAY AFTER SCHOOL, Lois Horne told me to go to Steve Trilling's office. Trilling was head of casting. When I got there, his secretary buzzed him through the intercom.

I heard him yell through the intercom. "He wants to see the kid! He wants to see the kid! Send her over to his office right away!"

"He" was Jack Warner.

I had never met Mr. Warner. Everyone was scared to death of him. He was a very tough man. But not knowing anything about the business, I never had any fear of the people who ran it. Obviously, I knew Mr. Warner was important. I probably knew, if I thought about it, that he could fire me. But I didn't care. There was nothing for me to do there anyway.

However, hearing Trilling's nervous orders gave me a little start; authority was authority.

I went over to Mr. Warner's office, where not one secretary but two showed me in. It was a very large room, impressively paneled in wood and furnished with antiques and a thick carpet.

Mr. Warner was a small, dapper fellow sitting back in his chair behind this great big desk. He was baldish, with a little thin moustache, dressed in an immaculately tailored suit. It was well known that he thought he was very funny. Someone had said that he told the worst jokes in the history of the world.

He flashed me a big smile, said hello, and told me to sit down.

I couldn't help looking around; I had never seen a formal, rich-looking office.

Mr. Warner didn't look mean, but he didn't stand up or get up out of his chair like a gentleman either. I didn't know what to expect.

"Hey, kid, I wanta talk to ya," he said.

"Yessir."

"What's your name *now?*"

"Mary Frances Reynolds."

"Do you like it?"

"I never thought about it. I guess I do." I didn't quite understand what he was leading up to.

Then he said, "Well, I'm changing it. You're now Debbie Morgan."

Just like that. I couldn't believe it. "I'm not Debbie Morgan. I'm Mary Frances Reynolds."

He smiled and said, "You're not anymore. I've changed your name. You're going to be a movie star and you're now Debbie Morgan."

I said, "Why would I be that?"

He looked at me strangely for a moment. "Because Dennis Morgan is a very big star and Debbie is a cute name for a little girl like you."

I said, "Who cares? He's a man and my name is Reynolds. That's my father's name."

"No one is a star with the name Reynolds. Dennis Morgan is a big star. And Mary is very plain," he added.

"Then you can call me Frannie. My friends call me Frannie."

"*Frannie?!* You ever hear of a star named Frannie?!"

I said, "Well, Frances is good."

"*Frances?!*" He said, "No, forget it. You're Debbie."

I could feel my back stiffening. I said, "Well, what's your name?"

"Whattaya mean, what's my name? What's the name up on the water tower?"

"Warner," I answered.

"Well . . ."

"So, are you keeping it or is somebody changing it?"

"Wait a minute, kid. I'll tell you what I'll do . . ."

I interrupted him. "How would your father like it if somebody changed your name?"

Something about that amused him. Little did I know that his father had had a Russian Jewish name.

"Because my father's last name is Reynolds and I'm keeping it."

"Okay, okay, you can keep Reynolds but I'm changing your first name to Debbie. You'll be Debbie Reynolds. You work for me, kid. I hold the contract."

"That's not fair," I protested.

"Listen, kid, every little girl in America would thank her lucky stars to be where you are and be called Debbie."

Then Mr. Warner laughed. "You'll do fine, kid, don't worry."

I wasn't worried. I was furious. When I left his office that day, I swore I'd never answer to the name Debbie as long as I lived. And for a long time I didn't. People would call me Debbie. I'd just keep on walking until they called me Mary Frances or Frannie.

I went over to Solly Baiano's office and complained to him. To console me, he told me the story about changing Judy Turner's name to Lana. But that didn't help. I wasn't Lana Turner. She was a movie star. I was going to be a gym teacher.

When September came, reality set in. Going to school on the lot meant not going to high school in Burbank. It never occurred to me I wouldn't be going back with my friends. No public school meant no athletics, no band, no playing at the Prom, no clubs. I wasn't about to give any of that up.

Mother went down to the studio to see Mr. Orr.

"Mary Frances wants to go to the public school and be with her pals."

"Mary Frances, or rather, uh, Debbie, is under contract to us here at Warner Brothers, Mrs. Reynolds. The law says we provide the school."

"Well, she's going to be one very unhappy little girl you've got under contract," Mother replied.

They compromised. Three hours of school on the lot every day, and then if I had nothing else to do, I could go to public school also. Mother went off to John Burroughs High School and made arrangements. When I finished my day at the studio, I'd go across the street and take the twenty-minute bus ride to Burroughs.

But changes were in store. Nothing, no matter how it appeared, was going to be that simple anymore.

Being under contract to Warner Brothers had in no way affected Frannie, as far as I was concerned. I was the same totally innocent, virginal, funny little thing they saw at the Miss Burbank Contest.

But my first day back at John Burroughs I discovered there were others who saw things differently.

"How's our movie star?" Arlene Peavey asked when I sat down with the other girls at lunch in the school cafeteria.

I was surprised by the sound of her question, but I made some joke about how it was like being in jail.

Nobody laughed. It wasn't funny. But I was Miss Personality. That was how they accepted me. If Miss Personality's joke fell flat, she kept right on going.

No sooner had I started my sandwich when Arlene finished hers. So did Sandy Ulrich.

"I think I'll go out and sit on the steps and see what's goin' on," Arlene said to Sandy. With that they got up and left. Three others soon followed. No one said so much as "See you later."

It was like a worst dream come true. I felt really bad. It was very important for me to be liked. I thought these girls were my friends. I still wasn't quite sure what happened. Had I said something that bothered someone? But who? What?

After lunch I went to my locker and got my books for the next class. Just outside the classroom, standing around, waiting for the bell, were Sandy and Arlene and the rest of the crowd. When I went over to join them, Arlene and Sandy looked at each other and went into the classroom.

"What's wrong with them?" I asked someone else.

"Nothing that I know of," she answered. "What's wrong with you, Frannie?" she asked, looking at me as if there were.

"Nothing's wrong with me," I said in a voice that was pleading, holding back the tears. Later that day, in phys. ed. with Miss Rutledge, my friend Jeanette remained the same. My friends Diane and Barbara remained the same. In band practice, no one seemed any different. But that didn't matter, because something was wrong.

I didn't say anything to Mother that night. I lay in bed thinking about it.

I decided the next day at lunch that I would act as if nothing had happened. I sat down with my tray, made some crack about my lunch, and Arlene, Sandy, and another girl got up and moved to another table.

They didn't like the fact that I had been signed by Warners—as if I had done it on purpose. It was a shock to all of us, to me especially. They probably thought they were more the type. I thought they were.

I went home and told Mother.

"Never be one of the flock, Mary Frances," she counseled. "Always be the shepherd and not the sheep."

"But I don't want to lose my friends over a movie contract that I can't get out of," I argued, the tears running down my cheeks.

"Those girls are not your friends. They're just jealous and that's life." Mother was both sympathetic and supportive.

I knew she was right. Thinking about what she had said to me, I got angry. Then I got over it. But I never forgot it.

Right after school started, Bill Orr made arrangements for me to be a morning disc jockey on KFWB, the radio station Warners owned in Los Angeles. I'd choose the records and introduce them. The audience would be kids my age.

I liked that. The show ran from 6:30 to 8:00, five days a week. I'd get up at 4:30 every morning when my father did, and catch the 5:30 bus that went over the Cahuenga Pass into Los Angeles.

When the show was over, I'd take the bus back to Burbank and go to class with Lois Horne.

Finally they found something for me to do. A bit in a picture called *June Bride*, starring Bette Davis and Robert Montgomery. Doris Day and Dorothy Malone were also in the picture. I played an extra in a wedding scene. When the camera panned, I was standing there.

The job was only a couple of days. When it came time to shoot a love scene between Davis and Montgomery, the set was closed to everyone except the two stars and the crew. However, I would sneak in during the lunch break and go up on the catwalk, about twenty feet above, and hide so that I could watch the shooting when they resumed.

"Don't make a sound, kid," warned Joe, one of the lighting crew. "If she knew you were up here, they'd have both our heads."

I stood there, still as a rock, elbows leaning on the railing, my hands supporting my face, staring down.

Two famous movie stars were lying there in a bright patch of light on that huge, cavernous stage, surrounded by the dark outline of lights, cameras, equipment, and the crew. Davis was reclining, dreamy-eyed, on a thick and sumptuous fur rug. Robert Montgomery, handsome and dashing, would kiss her tenderly. The two of them had so much passion it looked real. I was mesmerized.

The director called: "Action" and they began. Robert Montgomery whispered something in her ear. She laughed coquettishly. He leaned in and kissed her neck. She responded. The director said: "Cut!" and they stopped. He said something to Davis and Montgomery. They re-adjusted their positions. The director again called "Action" and they began once more. Same thing. The whisper. The laugh. The kiss. At which point one of my elbows accidentally slipped from the railing, throwing me slightly off balance, and one of my shoes made the slightest knocking sound on the metal walk.

Davis stopped the kiss. She threw Montgomery off and sat up ramrod straight.

"What's that?!" She looked skyward.

So did everyone else down below.

"Someone's up thah! Who's up thah? Someone's watching! This is supposed to be a closed set!"

I was terrified. Joe the lighting man muttered very loudly under his breath, "Beat it, kid."

I ran. I ran down that catwalk, down those stairs, with Bette Davis shouting at the roof, "This is supposed to be a closed *SETTT*! Who *IS* up thah?!"

My heart was pounding. She was furious. I thought she was going to kill me. I was going to be fired, machine-gunned, destroyed, and hung on the wall. That commanding voice of hers frightened the hell out of me.

It was in my contract that the studio could lay me off for six weeks after the first six months, which they did. They called it hiatus. That was fine with me. I persuaded Mother to go down to the studio and make it permanent. I was quitting.

When she told Bill Orr this, he responded by clarifying that Warners had me under contract, *their* contract. I wasn't going anywhere for as long as they wished to pick up the option, which they planned to do.

I was shocked. Everything went their way; the option was their option. That was the day we found out what a movie contract really was: They owned me. I was doubly shocked that they wanted to pick up my option.

But I was relieved to be free for at least a while. Christmas was coming up and I got a job working after school and weekends at J. C. Penney's in Burbank. I worked in the blouse department, which had a

Girl Scout division. I was very well informed about Scouting and for once felt I was actually earning my salary.

I loved working at Penney's more than at Warner Brothers. I was familiar and comfortable in that world. It was not dream work. It was down to earth.

Two weeks after I started, however, the Warners publicity department called the house for me one day. Mother told them I was at work. A few minutes later, they called back.

"Mrs. Reynolds, we've checked all over the studio and Debbie isn't here."

"No, she's not at the studio, she's at work!"

"But this is where she works, Mrs. Reynolds."

"Not now, she doesn't. You laid her off. She's working at Penney's for the Christmas rush."

"What?! Working at *Penney's?!*"

Well.

She was working at Penney's. Their little startlet! Everybody went nuts. There was a big luncheon which the studio wanted its starlets to attend. They were so upset they sent someone down to the store that day to get me. I wasn't going to leave. I had a job.

But they had a contract. I left my job. They put me back on salary immediately. No more hiatus.

". . . We had a script going, The Daughter of Rosie O'Grady. *It was a vaudeville story. This man has two daughters and is very protective of them knowing how Show Business is. The older sister is in the Act and the youngest sister is not. I said to Ed Jacobs, the producer, 'Listen, we got a little girl here on the lot who I think is dynamite. Write in a third role.' I had him meet Debbie. He calls and says, 'Yeah, she's cute; I'll put something in there.' So he did, and Debbie had about five snappers and all of them came off. We went to the preview and we laughed at all of them."*

—WILLIAM ORR

After Christmas, Sophie Rosenstein told me that they had written something for me into a picture starring June Haver, called *The Daughter of Rosie O'Grady.* I was the cute little sister who was always popping in and out of a scene. Sophie worked with me on it, and then introduced me to David Butler, who was directing it.

David Butler was a big, dear, jolly man who weighed about three hundred pounds. He understood that I had no idea how to approach a role. "Now don't try and act," he advised like a kindly uncle. "Just be you. They've written this to fit you; so just say the words the way you'd say them."

It was also Gordon MacRae's and Gene Nelson's first picture. I had never met Gordon, who was a few years older than I was, until we started rehearsals. The first day, during a break, I was sitting in the little schoolroom on the set studying my lines, when Gordon came in and sat down beside me. We chatted about the picture. He asked me about myself, my family, where I came from. It was very pleasant until Lois Horne appeared, out of nowhere, in the doorway.

"What are you doing here? GET OUT!" she said very coldly to Gordon. He jumped up, a little stunned. "She's only sixteen, you know. In the future stay away from her if you want to work on this lot."

"But, Lois! I was just talking to the kid," he said in defense.

"Never mind, Mr. MacRae. If I catch you with her again I'll go straight to Mr. Warner." Lois's Bryn Mawr personality could be very haughty. She was steely-eyed.

Gordon backed away from me with real fright on his face.

"But I'm a married man with four children!" he said to her.

"That doesn't mean a thing to me. I knew a faggot who had seven," she snapped. "Now get out of here!"

He was gone in a flash.

"Did I do something wrong?" I asked.

"No, dear, you're just fine. Mr. Warner just doesn't like any men in the schoolroom unless it's a parent."

Gordon obviously got the message. He steered clear of me after that. He never even got close enough to speak.

I loved being on the set. I went to the studio every morning knowing my lines, and I did exactly as I was told, repeating the words as if Mary Frances were saying them. Everyone was very patient with me. The rowdy little girl with the personality was adorable.

During makeup they discovered a minor problem. I had ears that stuck out like my father's. I also had baby-fine hair that couldn't hide them. In the picture, they wanted me to wear my hair down. The ears, peeking through my waves like an elf's, spoiled the illusion. They decided to solve the matter by gluing the ears back with liquid adhesive.

We came to shoot a scene where the father is giving his daughters a serious talk. I sat there, poised and quiet, listening intently under the hot lights. As the camera rolled on, I could feel the back of my ear pulling on the skin of my head. It was itchy. Finally the ear started to take on a life of it's own.

Ccccchhh-ccccchhh-ccchhh-POP! It returned to its normal position.

"CUT!" David Butler yelled. "GLUE HER EARS BACK!"

My face must have turned beet red. Everybody looked at me as if I had two heads. I was horrified.

The makeup man came on the set with the liquid adhesive. He applied it and then blew on it with a portable hair dryer while the cast and crew sat around and watched. I felt ridiculous with my ears holding everybody up.

Shooting resumed. I was afraid to move my head. Every move, every gesture I made, was done as if I were balancing a glass of water on top of my head, wondering when it was going to drop.

Back to the scene. Camera, action. We get through the father's speech. Now it's June Haver's line.

Ccchhh-ccchhh-ccchhh-POP! The ear flies again.

"CUT!" David Butler yelled again. This time it was really annoying him. "Will somebody please GLUE her ears back so we can at least finish shooting this scene!"

Again the makeup man rushed onto the set with the glue and the dryer, while everyone took a break and waited. I didn't love this kind of attention.

We made it through on the third try. But how was I going to get through an entire shooting schedule without having to go through additional humiliations?

I went home that night and stood in front of the bathroom mirror. No matter how I brushed my hair, up, down, or tied back, the tops of my ears peered out like sore thumbs. They always had and I had never noticed it.

I complained about it to Mother.

"Well, you could pin 'em back with plastic surgery like they did to Clark Gable's," she joked.

But it wasn't funny to me, so I asked Lois Horne about a plastic surgeon. She directed me to Dr. MacDougal in North Hollywood.

I made an appointment to meet the doctor. Plastic surgery was a very new art in those days. Dr. MacDougal himself had never done a pair of ears except in a mortuary when he was training.

Our family doctor, Dr. Levy, agreed to assist Dr. MacDougal.

They did it in the doctor's office with local anesthesia and me sitting up. I didn't feel a thing. They cut the cartilage in the back of each ear and then laid the ear back until it was small enough.

"Is that enough?" Dr. MacDougal would say to Dr. Levy.

Dr. Levy would look closely and ponder. "No, take a little more out."

So they'd slice again, like someone's ham or turkey.

That was my first and last plastic surgery. They wrapped my head in a huge helmet of gauze and sent me home with an aspirin. As the anesthetic wore off, my ears began to throb. It was the worst pain ever.

When my father came home, he couldn't help but notice Sis was wearing a white helmet.

"What's happened to you? Brain surgery?"

He was not amused. But he knew it was too late.

The drugstore across the street from the studio gate was a gathering place. The bus stopped right in front, so I would often wait inside for it. It was an intermediate place for me, coming from the world behind the walls of Warners to the schoolday world where I was Frannie again. It was a halfway house.

I loved to sit at the fountain and have a milk shake, talking with the other starlets who were waiting for their buses.

Dorothy Malone and I would often chat. We were both from Texas, so we had that in common. She was only a few years older, but in my eyes, *very* grown-up. She'd discuss the business and ask me questions like "How do you like acting?" She talked to me as if I knew something, which impressed me. I felt very grown-up too—for a few minutes.

It was at the drugstore that a man named Wilt Melnick came up to me at the counter and told me that I needed an agent. I was sixteen and a half.

Wilt explained to me what an agent was. He was with the Louis Schurr Agency. Louis Schurr was very famous; he was Bob Hope's agent until the day he died. He was small, round, and bald, with a neck that looked too big for his head. Every time he took a girl out, he presented her with a white mink coat when he picked her up for the date. When he dropped her off at the end of the evening, he asked for the coat back.

I was too young to have heard of Louis Schurr, so when Wilt Melnick mentioned his name, I was unimpressed. But after our conversation that day, he talked to my mother and to Solly Baiano. I signed with Wilt.

CHAPTER 8

". . . A *few months later, Debbie's option was just about up. Al Tres-*
cone, the talent scout from MGM, calls me on the phone and he says,
'That little girl we saw in that beauty contest. Are you going to keep
her?'

"I said, 'I don't know yet, Al, but probably, because she's very good*
in what she does. She doesn't have many chances to do anything because
we don't use many ingenues.'

"So he says, 'Well, I want her to meet some people here.'*

"So I told her maybe we could go to Metro and see Al Trescone. I says*
to her, 'Now don't be afraid. Be yourself.'

"Al introduced her to several big shots—Jack Cummings, Eddie*
Mannix. She did her song for them. She was so cute in that. Al called
me a day or two later and said, 'Are you going to drop this girl? Because
we want her.'

"I said, 'Well, why don't we make a deal. I'll sell her to you cheap.'*
He had something for her but I wanted to keep part of her because I liked
Debbie. I knew she could make us a lot of money someday. But the
studio wouldn't go for it. I finally told Warner, 'We're going to lose her.'

"He said, 'Well, if they want to sign her, let 'em sign her.' Okay.*

"She signed for that one picture with an option. They wanted that*
option. Anybody who looked promising might be worth millions. And she
was. From then on, she was right in the heart of the city. . . ."

—Solly Baiano

ONE MORNING I WAS TOLD that Solly wanted to see me
in his office.

"Remember Al Trescone at the beauty contest?"

"Yes," I answered, but vaguely.

"Remember we tossed a coin for you? Well, there's a movie at
MGM and you might go there."

Oh. A movie at MGM.

"I'll take you over there tomorrow morning. They're looking for someone to do a record impression, so bring along a record.

"You're going to meet some important people; just be yourself and do the impression like you were in your living room."

Metro-Goldwyn-Mayer Studios in the year 1949 was the most glamorous, most glorious place in the motion-picture industry. L. B. Mayer, its head, made the highest individual income in the United States. He was, and had been for the twenty years preceding, the greatest, most formidable mogul of them all, the undisputed King of Hollywood. He had under contract, it was said, "more stars than there are in heaven," many of whom, it should be noted, were created right there on the lot at Culver City.

When Solly and I arrived, a receptionist took us to Jack Cummings's office. It was large and beautiful, all white and decorated like someone's comfortable living room, with a fireplace and a desk. Solly introduced me. There were Cummings, Eddie Mannix, who was the number-two man at the studio after Mr. Mayer, and Burt Grady, the head of the talent department. It was Grady who made the famous evaluation of Fred Astaire's screen test: "Can't act, can't sing, can dance a little." There were also director Richard Thorpe; screenwriter George Wells; Roger Edens, the musical director who wrote Judy Garland's "Born in a Trunk," "Dear Mr. Gable," "Moses Supposes," and a lot of other famous and brilliant material; and Al Trescone. All men and this little girl and her record.

After the introductions, Mannix, a big burly man who started out in the business as a bouncer for the Schencks at Palisades Park, spoke in a gravelly voice like B. S. Pulley's and very gently said, "Do you sing?"

"No," I said. "Mr. Baiano told me you wanted someone who did it off a record."

Jack Cummings said, "Yes, that's right. There's a record player right behind you."

I put the record on, turned around to face them, and did my impression full out. They all smiled at the end, so I knew they liked it. Jack Cummings, with a big smile, thanked me and asked me to have a seat.

"We are doing a musical picture about Bert Kalmar and Harry Ruby," Jack Cummings said, still smiling. "Did you ever hear of them?"

"No," I said.

Everyone smiled.

"They were famous songwriters," Cummings explained. "And there's a part in the picture for a little girl to play Helen Kane. D'you ever hear of her?"

"No," I answered.

"No, of course she hasn't," Roger Edens added and put on a record to play me her voice. She had a high, squeaky voice.

"She sings so funny," I said.

"You think you could imitate her?" Jack Cummings asked, still smiling.

"Of course, it's easy to do that."

Wilt Melnick negotiated the deal. The picture was called *Three Little Words*. Two weeks at $350 per. That's also when I found out that Warners had not picked up my option for another six months.

Because I was still underage, Mother had to come to the studio with me every day. Daddy would hitchhike to work in Los Angeles, leaving us the car to drive to Culver City every morning at six. Despite the fact that her daughter was making a movie with Fred Astaire and Red Skelton (and Vera-Ellen and Arlene Dahl), having to spend her days at the studio waiting around was not her idea of a fun time, and she was not impressed.

I was very impressed to be in a picture with Astaire and Skelton. I had only one scene with them. They're two songwriters playing a tune on a piano that's out on the street in the process of being moved. I come out of a brownstone building, dressed in a sailor suit, kerchief, and beret, with a black wig on my head, and saunter down the steps to their side just as Fred Astaire finishes the first line of the song: "I wanna be loved by you, by you and nobody else but you. I wanna be loved by you alone." At which point I sing "Boop-boop-ee-dooo." They look at me like I'm crazy. Astaire sings the next line and I finish it with the tag: Boop-boop-ee-doop! Skelton turns from the piano, looks at me like I'm weird, then looks at Astaire. A light bulb goes off in his head and he says to Skelton: "Yeah, that's it; the kid's star is born." Fade out, fade in, the kid is on a Broadway stage. Carleton Carpenter is sitting on a park bench trying to read a magazine and I am singing (lip-synching) Helen Kane's voice: "I Wanna Be Loved by You."

It was two days' work: one in the street and one on the stage, with the number set by Astaire's choreographer Hermes Pan. Mr. Mayer saw the dailies and said, "Sign the kid." MGM picked up its option and signed me to a seven-year contract starting at $300 a week.

After two weeks of hanging around MGM Studios, Mother had had it. "I can't spend my life waiting around a movie set for you," she said. "You wanna be in pictures, you'll have to take the bus, that's all there is to that."

So I'd get up at 4:30, have breakfast, and then catch the bus over the hill. I had to take three buses to get to MGM in those days. The bus rides were an hour and a half. I was exhausted by the time I got there.

MGM was turning out, on the average, two feature films a week. The Thalberg Building had a floor of writers, a floor of producers, and a floor of directors. All these people flowed up and down all day sharing, comparing, and teaching. They were creating stars.

Mr. Mayer ate his chicken soup in the commissary with all the workers. He believed that MGM was a family. He was Papa. Carpenters, cameramen, writers, directors, stars, and Mr. Mayer, the boss, sitting at his own little alcove and oval table, right there for them to see.

He was in the business of making movies and movie stars. He had his own philosophy about family and company. Despite the fact that his own politics was several miles to the right of center, it was run a little like Russia: Everything was for the Studio.

Every so often, he'd give a speech to the workers. Standing up on a platform, he'd tell us, "This is the best studio in the entire business and it's all because of you. You're all wonderful and you make the greatest movies here."

Where Warners had seemed like a lot of older people to this teenager, MGM was younger people. Peter Lawford would be driving by with his surfboard sticking up out of his Cadillac convertible. June Allyson would be flipping down the street in her full skirt. Hedy Lamarr in full costume. It was like going to work in a movie, but even better. I saw every star.

I started classes first thing in the morning. They began with calisthenics, including stretching and some barre work. After that we had a fifteen-minute rest and then came ballet with Janet Bennett. I loved it but I couldn't do it.

Unlike Warners where I took ballet alone with my teacher, here the class nearly always included Cyd Charisse, Vera-Ellen, Ann Miller, Leslie Caron, and for a touch of spice, Zsa Zsa Gabor.

Zsa Zsa would come in her leotard, wearing her pearls and her diamond pin, and talk all the way through. She never did one thing right. If you can't have fun with Zsa Zsa and Ann Miller, then you don't have fun in life.

Cyd did everything perfectly. Her leg went over her head and into the sky. Vera-Ellen, the same way. I would look at their extensions and laugh because I could never do that.

Everyone was so nice. "Don't bend that way, Debbie, bend this way; put your arms this way. Don't break your wrist."

Zizi Jeanmaire was in this class sometimes. And Grace Kelly. Occasionally Elizabeth Taylor would come. Many of the big stars were usually too busy working, like Elizabeth and Lana and Ava Gardner who went from one picture to the next.

If you didn't like it, you had to be bananas. If you didn't learn from it, you had to be a moron. And I was not a moron.

There were only three of us left in the MGM schoolhouse: Claude Jarman, Jr., who did *The Yearling*, Elizabeth Taylor, and I. The first day I was there, Elizabeth appeared at the door of the schoolhouse with her books under her arms.

"Hi, I'm Elizabeth. Who are you?" she asked, flopping down at her desk.

"I'm Debbie Reynolds."

"Oh. Isn't this awful? Don't you hate school?"

"No."

"You're kidding! What's to like?"

"Well, I'm studying so I can keep straight A's now, so I can go on to college."

"College? Why?"

"I'm going to be a gym teacher. You have to go to college for that."

Elizabeth looked at me funny, with those eyes. "Aren't you in the movies?" she asked.

"Well, only for a short time."

"Whattaya mean a short time?"

"I'm going to get a scholarship to USC and become a gym teacher," I informed her.

"Why do you want to be a gym teacher?" she asked. "How boring."

"Why is it so boring? Is it better to be a movie star?"

"Well, I don't know," she answered. "I've always been a movie star," and then she added in afterthought, "I wonder what it would be like to be a gym teacher."

At first it was very hard to carry on a conversation with Elizabeth because her eyes were so incredibly violet blue. She was so gorgeous even women found themselves staring, not realizing. She stopped everybody cold, she was so magnificent-looking.

It was always girltalk with Elizabeth, flippant, light, casual. She was

fun and outgoing and not at all conceited. She wanted to know what it
was like to go to a basketball game, or to go on a date to a drive-in;
simple things that would never happen in her life. We got along great,
like two schoolgirls. She was good in English and I was good in math.
When it came time for the tests, she had no qualms about getting a look
at my answers and I had no qualms about showing her.

It didn't occur to me then, but being at MGM was like going to a
university. You could get out of college in four years, but some of us
were at this university for ten and fifteen. You never stopped studying.
Ballet, tap, modern dance. Placing the voice properly; how to sing; how
to walk and move; how to model, how to hold your hands, how to hold
your head, knowing the angle right for the camera; how to do makeup,
how to do hair.

Anywhere you walked on the lot there was activity, and often music.
Maestro Shapiro, a portly Italian, the voice teacher, was in an office
near the barbershop and newsstand, only half a block down the main
street from the commissary. In the background at all times was someone
doing classical scales. Janie Powell or, Kathryn Grayson, Howard Keel
or Mario Lanza.

Just to the left when you came in the gate was the music department. André Previn, Conrad Salinger, Johnny Green, Roger Edens,
Lena Horne's husband, Lenny Hayton, and Bobby Tucker were there.
You might hear André Previn on the piano, or Connie Salinger. Everyone had the windows of their offices opened because there was still no
air conditioning at that time.

Bobby Tucker taught phrasing. He was the first man I met who was
married to a man. His closest friend was Johnny Payne who stayed
home and took care of the house. I didn't know this until Bobby invited
me to dinner one night. Johnny answered the door in an apron. Many
men are marvelous chefs and naturally wear aprons in the kitchen, but
Mary Frances aged seventeen from Burbank didn't know that. The next
day I asked someone on the lot about Johnny.

"They're married, Debbie. They live together," I was told matter-of-
factly.

"How can a man and a man be married?" I thought my friend was
kidding.

"Because they're homosexuals," she answered simply.

"Homo-sexuals? What does that mean?"

"Well," my friend shrugged, "they're just men who *like* men."

Oh.

Bobby Tucker, in the meantime, coached me in phrasing. How to take apart a lyric of a popular song like Porter's or Gershwin's, to find its intent; and then how to phrase and sing that lyric. He was a wonderful teacher and a sweet man.

My drama coach, who was also everybody's drama coach, was Lillian Burns. A tiny woman, very smartly dressed, with short dark hair that she wore in bangs, she always sat upright, back straight, on an ottoman in her office. Despite her size, she had a theatricality that was larger than life. She spoke in a manner comparable only to Bette Davis's—clear, definite, and slightly dramatic. When she described a scene, she would emote it, with all the necessary passion and tenderness. Highly dedicated and as brilliant as a woman could be, obviously born to teach, she took her responsibilities very, very seriously. Not me. I was having fun. Her goal for her actors and actresses was for them to excel. She wanted to get the drama out of me. Not me.

She gave me a scene to do from the picture *Claudia*.

"Now when you do this scene, darling," Lillian said in her careful and gentle way, "I want you to cry."

"But, Lillian!" I protested. "I can't do that."

"Well, why not?" she wanted to know, looking at me quizzically.

"Because I don't cry."

"Then you'll have to learn how to, darling," she advised.

"I don't want to do drama," I replied. "I only want to do comedy. I'm not going to do drama ever," I stated.

"Of course you are," Lillian added patiently. I didn't want to learn to cry as an actress. That was revealing an emotion. It was much too private and I didn't like the idea. I wanted to be funny.

Lillian was a very strong, outspoken, and demanding coach. She was always definite about what her students were going to do. I couldn't have cared less. Her mannerisms were so extreme that I just wanted to impersonate her. Which I often did, sometimes almost making her laugh herself right off her ottoman. I'd do thirty seconds of Lillian and then fall back flat on the couch. I'd talk through my hour, telling her jokes and gossip, and then end it all with a pratfall. That was how I got around her.

By sheer force of will I avoided her coaching. Almost ten years were to pass before I took advantage of her great talent. I had no idea when I first went to her office that she was the most powerful woman in the movie industry. She had a direct line to Mr. Mayer and expressed her ideas and opinions freely in front of him. It was Lillian who supervised the tests and decided who would get the star treatment. In most cases, if

Mr. Mayer wanted to sign someone and Lillian said no, they didn't get signed.

Everybody at MGM was like your brother or your best friend. I felt very much at home with Mr. Mayer's family. I didn't feel strange or alone or untalented, but as if I should be there, even though I didn't yet know enough. I met poets, writers, and composers; people who were so interesting and intelligent—and far beyond me. I knew that. But I wanted to learn. I wanted to be able to talk to them intelligently. I found myself becoming interested because it was interesting. It changed me so that I no longer felt like an outsider as I had at Warners.

I used to spend time with Charley Shram, who ran the makeup lab where they made false ears, scars, noses, and all the other character makeup and special effects. Charley showed me how to pour the rubber to make the pieces. And Bill Tuttle would talk to me about how to sharpen my eyebrow pencil and how to put on my makeup, using sponges for applications. Or I'd be in Helen Rose's office studying the sketches and fashions; or in the wardrobe department looking at all the beautiful costumes. Anything to absorb the whole atmosphere of the place. One day during my wanderings, I was passing the commissary when Howard Strickling, the head of publicity, came out the door followed by another man. He grabbed me by the elbow, swung me around, and there was Clark Gable. "Clark," he said, "I want you to meet our new star of the lot, Debbie Reynolds."

Mr. Gable looked down at me with that kind of crooked little grin of his, and in that famous voice he said, "Well, kid, you'll find it an interesting life."

I was thunderstruck and thrilled and speechless. Very few people have ever been around me when I've had nothing to say. Even in the midst of labor, I've had plenty to say. Mother said I was born talking. But not in front of Mr. Gable.

It was a small town of very creative people. The main street ran from the gate and curved through the studio; off of it fed other streets. There was a street of rehearsal halls, A, B, and C, where Gene Kelly and Fred Astaire, Roland Petit and eventually Elvis Presley worked. Down below the rehearsal halls were the bathrooms, where the assistant director sat and wrote down when you arrived to go to the bathroom. I resented that and would take a pen and cross my time out whenever I had the chance. The school was also on that street, as well as the hospital and the fire station. I would often rehearse something by myself on the back lot. Here were the Andy Hardy street and the *Meet Me in St.*

Louis street with the tall Victorian houses and the streetcar tracks running down the middle. At the end was the huge train station with real trains, where they shot Judy Garland singing "On the Atchison, Topeka and the Santa Fe." Beyond that was the lake, with the Showboat on it, the whole set of *Hans Christian Andersen,* and the Esther Williams swimming pool. I would often take my lunch out there.

One of my early friends at MGM was Alma Garris. We first met when she was working as my stand-in on *Three Little Words.* She was also a good friend of Dorothy Kingsley, the screenwriter responsible for a number of MGM musicals including several of the Esther Williams pictures.

One Sunday afternoon I was invited by Alma to a party at Dorothy's. Alma and I drove over to Brentwood, where we ended up on a tiny street with a cul de sac surrounded by tall hedges. Dorothy was very wealthy. She was one of the most successful writers in the business, and in addition she was married to a very rich businessman.

A maid answered the door and led us through the big house out to the poolside where everyone was. Dorothy, a delicate and lovely woman, greeted us warmly. Around the pool and seated at tables eating were actors and directors and producers with their families. Dorothy took me around and introduced me to everyone. It was elegant yet casual. What was occurring, although I was unaware of it then, was that Alma was giving Dorothy a chance to watch me and get to know me, for she was at that moment writing a script for Jane Powell and Ricardo Montalban. The picture was called *Two Weeks with Love.*

A few weeks later, I was taken to meet Mr. Mayer in his office. Mr. Mayer had what must have been the biggest office in the history of Hollywood. You entered this enormous room, all in white, for what some people called the "quarter-mile walk" to a desk the size of a small helicopter pad, all highly polished and shining. Because Mr. Mayer was not very tall (about five five), and rather roundish and portly, he had his desk built on a platform, lest some big temperamental star or director come in and forget who was boss. His thinning silver-white hair was brushed back against his head and he was wearing wire-rim glasses. He rose when I entered and smiled, bowing and gesturing to a chair in front of him.

He seemed rather cuddly and sweet, although other people have expressed different opinions about Mr. Mayer. For many he was nothing less than a tyrant, who ruled his studio with an iron hand. But he was always nice to me and from what I could see, he was generally extremely polite and solicitous in the company of women.

He asked me if I was happy at MGM. And did I like my classes? He wanted me to have the best that the studio had to offer, which was, he added, the best that any studio could offer anybody. He told me that I was going to have a wonderful career and that they were putting me in a picture written by a very great writer, Dorothy Kingsley.

When he was finished, he told me that if I ever had a serious problem, I was to call on him and he would do everything in his power to help me.

Then he thanked me for coming to see him.

Two Weeks with Love starred Janie Powell and Ricardo Montalban. I was Janie's little sister, Melba Robinson. I had to wear flats because Janie, who's barely five feet tall, is an inch shorter than I am. It was a secondary role, and easy to play because the character was so like me— a little girl who was amusing and always getting into a bit of trouble in the family; Janie, the older, more sophisticated sister, was always putting me in my place.

Ricardo played the man Janie falls in love with. The whole thing was like going to a party every day. Louis Calhern played our father. He also used to bring his lunch to the set. I brought mine to save money. Louis brought his because he was on a special diet after having suffered a heart attack.

Mother always made me sandwiches of ground-up bologna and pickle with mayonnaise on white bread. Sometimes she'd throw in a peanut-butter sandwich with extra pickles and potato chips. I'd spend a dime and get a carton of milk. Louis could eat only the white of the egg and the white meat of the chicken. His wife improvised and prepared fabulous lunches of these ingredients, including fancy homemade cookies. They looked delicious, but he thought they were pretty boring. So we'd trade. I'd eat his lunch and he'd eat mine. And he never looked better.

Ann Harding played our mother. She had a very gentle, ethereal, rather Lillian Gish/Margaret Sullavan manner, with a searching quality to her voice—high and quiet, and breathless at all times. No matter what the scene, she maintained this strange, sweet, whispering sound.

I found her fascinating. I was also a quick-study mimic. At the beginning of the day I'd come up behind her on the set and say, in the identical high, breathless whisper, "Good morning, Ann."

She'd turn, look at me, and repeat innocently, "Good morning, Debbie."

She didn't realize I was sounding exactly like her. Everybody else on the set did, of course. Finally someone would say, "Oh, com'on, Debbie . . ."

"What? What is it?" I'd ask in the same strange, other-worldly whisper.

She never got it. Never.

They teamed Carleton Carpenter and me in a new version of an old song from 1914, "Abba Dabba Honeymoon." Carleton was a dancer, but I wasn't. Nick Castle staged the number. We swung in a tree and on a porch and did a little waltz clog, which is almost like a jitterbug. It was such a simple dance that it was a breeze to do.

Busby Berkeley was brought in to shoot it. It was kind of a comeback film for him. I had no idea who the great Busby Berkeley was.

Buz would strap himself on his crane and go miles up into the air so you could barely see him. There were stories about how in the past he'd be drinking and fall off if they didn't tie him on. He'd fall asleep while they were doing the lighting. Carleton used to sing, "Somewhere there's Busby, how high the boom . . ." They'd have to wake him up when they were ready to shoot.

Janie Powell and I were born on the same day, April 1. I turned eighteen and she turned twenty-one while we were making the picture. She could drink and I could drive. There was a birthday cake for each of us on the set, and Mr. Mayer came down to wish us a Happy Birthday. *Two Weeks* was a lot of fun. Everyone kidded around all the time. It was a picnic, and I was being paid three hundred a week.

Grandma and Grandpa Harman were staying with us in Burbank during the shooting. They'd come over to the set, sit all day and watch. Grandpa was very hard of hearing and in the habit of expressing himself very loudly. Seeing the apple of his eye performing a musical number before a movie camera would sometimes get him so excited, he'd start talking about it with Grandma in a voice so loud it overrode the dialogue.

About that time Daddy decided that I should get a car and drive myself over to Culver City every day. He found a four-door 1932 Chevy for $50, which was big money, pulled the motor out himself, and spent another $15 overhauling it. Mother upholstered the whole interior with some pieces of chintz she had left over. She made curtains for it, and put a little vase for flowers on the dashboard. Billy painted it for me. It had a stick shift, a starter, and a clutch. The back door kept falling off, and the engine made so much noise that they tried to get me to park it off the lot at MGM because they claimed I was interrupting shooting.

But I didn't care. I was thrilled to have it.

It was the end of high school and Mother had made arrangements with the Los Angeles school board for me to graduate with my class in Burbank. But first Elizabeth and I had to take our exams downtown at University High.

"Where're you going tonight?" she asked as we were leaving the building after our exams.

"I'm going to the candelight ceremony."

"Oh, what's that?" She still had that same little voice.

"That's where all the girls from the class go and light candles to symbolize going on to a new life."

"Oh, wouldn't that be fun. With real friends," she said wistfully. She started to cry. I felt so terrible for her, I did too. "You have real friends."

"So do you, Elizabeth," I said to console her.

"No, I mean school friends. Your own age. I don't. I've always been a star; I don't think it's fair." She made my heart hurt.

Elizabeth went to graduation at University High, but she wasn't one of the class really. It was more like making a personal appearance. Everybody wanted her autograph. Once her brother had tried to take her to a prom at his high school in North Hollywood. They were so mobbed by fans that they had to turn around and go home.

There was no teenage girl's life for Elizabeth. She didn't have a youth. She had been a star from the time she was twelve.

The Korean War was going on, and weekends a group of us entertained for the USO at different army and air-force bases. Mostly we went to Travis Air Force Base where the soldiers were ambulanced in and shipped out. There were Howard Keel, Carleton Carpenter, Arthur Loew, Jr., Keenan Wynn, Joey Bishop, and myself among others. I'd sing "I Wanna Be Loved by You" and tickle the boys' stomachs. Carleton and I would sing "Abba Dabba" and "Row Row Row."

Once I was part of a group that included Paul Robeson, the great basso who sang "Ol' Man River" in the 1930s stage production of *Showboat*. One day we visited a psychiatric ward for soldiers who had been shell-shocked or suffered mental breakdowns from their war experiences. Most of the boys were seated on the floor of the large room when we entered. As we entertained, they sat quietly, some of them rocking to the music. There was one fellow, a young black man, who, we'd been told, hadn't uttered so much as a word in several months.

When it came Robeson's turn to perform, he did a couple of his famous songs and then went into a jazz number called "Straighten Up and Fly Right," which Ella Fitzgerald had made famous.

> "Straighten up and fly right.
> Straighten up and be right.
> Straighten up and fly right;
> Cool down, papa, don't you blow your top."

He was snapping his fingers to the beat as he sang. Soon we noticed that the silent boy had started bopping his head and snapping his fingers to the song. The medical staff was amazed and visibly joyous at the break-through. Robeson kept on repeating the song for him.

In a matter of minutes, the boy started to move his arms and then his body. Then he stood up and started to dance. Everybody in the room was clapping and snapping for the boy, as he danced, first in place and then out into the room. He danced so hard, with abandon, almost as if in a frenzy, from one side of the room to the other.

For maybe fifteen minutes this went on, until in near frenzy, the young man whirled himself into a glass door, with a loud crashing sound. Blood gushed from his head. Robeson held the boy in his arms while a doctor cleaned the wound, a crowd of us standing in a tight circle around them as the singer comforted the injured boy.

Suddenly the boy, looking up at Paul Robeson, with great pain in his eyes, miraculously spoke his first words since he'd come to the hos-pital. "I'm sorry. I'm sorry. . . ."

"It's okay, it's okay," Robeson repeated, and again the boy said, "I'm sorry."

When the gash was cleaned, Robeson sat the young man down on the floor again with all of us, in a large circle, like group therapy, keeping the boy talking. Every one in the group was overwhelmed with emotion. When I got home, I went out and bought a record player, that song, plus as many records as I could find that had a beat, and sent them to the recovering boy. After that, the doctors started using re-corded music as therapy for the boys in the psychiatric ward.

When I was old enough, and could afford to get my own apartment, Daddy didn't want me to leave. He always said that I could have any friends to the house, as long as I allowed him to do the providing and went along with his rules.

But my father was raised to be prejudiced. One of my friends was possibly gay. Daddy didn't like him and said so. The boy seemed odd and effeminate to him.

"Well, he is different, Daddy," I countered.

"What does different mean?" he asked sharply. "Is he a faggot?"

"Well, I don't know. I've never asked him. We don't discuss it. He's my friend."

The matter was dropped.

My brother had been drafted when I was seventeen and was stationed at Fort Ord in Monterey, along with David Jansen and Dick Long. Weekends when I didn't have USO dates I would go up and entertain. One of Billy's friends, Rudy Render, who worked for the general, played accompaniment for me. Rudy, who was black, was an excellent professional musician in his own right. We became fast friends, and the friendship grew and grew.

One weekend Billy came home on leave and invited Rudy to dinner. No one had bothered to tell my father Rudy was black. He arrived just as we were sitting down to dinner.

Daddy took one look at Rudy and got up from the table. Billy, Mother, and I were mortally embarrassed. Mother said something about Daddy having an upset stomach, and it was covered up. But he never came back to the table.

After Rudy left that night, we went out to see Daddy, who was tinkering with a machine he was repairing in the garage. I asked him why he had left the table during dinner.

Without looking up from his work, he said, "I can take anything but not a nigger." We were all outraged.

"We can't live here if we're not free to have our friends." We decided on the spot that we'd move out. And we did. That night, the three of us checked into a motel.

The next morning Daddy, full of remorse, found us. But we told him that we couldn't live like that, that he'd have to live by himself.

I think he was shocked by our ultimatum, and maybe a little worried. "Come back," he said. "Any friend is welcome."

The four of us sat down and had a family meeting. It was the first time we had ever talked about anything together. I reminded Daddy of our original agreement—that any "friend" of mine could come to the house, as long as we lived with what Daddy could provide and pay for himself.

He said that was all right with him.

"But Rudy is a friend, Daddy," I said.

"I know that."

"And he is black, Daddy; colored."

"Any friend is welcome," he said, reaffirming his promise.

A few months later, Rudy, who was from Indiana, was in a very serious automobile accident in Los Angeles. He had fractured his back and needed to stay in bed for a few weeks. He had no place to stay. Mother and Daddy had recently done over the garage and made it into a small "guesthouse" with twin beds and a kitchenette. Rudy moved in there and Mother nursed him for three weeks.

I was working or traveling during most of that time and so Daddy had to help Mother with Rudy. He grew attached to Rudy and began to think of him as a son. In time Rudy became as close to my father as anyone he ever knew, other than my brother and myself. Rudy called me the night Daddy died, years later, and sobbed so much I had to hang up because I was having a hard time controlling myself. For Rudy it was like losing his own father.

That year I also went overseas to Korea to entertain the troops. I had never seen death, or smelled death. I had never had dying boys grab at my shirts screaming, "Oh God, oh God, oh God . . ." I would look down and it would be a boy my age, in terrible pain, having been hit by a flamethrower, burned like charcoal, covered with salve, lying on a stretcher.

The first time it happened I had to go out and throw up. I fell sobbing uncontrollably against a wall. Keenan Wynn came over and put his arms around me.

"That's war, kid," he said. "You don't have to come back if you don't want to; it's all right."

I didn't want to go inside again. But all I could think was, if they can have it done to them, I can at least do my job.

The smell and the pain and the death was all around us. I'd be singing and some boy would succumb. We had to act as if we didn't notice, as if it didn't bother us. It wasn't good to cry in front of the soldiers.

Two Weeks with Love was released during the Christmas season in December 1950. That little bitty number of mine and Carleton's horsing around the swing and the porch singing about Abba Dabba Honeymoons turned out to be the showstopper in the picture. A record of it was released and it went on to sell a million copies.

Shortly after we'd finished shooting the film, Grandma and Grandpa went back to El Paso.

By the time it was released, Grandpa was a very sick man with heart disease. The doctor's orders were for him to stay in the house and not even walk, except to go from one room to another.

But Grandpa wanted to see little Mary Frances's movie, and on opening night, my uncle took him. As soon as my name came up on the screen the whole theater knew that was Owen Harman's granddaughter. According to my uncle, every time I appeared, everything I did, Grandpa applauded and shouted for joy. When Carleton and I sang "Abba Dabba," he was so delighted, he just roared with laughter.

When they got home after the show, Grandpa was worn out from all the laughing. He couldn't stop talking about how proud he was of his adorable granddaughter. His feet were a little cold, so he put them up by a small stove and Grandma covered them with a blanket. Grandpa felt a little hungry. Grandma went into the kitchen to fix something for him. A couple of minutes later she heard a gasp and a loud noise from the next room. She went in to see. Grandpa was in Heaven.

The studio sent Carleton and me out on the vaudeville circuit to publicize the picture. They paid us $1,500 a week for playing five or six shows a day—an hour or so between each showing of the picture. We were the opening act for some big band and a name. Phil Silvers, or a star like that, would be with the band.

Roger Edens put our act together, and Nick Castle staged it. It was probably the worst act in the history of vaudeville. Carleton and I opened the show doing "Row Row Row" and closed with "Abba Dabba." We also sang "You'll Have to Get Under" and "Oogie Oogie Wah Wah." Off-the-wall songs like these are hard to find. Cute. So cute you could throw up. Nick Castle told us, "With these songs, kids, from here your careers can only go up."

Carleton and I became friends, as well as partners. He called me "Little Creature," because I was practically half his size. He thought he knew everything about show business, and he did; or at least more than I. He felt I wasn't equal to him, and that he should be touring with someone who was. But despite the fact that it hurt my feelings and I didn't appreciate his attitude toward me professionally, there was nothing I could about it. Then one day at the Capitol Theatre in Washington, fate stepped in and did it for me.

Our final bow was choreographed so that Carleton would kick up his leg so high that I could duck under it and then take my bow. This time he kicked so high that as I went under, he went off balance and fell right into the orchestra pit. The sight of all those arms and legs flailing in the pit was so funny, I cracked up.

As soon as we got offstage, he let me have it. "You don't laugh when I fall into the orchestra pit. Couldn't you see it was an accident?" He was livid.

"Oh, really? You should keep it in."

He failed to see the humor.

The kids were always there to see us on the tours. The audience really hooked me. I suddenly realized that I enjoyed performing. Up until then I was always thinking about getting out of the business. Now I was always thinking about staying *in*.

Carleton and I would stand by the stage door for a couple of hours after every show, signing special pictures the studio had made up for us. In those days you were *taught* to give an autograph to everybody. I pass that along to all the new stars who are aloof and think that fans are an imposition. It takes longer to say no than it does to sign an autograph. I thought it was exciting that five or six hundred people would line up to see me. It was very surprising to me how popular I'd become.

CHAPTER 9

LIVING AT HOME and banking most of my salary, I really wanted to help out in some way with the family finances. Daddy wouldn't have it. "If I can't afford it, we can't have it" was the official rule.

I suggested I be allowed to pay for our food since I could now afford more than chopped-up bologna and mashed potatoes.

Uh-uh. Daddy remained steadfast. His argument was always: "I still don't know what you're doing over there that they pay you all that money. When are you going to go out and get a real job?" In other words, don't talk about it.

Finally, with Mother's help, I persuaded him to let me buy us a steak once a week, but *only* once a week.

That night we had a two-inch-thick T-bone steak. Daddy didn't leave a morsel on the bone.

"Abba Dabba" had sold more than a million copies and I received about $15,000 in royalties in two checks. That summer I decided to buy my father a set of golf clubs and a red 1951 MG convertible with the tire on the back.

I had the dealer wrap a big ribbon around it and I drove it up in front of the house on a Saturday afternoon.

If I'd asked him, he'd have said no. But when I was a small child living near the border in El Paso, he always used to tell me of a special tradition the Mexicans had about gift giving. If you turned down a gift, it was an insult.

When I handed him the keys that afternoon, I said, "Daddy, this is for the next time you need to drive yourself to work. It's a gift and if you turn it down, I will be insulted."

I thought he'd be very angry with me. But he laughed and he grumbled—and accepted it. He loved it too. It was the last thing he would accept from me for years. He was the man; he was the father, he had to provide.

A few weeks later, he got into his little roadster and went off to Texas to visit his brothers and sisters. His golf clubs in the back, he looked so fabulous and young driving away, instead of the burdened, overworked man who had brought us from Texas. I was so happy to be able to do that for him.

The MG cost $2,000. With the rest of the first check I bought mother a new stove, and me a closet. The original one in my room was like a hall closet, it was so tiny. I did buy clothes now. And shoes, shoes, shoes.

The following year I received my second royalty check, and so when Daddy went on his vacation, we dug up the backyard and put in a swimming pool with "Abba Dabba Honeymoon" written on its steps. When he came home and saw it, he really flipped out. He hated it.

Of course it was too late. However, the year I married and moved away, he filled the pool with dirt and it remained that way for the next twenty years, until they sold the house.

Careers were created, developed, and produced at MGM, just like pictures. While Carleton and I were still playing the Loew's circuit, Mr. Mayer had a conference in his office with Lillian Burns about the future of Mary Frances. Mr. Mayer was a great believer in young talent and always took a great personal interest, even then, in his twenty-sixth year as head of the studio. Elizabeth Taylor had been signed when she was eleven. Mickey Rooney, Roddy McDowall, Janie Powell, Dean Stockwell, Margaret O'Brien, Van Johnson, Peter Lawford, Lana Turner, Ava Gardner, June Allyson, Judy Garland, Pier Angeli, Leslie Caron, to name a few, were all still kids when they first went to work at Metro.

Frannie, it happened, was the last of the babies.

"Lilly," Mr. Mayer asked, "do you think the little girl could be an actress?"

"Yes, I think she could be a very good actress. Not tomorrow morning," Lillian added bluntly, "but the talent's all there."

"Do you think she could do *Peg o' My Heart?* he continued, thinking out loud. The play, which had been written almost forty years before, had starred the great stage actress Laurette Taylor.

Lillian told me this years later. The star-making machinery had been set in motion. I didn't know that. Raised to say "Yes, sir, "Yes, ma'am," I never knew I could say no. I was signing my autographs "Debbie," and demanding that everyone call me Frannie.

But I was beginning to realize that it was exciting and challenging. All I really knew at that time, however, was that I had to keep up with the schedule.

*   *   *

From the time I was first at the studio, I was encouraged to study everything. Mr. Mayer let me run a movie as often as I wished. Some nights I'd run two. I'd watch Davis to see how she moved her hands; Hepburn to study how she walked. If there were something, even a gesture I wanted to see again, the projectionist would stop the film and run it over.

That's when Lillian really came into my life. I felt comfortable with her. I'd ask her a lot of questions about performing—why I would have to study this or practice that.

"They're paying you to learn and what else have you got that's better to do?" she'd ask.

This wasn't pie-in-the-sky dream talk or flattery. At least I knew that. This was someone's plan.

There were dozens of magazines in the early 1950s. It was a requirement with Mr. Mayer that his girls be on the cover of all of them: *Life, Look, Collier's, Saturday Evening Post, Cosmopolitan, Redbook, Ladies' Home Journal, Woman's Home Companion, Modern Screen, Photoplay, Motion Picture, Screen Stories.* The studio supplied covers of its stars all over the world: Elizabeth Taylor, Janie Powell, Kathryn Grayson, Grace Kelly, Ann Miller, Greer Garson, June Allyson, Debbie Reynolds, Donna Reed.

We had to be photographed once a month. Virgil Apgar was the staff photographer. I'd go to his bungalow early in the morning and spend the entire day. Helen Rose provided the wardrobe.

Ann Straus of the publicity department was the fashion coordinator and in charge of all still photography. She would work with us on posing; how to stand, how to sit, how to hold our hands, how to look pretty.

We'd wear every mink coat, every jacket, every scarf, every everything. They'd just change the top and do a hundred covers in a day: layouts at home, on bicycles, romping in the surf, petting the dog, picking up bunny rabbits, feeding a horse.

They taught us how to smile. Think of something, they'd tell you—ice cream . . . sex. If you think of nothing, that's what it looks like.

Magazines were dependent upon the studio publicity department. Within months my picture was on a dozen covers. Within a year, it was on dozens. Within two years Elizabeth and I were on more magazine covers than anyone else in the world.

Every new starlet had to meet the press and give interviews. Louella

Parsons came first. She was a brilliant woman, driven and very much supported by her publisher, William Randolph Hearst. Her column ran in hundreds of papers as well as a movie magazine, and she had a radio show the whole world listened to. She was the First and Most Powerful Woman in Hollywood. She was also the most interesting reporter because she never seemed to listen to anything and she never asked anything.

Short and stout, with tightly set brunette hair, a round face, and an eternally smiling voice that sounded like a raspy Liberace, Louella almost always wore furs over a brocade or lace formal.

Louella like to tipple. Her husband, Dr. Martin, whom everyone called Docky, was a very agreeable man and very dear to her. Docky didn't like her to drink although he didn't mind if he had a few himself.

She'd wander into a party like a lost soul, Docky following close behind, and you'd think: Oh, the poor thing doesn't know what she's doing.

"Now, Debbie, I'll just have a glass of water," she would fairly gush, when I'd ask her what she wanted to drink.

I'd bring her the glass of water, which was always vodka over ice in a huge tumbler. She'd drink the whole glass in no time and ask for another.

"Hello, how are you, dear?" she'd say with a big smile. If anything was said, it was small talk, nothing of substance and never gossip. Before the evening was out, she might just fall over and go to sleep with her head on the plate.

I don't think I ever heard Louella actually ask anyone a question— Are you pregnant? Are you having an affair? Are you anything? I always thought she was drunk. So did everybody else. People who were afraid of her would take one look at that lady with her head on the table and say anything. But the next day, in headlines, there it would be in all the Hearst papers throughout the world—everything that was said while she was sleeping. I'd never say a word, anything, in front of her that I didn't want in print.

I met Louella right away; day one. And Hedda Hopper and Mike Connolly and Harrison Carroll and Sidney Skolsky. They were god-almighty. Some, like Harrison Carroll, were nice guys. Others, like Mike Connolly of the *Hollywood Reporter*, could be real snoops and gossips.

Hedda Hopper looked rather like a combination of June Havoc and Gypsy Rose Lee. She was always well groomed and well dressed. She always wore pinks and lavenders, and of course her hats, which tended toward the outrageous.

She also had a very sharp tongue. Hedda could and would hit you head-on. You had to really like her to put up with her because she could be the Bitch of the World.

All the studios had their young, up-and-coming stars going out all the time. We had to go to every opening, every premiere, every cocktail party, to be seen and photographed. The studios arranged a lot of these. They also arranged the dates. Sometimes you went with Tab Hunter because you looked darling together. Sometimes you went with just the publicists. Jimmy Mahoney and Rick Ingersoll were two young press agents who often escorted me.

It wasn't long before people were asking me out without the suggestion of the publicity department. One of my first dates was Arthur Loew, Jr., whose family were the majority stockholders in MGM. He was long and skinny, with a very zany humor like Steve Martin's.

We went to a very chic restaurant on the Strip called LaRue.

The dress I wore was one of those cheapos I loved to buy on sale. It was black with white polka dots and had a sheer little coat with a net effect. I thought it was fabulous. It cost about thirteen dollars.

This was also my first visit to an expensive restaurant where the maître d' seats you.

We walked in and stood at the edge of the dining room. It was quietly elegant. The diners all looked very glamorous and sophisticated to me. I pretended not to notice so I wouldn't stare. Arthur and I were having a very animated conversation when a suave-looking man in a tuxedo jacket approached us.

We were seated and given our menus. The maître d' left, and another man—the captain, it turned out—came over to our table.

"Good evening, Mr. Loew," he said in a voice like Charles Boyer's.

"Good evening," said Arthur.

"And what would the lady like to drink?" the captain inquired.

"Oh, I think I'll have a glass of milk."

The captain looked at Arthur. Arthur looked at me. "Uh, Debbie, I think he means a before-dinner drink."

"No, milk is fine."

"Uh, wouldn't you rather have milk with your dinner?" Arthur asked, "and have maybe . . . a Coca-Cola now?"

The maître d' looked at Arthur with a wan smile, as if I weren't there.

"And you, Mr. Loew?"

Arthur ordered a cocktail. The captain thanked him, bowed like a diplomat, and left.

I opened my menu. It was in French. I looked around the room. Other people were reading their menus and ordering as if they were living in France. I was dead. Not to mention the three forks and two knives set before me. I didn't know what all that was for.

If Arthur noticed my embarrassment, he didn't let on.

Driving me home after dinner he told me that he'd like to date me again.

"I don't think that will be possible, Arthur," I said.

"But why?" he asked, as if I'd made him feel he'd done something wrong.

I didn't know what to say. I didn't want to tell him. "Because all the girls tell me you're a wolf."

"*Wooolf?*" he repeated, as if he had never heard the word before.

"Well, yes. That's what I've been told and that wouldn't work out."

"But Debbie . . ."

"I mean we've had a nice night tonight and I really think . . ." Then I just blurted it out. "I don't like fancy restaurants and I felt very uncomfortable and I don't know what you're gonna wanna to do to me."

"I don't want to do anything to you. I just want to go to the movies and not be a lonely guy. I think you're really fun and I'd like to do whatever you want to do."

"Well, I'd rather go bowling," I said.

"Fine. Then I'd like to go bowling too."

I didn't know what to say. We'd just reached the top of Mulholland Drive on our way over the hill to the Valley. Arthur Loew was a man-about-town. I didn't know what was going on.

"Look, Arthur," I said, "you wouldn't like bowling because you're very rich and you're the son of the people who own all this. You can go out with Janet Leigh or Mona Freeman. . . ."

"Debbie, that's not the point. I just like you as a person. . . ."

It was another fifteen or twenty minutes to the house in Burbank, where my father might just very possibly be waiting up in the kitchen in his pajamas, with a baseball bat, waiting for me to get home.

"Arthur, the point is, you frighten me. I've heard about you."

"But what have I done wrong tonight?"

"Nothing, but you might." I was staring out the windshield, counting the blocks to the house.

Arthur was befuddled. "I think you should give me a chance," he said.

In very few minutes we were back on Evergreen Street, where the light was on over the front door at number 1034. I said good-night and before Arthur could even shake my hand, I was out of the car and into the house. Frannie, home safe and sound.

Arthur did ask me out again, and we went to a movie, in blue jeans. He bought me popcorn and I was happy. We dated quite a few times after that. And he was never a wolf and he never did scare me. We had a good time together and he couldn't have been kinder. He later married Ty Power's widow and adopted his son. I can't believe what he put up with, when I look back.

I had a blind date one night with John Barrymore, Jr., to go to a pizza palace in Encino. John was a nice-looking guy and a very considerate date. On our way home, he hadn't been drinking but he got sick. He drove along Ventura Boulevard with his head out the window, he felt so nauseated.

"Look, Debbie," he said as we were nearing the house, "I feel so bad I don't think I can make the drive back over to West Hollywood. D'you think your parents would let me sleep on the couch?"

I didn't see why not. He was miserable. We got into the house about 10:30. Mother was still up. I asked her. She said it was fine and went to get some sheets and a blanket while I warmed some milk for John in the kitchen. A couple of minutes later Daddy, who had been asleep, came in barefooted in his little Carter pajamas.

He took one look at John. "What's goin' on?" He was not pleased.

"John got real sick at the restaurant, Daddy, and he's going to sleep on the couch overnight. He's too sick to . . ."

"No, he can go," Daddy said without letting me finish.

John raised his head, looking miserable. "I'm sorry, Mr. Reynolds. I just feel so bad. I'll only stay for a few hours," he said.

"No, you can sleep at home. You'll be fine."

That was final. John got up and dragged himself to his car. What could I say?

I never dated John Barrymore, Jr., again. I'm not sure I even saw him again until about ten years later in Trader Vic's restaurant in New York. I didn't recognize him when he first came up to the table and introduced himself. He had grown a beard and his hair had turned white.

He reminded me of the night Daddy threw him out. "You know, he was the only one I ever met who saw right through me. I had it all planned that night. I was going to wait until everyone was asleep and then I was going to get into your bed." He laughed. "I wasn't sick."

It was an act. I never forgot that story. Never try to think like a man. He didn't have a bad stomach. He had a hot something else.

Everyone met at the parties. They'd invite writers and directors and producers and all the stars. That was how I met Hugh O'Brian, who was at Universal, as were Piper Laurie, Rock Hudson, and Tony Curtis, and Lori Nelson, who became a close friend.

The publicity department would say, "We'd like you to go out with Rock." The limousine would pick him up and then pick me up and we'd be off to an opening at the Cocoanut Grove or Grauman's Chinese.

They preferred that we date people from our own studio, but there weren't as many boys available at MGM. We had Rod Taylor, Richard Anderson, John Ericson. There were quite a few, however, at Twentieth Century-Fox, including Tab, Bob Wagner, Jeff Hunter, Craig Hill, and Don Murray.

I immediately had this great social life. All through school no one asked me out and now I was dating these gorgeous young movie actors.

It was the best time ever for Frannie. There was no pressure, no need for conversation. There was no worry of anyone being fresh and not taking me home. Someone from publicity went along as chaperone.

The publicity parties were photo opportunities but they were real parties also. I met people who were doing the same thing I was doing; people who understood the pressures. People would talk about their work: "What script are you doing?" "I'm going to be doing a Gary Cooper picture"; or gossip about the director, the producer, or another actor.

Sometimes two people really clicked. Tony Curtis and Janet Leigh met one day when we were entertaining at Edwards Air Force Base. Janet was something to behold; beautiful as well as talented. Not jealous, not vindictive, not a bitch, not boring; she's a guileless, dear, terrific lady. Tony was a big, macho, Rambo-type guy; stunning, with gorgeous blue eyes and an ego on steroids. But he took one look at her and it was like the Fourth of July tripled.

Janet had the world trying to get her, but Tony wanted her and she didn't have a prayer. It was physical; it was sexual. It was like dynamite. He got her and he married her.

*   *   *

There was never anything like that in my life, although for me, more importantly, there was Bob Wagner. I met RJ, as he was known to his friends and family, on a prearranged studio date when I was eighteen, not long after I'd finished making *Two Weeks with Love*. It was a double date and we were each with the other person.

All the boys I dated were a lot of fun as well as good-looking, since most of them were actors too. Most of them had come to the business as I had. They had to learn. But RJ was different. He was amusing and bright but with a different energy from mine. He was sensitive and charming and two years older. He dressed beautifully. To me he was perfect. I was the clown and he was the sophisticated, dashing young fellow. RJ was classy. From almost the first I felt he was the one boy I would love to marry and whose children I would like to have.

We dated casually at first. There were always premieres during the week. Weekends there were always parties.

In the beginning, if it was a date date and not business, my parents insisted that he come to pick me up. They liked a boy to come in, say hello, and then I could go. I had to be delivered back by a certain time, too. At eighteen it was 11:30, and midnight if it was something special. RJ lived with his parents on Stone Canyon in Bel Air. Burbank was a long drive. It wasn't twenty minutes by freeway the way it is today. To date me was a challenge for anybody. To get to my house from his was a good hour's drive. He was on the road half the night!

One night we were going to a party in Beverly Hills, and because he had an early call at Twentieth the next morning, he asked if I could drive over to Bel Air and spend the night. Mother understood those situations by that time and allowed it.

Mr. and Mrs. Wagner—Chad and Dude—were soft-spoken, friendly people. Chad was a very beautiful woman. Dude, RJ's father, was in oil. They lived in a spacious house with a stone front and beautifully landscaped grounds.

It was the type of home I guess every young girl might dream of having. They lived in an environment totally unlike any that I knew. It was comfortable, warm but genteel. I knew that RJ and I could have a home like that.

Chad and Dude took to me just as if I were their daughter. That night Dude slept in RJ's room and I slept in their bedroom with Chad.

We were served breakfast in a lovely room overlooking the garden and chatted with RJ's mother. She talked to me like an old friend, telling me stories about her son, whom she adored.

I drove out of Stone Canyon that morning feeling that I'd made new friends. From the moment I entered RJ's world, I was impressed. I discovered what I could want, what I could fantasize having as a married woman.

RJ, I soon learned, was very popular with everybody. One weekend he asked me to go to a houseparty in Lake Arrowhead. Mother said yes. "If you can't be trusted by now, it's too late anyway," she said to me the night before.

Our host was a man named Watson Webb, who was the head cutter at Twentieth. He was also the scion of a very wealthy and social eastern family and owned an enormous lodge that slept twelve or fifteen, right on the lake.

There were eight or ten guests that weekend including Tyrone Power and his French wife (whom he would soon divorce), Annabella, Tab Hunter, and Clifton Webb. Tab, RJ, and I were by far the youngest.

Watson, who looked every inch the silver-haired patrician, was a wonderful host. He planned the weekends for fun and relaxation. We got up the next morning at 5:30 to be ready for water-skiing at 6:30 when the lake was smooth as glass. After a few hours of water-skiing and sunning on the dock, we all hiked up the hill to lunch on the terrace. It was a lively, talkative group of very witty people, who told the best show-business stories. There was so much to absorb, to learn.

Clifton Webb was a funny, funny man who delighted in young people. He loved to share his knowledge and experiences with the less knowledgeable like myself. This was not always true of older, distinguished actors. Charles Laughton, for example, required a bit of a nod and a bow from his younger colleagues, and in turn nodded back. Clifton, who was a bachelor all his life, loved young people as if they were his children.

It was another world for me. I felt privileged to be invited back again and again even without RJ. Often I was the only female present in a group of six or eight, most of the men perennial bachelors, and all of them in the business. At night after dinner, everyone would pitch in to clean up and wash the dishes. There would be a roaring fire in the fireplace and people would stand around Watson's player piano and sing. One night Noel Coward and Clifton sang a duet of one of Noel's songs. I would sing something, often as an impersonation of one of the other guests. For me, these were brilliant weekends spent with the the the wittiest teachers. And I was their student.

CHAPTER 10

ONE AFTERNOON in the early spring of 1951, I was called to Mr. Mayer's office. I took my seat as he indicated and he sat down, clasped his hands on his vest, and looked at me with a smile on his face.

"Debbie," he said, "you are a very talented little girl and I have a surprise for you today. You are going to make a picture with Gene Kelly and Donald O'Connor."

I thought, "Gene Kelly!" Every matinee I ever loved was with Gene Kelly! And Donald O'Connor!

Mr. Mayer continued, "And today Gene Kelly is coming to see you here."

Almost immediately after that, his secretary, Mrs. Koverman, informed Mr. Mayer that Gene Kelly had arrived.

"Send him in," the boss instructed.

Gene Kelly entered, greeting L.B. (as he was called by many of his employees) with a warm hello. He had the same natural charm that had totally captivated me in the Burbank movie house only three years before.

Mr. Mayer introduced us and he took a seat. Mr. Mayer, still very much the grandfather beaming with pride at the sight of two of his "children," again with his hands clasped before him, said to Gene, "So here's your leading lady."

Gene Kelly looked at me suddenly and very seriously. "Whaaat?"

Mr. Mayer repeated himself. "So here's the girl—*Singin' in the Rain*—your leading lady."

Gene stared at me and stared at me. "Do you dance?" he asked.

"No," I replied tentatively, adding, "Well, a little."

Looking at me as if he were making an appraisal, he continued, "Do you sing?"

"No." Well, I sang, I thought to myself, in that I could do harmony, but . . .

Gene looked at Mr. Mayer in shock. "L.B., w-w-w-whaaat are you doing to me?" He was very upset. Without waiting for L.B.'s answer, he said to me, "Stand up."

I stood up.

"Can you do a time step?" he asked.

"Yes, I can do a time step," I said confidently, hoping that would relieve him a bit.

"Okay," he nodded, "can I see it?"

So I did a waltz clog.

"That's not a time step, that's a waltz clog," he corrected me with distress in his voice. I didn't know. I thought a time step was a waltz clog.

"Can you do a maxi ford?" he continued.

A maxi ford? "I don't know that car," I answered meekly.

"That's not a car, that's a *step!*" It also happened to be, I later found out, Gene Kelly's favorite step.

It didn't matter to Mr. Mayer. Gene Kelly had been told he had me and he *had* me. When I told Mother that night that my next film was going to be *Singin' in the Rain* with Donald O'Connor and Gene Kelly, I was bursting with excitement and anticipation. It hadn't occurred to me that I had to *dance* with them and be as *good* as they were.

However, I soon found out I should have been thinking, "Just go take gas; turn on the carbon monoxide and just close the door." Because I was about to start something more difficult, more exhausting, more horrendous than any experience I'd ever known in my short and very sheltered experience.

We started rehearsals just two weeks after my nineteenth birthday. The studio had three months to turn me into a dancer. Both Gene and Donald had been dancing all their lives. I was assigned three teachers: Ernie Flatt, who taught me tap and later became the choreographer of *The Carol Burnett Show*; Carol Haney, who was Gene's assistant on the picture and went on to star in *The Pajama Game* on Broadway, and Jeanne Coyne, who later married Gene.

For the next three months I was locked in a sound stage for seven, eight hours a day with my three teachers taking shifts. Having been a gymnast made me strong, but soon I was overwhelmed and intimidated.

Carol Haney was assistant choreographer because Gene was also directing the picture and didn't have time to do it all. Gene had certain steps he liked to do. Donald, who was working on "Make 'Em Laugh," had certain steps *he* always did; and so Carol assembled everything for Gene to approve.

Meanwhile, I was taking a two-hour class with Ernie. Then a two-hour class with Carol. Carol would go on to take care of something else, and Jeanne would come in to teach me. I was dancing eight hours a day, nonstop. That's all I did.

I had to learn every step Gene was going to use and every step Donald was going to use, in whatever sequence they put them to make the dance. I didn't know any of their steps, of course. These were very difficult tap combinations. It's a very hard thing to learn tap. You have to get your ankles very loose first. The fronts of your feet have to become like balloons. Your brain has to work very fast. It takes years to perfect. And I had three months.

Gene would come in to rehearsals, look at me, and ask me to do a maxi ford, the traveling time step, or a combination of the steps they were teaching me. He was never satisfied. I never got a compliment. Ever.

I was afraid of him. He was so strict, so unyielding, and so serious all the time. He had an enormous burden of creativity on his back. Who had time for a crying nineteen-year-old who didn't know how to sing or dance?

In my opinion, I was being thrown to the lions. At first the frustration of mastering the dance infuriated me. One day I was feeling so defeated that I flew into a rage right on the stage, shouting and swearing. I took off my tap shoes and hurled them at the stage mirror and shattered it. Everyone stopped. People were shocked, staring at me as I walked out of the rehearsal hall.

I was so ashamed of my behavior. I went home that night and talked about it with Mother, asking her to help me, to remind me whenever I was getting toward the boiling point.

After that I found myself crying on the soundstage, doing everything in my power to hold back the tears. My feet were killing me. I was so overwhelmed, so intimidated. I couldn't understand why Gene was being so hard on me. I know why now. He was stuck with me. He knew he needed to drive me and so he did. But I didn't know the word *quit*. In my mind, I just had to do it.

After we'd finish a session and I was alone on the rehearsal stage, I'd just walk around and sob to myself. My teachers were all nice to me, and even fun. But I felt inept and exhausted all the time. One day I was lying under the piano sobbing when I heard a voice ask, "Why are you crying?"

"Because I'll never learn any of it," I said, tears still rushing forth. "I can't do it anymore. I feel like I'm going to die, it's so hard. I can't . . . I can't . . ."

"No, you're not going to die," the man said gently. "That's what it is to learn how to dance."

Taking my hands from my eyes I saw a man's pant leg. I pulled myself together to look up. It was Fred Astaire looking down on me, his brow creased with concern.

"You come watch me," he said, as he lent a hand to help me up. "You watch how hard I work. I don't cry," he explained, "but I do get frustrated and upset and I'm going to let you watch."

He took me into his rehearsal hall with Hermes Pan, his choreographer, and his drummer. They were rehearsing for *Royal Wedding*. Now Fred Astaire *never* let even Mr. Mayer watch him rehearse. He was a taskmaster and I saw that. I sat and watched them work until he too was totally frustrated with what he was doing. I knew that it was time for me to leave. But I left thinking that I wasn't alone; it's hard for everybody if it's hard for Fred Astaire.

His gesture was an enormous help to me. It was another step in seeing that MGM was a university of hard work and pain and wonderful creativity.

As production grew closer, the pressure intensified. There were scenes to learn and rehearse, costumes to be fitted, and songs to be recorded. The days seemed even longer and harder. I would be so tired that instead of making the long trip back to Burbank, some nights I'd sleep in my little dressing room on the floor, with a guard stationed by the studio outside my door. Other nights I'd stay with Lois Horne, my teacher from Warners, who lived nearby in Westwood.

Shooting began on June 19, 1951. I thought I was good at lip-synching until we went before the camera. Then the pressure was on like nothing I'd ever known. Putting the song together with the dancing takes a very special precision. They had one man on the set who did nothing but watch our lips. If there was one mistake, it was "CUT!" and we'd have to start all over again.

Now I had to remember not only the dance steps but where to breathe in my already recorded phrasing of the song. When I wasn't in front of the camera, I was off somewhere sitting listening to a record, mouthing it.

We started shooting the party number, where I did a dance with the girls:

"All I do is dream of you
The whole day through. . . ."

It's the scene where the girls and I are hired to entertain for the evening at a Hollywood party. The girls come in, throwing flowers in front of a big cake. The cake stops and I emerge from it.

By this time my brains were fried, my eyes were crossed inside, and my hand was squeezing my butt just to keep my concentration on the lip-synch, the steps, and the spacing. In my mind I'm thinking: "Double tap, double tap/sli*iiiide* tap! double tap, double tap/sliiiide tap!" My mind was racing.

Meanwhile, Gene is off camera with a microphone yelling: "SMILE DAMNIT, SMILE!!"

Smile! I'm smiling.

"DON'T LOOK SO PANICKED!"

Don't look so panicked, I'm thinking. Double tap, double tap/sliiiide, tap! Double tap, double ta . . .

"SMILE DAMNIT, SMILE!"

"I'm smiling, I'm smiling double tap, double tap/sliiiide . . . smile damnit, smile double tap, double tap . . .

Once in production, Gene would get mad at Donald and tear into him. "You're so stupid, you're not doing the step right! You're stupid!"

It wasn't until thirty-five years later that Donald told me the reason Gene always picked on him: It was because he was always mad at me. But he realized if he kept screaming at me I'd probably hold up production with my tears. So he screamed at Donald, who wouldn't cry.

The toughest scenes were done with Donald and Gene. Gene was in great condition. His legs were like pistons; he had the strongest thighs of any man alive. Donald was slim and not nearly as muscular but very strong. My body was strong from sports and barre work. Fortunately I didn't have to build the body, but I was still worn out.

The couch scene ("Good Morning") was the hardest scene I've ever done. Up the stairs, down the stairs. Up the couch, over the couch. We went over that couch hundreds of times. We had been shooting from eight o'clock in the morning. Gene was never satisfied. My feet were bleeding but he was relentless; take after take, he would never give up.

About eleven o'clock at night we finished a take and I just fell over. I just lay on the ground and with barely enough breath to talk, I said, "I can't do it again."

"All right! That's a wrap!" Gene said.

I was driven home that night. The next morning I couldn't get out of bed. I couldn't move. I couldn't walk.

Mother called Dr. Levy to come over and see me.

"What's wrong with you, Mary Frances?" he asked.

"I can't move I'm so tired." I felt as if I'd just crossed a desert.

He checked me over. My heartbeat was slow. "That's ridiculous!" he said. "You'll have to stay in bed for two days."

"But I can't, Dr. Levy. We're shooting a picture. . . ."

"You don't stay in bed, you may not live to finish that picture," he replied.

Mother called the studio. Hundreds of extras, musical numbers costing thousands of dollars, and Mary Frances is tired. Arthur Freed, the producer, called Dr. Levy.

"You don't understand; we have a major motion picture going here and Debbie has to report."

"No, she doesn't," said Dr. Levy. "She's exhausted and she's not going to. It's medically unsound."

"She's only nineteen years old! Get her ass in here!"

"She's staying right where she is," countered the good doctor.

Everyone flipped out. Gene Kelly, Arthur Freed, the insurance company. Dr. Blank from the studio called Dr. Levy informing him that he'd take over my case. He'd give me some "vitamin" shots and I'd feel fine.

Again Dr. Levy said, "No way. Rest is what she needs. You can keep your shots." Which probably saved my life. It was Dr. Blank who administered all the "vitamins" that got Judy Garland and a lot of other people started on the road to complete addiction.

So they rearranged the schedule for two days.

The picture was directed by Stanley Donen and Gene. Stanley handled the technical end, working with Gene in setting up the shots. Gene directed all the actors. They worked very well together.

I felt under the gun so much of the time that I missed just about anything that didn't have to do with my performance. Jean Hagen was wonderful and very nice to me. The role she played, a caricature, was not at all like Jean's personality. She modeled it after Judy Holliday. She should have won the Academy Award she was nominated for. In the picture, my character was supposed to dub the "squeaky" voice of Jean's character while she sang. Jean's real voice, however, was lovely and she dubbed herself.

I sang "You Are My Lucky Star" with Gene Kelly. But it was a very rangy song and done in his key. My part did not come out well, so my singing voice was dubbed in by Betty Royce after the picture was finished.

Shooting ended on November 21, eight months after rehearsals had begun.

Ironically, the man whose vision and instinct had made it all possible for me was no longer there. L.B. Mayer, after twenty-seven years as production head of the studio that bore his name, had been ousted in a power struggle with an ancient rival, Nicholas Schenck, the chairman of Loew's. Mr. Mayer passed through the studio gates for the last time on June 21, the third day of shooting *Singin' in the Rain*. He was replaced by producer/screenwriter Dore Schary. Schary presided over what turned out to be the beginning of a dismal end to a long and legendary era in the history of American film.

Singin' in the Rain and childbirth were the hardest things I ever had to do in my life. The pain from childbirth was in the lower body but in *Singin' in the Rain* it was everywhere—especially my feet and my brain. As soon as shooting was completed, I went up to Lake Tahoe for a week's rest. My friend Jeanette went with me. She'd get up in the morning, go water-skiing, play tennis, and bring me my breakfast at noon. My first day there I slept for eighteen hours.

CHAPTER 11

TEN DAYS LATER I was back at the studio to work on *Mr. Imperium* with Lana Turner and Ezio Pinza. Marjorie Main of the "Ma Kettle" series played my aunt.

In the story Marjorie runs a boarding house/resort cottage in the Italian Alps where people go for a vacation. I come to live with her as a young girl after losing my parents. Lana plays a movie star who's come up to the mountains for a rest. Ezio Pinza plays opposite her as a king who's in exile and who also comes up to the mountains for a rest. They meet and *voilà!* fall in love. Such a script.

The real movie was offscreen. Marjorie Main was certainly a funny one. She was a wonderful woman, but completely eccentric. When Marjorie wasn't on the set, she wore gloves all the time to avoid germs. Often she'd wear a mask over her mouth and nose.

Marjorie was an older woman who, it so happened, had a real-life bladder problem. She'd be saying her lines on camera, and nature would call. Continuing on with her lines, as if it were part of the movie, she'd walk right off the set into her dressing room. You'd hear the toilet seat go up, the toilet seat go down, the flushing, and Marjorie was still saying her lines. Then she'd come right back on the set, as if we hadn't cut, and finish the scene.

She always knew her lines right down to a *t*. Her only problem was nature calling at any odd moment, so the studio provided her with her own bathroom. No one else had a private toilet, not even the stars. (Mario Lanza couldn't be bothered with the walk. He'd just go off into the corner of the set and pee. Finally they got him a bucket and he used it.)

Marjorie was a widow. She had been married for a long time to a man named Horace, and she wasn't about to let a little thing like death separate them. Everywhere that Marjorie went, Horace went.

The first time I was aware of it was during a break on the set. I was sitting in the chair next to her one day when I heard her say, "Horace, this is a very warm day and I'm tired. Why don't you get me a glass of water?"

And Horace would go and get her a glass of water. In her mind, that is. Then another time during lunch break, I passed Marjorie in the commissary, where she was seated at the counter. Horace sat next to her.

"Say hello to Horace," she said to the waitress.

"Uh . . . hello, Horace," the waitress said.

"I'll have the ham and Swiss on rye toast and Horace will have the egg salad."

She had a house in Palm Springs and every weekend she'd pile her food and supplies into the back of an old car. "We're going to the desert," she'd say to whoever was around. "Com'on, Horace, get in."

It was bizarre. I'd never worked with anyone who'd gone over the edge and thought it was perfectly normal. She was Off. Her. Rocker. But she could put on a costume and know her lines; that was all that counted. She had a great career.

I was very impressed to be working with Lana Turner. The first day she emerged from her dressing room onto the set, it was an entrance, a triumph in shimmering platinum.

Lana was a big star. She got the full treatment. She was catered to. A car picked her up in the morning and brought her to the studio. Her dressing room was the biggest on the set. Lunch was brought to her on a silver tray. She had a maid as well as a wardrobe woman at her service at all times. She didn't have to take a step to get anything. Mention it and she had it.

Lana had a lot of things on her mind during the making of this picture. For one thing she was pregnant and suffering a little from morning sickness. She was married to a millionaire playboy named Bob Topping at the time and didn't seem very happy about it. He wasn't very nice to her. But she really wanted this baby.

She wasn't in the ideal state to be working. But the studio insisted. In those days you did what you were told or they cut your money off and put you on suspension. Besides, millionaire or no, Mr. Topping, it seems, was always short of cash. Lana needed the money.

Yet with me she was very patient and even, in a way, maternal, which is not really Lana's thing. The pregnancy must have brought that out and I was the lucky benefactor.

This was my sixth film but acting was still very new. Lana would go over some of the difficult scenes with me. She'd give me tips on working with the camera. "Don't turn your body that far away from the camera, Debbie dear; it's a bad angle." Sometimes I'd visit her in her dressing room just to cheer her up.

*   *   *

Ezio Pinza was fresh from Broadway and his starring role in *South Pacific*. I didn't know from Broadway. I didn't know Pinza was the greatest baritone in all the world. To me he was a big, unattractive, oversexed kind of man who was the most conceited egomaniac I'd ever met.

Every chance he got, right there on the set, he'd be groping Lana, who was forever maneuvering to keep her body out of his hands. Back in her dressing room she'd be seething with rage.

"He's dreadful. He's a slime! I can't stand being within ten feet of him!"

This was a problem because the script called for a hot and heavy romance between them.

One day they had a kissing scene to do. Without showing her disgust, Lana very compliantly took her place before the camera. Pinza, with all the self-confidence and aplomb of a Latin lover, took his. They exchanged dialogue as he took her in his arms. Then, unleashing his idea of passion, he absolutely overwhelmed her with a big, rapacious, wet kiss.

Lana jerked back, pushing his head away, and violently wiped her mouth with the back of her hand.

"Bleee-whaaa! CUT!" she shouted. "Ezio! Just kiss me, don't *eat* me!"

Pinza, unfazed, looked at her with a sly grin. They had to do another take.

The dialogue was exchanged. Pinza moved in for the kiss; Lana, totally hiding her revulsion, was prepared. *WHAP!* Pinza did it again! This time Lana went along. It was either that or face being humiliated once more.

Back in her dressing room she was furious.

"Ugh! He's such a pig! I hope they got that shot because I'll never do another kiss with him again as long as I live!"

The two stars fought throughout the whole picture. Pinza couldn't have cared less. He thought all women fell at his feet anyway. Obviously, the man did not have a mirror. He thought that he was the biggest star in the world and that Lana was lucky to be working with him. He never even noticed the rest of us. He certainly never noticed me—or even Marjorie Main running around with a mask over half her face.

Mr. Imperium bombed at the box office. Lana lost her baby, eventually divorced her husband, and started spending time with a Mr. Stompanato. Ezio Pinza went back to the concert stage, where he could actually have the world at his feet, and Marjorie put Horace in the car and went back to Palm Springs.

I felt that it was all a big game, a kick. Every new picture I made, I'd be thinking "I'm watching this!" I didn't realize that I was being swept up into it; that I was never going to get out of it.

Just one week after my twentieth birthday, in April 1952, *Singin' in the Rain* premiered in Hollywood. RJ and I went together in an old car like the one in the movie. I had been to many premieres by then, but this one was mine.

There was I, in my Helen Rose dress, on the arm of RJ Wagner, he looking so darling and handsome, the crowds cheering us and calling to us as we entered the theater under a blaze of photographers' flashbulbs.

But once the theater lights dimmed and the curtains parted, all the glamour and hoopla faded away. I was suddenly alone in the dark. I remember sitting there, taking slow careful breaths, a little stiff with anticipation, wondering what it would all look like—all those eight months—agony and exhaustion, tears and pain, all the anxiety about getting the steps right, getting the lip-synch right, smiling, DAMNIT, smiling.

Then suddenly the screen lit up with this amazing movie. And there she was, popping out of that cake, dancing up and down those stairs, singing and smiling and holding her own with those two dancing ge-niuses. If there was ever a single moment when Mary Frances was trans-formed into Debbie, it might have been then. I thought, hey, I'm good! All that pain and the kid is good! I was amazed. To this day I am amazed at what I accomplished in so short a time. I knew then and there where I belonged. Gene had pushed and the girl was good.

A few days after the picture opened, I was called into Benny Thau's office. Benny Thau had been with MGM since the 1920s when he was hired by Mr. Mayer for the casting office. By the time Mr. Mayer left the studio, Benny and Eddie Mannix were his top executives. Benny was a small man with a face like stone. People said he had ice water in his veins.

"Now, Debbie, I want you to run the movie and listen to your voice. You have to study now. We have to lower your voice. It was all right for that role. You were a little girl. But we want to move your career ahead, so you'll have to lower it."

He was right of course. I ran the picture. My voice could get real high and real squeaky at certain moments. It was time to take Gertrude Fogler seriously.

1. Mary Frances, six months old,
El Paso, Texas, 1932

2. Billy and I, five and three and a
half years old

3. The Girl Scout cookie-sales champion, age thirteen, Burbank

4. My first—and only—prom. The tall, handsome boy is my first boyfriend, Jerry Odens. Mother added the black net and pink tulle. My black and gold sandals were $1.99 from Standard Shoes.

5. Miss Burbank 1948—crown, robes, and throne courtesy of the Warner Brothers wardrobe and props departments

6. Warner Brothers' two youngest starlets, Alice Kelly and me, with the studio teacher, Lois Horne

7. *Below*, on the set with June Haver and Marcia Mae Jones in my first picture, *The Daughter of Rosie O'Grady*, Warners, 1948

8. With Fred Astaire and Red Skelton in *Three Little Words*, my first film at MGM, 1949

9. Janie Powell and I blowing out the candles in *Two Weeks with Love*, MGM, 1950. She turned twenty-one and I turned eighteen on the same day.

11. *Above*, with the boys in Korea, age eighteen

10. *Left*, Carleton Carpenter and I, "Boop-boop-bee-doop," Korea, 1950

12. Ezio Pinza, Lana Turner, Marjorie Main, and I on the set of *Mr. Imperium*. Pinza thought he was God's gift to women. Lana had some other ideas about that.

13. Linda Christian and Edmund Purdom, on screen and off, *Athena*, MGM, 1953

14. Leon Tyler and I dancing at Jeanette Johnson's Flapper Party. I'd just met Eddie and he arrived later.

15. *Above*, RJ, his mother and dad, and I, visiting him on location. You can see from our expressions how much he was loved.

16. *Left*, Lillian Burns Sidney trying to be my drama coach, MGM studios, 1951

17. *Right*, Gene Kelly and I in *Singin' in the Rain*

18. "Double-tap, double-tap, *sliiiide*, step . . ." Making that film was as painful as giving birth.

19. Gene, Donald, and I filming the opening of *Singin' in the Rain*

20. *Right*, with Joan Crawford

21. Eddie, I, mother, and Louella Parsons at the Sands Hotel, 1954. Louella had taken to calling us "America's Sweethearts."

22. Engaged to Eddie, with Bernie Rich and Margie Duncan at the Stork Club in New York

Gertrude Fogler was about age eighty then. She was a tiny woman, about four feet ten. She dressed simply, wore no makeup, and pinned her gray hair up in back. It was she who taught Grace Kelly French before she married Prince Rainier. It was Gertrude who worked long and hard and ultimately unsuccessfully to get Ricardo Montalban and Fernando Lamas to speak without an accent. That, of course, never happened. She was a brilliant woman who ate nuts and yogurt all day, long before it was popular; and who worked almost right up till the end of her ninety-eight years.

Studying with Gertrude was like studying to be a doctor. It could be so boring I used to spit on my eyelids to stay awake. She made me study the entire chest frame, the diaphragm, the rib cage, the anatomy.

I sat up straight in a hardback chair for hours in her little green bungalow. I'd have to lie on the floor and bounce a book on my diaphragm.

"Your voice is dreadful! Now put it here!" she'd say, placing her palm under my rib cage. "Feel the resonance? Feel!"

She must have felt like giving up on me a million times but she'd never let me get out of it. We got rid of that Texas accent. She finally placed my voice in its proper channel.

Everybody had to study with Gertrude, and everybody spoke beautifully.

In the Star System, the Moguls were the bosses. Goldwyn, Warner, Cohn, Mayer, Zanuck. You did what you were told or they fired your ass. Except for Garbo, Hepburn, Tracy, and very few others. The time came when even Gable was fired. He drove off the lot alone in 1957.

At the beginning of a career, a lot of the bosses' directions were carried out in the makeup department. At MGM, makeup was an institution, a whole other world. You'd walk in at six o'clock in the morning, looking as if you'd just rolled out of bed, hair hanging limp or askew, and there they were, all of them, all at the same time: Elizabeth Taylor, June Allyson, Jane Powell, Janet Leigh, Hedy Lamarr, Grace Kelly, Pier Angeli, Leslie Caron, Ann Miller, Cyd Charisse, Kathryn Grayson, Lana Turner, Ava Gardner, Esther Williams, Greer Garson. It was an amazing sight. And very interesting to see that at that hour, after a night of sleep, they all looked like me. They weren't that beautiful in the A.M. The ingredients were there, but the beauty had to be brought out with the proper makeup.

We all had to do what the average woman has to do.

First we went into individual cubicles. Every girl had her own makeup person. The beauty wasn't all cosmetic, but the cosmetics definitely enhanced.

At first I didn't like what they did to me. I didn't feel I should be made up. It wasn't my personality. It wasn't Frannie. Glamour was for Marilyn Monroe and Lana Turner, I thought.

The brunettes needed less makeup and the blondes looked worse in the morning. The brunettes walked in looking better from the start, and they became gorgeous. The blondes took longer. Until a blonde emphasizes her eyelashes and puts on her eyebrows, she looks as if everything has disappeared overnight. In those days the eyebrows were plucked so much they often never grew back.

We came out of our cubicles for hairdressing looking good because the face was up. Hair was done in a great big open room with one long table. There were lights across the top and in strips down along the sides of the mirrors. Alongside were the hairdryers with the large glass bubbles.

First the stylists would wash our hair and then wet-dress it. There were no rollers in those days. They'd twirl the hair and curl it with a hot iron. Then we'd have to sit under a dryer for forty minutes. When we finished with the dryer, they'd take the hot iron to smooth every bit of hair so that it looked perfect for the camera.

There might be twenty hairdressers dealing with twenty stars at the same time in the same room. Sidney Guilaroff, a cigarette constantly in his hand and carrying the gold cigarette case given to him by Greta Garbo, oversaw everything. Sidney always did certain people like Elizabeth and Lana. Vera-Ellen would be sitting with her legs up, but never with her feet crossed at the ankle because it hurt circulation. Ann Miller would be talking a mile a minute; Greer Garson would be off in her corner reading poetry. All the ladies were chatting and gossiping, yakety-yak, just like a beauty parlor. It was the movie-star morning rap.

"You know who's going with George, don't you?"

"Oh, she's been sleeping with him for years."

"He divorced her and then started seeing her sister. . . ."

Everyone was buzzing. When Grace got engaged, it was all buzz-buzz. Ava and Frank, buzz-buzz; Lana with Johnny Stompanato, buzz-buzz. Careers beginning, peaking, stopping, and falling; it was all right there. All about Hollywood; what's going on and with whom. No matter how new, how young, or how small, loan-outs, new stars, no matter how they got there—limousine, bicycle, or bus—that's where all the girls went in the morning.

In the beginning I just sat there agog, taking it all in, half the time not even knowing what I was listening to. With all these stars in one room, what did I have to say? My baseball glove wore out?

It was an intense two and a half hours. We came en masse, like so many working girls of all ages, often bedraggled, no eyebrows, the hair awful, no face, and we were sent out as *They*, the miraculous-looking MGM stars.

The psychological power of the makeup department was not easily forgotten. When I first went to MGM, they wanted me to have my nose fixed. I thought my nose was fine and I refused. I wasn't against that sort of thing; witness my ears. But only if necessary.

Others were less fortunate. One famous star took their advice and ended up with a nose job that was so bad, she forever after had to wear a "piece" to build it up for the camera. Vera-Ellen was told that she was too fat, that her top thighs were too heavy. No matter how she exercised, the fat remained. Vera-Ellen was never fat, but she was insecure and wanted to please so she believed them. Which was the worst thing she could have done. She cut way back on her food intake. After that she drank coffee all day and ate only a steak and a vegetable at night. Her legs became absolutely angular. That regimen started her on the road to deeper, more intractable psychological problems. Her life eventually turned into a tragedy, and the diet killed her.

I was doing all my growing up in very grown-up places. From the Girl Scouts to the jet set. Everything was new and more fantastic.

Not long after *Singin' in the Rain* was released, Hugh O'Brian, who was under contract to Universal, invited me to a party at Marion Davies's. I'd heard her name. Other than that, I knew nothing about her. But Hugh filled me in.

Marion Davies had been a famous silent-screen comedienne in the 1920s. She was also the mistress, for thirty-five years, of the legendary William Randolph Hearst and hostess to the world (including Churchill and George Bernard Shaw) at his fabled castle at San Simeon. Their relationship was immortalized in Orson Welles's *Citizen Kane*.

Hearst was almost ninety when he died in August 1951. Only a few months later Marion married Horace Brown, an airline captain, a man about her own age. People were shocked, forgetting that maid Marion had always been a bridesmaid but never a bride.

The party we were going to was her first since Hearst had died. It was in honor of Johnnie Ray, who, except for a boy named Eddie Fisher, was the hottest recording star in the world.

All Hollywood was going to be there. It was formal. I needed something new. Helen Rose designed a dress—black-velvet V-neck top with sleeves below the elbow, cinched waist, and a white-lace full skirt. If I had been going to a premiere, the studio would have made it and paid for it. But this was purely social, so Mother made the skirt and a neighbor, Mrs. Kropf, made the top because she was better at tailoring. Janie Powell loaned me an evening bag and an ermine jacket. And Lillian Burns, who in private life was married to director George Sidney, lent me an emerald ring to wear.

Marion Davies lived on a huge estate in Beverly Hills. The house was up a long driveway lined with dozens of tall palms—a U-shaped, pink, three-story Mediterranean mansion.

We entered a foyer two stories high. Off the foyer were enormous rooms with fifteen-foot ceilings, decorated for the party to resemble New York's El Morocco, Stork Club, and "21." There were orchestras in every room and food everywhere—French, Italian, Oriental, Mexican.

These rooms all opened on to a vast sweeping terrace with a hundred-foot-long pool in three tiers that ran down to the formal gardens. The garden paths were carpeted with synthetic grass; a circus tent was erected near a fishpond. The place was jammed with guests, more than seven hundred, drinking cocktails served by butlers with sterling-silver trays. Everywhere you looked, it was wall-to-wall stars. Joan Crawford, Ava Gardner, Charlton Heston, Gary Cooper, Red Skelton, Lena Horne, Jack Benny, Merle Oberon, Gregory Peck, Clark Gable, Dinah Shore, just dozens and dozens of famous faces. *Life* magazine was covering it for a special piece.

It was like being in a nightclub and a museum at the same time. People toured the house, inspecting the gilt-framed old masters hanging gallery-style alongside amazing oil portraits of Marion in costume for her different film roles—always a lovely young woman with big, almost innocent round eyes and short platinum-blond hair.

Every few minutes after we first arrived, I'd ask Hugh to point out our hostess in the crowd, but she was nowhere in sight. About an hour later, we were standing in the "El Morocco" room when suddenly there was a moment's hush. Someone had spotted her.

"Marion darling!" a woman shouted above the voices of the crowd.

At the top of the grand staircase, leaning on the arm of a big, husky-looking man, stood a small mature woman of fifty-four. She had short blond hair nicely done in a wave.

Dressed in a simple white-satin strapless gown, she was drenched in, covered with, fabulous jewels. Three quarters of a million dollars' worth: huge diamond teardrop earrings, bracelets of rubies and diamonds running up her frail arms, a necklace of diamonds *and* a necklace of rubies to match an enormous ruby ring that she wore with her simple gold wedding band.

An almost audible gasp filled the room and everyone burst out in applause. They cheered as she descended the stairs slowly, like returning royalty, her jewels shimmering like a chandelier. People were thrilled. It was like, "Look, she's actually *walking!*"

She was beautifully made up, although she looked kind of old to me. But I was twenty and thought forty was old. Now that I'm in my fifties, I realize she looked great.

When she reached the bottom step, she was greeted by Johnnie Ray, who took her hand and kissed it. Then the two of them made a receiving line.

She shook the hand of nearly everyone present. After that she stood for more than an hour, posing for photographers with group after group of guests. She was very gracious, but it looked as if she were making a personal appearance in her own house.

By that time, however, everything was roaring along. Brod Crawford was doing alcoholic acrobatics on the terrace. Diana Dors caused a small sensation by "accidentally" falling into the fishpond. She emerged, soaked through to the skin, just in time for the photographers. Clark Gable danced cheek to cheek with Kay Spreckels, whom he would eventually marry. People partied into the night, everybody, that is, except Marion, who, almost like a ghost of a more glorious past, retreated back to the privacy of her bedroom hours before the final guests emptied out of her palace.

The evening was like riding the carousel. I got this beautiful, wonderful chance to get on and ride and reach for the gold ring. And so I did.

Meanwhile, the studio was creating a career for me. They teamed Donald O'Connor and me again and sent us on location to New York City for *I Love Melvin*. That same year I also did *The Affairs of Dobie Gillis* with Bobby Van and Bobby Fosse; *Give a Girl a Break* with Marge and Gower Champion and again Bobby Fosse; and then was loaned out to RKO for *Susan Slept Here* with Dick Powell. The picture was produced by Harriet Parsons, Louella's daughter. When that was finished, I went right back to MGM to do *Athena*. Five pictures in about fifteen months.

Athena was my eleventh picture and the first one I didn't want to do. Previously I had been observing while I was doing. On this one I now knew enough to realize I hated the script. It was about a family of back-to-nature health nuts. The cast included Edmund Purdom, Janie Powell, Vic Damone, and a small horde of musclemen and body builders led by Steve Reeves, who later went on to *Hercules* fame.

The only relief on the set was the action going on off camera. Linda Christian, who was Mrs. Tyrone Power at the time, was also in the picture. An exotic combination of cultures, the daughter of a Dutch father and a Mexican mother, Linda had a very bright and exciting European quality. She was earthy and exuded sexuality.

Linda didn't mingle, although she wasn't aloof. She looked as if her mind was always working on more worldly matters, like whom she wanted to meet. Linda was noted for her flamboyant love relationships. She was a temptress. And right before our eyes, we saw the tempted, who in this case was playing opposite Linda, Edmund Purdom.

Edmund was a gorgeous, debonair Englishman. He was *ool-weeze a veddy nahce yoong mahn. But ek-chu-lee kwaht af-fick-ted* in a way that didn't suit a young man in Hollywood at that time. Had he stayed in England and met Cubby Broccoli a few years later, he'd have made a perfect James Bond.

So you could say Edmund was prior to his time; except to Linda. His timing was perfect for her. They fell in love.

Everyone had a little trailer on the set, a little box that was a dressing room. Linda and Edmund would go into his little room, close the door, and be gone for quite awhile. It was soon the gossip of the lot. After all, he was not exactly a big star and Linda was very much married to Tyrone Power.

Tyrone Power, as a star, was right up there with Clark Gable and Gary Cooper. And being in his physical presence was almost overwhelming, he was so beautiful, so charming, so gentle, so sensitive, and so kind—to everybody. He was not the sort of husband most women would risk losing.

Sometimes Tyrone would drive over from Twentieth Century-Fox where he worked to have lunch with Linda. We were all thrilled just to see him, he was so sensational-looking. Linda always seemed quite pleased to see him too.

One day we were shooting in a Santa Fe-style setting on Lot 2. It was a huge area with wonderful gardens and landscaping, as well as a lovely pond. It was like being in a park.

Linda and Edmund must have had a special appreciation for it too, because that day during the lunch break, the two casually wandered off down a garden path, and were gone. Those of us who didn't eat in the commissary would eat outside on the set, and then often go for a stroll. But no one went near the pond that day. Even I knew that Linda and Edmund's picnic was strictly private in nature.

That day I was also giving an interview.

So I was sitting there, the fount of wisdom on matters romantic, when I looked up and saw Tyrone Power's car on the lot, driving very slowly down the road toward us.

Omigod, I thought; Linda obviously hadn't been expecting him. What if he went looking for her!

The only solution was to warn her. I excused myself very discreetly from my interviewer. I jumped on my bicycle, which I always used for getting around the studio, and started pedaling like mad.

I rode all around the pond and into the surrounding woods, with no Linda and Edmund in sight. What if Tyrone decided to look in the woods, I wondered.

"Linda! Linda!" I called frantically.

Nothing.

I rode over by the swimming pool, thinking maybe they were taking a little sun. Forget it. I turned the corner on the path near where they shot the exteriors for *Mrs. Miniver*, and on the other side of the small field, my eye caught a clump of bushes in a steady jiggling motion.

That must be it, I thought.

First in a loud whisper, not wanting, under any circumstances, for Tyrone to hear, I called: "Linda! Linda! Linda!" Yoo-hoo.

Nothing.

The bushes kept shaking away. Call it intuition, for that's all it could have been at that point in my life, but I knew that was no squirrel looking for acorns.

"*Linda!* Linda! Your husband's here!" I yelled.

The bushes stopped. A few seconds later, she materialized, smoothing her dress, shaking her hair back in place, walking very quickly in my direction.

"He's on the set," I said to her, wide-eyed, almost gasping from anticipation.

"Thank you for telling me, Debbie," she said very seriously, walking quickly across the field.

When Linda and I returned to the set, Tyrone was standing there in conversation with a several people.

"Oh, darling, it's so unexpected," she cooed, rushing up to him.

"You didn't let me know you were coming," she added, throwing her arms around him like the adoring wife.

"I wanted to surprise you, baby," he said, kissing her.

They looked like Hollywood's dream couple, standing there. My heart was pounding and he wasn't even my husband.

Nor was Tyrone Linda's husband for very much longer. The Christian-Purdom romance continued to blossom. They divorced their spouses, got married and went off to Rome to live.

Vic Damone played my boyfriend in the picture. He wasn't much older than I but he seemed worldly to me. A worldly man I connected with sex. It was all in my mind but it was *in* my mind.

I got around it with Vic by becoming like a sister to him. He'd tell me all about his girlfriends. He'd tell me what he did the night before and the night before and the night before that.

He'd tell me everything, wild stories. He liked redheads. Real redheads. Red all over. Vic made a very big point of it. He wanted me to know. I'm sure he was trying to shock me, and he did. It was the first time, possibly the only time, I ever discussed pubic hair with a man. I did my best to laugh about it, but it made me feel very uncomfortable.

By then, I had been dating RJ for more than a year and a half. We went out two or three nights a week to premieres and opening. Sometimes we'd go to Watson Webb's in Arrowhead, or to a party, like a big western evening at Alan Ladd's ranch out in the valley. RJ liked to dance and to swim. We'd go water-skiing together, or play tennis. Often we'd go over to Clifton Webb's house and be entertained for hours with his wonderful stories.

I dated others, but compared to RJ they were really "friends." It was social. RJ I considered my steady. He was sensitive and charming but not bossy. He liked strong women. I could make the date. Tennis, bowling, a party. "RJ, I'd like to go bowling Thursday night; are you free?"

RJ was different from all the other boys I went out with. I wasn't afraid of him. I trusted him. After the first few dates he kissed me goodnight. I loved the way he kissed, although my responses were shy and tentative. I felt safe and comfortable with him. He was the ideal Frannie would grow up and marry. I knew he'd never push things too far.

Frannie was now almost twenty-one. RJ was two years older. Like any normal, healthy red-blooded American boy, he had more in mind than a quick kiss inside the front door at the end of a night. He didn't say so, but even I knew that. We kissed, of course, and the most exciting thing would be when he put his hand on the top of my chest—not anywhere near my breast—where he could feel my heartbeat.

I wanted to step out into that adventuresome land, and fantasized what it would be like. But if he held me too close while we were dancing, and if I felt the impression of his body against mine, it frightened me. I had been taught to stay away from sex or otherwise go to hell. But if I was going to marry RJ and be the mother of his children, it was going to be right.

At one point in our relationship, he was going away on location to northern California. He called me at the studio and asked me if I'd have dinner with him that night. I had to say no because I had a lot of dialogue to prepare for the next day.

RJ said he had to see me. I told him to come to the house after dinner. He arrived about eight o'clock. Everybody was at home in the little house, so we went outside.

The sun had just gone down. We sat in a couple of wrought-iron chairs by the pool. RJ turned his chair very close to face mine. Our knees touched. He leaned forward and taking my hands, looked into my eyes.

He told me how much he liked looking at me, how much he was going to miss me.

Nervously making small talk to avoid anything more serious, I told him I was overweight.

He nuzzled closer so that his lips brushed my ear. "I think you are the perfect weight," he whispered.

I moved away just slightly. "RJ, remember there are neighbors." What if the neighbors. . . ?

"Why don't we go out for a ride?" he asked.

I was torn. Was that desire? We couldn't continue to sit out there. It was getting dark. I wouldn't have put it past my father to come outside and say something, despite the fact that both he and Mother liked RJ.

We sat there for a few more minutes. Should I or shouldn't I lose six pounds? Could we or couldn't we go for a short ride? How long would it be before we'd see each other again? Maybe I could go up north and visit some weekend. Maybe I could go up north with Chad and Dude. Maybe.

He kissed me good-night. Don't worry, Debbie. It's dark, Debbie. The only way the neighbors would see anything would be if they used a flashlight.

Just as that thought flashed across my mind, somebody—either my mother or my father—flicked on the light over the back door.

*   *   *

Three days after RJ left, there was an envelope with his handwriting in the mailbox. The return address was Pinecrest Lodge ("on beautiful Strawberry Lake"), Tuolumne County, California.

Debbie Darling:

Well, I've been gone for exactly 24 hours and I miss you terribly. Isn't that the end?

You were so cute last night when we were outside talking. You really looked wonderful. I wanted to kiss you so many times but those neighbors, they have got to go or we'll have to pick another spot.

Tomorrow we are going to rehearse and then the next day we will start to shoot. Maybe after this picture, I'll be able to own you because I am sure I love you.

Will write again soon. Until then, take it easy and remember, I love you.

RJ

P.S. Think you look great at 106, so don't lose, don't gain, you look just right.

I did go with his parents that summer to visit RJ on the set. And the first day he was home from location, he came over to have lunch with me in the commissary. He was going right into a new picture, *Titanic* with Clifton Webb and Barbara Stanwyck. He was very excited to be working in a picture with Clifton.

The first couple of weeks he was home, he came over to the studio for lunch a few times and we went out over the weekends. He told me then that he'd been thinking about me a lot while he was away. He wanted us to spend more time alone together.

I knew what he meant although I didn't want to think about it.

I didn't see it at first, but something was changing for us. It was RJ. One weekend he didn't ask me out. I didn't think anything of it at the time. I did notice, after the third time, that he would be late for a date, which wasn't like him.

One Friday morning in makeup, one of the girls asked me what RJ and I were doing that weekend. I realized when she asked that there weren't any plans.

"He's probably working," I commented. "He's shooting a picture."

"Yeah, that picture should be some *experience* for him," my friend remarked.

I didn't like the way she said that. "Experience?"

"Well, after all, Debbie, he's making a movie with Barbara Stanwyck. She's a great woman. . . ."

I still didn't get it.

As the weeks passed, he came fewer and fewer times for lunch at the studio commissary. He "couldn't get away."

I asked him to a Halloween costume party. He said yes. I planned for us to go as clowns. He said fine.

That night he was late again picking me up. I had his costume ready; he was supposed to change at the house. But he'd decided he didn't want to go as a clown. He wanted to be Cary Grant and go as someone dashing. I wanted him to go as a clown. He gave in to me and put on the outfit. But he wouldn't wear the makeup.

It turned out to be one of those outrageous parties. There were guys dressed as drag queens in feather boas, people practically nude in skimpy little costumes. RJ and I had no fun at all. He was very quiet. I tried to have a good time dancing and clowning. But I could feel that he didn't want to be in costume and he didn't want to be there. He'd gone because he felt obligated.

Driving home that night, he told me. "I think we're too young . . . to go out this much together."

I said nothing. I knew what he was really saying.

He broke the silence. "You know, you're not willing to commit that much to me."

"You mean go to bed with you," I said, clarifying.

"Well . . . passion can't always be hidden. I have to be with you more. I have to touch you more."

"Well to me, RJ, it's a sin. Unless you're married."

He didn't say anything to that. I'm sure he knew I wasn't trying to get him to marry me. But I really thought if a boy didn't want to be with me unless he could sleep with me, then he was only interested in the physical.

"I think we should date less," he blurted out very seriously.

I said, "Fine."

I was so mad. I knew I had lost him; riding along in the front seat of his car, the two of us in our striped, baggy costumes; me, this tomboyish starlet with no experience, wearing a red rubber nose and full clown makeup. I said nothing more, and just stared straight ahead.

When we got to the house, he walked me to the door and kissed me lightly on the lips. Looking very sullen, he said good night.

Good night.

I went inside and stood behind the window curtain watching him drive away.

We saw each other a couple of times after that. He was too kind to just end it. He's the kindest man living. He didn't want to be with the clown; he was enamored of Barbara. I couldn't compete with that.

I was really crushed by the loss of his friendship. By myself, I would cry about it. But I never discussed it with anyone—my mother, my girlfriends; no one. Sometimes I wanted to call him and say, "Okay, I'll go to bed with you." But I knew I couldn't.

I couldn't avoid the reality that I lived in a house that was very repressed in terms of sexual relationships. I wanted to get beyond that, but I couldn't just force myself.

Had we gone to bed together, he would eventually have left anyway. Then I would really have been destroyed. I would have had to face the fact that RJ was attracted to a different, more sexual kind of woman.

When he met Natalie Wood a few years later, she didn't put up any of my barriers. They could go away on weekends together and share intimacy. When they got married, I thought, "Lucky her." RJ was a wonderful light in her life because he is naturally loving and giving.

He was the one I loved, in my fashion. I can't say that I've forgotten him. I still see his picture, thirty-five years later, and think that's my idea of a terrific-looking, wonderful man. It was a fantasy never realized.

CHAPTER 12

1954. *Modern Screen* magazine's ten most popular young female stars that year were Debbie Reynolds, Grace Kelly, Elizabeth Taylor, Doris Day, June Allyson, Marilyn Monroe, Ann Blyth, Janet Leigh, Jane Powell, and Pier Angeli. In that order. The most popular males were Rock Hudson, Marlon Brando, Tony Curtis, Tab Hunter, Robert Wagner, and William Holden. That year, I made three pictures for Metro and was loaned out to Howard Hughes for a fourth (*Susan Slept Here*) at RKO. I was Debbie now to almost everyone but my family and my oldest friends. I no longer thought about my future as a gym teacher.

"Now there's a nice boy," Mother would say, her eyes glued to the television set in the living room, watching Eddie Fisher. Mother never passed judgment on the boys I dated, although she had her favorites like RJ or Bob Neal, a wealthy Texas boy who spent a lot of time in Hollywood. Besides, the youth she missed by marrying young, she was experiencing through me. Maybe this was the kind of boy she would have dated, all things being equal.

Eddie.

He had a fifteen-minute television show called *Coke Time* two or three nights a week. He was the heartthrob of America, bigger even, for that moment, than Sinatra; bigger than all of them until Elvis. He had not only his television show but something like twenty-seven gold records.

In 1953, a fan-magazine interviewer asked whom he'd like to meet most in Hollywood. His answer: Debbie Reynolds. I wasn't interested in Eddie Fisher. I'd watched him a couple of times with Mother. He had a wonderful voice. He was cute. But when his show was on the air, I'd be getting ready or running out the door for a date with RJ.

I first met Eddie on the set of *Athena* in 1954. Joe Pasternak, the producer of the picture, was giving him a tour of the studio.

He was boyish with dark-brown curly hair, a slim figure, a warm smile. I thought he was adorable. He was the boy from South Philadelphia, being wooed by Metro-Goldwyn-Mayer to be a movie star, and he was charming.

He was also in town to open as the headliner at the Cocoanut Grove at the Ambassador Hotel in Hollywood.

He asked if he could call me. I said yes. Why not? Sounds like fun.

Mother answered the phone when he called that night.

"Is Debbie there?"

"Who's calling?"

"Eddie Fisher."

"Eddie Fisher?! Sure, and I'm Lauren Bacall," she cracked. Mother could not believe it. Her sweetheart on TV was calling me.

He asked me if I'd be his date on his opening night. I said yes.

The Cocoanut Grove was very glamorous. It had been a top night-club on the Hollywood scene since the mid-1920s. An opening there was an event, star-studded; the kind of thing that doesn't exist in Hollywood anymore. The studios saw to it that their stars were there, dressed to kill. The men wore tuxedos. Helen Rose designed a strapless, red-lace dress for me. I wore a single strand of my own pearls, borrowed Janie Powell's ermine jacket, and carried an evening bag from Lillian.

Eddie had arranged to have his friend Mike Todd pick me up and escort me to the club. We had a ringside table. The house was packed with stars, including Gordon and Sheila MacRae, Jeff Chandler and Gloria DeHaven, Dan Dailey, Joan Crawford, and Johnnie Ray.

The evening was electric. If it had been a script for an MGM musical, we couldn't have had a better location for being seen, not only by the performer but by the audience and the press. Eddie gave a great show, singing some of his songs to me. It was so romantic. I loved it.

In the bright, almost hot blue glow of the photographers' flashbulbs, Eddie's life and my life were suddenly transformed into one. It didn't feel that way then. It was just exciting, like a wonderful party. I remember looking at him, thinking how handsome he was. I even found myself imagining falling in love with him. He was like the white knight; the handsome, sweet, attentive prince. I was twenty-two, going on seventeen. How perfect.

What's more, like a good MGM musical script, there was a subplot being played at the next table. Eddie had invited Pier Angeli, who happened to be a close friend of mine, to be his date also. He just hadn't met me when he asked her.

Pier and I saw each other but she didn't know Eddie had asked me.

So there I was, with Mike Todd, completely oblivious. And there sat Pier thinking she was with Eddie Fisher too. Until Eddie came down to my table and the photographers descended on us.

When Pier realized what he had done, she left. She also never told me about it until long after it could have made a difference in my life.

That night after the show, Eddie and I and Mike Todd went out for drinks. Except I didn't drink and neither did Eddie. We had Cokes. The two men liked each other very much. Eddie was very sweet and very attentive to me. So was Mike. I not only felt very flattered, I had a great time with them.

Later on, Eddie, without Mike, took me back to Burbank in his limousine. He told me how much he'd like to see me again and asked if he could call me.

Yes.

When we got to the house, he walked me to the door, kissed me gently, and asked if he could call me tomorrow.

Yes.

The next morning there were two dozen roses on my doorstep. The morning papers were filled with pictures of Eddie's opening—and us. He called that afternoon to ask if I could come to see him at the Cocoanut Grove again. I went the following night.

The morning after that, there was another huge arrangement of flowers at the door.

That afternoon he called. When could he see me again? What about tomorrow night? Okay.

That night on the way home, he slipped me a small, narrow gift-wrapped package.

"What's this?"

"Open it," he said.

Under the wrapping was a red-velvet box.

"It's beautiful," I said, running my fingers over the box.

"Open it, open the box," he said, pleased but impatient.

Inside was a pearl and diamond bracelet!

Bob Neal had once given me a little cross of diamonds as a birthday gift, but no man had ever given me jewelry.

He invited my family to come see his closing show. Daddy wasn't interested, but Mother and Grandma Harman, who was up from El Paso visiting for a few weeks, were enthralled.

The Grove seemed more jammed that night than at the opening, with people standing against the walls and others seated on the floor between the tables. When Eddie came out onstage for his opening number, the audience exploded with enthusiasm. They cheered him when he finished the song. He made a few remarks and they cheered some more. Then he sang to me, a new song by Irving Berlin, "Count Your Blessings." They cheered him again. Irving Berlin came out on the floor and placed an affectionate arm around Eddie's shoulders. He sang an impromptu chorus of "White Christmas." Everyone cheered again.

The next night we went with Mike Todd and Evelyn Keyes to the Mocambo for Joe E. Lewis's opening. Earl Wilson, the columnist from the *New York Post*, sat with us.

Something was happening. After six years in the movie business, I had been trained to oblige the press and their columnists. I was used to their interest and their questions. But never had anyone followed me around. Now they were everywhere. Now whenever I walked out the front door, or got out of my car, they were there en masse, practically hanging from the trees. The phone was ringing off the hook at my parents' house. They all wanted to know about Eddie and me.

Two fish. At sea in a goldfish bowl.

On our third actual date as two people not being followed, we double-dated with Lori Nelson and Eddie's close friend Joey Forman. Lori and I decided we'd make dinner for the boys. The four of us had a great time together. Joey was a comic. Lori and I had been friends for years by then, and Eddie and Joey had grown up together.

We were sitting around on the floor of Joey's tiny living room when Eddie pulled out a crumpled-up, worn-looking piece of Kleenex, and handed it to me.

"What's this for?" I asked, not getting the joke.

Eddie shrugged with a sly grin on his face. "Pull it apart, Frannie," he said, using my real name, as he did at certain moments.

What was it? A piece of candy? I gingerly pulled apart the ends of the tissue. There before my eyes was a diamond—a huge emerald-cut diamond ring. It was so big all I could think of was Marion Davies.

I stared. I probably mugged too because I couldn't sort out in my mind what was happening.

"Whaaa. . . ?" I still didn't get the joke. "Whose is this anyway?"

"Whatsamattah, eleven carats isn't big enough for you?" Joey cracked.

So this was what eleven carats looked like. I looked at Lori, whose eyes were bulging in disbelief.

"Eddie? What is this?" Staring at the ice-blue solitaire.

"That's your engagement ring," he answered coyly.

I looked at Lori. She was looking at the rock. She looked at me. We both started to cry. And then laugh.

Somebody said: "Oh, my God!"

Eddie said, "Well, aren't you going to try it on?"

I slipped it on the third finger of my right hand.

"The left hand, the left hand," Eddie corrected me.

I put it on the left hand.

"Well. . . ?" Eddie looked at me with the same silly grin, waiting.

"Well what?"

"Well, what'd you say?"

What could I say? Was he asking me to marry him? He was. An eleven-carat diamond! I was in shock. But I put it on. Everybody gawked. I gawked. It was like wearing high heels for the first time. Was this me?

Eddie bent over and kissed me. He was like a schoolboy.

That was it. He didn't ask me and I didn't say anything. It was like getting into a mind-set.

Driving me home that night, he wanted to know *when*. We had known each other for less than two weeks.

"We should wait a bit and give us time to get to know each other more," I said. I knew I liked him. Since the first night at the Cocoanut Grove, it seemed as if we were *together* in the world.

"Of course, we can take all the time we want," he said. "But I'm sure of one thing."

"What?" I asked, looking at his profile lighted by the headlights of an oncoming car; his soft brown eyes shining.

"I want you to be my wife."

Hearing those words stunned me. That was something RJ never had said.

A couple of days later I drove over to Bel Air to see RJ at his parents' house. There was the thought in the back of my mind that we had left something unfinished. He was standing on the lawn when I turned into his driveway.

I had a fantasy that I would tell him about Eddie and he would say to me, "Well, let's sit down and talk about this because I'm in love with you too." Or I would have to face reality and get rid of my schoolgirl crush forever.

RJ smiled when I told him I had met this terrific, adorable boy and that we were going to get engaged.

He told me he was very happy for me. I could see that he was. He stood there, casually leaning against the side of my car, his arms folded in front of him, his brow slightly furrowed, the very picture of the patrician young man. But there wasn't one cloud that came into his eyes. I was still looking for it. But there was nothing there.

I drove away from him that day thinking that now my dreams could be put aside. I could move on to a man who said he really loved me, with the commitment of marriage.

Except for Lori and Joey and my parents knowing, we decided to keep the engagement secret for a while.

I wanted a long engagement. We needed time to date; to go out and be together. I had never done that, except very innocently with RJ. Eddie had. He had had a number of women in his life. Full-fledged lovers.

Eddie very soon was educating me, as far as kissing and holding each other, and not being afraid. He was fresh and forward and aggressive in touching me. But now, somehow, it was all right. That was because of Eddie. I trusted him. He would hold me close and kiss me in a different manner from anyone before. He would kiss my ear. I didn't even know about that.

It had to be a slow courtship for me, but he was sensitive to that. I wanted to be a virgin bride; that was important to me. He was a man who had women throwing themselves at him everywhere he went.

With me he was kittenish and affectionate. He called me his "bunny" and his "little rabbit," or his *shiksa*, and nibbled at my ear with sweet kisses. It all seemed very beautiful to me.

In considering marriage, we also had to consider Eddie's fans. That was something Milton Blackstone, his manager, was going to be thinking about. Eddie was the number-one teen idol in the world. He was a multimillion-dollar entity. Milton got one half. It was always considered bad for business for a boy in his position to be married. It might threaten his popularity. This was the kind of thought Milton would have. I understood; MGM taught me that.

Besides, I hadn't met his family, all of whom lived in Philadelphia. And it wasn't as if we were going to have much time together, anyway. It was summertime. His show was on hiatus and he was booked solid until the end of the year. I was doing one picture after another.

There was the additional problem of where we would live. I was under contract. I had to live on the West Coast, at least most of the time. He was under contract to NBC and his show came from New York. We also had to decide where we would marry and what kind of wedding. And something else that never crossed my mind.

A few days after Eddie gave me the ring, driving home one night, out of nowhere, he said, "You realize what I am, don't you?"

I stared at him. I didn't know what he was talking about. "What . . . you . . . are?" I guessed. "You're a singer."

"You know I'm Jewish," he replied very quietly.

I looked over at him. I could see that the subject made him very nervous. "So, what does that have to do with anything?"

"Well, you're a Christian. People will talk, you know. Do you think you can handle it?"

"I don't care if they do."

"You can say that because you've got blond hair and blue eyes."

"I can say that because I believe that." I refused to consider it a problem.

"If we eventually settle down here, and raise a family, you know we'll have to join Hillcrest."

Hillcrest is *the* country club in Los Angeles for wealthy and socially prominent Jews, including a lot of show-business greats.

"Nothing would make me happier," I said.

"Bob Wagner would belong to the L.A. Country Club."

Bob Wagner? I couldn't believe Eddie was saying his name. How did he know about Bob Wagner? Nobody knew how I felt about RJ, not even RJ.

"Bob Wagner couldn't join either. They don't take actors."

Eddie had reason to believe otherwise. I thought it was all nonsense. I would have to learn.

The first week in July Eddie had a date to play the Sands in Las Vegas. I went with Louella Parsons and Jimmy McHugh, the songwriter, who was also a good friend of Eddie's. Louella's husband had passed away and Jimmy often escorted her.

The three of us stayed at the Desert Inn. Eddie and I had decided that I wouldn't wear the ring, at least not in public, until we officially announced.

On Monday, July 5, United Press reported over its wire services that Eddie and I were "headed for the altar in Las Vegas." The following day, the *New York Herald Tribune*, with picture, announced that our "marriage was near." Soon everyone was on the bandwagon—Walter Winchell, Ed Sullivan, Hedda Hopper, Leonard Lyons, Louis Sobel, Harrison Carroll, Earl Wilson, and on and on. We had known each other less than a month! Everyone was already speculating about whether or not we'd marry—not just with a couple of lines in their columns, but with headlines and photo layouts! Literally overnight, we became the ideal young American lovers.

Every step we took was recorded. Both Eddie and I were already famous in our own right, but this was like a wonderful tidal wave that was always on the crest. It wasn't real life. Part of me loved it. Part of him loved it.

After his stint in Vegas, Eddie came back to Los Angeles to do a concert at the Hollywood Bowl with André Kostelanetz. He had arranged for me to attend the show with Irving Berlin and General David Sarnoff, the founder of RCA, which owned NBC.

There were often a number of much older, very successful men around Eddie, including Eddie Cantor, who is generally credited with having discovered him. Eddie attracted that. He was the charming kid, like the son they might have wanted.

The Bowl concert was a sell-out—twenty thousand people bought tickets to listen to Eddie sing under the stars (and in front of the stars). We went backstage to see him before the performance.

Whenever Eddie was working, he was surrounded by people. Milton Blackstone, Eddie's manager, was always there, along with several of Eddie's childhood pals—like Joey Forman and Bernie Rich—who were now part of what was, I would soon learn, the inevitable entourage. Milton was nice, but already cool toward me.

That night at the Bowl there was also a strange man whom I had seen briefly in passing every night at the Sands. A frumpish-looking character, always in an unpressed navy suit. He was sinister, like a Vincent Price character in a murder movie.

"This is Dr. Max Jacobsen," Joey said as the doctor extended what was a warm, yet clammy hand. He smelled like medicine, which I thought was very peculiar, considering the place and the time of day.

"Who is *he?*" I asked Joey after the doctor had moved on.

"Oh, Eddie flies him in whenever he appears. He never opens without him."

"Why? What does he do?"

"Oh, he's his doctor."

"Is Eddie sick?" I asked.

"Nah, he just gives Eddie a vitamin shot before the performance, to give him a little more energy."

I looked across the room at Eddie huddling with Milton and Axel Stordahl, the conductor that night. He looked fine to me. He looked wonderful, as a matter of fact, and I said so.

"Yeah, yeah. It's just vitamins. Gives you a lift. We all get 'em. Even Milton. You should have Eddie get the doc to give you a shot sometime."

Uh-uh, I thought to myself.

I asked Eddie about Dr. Max the next day.

"Oh, he just gives me a shot before I go on," he said, as if it were nothing. "Vitamins. And female hormones."

"*Female* hormones? What do you need those for? You trying to grow longer nails?"

Eddie laughed. "Now, my little rabbit doesn't have to worry about a thing. Dr. Max is a genius. Everybody in the world goes to him."

There was so much else to think about. Eddie was leaving for a three-week European tour. The *Daily Sketch* in London announced on July 13 that we were engaged and that I might be accompanying him.

The morning after the *Daily Sketch* piece, we were barraged with phone calls from all over the world. The phone rang every time we hung it up.

It continued the next day. Mother stopped counting after call number forty.

Eddie and I had known each other for six weeks. But after seeing each other almost every night and talking to each other every day, sometimes for hours, it seemed like forever, as if I had never not known him.

The day before he was leaving Los Angeles, he arrived at the front door late in the afternoon with a six-week-old snow-white toy poodle. He'd named her Fanny after his latest hit record.

"I want you to keep her for us," he whispered as he handed her to me.

We went out to a quiet dinner that night. I had begun to realize that I was going to miss him.

"What's wrong, Mary Frances?" he asked, reaching across the table to take my hand in his.

I hesitated. "I don't know."

"I'm going to miss you," he said.

"I'm going to miss you too," I said. "It's going to be such a long time, Eddie." Then I blurted it out. "I've got your ring but you'll be thousands of miles away all day long. Everywhere I go someone's going to be asking me *when* or *where* or *what.* . . . I don't know what to think at this point. . . ."

"Wait a minute," he interrupted. "I've thought about that. We're going to talk every day I'm in New York and then we'll write each other while I'm overseas. In the meantime," he said, reaching into his jacket pocket, "I got you something to keep track of the days until we're together again."

He handed me another long velvet box. Another bracelet? No. It was the tiniest, most delicate gold and diamond wristwatch I had ever seen.

"It's a LaCoultre," he said watching my face. "The finest wristwatch in the world. There are only three of this style—one belongs to the queen of England, one to the wife of the president of France, and one for my little rabbit, Mary Frances, to watch the hours until I come back. When I do, we'll tell the world our secret."

I was dazzled dumb. Me and the queen of England.

Eddie kept his word. Every day before he left for London, he called. He sailed on August 7. On August 12 I received a cable.

DEBBIE REYNOLDS

1034 NORTH EVERGREEN ST

BURBANK CALIF-

JUST ARRIVED WONDERFUL CROSSING MISS YOU WROTE TWO

LETTERS DESTROYED SAME ALL I CAN SAY IS I LOVE YOU I LOVE

I LOVE YOU YOUR RABBIT FOR ALWAYS-

-EDDIE-

Two days later I received a special-delivery airmail letter from Eddie who was staying at the Savoy in London.

Dear Miss Debbie:

Just arrived here and was very happy—extremely happy I should say—to receive from ma little rabbit—five different pieces of mail! Very depressed and expecting to find nothing from her.

Altho they weren't very enlightening—just *hearing* from ma bunny was sufficient to say the least.

Everywhere we've been all of the people were extremely curious about "my wife" and why she wasn't with "her husband"—but everywhere I went there wasn't one moment *not one* that I didn't think of you. I've never been that way before and let me tell you—it'll never happen again—you're gonna marry me and not leave me for a moment—or I'll take back Fanny and stay with mother. You're in my thoughts every minute of the day and night. I love you too much and for always,

Edwin Jack

He called me the following day from London and asked if I could join him in New York at the end of the month. After that we'd make an announcement to the press that was issuing daily bulletins about us.

On Thursday, August 19, I received a cable from London:

LONDON IS WONDERFUL BUT LEAVING HAPPILY FOR IT BRINGS

ME THREE THOUSAND MILES CLOSER TO YOU ALL MY LOVE-

EDWIN JACK-

The following day came a cable from Gander, Newfoundland:

ARRIVED GANDER FOUR HOURS TO GO TO NEW YORK THEN YOU

DYING TO SEE YOU-

EDDIE-

The next morning, Saturday, Daddy picked up the *Los Angeles Mirror* from the front walk and brought it into the house. In bold headlines covering half the front page, it announced "ENGAGED STORY DENIED BY FISHER—Eddie plans flight to see Debbie."

I also received a couple of hundred fan letters. Among them was a small, ordinary-looking, white envelope with my name and address scrawled across the bottom. Inside, in the same blotchy-looking chicken-scratch was a note:

Dear Deb:
Thought you should know Eddies Father does *not* approve of him marrying a Gentile. Doesn't want him to be *hurt*. What about *you*—if you did? Does your Mother and Father want half-Jew grandchildren

No signature, naturally. It was postmarked Hollywood, August 18. It was the first of many. I never knew who wrote them, but I was getting to know what Eddie was talking about.

Five days later, the headline on the front page article of the *Los Angeles Examiner* read DEBBIE WILL FLY TO NY TO SEE EDDIE, under Harrison Carroll's by-line. He quoted Milton Blackstone saying that "the romance is very serious. I think Eddie finally realized his feelings during his recent trip to Rome, that he missed Debbie very much."

I felt relief. Had Milton given his stamp of approval? Did he like me now? Was I all right?

The following night Mother and I flew to New York. I was introduced to Eddie's mother while the flashbulbs popped. We stood there for fifteen minutes and posed while the reporters peppered us with the same questions over and over. Are you in love? Will you marry? When? Where? Are you engaged? Look this way, Debbie. Eddie, over here. Mrs. Reynolds, look at Debbie. Debbie, look toward Eddie's mother.

Mother and I checked into the Madison Hotel. Our suite was filled with flowers and gifts from Eddie: a little monkey's head with a card attached ("Guess who? ME!!!"), a little white rabbit ("Ma little rabbit"), a stuffed MGM lion whose name, according to the card, was "Dore Schary," two dozen long-stem roses ("Who loves you Babe??"), a box of Rumpelmayer's chocolates from Eddie's mother, Kate ("To a very sweet little girl, Eddie's Mom"), and an eight-ounce bottle of Arpège.

Friday night we went to the NBC studios to watch Eddie's show and after that we went to dinner, where we met Jennie Grossinger. Jennie had started the famous Catskill Mountain resort and had been one of Eddie's earliest supporters. She was beloved by everyone.

The next morning our arrival in New York was plastered all over the *Daily News*, the *Mirror*, the *Post*, the *Journal-American*, the *Telegram*, and the *Herald Tribune*.

That night Eddie picked me up at the hotel in his limousine, and with one of his publicity people, we drove over the George Washington Bridge to Palisades Amusement Park in New Jersey, where he was doing an open-air concert.

The original idea had been for me to watch his performance from backstage. The press agent told us on the ride over that it was going to be a good turnout at the park. The management had hired a lot of extra police, he said, to keep everything organized. Eddie asked how many. Oh, seventy-five to a hundred.

"A hundred extra policemen?!" I asked. "That's like a small army."

"So she doesn't know, huh, Eddie?" he asked, rolling his eyes.

The car pulled into the park and there they were. Thousands and thousands of teenagers, mostly girls, screeching, squealing at the sight of us. And there were the cops—it looked like hundreds—making a human barricade to let us through.

We got to the backstage entrance and they were all over us. You could physically feel them pressing all over the big heavy Cadillac. It's a peculiar experience; there's a strange threat of being smothered and crushed by all that adolescent, innocent humanity. It's monstrous.

They decided on the spot not to let me out of the car, for my own safety. A couple of dozen cops and as many reporters pushed the crowd back enough to let Eddie out. He seemed to take it in stride.

As soon as he was out of the car, a police car escorted us out of the crowd and when we reached an open roadway, the chauffeur stepped on it. We went to a restaurant nearby to wait out the hour or so until Eddie was to be picked up.

Sunday night, Eddie made an appearance on *The Ed Sullivan Show*, while I watched in the audience. Afterward he took us all to the Stork Club.

He and I had very little time together that weekend, between our mothers, the publicity people, and the crowds. We hardly noticed, caught up in the circus. But we did decide that when Eddie came out to California at the end of September, we'd announce our engagement.

Mother and I returned to Los Angeles on Monday morning. I had to report to the set on Tuesday.

There were a dozen roses and a telegram waiting for me at home.

HOW LIKE A WINTER HATH MY ABSENCE BEEN FROM THEE-

WILL SCHWARTZ

Three days later, this letter, typed out on Essex House stationery.

I had never wanted a way with words before. I had always thought I talked well enough. But now I know. . . . The feeling of you with me hasn't left even tho you're three days and three thousand miles away.

In the middle of a conversation, completely unrelated, I find myself thinking of you.

We're so lucky, cried she, in a moment of madness. But really, I'm so lucky . . . or maybe it's the aroma from these Romeo & Juliet cigars.

But the fact still stands, woman, I love you.

Edwin Jack

We're so lucky, cried she. I felt that way then.

I went to the studio every morning and came home every night to talk to Eddie in New York. We'd talk for literally hours sometimes. Every day was full of new plans, new experiences, and new stories to tell about our life together while the world was watching.

He was arriving on the eighteenth of September. A few days before, over the phone, it came out that he wasn't really sure if we should announce our engagement on the planned date.

It caught me off guard. "Why not?" I asked, hearing the defensiveness in my voice.

"Well, I don't know if this is the right time."

"You don't think next week is a good time to make it public?"

He was stumbling. "Well. I don't know. Sometimes I think yes, sometimes I . . . have my doubts."

Or course, he was vacillating, but being the naïve young girl that I was, I paid no attention. The next day he sent this wire:

MFR-

DOUBT IS NOT IN ITSELF A CRIME ALL MANNER OF DOUBT IN-
QUIRY ABOUT ALL MANNER OF OBJECTS DWELLS IN EVERY REA-
SONABLE MIND IT IS THE MYSTIC WORKING OF THE MIND ON
THE OBJECT IT IS GETTING TO KNOW ABOUT

-EJF-

Four days later I got another wire:

TOMORROW IS D DAY

UNSIGNED

Eddie arrived from New York at six in the morning. I took our little white poodle Fanny with me to meet him. There were none of the thousands of screaming girls at that hour, but there was a small crowd of press asking the same question: When?

It was a working weekend for Eddie and me. He was rehearsing for *The Colgate Comedy Hour* on television, and I had a personal appearance in San Diego on Saturday night. We spent Sunday afternoon alone together. Monday morning Mother told Louella, the wire services, and the world that Debbie and Eddie were engaged to marry the following June.

The news exploded in headlines. I had become Debbie-and-Eddie, and so had he. It was the ultimate romance; our coming of age. A couple of weeks later I went back to New York. Eddie and I were going to go down to Philadelphia to meet his family. He came from a family of seven children. He had four sisters, Miriam, Shaney, Eileen, and Nettie; and two brothers, Bunny and Saul.

The entire family had a party for us at his mother's house. I was the only Gentile. I felt as if I were in another country. There is a South Philadelphia accent that almost sounds like a foreign tongue. There were also elderly relatives who still spoke with the thick accent of the old country.

Kate was divorced from Eddie's father and remarried to a very dear man named Mr. Stupp. Mr. Stupp owned a very prosperous supermarket, so there was an array of food beyond anything I'd ever seen in our house. They all called Eddie Sonny-boy. They were shocked that Sonny-boy was marrying a *shiksa*, but they thought I was friendly and cute. "If Sonny-boy likes her, we'll like her."

Except for religion and geography, Eddie and I came from similar backgrounds—simple, family-oriented working people. Our mothers were perhaps a bit more ambitious—if you could call it that—than our fathers. I liked all his family, especially his older sister Miriam. Miriam stood by him in later years, for which I admired her very much. Unlike so many people in his life, she never asked for anything from Eddie, nor was she was one of the main recipients of his generosity.

I found my visit to Eddie's family fascinating. I decided that I would learn about the Jewish culture. I had no intention of converting, but if one day one of our children wanted to be part of the Jewish faith, I wanted to understand it. There were a lot of people who felt that Eddie should marry a nice Jewish girl who would stay home and raise the children to be nice Jewish children. I wanted to be able to do that for him too.

Back in New York that same weekend, Eddie and I went to the Copacabana with Margie Duncan and Bernie Rich, who were the only other couple we knew who were engaged. Margie and Bernie were childhood friends of Eddie's. All of them in their preteens had been performers on a local Philadelphia radio show.

Two weeks later Eddie came back out to California for our engagement party, which was given for us by Ida and Eddie Cantor at the Beverly Hills Hotel. There were five hundred guests. Eddie Cantor, being like an adopted father to Eddie, invited all his old show-business friends including Jack Benny, Jack Warner, and Groucho Marx. There were MGM stars, friends from the industry, the major newspaper columnists, all of Eddie's pals from South Philadelphia, and all of my friends, including school chums Jeanette Johnson and Camille Williams. There were forty-five photographers present and every one of them wanted a picture of me and Eddie kissing. The following week, *Life* magazine did a four-page layout of the party.

Eddie drove me home that night after the party. It was again one of the few times we had to ourselves. He was rehearsing the rest of the weekend for a television show and I went to work at the studio the following Monday morning.

That's all I remember about it. We were living a constantly overwhelming experience. In our situation, as Debbie-and-Eddie, the attention was extravagant. It became a day-to-day thing.

But I was still going home to the little house on Evergreen Street in Burbank every night. I still sometimes had to wait for the one bathroom we had. It was like having two lives; one inside the house and the other inside a movie.

We'd set June 17, 1955, as the wedding date. By that time we could have our lives organized enough so that we could live together. I thought eventually I'd leave the business and concentrate on being a wife and mother. Then we would not have to worry about where we'd live, we'd live wherever Eddie was working.

In the meantime we'd see each other over long weekends whenever I could go east or he could come to the West Coast. Eddie came out in December to spend Christmas with us.

From the beginning, he and Mother were very comfortable with one another. I think he liked Dad more, however. My father never gave a damn whether or not anyone liked him. He didn't really trust any man around his daughter. However, both my parents liked Eddie and welcomed him into the family.

On Christmas Day, 1954, Eddie came over in late morning to open presents. He seemed distracted and slightly nervous almost from the minute he arrived. He gave me a fabulous sheared red-nutria coat that looked and felt like beaver.

After lunch Eddie seemed to get more preoccupied. About midafternoon he jumped up from his chair, a big smile on his face, said, "Well, finally!" and headed for the front door.

"Your Christmas present," he said. "It's here!"

I thought the fur coat was my present. "But . . ." It was a fire-engine red 1955 Ford Thunderbird.

I had never seen one. In fact, few people had ever seen one since Ford had yet to ship any to its dealers. It was beautiful, two doors, low, white-leather interior, the new "wraparound" windshield.

The driver had personally driven it out to California from Detroit to deliver it on Christmas Day to me.

Eddie walked over to the driver's side and opened the door. "Merry Christmas, Miss Debbie," he said, offering me the seat.

CHAPTER 13

AFTER THE BEGINNING of the new year, I tried to get to New York to be with Eddie as much as possible. It was more difficult for him to come to the West Coast because of his three-times-weekly television schedule and his club or recording dates. I'd go with either my mother or Camille Williams or Lori Nelson. Lots of times the trips would be paid for by the studios, which then had use of us for publicity purposes.

On one such trip, Lori and I spent a couple of weeks giving interviews in the daytime, shopping, and going out with Eddie and his boys at night. Eddie cut a new record, "A Man Chases a Girl," in which I did uncredited backup, singing one line after the title: "until she catches him." It was released a few weeks later, and like all of his records, it became an instant hit.

Some weekends we'd go to Grossinger's. Jennie Grossinger treated Eddie like a son, and me like a daughter. She had taken the family farm in the Catskills and turned it into a resort, for Jewish people primarily although she didn't turn away Gentiles. She booked top entertainment and attracted a lot of show people.

Milton Blackstone had worked for Jennie in the forties as her publicity man. It was Milton who brought the teenage Eddie Fisher to her attention back in 1946, when she hired him to sing on weekends for room and board.

Rocky Marciano, who was the heavyweight boxing champion of the world, trained at Grossinger's. Eddie and I became good friends with him and his wife, Barbara.

I had never been a boxing fan, but after meeting Rocky, we went to all his fights. I won't say that I'm a big fan of bloodshed, but watching a real champion, it's a hell of a contest. After his last fight, when he retired, he gave Eddie his boxing gloves, bloodstains and all.

*   *   *

The trips to New York also gave me a real chance to see what Eddie's life was like. A lot about it was similar to mine. It was mainly work—either his TV show, or rehearsing for another, or a recording session or a concert or a club date. He went from one thing to the next to the next, with very little leisure in between.

Like all pop stars who earn most of their living performing live, Eddie was surrounded by a group of men, most of them his age. Milton Blackstone; lawyers, accountants, press agents; the boys, including Joey Forman and Bernie Rich; and of course the inevitable Max Jacobsen, to whom I was soon referring as Dr. Needles. They are necessary for a lot of things including the semblance of a social life, which is almost non-existent for a busy performer.

Eddie was very, very generous with his entourage. Milton took half of everything Eddie made, right off the top. With his own half, Eddie paid not only for his living expenses and whatever he shared with his family but also for the boys. Shirts, shoes, jackets, even cars; Eddie provided. When they went out on the town, whenever they traveled, Eddie picked up all the tabs. He was loyal—these boys had grown up together and Eddie happened to be the one who hit it big.

In New York Dr. Needles seemed to be around almost as much as the boys. The pockets of his dirty, rumpled old dark suit were always bulging with little vials and needles. Everybody in the group, it seemed, was administered to by Dr. Needles. If you had an earache, he'd give you a shot in the ear. If you had a cold in your nose, he'd give you a shot in the nose. Wherever it hurt, he'd stick the needle.

Thirty years ago few if any people knew that amphetamines were addictive and dangerous. Nor did anyone question why a twenty-six-year-old man needed a shot every time he went onstage.

Everybody swore by Dr. Needles. His New York waiting room was filled with Broadway stars, politicians, and socialites who had become dependent on his "miracle" drugs. President John F. Kennedy took him to the Summit with Khrushchev in Vienna in 1961.

In the spring of 1955, Eddie was booked for a show at the Palladium in London, and so he asked Mother and me to go along. Eddie brought me onstage after singing "A Man Chases a Girl" before the queen and the royal party. Later we were presented to the young queen and Prince Philip.

My first trip to Europe was a vacation for me. We toured London on a doubledecker bus, went to the Tower, Westminster Abbey, and the Houses of Parliament. One day Eddie hired a car to take us for a drive out into the British countryside. But there were still the dressing-room dinners surrounded by crowds of strangers. When Eddie finished his stint, he took me to Portugal for three days in the sun.

Cole Porter gave a dinner party for us while we were there. He was a tiny man, who dressed impeccably and carried a cane with a gold tip. The house he had leased was a small palace, filled with antiques, paintings, marble columns, and marble floors. The guests included the king and queen of Italy and the king and queen of Spain—all in exile of course.

We were still in England on my twenty-third birthday, for which Eddie surprised me with a party at the chic Embassy Club. It was a whirlwind, romantic time.

But when we got back to New York, Eddie told me that we might have to change our plans for the wedding.

I had my heart set on a big church ceremony, inviting all our friends and family. I'd already ordered a spectacular and very expensive wedding dress designed by Helen Rose. I splurged because I was going this way only once. Or so I thought.

"But why?" I asked, unable to mask my disappointment.

"Milton's got me on a tour those middle two weeks in June."

"But he knew we were planning on getting married on the seventeenth!"

"I know, Mary Frances, but you know Milton is only thinking of my future."

"I am your future too, aren't I?"

Eddie didn't say anything.

"Well, aren't I?"

"Of course you are," he said quietly. "But you know in this business how important it is to keep working."

"It's not like a wedding is going to take a month out of your life!" I said in exasperation.

Eddie just sat there like stone. I knew he was torn. Up to that point in his life, his career had always come first, which I respected as much as anybody could.

"You want to call everything off?" I asked.

"No!" he said. "Why can't we just elope? We can do it now, today, if you want."

"I don't want anything you don't want, Eddie, but I can't do it today. The studio would never stand for it."

We were sitting in his living room at the Essex House. There was a cold spring rain coming down outside the windows. It felt like that inside too.

"Look, we've got to follow Milton's plans. That's my business. He's my partner. He's the man who's responsible for everything I have, everything *we'll* have!"

In other words, what Milton says goes. I couldn't help being furious. Eddie wasn't taking any kind of a stand at all.

I got up, put on my coat.

"Where you going?"

I felt sad. "I think you need some time to think things over. We're not going to settle anything now."

"Don't leave," he said.

"I think I'd better, Eddie. Talk things over with Milton and then let me know what you decide."

He grabbed my hand as I reached for my bag. "You mean you won't elope with Harry?" he smiled. Harry, oddly, was one of my nicknames for him.

He was flirting but I wasn't in the mood. I was hurt. "Yes, I'd elope but not on a date set by Milton Blackstone." Eddie pulled me closer to kiss me. I turned my face away. "Not now, Eddie."

"Don't feel bad, Mary Frances," he said, letting go of me.

"I'm sorry. I can't help it right now." He followed me to the door, grabbing the handle before I could.

"Do you still love me, Mary Frances?" I looked at him smiling at me. I felt that I was being manipulated. He'd got his way, Milton had got his way; and now Eddie just wanted to make sure I still loved him.

"Yes. I do. But you've got some things to think about, so I'll just leave you alone."

Since we first got engaged our plans had gone from a big wedding to an elopement to a small wedding, to living in Beverly Hills to living in New York, to a big wedding and now to an elopement. What at first seemed like simple changes in busy schedules now seemed more like indecisiveness on Eddie's part. I never doubted that Eddie wanted to marry me. But now I was beginning to wonder if Milton Blackstone would ever allow it. I felt suddenly lost. Where did I really fit into the picture? Or didn't I?

Mother and I took an early plane back to Los Angeles the next day. Walter Winchell, the most widely read gossip columnist in the world, had written in the *New York Daily Mirror* that Eddie and I were through:

> . . . Eddie's too busy singing love songs and Debbie's too busy
> acting in love stories. Success has made it impossible for them to
> enjoy something worth more than success.

*   *   *

Someone had given him that item, and it wasn't I. Reporters were waiting for us at the airport.

"I love Eddie and Eddie loves me" was my statement.

Within days the press and the magazines were filled with new slants on the old story. To which Louella Parsons wrote, "If Debbie and Eddie aren't in love then neither were Romeo and Juliet."

Then there came the announcement that Coca-Cola had decided that Eddie could not move his show to the West Coast. That was followed by the report that Eddie had canceled our "honeymoon suite" on the S.S. *United States*.

Days passed. I heard nothing from Eddie. I was upset by this but I didn't call him. This was a decision about our whole lives and I was willing to wait.

I was leaving for a week to go to Korea and Honolulu to entertain the soldiers. Eddie sent me four dozen roses and told the press that we were still engaged. But the outside pressure on both of us didn't let up.

In early May 1955, I was assigned *The Tender Trap*, starring opposite Frank Sinatra. That meant I wouldn't be going anywhere for at least a couple of months.

Frank was fabulous to work with, lighthearted, sweet. His comeback had been accomplished and he was once again a huge star.

He was the consummate professional on the set. It was true that he didn't like shooting a scene a lot. He would try to get it in the first take, which is always better in comedy anyway. But he didn't have the hard-and-fast rule that has been ascribed to him—insisting that the scene be shot once and printed even if it was bad. He was also good with the crew and the guys. I felt very fortunate that he liked me. I never saw his dark side. Humphrey Bogart was alive then. He was the leader of the Pack. Everyone loved Bogart, especially the men.

Frank used to go with Bogart out on his boat on the weekends. They had high times. Monday mornings on the set Frank would always look a little worse for wear because they really partied. I always wanted to be invited but I never was.

I was very surprised when one day on the set he very seriously said, "I'd like to talk to you."

We went to lunch. He said to me, "You really love this boy?"

I said, "Yes."

He shook his head. "Very difficult life, to be married to a singer. Very hard."

"I know, but I've spent some time with him. I think I can live with it."

"You're not aware of what you're getting into, Debbie. It's a very hard life. I know. You should really think twice about this."

I was a little taken aback by his insistence. Frank had never spoken so gravely about anything with me before.

"I have thought about this, Frank," I said. I couldn't argue with him because I couldn't doubt his sincerity.

But I had thought about it, or thought I had. I was aware of the all-consuming aspects of Eddie's career. I didn't like a lot of things. I didn't like Dr. Needles. I wasn't crazy about Milton Blackstone. But I knew enough by then to understand that in show business people come and go. The work I could live with. It was tough and demanding and the hours were hardly convenient, but so was my father's work on the railroad. Only he was paid $35 a week, whereas Eddie got $35,000 or twice that. I didn't mention any of this to Frank, but I was thinking it.

"Well, you're too young," he said. "You'll never be able to make it work. I know."

That remark, no matter who might have said it, didn't sit lightly.

I felt very flattered that Frank took the time to say these things. It was very sweet of him to open himself up to me. He was trying to save me great heartache. He felt truly that being married to a big singing star was an impossibility. But I couldn't listen. I was in love. I was on top of the world.

In July Eddie came to California for a few weeks. There was no way to stop the stories in the press. Day after day: Will they? Won't they? Neither Eddie nor I said anything to anyone. The publicity was no longer just overwhelming, it was like a monster out of control.

I had never been uncertain of my feelings for him. To me, it was as if our lives had already become one. Nor did I ever doubt his intentions toward me. But I knew he had intense career pressures that confused him. I understood. I wanted him to have every possible out because I wanted him to make a decision about us and stick to it.

Eddie told me he was sure. He didn't want to wait any longer. He wanted us to marry soon; quietly and privately on a weekend, with just our families present. He said that Jennie Grossinger had offered her home for the wedding and that way there would be room to put up everyone. He apologized that there wouldn't be much time for a honeymoon for a few months because of work. But we'd make up for that after the first of the year.

The only time we both had a few free days was in late September. That would be it, we decided: late September, exactly a year from our engagement. I would ask the studio for a few months off and we would live in Eddie's apartment in New York until we could decide where we'd settle.

It was a relief to have the decision behind us. The temptation to tell the press, just to stop the endless questions, was enormous. But one word could have ruined our precious plans, so our secret became, in a way, our bond.

We spent the following two weeks going to parties, taking a tour of the just-opened Disneyland in Anaheim, attending the opening of Judy Garland's brilliant comeback revue at the Santa Monica Auditorium, and celebrating Eddie's twenty-seventh birthday with a small group including Mike Todd and Evelyn Keyes.

Mike Todd was living with Evelyn Keyes at the time, although they weren't married. Eddie and I spent quite a bit of time with them, but I didn't know they shared the same house. One early afternoon Eddie and I went by Mike's and Evelyn was there, in a bathrobe, looking as if she'd just got out of bed. I remember later asking Eddie if Evelyn didn't go home after a date with Mike.

"Yes, she goes home," he said curtly. "She lives *there*! They live together."

"But they're not married, are they?" I asked, confused.

"No. But they're grown-ups, Debbie. Not everybody has to be married to live together," he said as if speaking to a child.

I knew what he was telling me. I could tell by his tone of voice how he felt about it too. It didn't surprise me. Mike was his idol, his mentor. Mike was also twice our age and had a son, Mike junior, who was older than I was.

But I was thinking of Evelyn. It was obvious that she adored Mike. All women did. Eddie and I had gone to a party only a week before where we met Marlene Dietrich, looking like the screen legend that she was in a white-silk man-tailored suit. It was evident that she and Mike had been more than friends. They were so comfortable with each other. What if he decided to run off with Dietrich? I wondered. Then what would Evelyn do? Move out? I wouldn't have wanted to be in her position.

CHAPTER **14**

ON FRIDAY, SEPTEMBER 17, 1955, I flew by myself to New York. Eddie and I told the press I had come to see the Rocky Marciano–Archie Moore fight and maybe a couple of the World Series games between the Yankees and the Dodgers that were starting the following week.

There was now also the pressure of sex in our relationship. Eddie naturally had wanted us to go to bed, but I had resisted up to that point. I knew a lot of people outside marriage did, Mike and Evelyn, for example. But I just didn't want to be one of them. Premarital sex in those Dark Ages of the 1950s was considered immoral and it cheapened a woman in the eyes of society.

I was also afraid. My childhood fears about sex were very much a part of me. I was not prepared and I knew it. But now our wedding day was drawing near.

One night Eddie and I were coming from a cocktail party in his limousine heading down Fifth Avenue to his apartment on Central Park South. I sat with my head resting lightly on Eddie's shoulder, holding his hand. Within a week I would be his wife and his partner. Despite my nervousness about sex, I knew it was silly to put it off any longer. So I said to Eddie: "You really want to try it?"

"I think it's time," he said.

At the Essex House we got into the elevator with another, older couple. The first thing that came to my mind was that they were going to think Eddie and I were going up to his apartment to go to bed, which we were. That made me uncomfortable.

The elevator came to our floor, we got out, the doors closed, and I walked with Eddie down the hall to his apartment. Inside, I followed Eddie into his bedroom. It was dusk and the lights of the buildings around Central Park were just starting to blink on. I was silently waiting. For what, I wasn't sure. Eddie started taking off his clothes and so I took off mine. He got into bed and I got into bed. He made love to me.

It was quick and mechanical. It wasn't uncomfortable and it wasn't wonderful. It wasn't anything that I had dreamed about or read about or thought that it would be.

Eddie seemed disappointed from the moment we got into bed. He was rather strange about it. He seemed to be going through the motions, never cuddling, never kissing, not even holding me.

I felt very Little Girl, very out of the water, very stupid. I thought to myself, why did I bother? I didn't know what to do and it wasn't exciting. I could tell it certainly wasn't exciting for him either.

When it was over, he got out of bed and put his clothes back on. I watched for a moment, not knowing what I should do, then did the same. Then he took me back to my hotel, so that I could change for dinner, and left. Nothing was said.

I walked around my hotel suite getting ready in a kind of void. I felt cold and lost and frustrated, although there was no guilt, interestingly enough. Obviously it didn't work. I hadn't made him happy.

As I look back on it, I don't think he had the patience for being a lover; he preferred being catered to, and patted and cajoled; and mothered and made love to. But at that time, I looked to him for experience: He was the man. Although he knew I was a virgin, it was really brought home to him that night. I knew nothing and it shook him up. I blamed myself. I never had anyone to discuss it with.

All I knew was what I read. Yet I had foolishly thought a book would do it. I was still reading books when I married my second husband. I was still reading books long after that too.

It would be shocking, if it weren't so ridiculous—my not knowing. But I didn't, not having had experience. I didn't know why I was upset, or why I had a pain in my stomach. I didn't know why my body felt aching or longing. I finally learned about lovemaking from a man who taught me when I was forty. It's like learning how to dance; you've got to get the steps down.

We needed blood tests for the license and they had to be done ultra-privately, so two days before leaving the city, we went to Dr. Needles's office.

That was my first run-in with Max Jacobsen. I wouldn't let him take my blood. He was very annoyed but finally agreed to let his nurse do it. I couldn't stand to have him touch me.

Eddie said nothing to me about the incident so I don't know that the doctor even mentioned it.

On the Wednesday before the big day, we went up to a small courthouse near Grossinger's for the license.

Since I didn't have a wedding dress or the time to have one made, the solution was a dress I had worn in *The Tender Trap*. It was a beautiful Helen Rose design—white lace, ballerina length with full skirt; perfect.

However, it belonged to the studio and we wanted to borrow it without anyone knowing why.

That same Wednesday morning when Eddie and I were getting our marriage license three thousand miles away, Mother went over to the studio, up to wardrobe, and confided in a friend she had there. Her friend very casually took the dress, rolled it up, and packed it in a shopping bag. Mother walked off the lot with it, no questions asked. She then borrowed a veil from the girl across the street from us in Burbank.

My oldest childhood friend, Jeanette Johnson, was going to be my maid of honor. She and mother went out to a bridal shop and bought her a blue dress with the same skirt length as mine.

Mother, Daddy, Billy, and Jeanette, with the wedding trousseau under wraps, flew to New York just before the weekend. Someone had a suspicion and tipped off the press, who were waiting at the airport. Daddy told them they'd come to see the World Series.

It was also Rosh Hashanah, the Jewish New Year, which ended when the sun set on Monday. We planned the ceremony for seven-thirty that night in Jennie Grossinger's living room. It was performed by a local judge.

Jennie had all the furniture removed to provide room for seats. The walls were decked with white flowers and autumn leaves. The room was entirely lit by candles. There were about thirty-five guests, all family and close friends. Eddie's family got caught in traffic on their way out of Philadelphia and were more than an hour late.

A few minutes after nine o'clock we were ready. Standing at the top of the stairs with me, Jeanette got so nervous waiting, I had to calm her.

Finally the pianist and two violinists started to play the Wedding March. Daddy led me down the stairs and then arm in arm we walked to the altar of flowers. Milton Blackstone was Eddie's best man.

The judge read the rites. We said our "I do's," I took the ring on my finger, and then the judge concluded the ceremony by saying "the world had bad news last week" (President Eisenhower had had a heart attack) "and now it is receiving good news with the marriage of Debbie and Eddie." It took all of a hundred twenty seconds.

It was not sweet or pretty. It was fast and cold. Unlike most wedding parties, we did not then go to the reception. Instead, one news photographer was brought in and we repeated the short ceremony for him. Dozens of newspeople had been waiting for hours outside the gate of the inn for a picture or a quote. They had agreed among themselves to divide up the shots. The photographers got a longer marriage ceremony than we did.

Jennie Grossinger had her baker make us a five-tiered wedding cake that was big enough to feed 250 people. We drank toasts and then the reporters were invited in for some cake and champagne.

We spent our first night of marriage in a guesthouse on the grounds. Eddie was less businesslike than the first time we'd made love, but bells didn't go off and I didn't expect them to.

Now that we were married, I felt we had time to grow as lovers. The idea of marriage being something you had to work at seemed natural to me. When we were leaving the reception that night, Eddie's mother said to me, in front of the guests, "Just give a little and take a little and your life will be a happy one."

That made sense. I could do that. My mother and father had; so could I. I knew I could make my husband happy. Somehow I'd find the way.

Tuesday morning, we were on the front pages of newspapers all over the world.

The next week couldn't have been better planned by the MGM publicity department. We flew to Atlanta for a Coca-Cola convention. The master of ceremonies, who in retrospect reminds me of Archie Bunker, was from the Atlanta area and welcomed everyone with a rousing speech about Coca-Cola. When he finished his lavish praise of the company he turned to us.

"And I want to extend a warmest welcome to Eddie Fisher, and his sweet little bride, Debbie; and I want this couple to know how thrilled we are to have them here on only their third day of marriage as our guests. We want them to know that we, of this wonderful club of ours where no niggers and no Jews have ever held membership . . . and I want . . ."

That was his thank-you.

Eddie turned white and I found myself audibly laughing. Eddie kicked me. They obviously didn't know he was Jewish. The man went right along with his speech. No one so much as cleared his throat. Nobody even noticed when I laughed.

When it came time for me to say a few words, I couldn't resist. "Well, gentlemen, you broke all the rules today; free lunch on the house." They had no idea what I was talking about. "You see, in this wonderful club where no Jews are allowed, you've made my husband your honored exception. And as you see, he's not black."

There was a very large silence.

I was the only one who thought it was funny. Eddie didn't.

After the convention, we got on a plane to fly back to New York.

We fell into bed at six. At noon we were awakened by the manager telling us we were expected at Yankee Stadium for the opening game of the World Series. We had a half hour to get ready.

We got to Yankee Stadium just before the first ball. As we were entering our box to take our seats, they announced us over the loudspeaker.

With that, forty thousand people stood up and the rafters shook while they cheered and applauded us.

"We love you Debbie and Eddie!" they shouted.

It was amazing. Astonishing. The energy of forty thousand people directed at you for one moment—all that love—is indescribable. Both of us felt humbled. Eddie took my hand and squeezed it twice when they stood up cheering us. I looked at him and he winked at me, as if to say, "It's you and me now, kid." We were finally married.

Thursday we had the day off until the evening when we went to a banquet honoring General Sarnoff. Before dinner was over, we left to catch a train overnight to South Bend, Indiana, where Eddie was opening a new television station on the Notre Dame campus. That night we went to the campus ball where Eddie and I entertained. The following day we went to a Notre Dame game and flew back to New York.

We spent two days in New York. On Sunday we flew to Kansas City, where we visited former President Truman, who had a few years before declared Eddie to be his favorite G.I. On Monday we visited the Trumans at Independence, Missouri. That night we got on a plane to fly to Los Angeles.

We had been married a week. It had been hectic, but it was fun. We had very little time alone together, but we had a lifetime ahead of us.

When Eddie fell in love with me and told me he wanted to marry me, I thought everything would be just fabulous. I thought it would be like all the books I'd read and the movies I'd seen. And it was.

There had been bumps in the road in our yearlong engagement. But now we had finally started a life together. We were the modern version of Mary Pickford and Douglas Fairbanks. I forgot—or maybe I never knew—what happened to Mary Pickford and Douglas Fairbanks.

In Los Angeles, Mike Todd gave a huge reception for us in a tent on the estate he was renting on South Carolwood Drive. There were hundreds of guests. The Gary Coopers, the Dean Martins, Lucy and Desi, Milton Berle, Frank Sinatra, the Goldwyns, the Goetzes, the Selznicks, Edie Adams and Ernie Kovacs—and on and on.

Eddie was also doing a TV show with Eddie Cantor while we were in California. Milton Blackstone asked if I'd like to do the show with the two Eddies. I'd love to. But first I'd have to ask permission from the studio.

In those days MGM did not allow its stars to do television regularly. To the movie industry, television was degrading (by potential overexposure) to their stars and harmful to their box-office magnetism. No way were they going to allow that.

I told Milton Blackstone I had to ask the studio. When Eddie heard, he got very upset. Why couldn't I? I was his wife!

I agreed. I went to see Benny Thau at his office. It was often said that Benny Thau was so cold he peed ice, but he was always kind to me. However, they were paying me my $450 a week salary and loaning me out to Howard Hughes for $170,000 a picture.

He said no, I couldn't be on TV with Eddie even if he was my husband. Oh, please, Mr. Thau, we're only going to do one short number together. No, Debbie, MGM will not allow it.

I decided to do it anyway. I had already had the dress made. How could one little appearance harm anything?

The day we were doing the show, I happened to wear my little diamond cross. After our first run-through, Milton Blackstone said, "You'll have to take that cross off. It shows you don't like Jews," he reproached me.

I looked at him, thinking, this man is so prejudiced by his own prejudice, he's silly.

He gave me a dead stare with those small puffy eyes. "It has to go, Debbie. It'll hurt Eddie."

I never cared for Milton Blackstone after that incident. I saw him differently, more clearly. In time I came to think he had mishandled Eddie's career. He took his 50 percent as fast as he could get it and never gave any wisdom to Eddie. Instead of getting him a therapist, he got him Dr. Max Jacobsen, ruiner of lives.

I did what Milton said that day. That was stupid of me because it set a precedent for the future. But I didn't want to make trouble for Eddie with his manager. I wanted to be the good wife, subservient, accommodating. From then on, he told me what to wear and how to dress and how to speak whenever I was doing anything with Eddie.

The show with Eddie Cantor was a lot of fun and a big hit. Then all hell broke loose. Benny Thau hit the ceiling. He called Eddie in for a private meeting and told him he was threatening his own future in the movies. Eddie was furious that Benny Thau could control me.

"Maybe you should just quit the whole thing. If I have to travel, I want you with me and not working."

"I want to do what you want, Eddie," I told him. "I don't mind breaking the contract."

I didn't think he really meant that he wanted me to quit. But he did have a need to feel powerful at that moment and so I let him. I also believed that if, as my husband, he didn't want me to work, then I shouldn't work. I thought that was how you made a good marriage.

Eddie cooled off shortly. He didn't want me tearing up my contract with MGM. "In the future, we'll just make sure we get their approval."

I knew they'd never give approval, and they never did. Eddie didn't really understand how it worked in the industry. If you were signed, they owned you. He only understood that he wanted to make movies and people like Benny Thau could have something to say about that.

After the little contretemps with Metro, Eddie and I went back to New York to set up housekeeping in his three-room apartment at the Essex House.

Eddie had a strenuous daily work schedule and there was nothing for me to do. I didn't really know anyone. I thought, fine, it'll give me a chance to become his wife. I'll shop, cook, sit in on his rehearsals or his recording sessions. This would be marital bliss.

Things are never that simple. Eddie didn't really like me to sit in on his rehearsals or his recording sessions. Nor did he like me getting involved in anything that took me away from home, because he liked knowing where I was.

I was spending my time at the local Gristede's Market discovering sliced fruit in a jar, or on the phone to my mother in California asking her how to bake a chicken leg. I did not have nor do I now have any talent in the kitchen. I did learn how to slap together a hamburger and boil water. I was undaunted at first, preparing Eddie's meal each evening.

This activity was soon complicated by the fact that I never knew when Eddie was going to get home. Would it be six o'clock after his rehearsal, or eight-thirty after his show, or three in the morning after his recording session? I found out by waiting. Shopping, sitting around, and waiting.

This was the way he lived. He couldn't be expected to change. This was his work schedule. I understood that completely. Eddie, as a live performer, lived on the other side of the clock—as I do today, at the time of this writing. I'd put his dinner in the refrigerator and go to bed; when he came home, he'd wake me. I'd get up and heat his dinner.

Other nights, after a session, he might come home with three or four of the boys and sit up till dawn, playing cards. In the beginning, I'd fix something for them to eat, and sit and watch. No one ever asked me to play or to take part in any way. I was still not included—only guys with guys. I felt like Marilyn Monroe with Joe DiMaggio—only good at serving sandwiches.

I complained about this to Eddie in the beginning. He was considerate but he wasn't interested in my joining in. This was something he did with the boys.

I understood. But it was so lonely. I begged him to let me watch his rehearsals or watch him record. I promised I'd stay out of the way. He was very sweet about it. The sessions were long, he explained, and very boring to the spectator. He was concerned that I would be more unhappy there. But he took me along the next time. He was right. They were long and boring. I'd fall asleep sitting up. But I *was* spending time with my husband.

Spending time with my husband, I soon realized, also meant spending a lot of time with the boys. They were always there. After all, they lived off Eddie. They made him laugh and gave no small amount of ego massage. None of the group was crazy about Eddie having a wife. Maybe some of them wouldn't be needed if he spent more time with me.

I tried to make friends with them, but I was Mary Frances again, back in El Paso, scuffing up dust with my bare feet because the boys wouldn't let me play.

I couldn't imagine what I could do about it. When I mentioned it, Eddie'd say, don't be ridiculous; nobody's leaving you out.

Before we were married he put me ahead of them. I was the movie star, Debbie Reynolds. He took me, and the boys had to wait. Now it was different.

I didn't complain for long. It was getting me nowhere anyway. I'd concentrate harder on being the dutiful wife. I knew this was what was required of me. I'd get used to it.

CHAPTER 15

I HAD TO BE BACK in California in January 1956 to start a new picture, *The Catered Affair* with Bette Davis and Ernest Borgnine. Milton Blackstone made arrangements for Eddie to work on both coasts. We were moving west.

I had to find us a house to rent, which I loved doing. One morning the real-estate broker told me she was taking me to a "dream house," a completely furnished honeymoon cottage way out Sunset Boulevard almost to the ocean; it was a good half hour's drive from Beverly Hills. There were no other houses in sight.

I fell in love with it. The house went in every direction. There was a sixty-foot-long sunken living room, with exposed roughhewn beams painted white. A couple of steps led down to a den and a couple of steps more led down to a small projection area to run movies. There was a library with shelves stacked high with books.

At one end of the house was the master bedroom, all in white wood paneling, again with roughhewn beams, and bay windows. There were a fully equipped kitchen, guest bedrooms, and three maid's rooms.

Behind the house was an enormous Early American–style playhouse, also fully furnished, with a pool table and a barbecue. If we took it on a year's lease, the owner would even put in a swimming pool!

I wanted it. It all depended on Eddie. I warned him ahead of time about the drive. But he took one look at it and fell in love with it too.

As soon as we moved in I went right to work on *The Catered Affair*. The picture was a reflection of the new regime at MGM under Dore Schary. Serious. The story was first written as a script for television by Paddy Chayefsky, who was very hot. It was adapted for the screen by Gore Vidal, also a top writer. It was starring Ernie Borgnine, fresh from his Award-winning role in *Marty*, Bette Davis, Barry Fitzgerald, Rod Taylor, and me.

We're a family in the Bronx. It's a life of bare light bulbs hanging from the ceiling and dishpan hands, as seen through the grainy, black-and-white camera eye of Richard Brooks, the director.

Brooks was a *serious* director and he was intending to make a serious film. He did not want me. But Schary and Thau said, sorry, you have her.

I felt I was right for it. I understood the girl; the worlds we came from were not far apart.

"She can't do it. She can't act, she's cute, and she's wrong for the part," Brooks was said to have protested.

He wanted someone very understated, someone not known; someone not connected with Eddie Fisher. But the studio loved it.

He called me Miss Hollywood and Debbie Darling and Debbie Dimples. Maybe he thought I was going to play star. I was upset all the time.

One day I was doing a scene with Joan Camden, who played my friend in the picture. It was a very serious moment: I was telling her how I felt about getting married.

The director was standing behind the camera. "You have to cry in this scene, Debbie Darling."

I couldn't just cry. I did not know the technique of how to cry on cue. I never wanted to know. Now that's all I was hearing.

"Com'on, Miss Dimples. Cry! You have to cry!"

"Please don't yell at me!"

"Cry, Miss Hollywood!"

Joan, who was a very good dramatic actress, much better than I, kept saying, "Don't let it bother you. Just look at me and let's just be it."

All of the cast were so supportive of me under the circumstances. One lunch break Bette Davis invited me into her trailer.

"Debbie," she said, "don't let anyone bah-thah you. You're quite good. Just do the scene. And don't cry if you can't." Then she rehearsed me in the scene.

"Never be afraid of the greats. Only work with the greats. They'll make you great."

You learn when you work with Bette Davis. We had a scene together, mother and daughter, where she's cooking fish and talking to me. We rehearsed that bit for two weeks. Everything had to be timed. Turn on the gas jets on one line. Pick up the spatula on another. Put it down on the third. It had to look very natural. It's very tricky working with props in movies because the different shots have to match. In the end it just looked like the two of us having a conversation. Davis is a perfectionist, and brilliant. To this day I am grateful for her many lessons.

Ernie Borgnine also worked with me, rehearsing me in my scenes with him. When it came to actual shooting, the director worked hard with me too. But he intimidated me throughout the production and I hated it.

The picture was a success critically but not at the box office. With the coming of television and the departure of Mr. Mayer, we were seeing an era come to a close.

And all of a sudden we were left without him or the rest of the family who made it all happen. The directors, the lighting men, the wardrobe people, the makeup people.

They were gone and there we were, standing alone, in the midst of fame.

By 1956, the studio had let a lot of contracts lapse. Gable got into his car one day and drove off the lot after twenty-five years at MGM. Ava Gardner moved to Europe. Lana. June. Van. People whose faces and talents had earned millions and millions for the studio (and do even to this day, thirty years later)—gone. Mickey and Judy had already left and made new careers for themselves.

It wasn't as if people didn't have money. But they had no place to go. All of a sudden the party was over and many of us were without a public.

We all reacted like abandoned children. Musicals were over. A lot of people probably could have gone straight into television except we had been taught *never* to go on television. Some people went home and shook. Others waited by their telephones.

I didn't care what happened to me because I was committed to being a wife and mother. I felt I could leave the work behind me. As it happened, being a famous new wife, I was such big box office that they had no intention of letting my contract lapse. Even if they didn't have a picture for me, they could loan me out to another studio and make a fortune.

Meanwhile I was busy setting up my new home. One Friday in the middle of January 1956, Edward R. Murrow interviewed us on *Person to Person*.

But between my working and Eddie's club and concert bookings, we had very little time to entertain those first few weeks.

Many of those nights I went home from the studio to an empty house, except for Eddie's boxer dog. Fanny, the poodle Eddie had given me, had remained at home with my mother. Eddie would be in New York or on the road. Our cozy little house became the large house that it was. I'd spend most of my time in my bedroom with a fire going and the dog at the foot of the bed.

The isolated house was surrounded by all the natural noises of life.

Squirrels, raccoons, deer, coyotes, waking me out of a sound sleep, my heart pounding, terrified suddenly that somebody was coming through the door—the Dutch door with a little slide lock on the bottom and a little slide lock on the top.

Sometimes Rudy Render would come out and spend the evening. He would play the piano and we would sing songs. We were young and happy. Sometimes he'd stay over. I got to know the two cops who patroled that part of Sunset. They came down the driveway a couple of times a night, which was reassuring.

Often Eddie would come home for a long weekend with the boys in tow. It was just like New York. They'd sit up till three or four in the morning playing cards. I'd make them grilled-cheese sandwiches with pickles. That's what I made best. It gives you an idea of how my cooking had progressed.

Philadelphia days and the record business—that was the conversation. No one would ever look at me and say, "Well, Debbie, that was when we were kids and were doing the local radio show." They'd just ignore me.

Eddie would, to a great degree, ignore me also. Small wonder I felt completely left out.

The Thunderbird was in the garage and the diamond was in the drawer. And I was alone. I couldn't even have my friends over because he was having his friends over. I could have pushed the point but I wanted the marriage to be happy.

I didn't understand why I was in this situation and I didn't like it. I was spoiled too. Other people found me bright and amusing. After all, that was how my career happened.

I never discussed the problem with anybody. I wasn't always sure that something was wrong. Maybe this was the way marriage was supposed to be. I was always trying to satisfy Eddie sexually. Until one night when I was going to bed and I asked him if he wanted to make love.

"Yes," he said, "I'll be in in a little while, so get started without me."

Get started without me? I didn't even know where it was. He said it so seriously I thought he meant it. I felt so stupid and confused.

These weren't things I could discuss with my mother. I kept telling myself that it would all work out. I have a very strong optimistic side anyway; a very strong faith.

As married people, our lives in Hollywood were opened up to a society unlike anything either of us had ever known. We were the hot-young couple, so they loved having us. The Goetzes, the Goldwyns, the Warners, the Mervyn LeRoys; the very rich and the very famous were invited. Nobody else. I loved every minute of it. It was very stimulating and very worldly, full of brilliant and interesting people.

The entertainers were often the entertainment at the parties. Gary Cooper's wife, Rocky, used to hire the piano player from MGM who knew everyone's repertoire and the key we sang it in. Merman sang, Garland sang, Sinatra sang, Noel Coward sang, and so did Reynolds.

By then, I knew a lot of people in the movie business. It was a whole new world for Eddie. When he was in town for more than a weekend, we'd go out all the time. We began spending time with Dean and Jeanne Martin, Edie and Ernie Kovacs, the Sammy Cahns, Cloris Leachman and George Englund, Tony Curtis and Janet Leigh, Mike Todd and Evelyn Keyes. We'd go to each other's houses or out to dinner. Eddie wouldn't invite the boys to the Star parties, so I was his companion.

It was a lot of fun and we were, at times, really very happy during those early days.

The men often played cards, for big stakes—ten, fifteen, even twenty thousand dollars in a night! The women would end up talking with each other until the wee hours.

It didn't always seem like a big party. Eddie, I discovered early on, was a moody boy. I had had a glimpse of that a couple of times when we were engaged and he was undecided about our future plans. I'd had another indication after the Coca-Cola convention.

After we were married, he would often be aloof. I had never known anyone who'd withdraw like that. I'd ask him, "Did I say something wrong? Did I do something wrong?"

Sometimes he'd say no, and sometimes he'd say nothing.

But he never gave any reason or explanation. He was always like that, very up or very down. He was depressed and wanted to be alone. I, in turn, was getting the clear impression that it had something to do with the way he felt about me.

Then one night, after we'd moved to Los Angeles and we were out at the Mocambo, I got a good, hard look at my new reality.

It started out innocently. Mocambo was packed with friends that night. There was a singer performing. Afterward Dean Martin, who was in the audience, got up onstage and started ad-libbing at certain people at the tables. I responded with some ad libs; one thing led to another, and the two of us ended up on stage kibbitzing and clowning around.

The audience was hysterical, screaming with laughter. Dean and I were having the best time. Dean was making outrageous remarks and I was doing pratfalls and shtick. We were Sid Caesar and Imogene Coca, Red Skelton and Patsy Kelly, on a high from the huge applause. It was just a very funny night. Everyone had a ball.

Except Eddie. Eddie had a terrible time. He wasn't onstage. He was in the audience. Evidently while I was up there, he wasn't laughing. I didn't notice when I got back to our table. It wasn't until later on when we were in the car on our way home.

We couldn't have been twenty feet down the road from the Mocambo when Eddie went into a tirade about how awful I was. I had been having such a good time his words were like a punch in the face.

"I've never been so embarrassed in my life," he said again and again.

"But, Eddie, how can you say that? The audience . . . they were hysterical. We had a great time."

"*You* had a great time but you were embarrassing!"

"That's not true!" I protested.

It wasn't true. I know when I'm funny; I have an instinct for comedy. I was born funny. I could always make people laugh, and now here's this man, this man that I love, telling me that I'm not funny; that I should be quite and sit in the corner. And shuttup.

"Then if I was embarrassing, what was Dean?"

Eddie hesitated for a moment. "Well, he was funny."

"Oh. We both were onstage, you know."

"Well, you weren't in the audience," he huffed. "You don't know what it was like for me to see my wife up there embarrassing herself. Embarrassing *me*!"

He told me off all the way home, banging the steering wheel to make his point, consumed by his fury, charging the air all around us.

I felt put down and destroyed. I was so angry, yet drained—as if he had slapped my face, thrown me out of the car, and run over me.

Nothing more was said that night, about anything. We went to bed. Eddie somehow fell right to sleep. I lay there, staring at the inside of the bed's canopy, listening to his sleeping breaths, wondering what he would say in the morning; wondering how long it would take before the heavy feelings would fade. Would it be dropped and forgotten?

But how could I forget? I had never before been slapped down for being myself. It hurt.

The sun was about to break through by the time I fell asleep. When I woke up in the late morning, Eddie had gone to play golf. I was glad he was out of the house. At least I'd have some relief from his objections.

I still felt as beaten down and confused, and with no one to turn to, I thought, Dean; I'll call Dean and ask him what he thought.

"Whatta you puttin' me on?" he said. "It was the funniest!"

Was he just trying to protect my feelings? I couldn't get Eddie's rantings out of my mind.

"Dean, I have to ask you a question. And you've got to be truthful with me, no matter what. Was I embarrassing to you last night? Because somebody I know thought I was. And that I should have sat down and kept quiet."

There was a quick pause on Dean's end. He didn't know how to answer. "Who was this anyway?" he asked.

"Actually, it was Eddie. He just said I wasn't at all funny."

"Well, kid, what does he know? Let him sing. He's a singer."

Dean passed it off and I felt reassured by his words. But I was still very upset. It seemed as if Eddie didn't like what came naturally to me.

I can say this now, but I didn't know it then. Looking back, I realize Eddie never felt differently. I would try not to notice what I couldn't help but notice. But every time we went out, if I entertained or joked around, I was always reprimanded, like a smack on the hand.

It was a slow process; a kind of deteriorating, mental picking. I was becoming, for the first time in my life, self-conscious of everything I said, always afraid he wouldn't like it.

I grew up thinking the way to handle a problem was to make everybody happy. It was now my duty, as his wife, to make Eddie happy. I didn't mind; I was trained to have a boss. I took full responsibility.

I didn't agree with him, yet I couldn't see how it was his problem. It wasn't until many years later that it occurred to me he probably hated my being funny. Because he wasn't. So what? In those days I never thought I could sing. He could. After he married me and we were living in the thick of the social and night life, the repartee was always between me and Frank Sinatra, or Sammy Davis, or Dean Martin, or whoever, but not Eddie.

Perhaps he felt like an outsider, although he wasn't. Everybody embraced him. He became good buddies with several people, including Dean. But somewhere deep inside, I think he always felt South Philly, the little boy who sold vegetables; who sang on the radio on Saturday mornings. He was insecure. I was too young, or dumb, to see that. I saw quite the opposite. My husband was the man who was chased by screaming teenagers everywhere he went, a man adored by greats like Eddie Cantor, Irving Berlin, General Sarnoff; even Presidents Truman and Eisenhower. He was sought after.

And, according to him, I was embarrassing.

CHAPTER 16

I DIDN'T GO INTO MARRIAGE with great expectations, although right away I loved our social life, our home, and the dream of having a family. We were really very lucky people. As far as marriage being a difficult road—that came with the territory.

I only had to look around to see that other people had problems. Elizabeth was already divorced from Nicky Hilton, who had treated her so terribly. By the time I married Eddie, she was remarried, to Michael Wilding, and by then that marriage was also in trouble. Leslie Caron was in her first marriage, to the meat-packing heir, Geordie Hormel, a union that was hardly bliss. And Pier Angeli had not long before stepped over the threshold into a disastrous marriage to Vic Damone.

Shortly after Eddie and I were married, he and Milton Blackstone signed a deal with RKO to make his first picture. I was loaned out by MGM to co-star in this remake of *Bachelor Mother* called *Bundle of Joy*. They were cashing in on the Debbie-Eddie phenomenon. I played a clerk in a department store who finds a baby whom everyone thinks is really mine. Eddie played the son of the owner of the department store, who was Adolph Menjou.

I was pregnant when we started shooting. Eddie was very happy about the news. He was proud of me and I was overjoyed with the prospect of giving him the son he wanted, and of being a mother. I wanted a large family—four or six children. When the time came, I would give up my career and stay home to take care of my family.

In the meantime, we had business to attend to: making *Bundle of Joy*. Eddie, everyone soon discovered, was not an actor. He was charming and cute but he wasn't trained. When you don't know what you're doing, but are already a big star, you tend not to listen. You think you know it all. Eddie was a big star.

I felt our celebrity was equal. In other words, I wasn't in awe of him. We were now working together in my field. Eddie could get very self-conscious shooting a scene. If he forgot one word of dialogue, he'd blame somebody. If we were doing a scene together and things didn't go right, it was my fault. If a scene didn't go well, I'd say, let's rehearse it.

"No. That's not the way I work," he'd snap.

Everyone has to rehearse. That's the way it's done.

"That's not the way I work."

I only knew about rehearsing and rehearsing until you get it right. I don't believe in rehearsing on camera.

This argument went on, on the set, with everybody standing there. I would never fight him, only suggest.

But Eddie wasn't interested in suggestions. Adolph Menjou, who by then had made about a hundred pictures and was the consummate pro, didn't care for Eddie one little bit.

My reaction was to overcompensate. I maintained a constant state of smiling adorableness so the crew and everyone else, I hoped, would overlook the problem.

However, *I* couldn't overlook the problem; I went home with it every night and returned with it every morning.

You could cut the tension with a knife. One morning driving to the studio we managed to get into an incredible argument over whether or not Jesus was born a Jew. Eddie claimed he was not. Eddie had never heard of the King of the Jews. There we are, America's sweethearts, at six A.M., driving down Melrose Avenue in Hollywood, arguing about Jesus being a Jew.

Yes, he is.

No, he's not.

Eddie was adamant.

So was I.

Finally, several blocks from the studio, I couldn't take it anymore. "Stop the car!" I shouted over his voice. "Stop the car and let me out!"

He slammed on the brakes. I got out and slammed the door behind me. He drove away in a fury, and I walked to work, so upset I was shaking.

Dr. Needles was there too. Eddie flew him in and put him up at the Beverly Hills Hotel.

Bundle of Joy was not an "up" experience for the newlyweds, a good argument against spouses spending all their time with each other. Except in public now, Eddie often tended to ignore me. Completely. He had a way of just erasing me from a situation. I might be sitting with a friend when he'd come into the room, say hello to the friend, and as soon as I'd start to say something, he'd leave. Or he'd interrupt and talk directly to the friend. It wasn't always obvious and I'd pretend not to notice, but it was as if I weren't there. It was humiliating. I was afraid to ask about it because I didn't think I could take hearing the answer. Obviously I had done something wrong.

Or maybe I hadn't, although he'd never say. He'd get into dark moods for several days. I couldn't talk him out of it.

I adapted. When Eddie was in the room, I was the quiet one, and when he was gone I was myself: Frannie the clown. The only thing to do was to be a good, devoted wife. I had committed myself to this man. I was bearing his child.

Margie Duncan, who by now had married Bernie Rich, and was expecting too, would often come over to the house when Bernie did, which was great company for me.

She and I decided that since we were both married to Jewish boys, we'd have Passover seder together and invite their friends. We read up on it and bought all the kosher foods for the seder.

Despite my lack of talent for cooking, for that holiday I wanted everything to be right and perfect. I was going all out. This would be the first of many seders at Debbie and Eddie's.

There were about fourteen or sixteen of us for the supper. The table was beautiful and we were proud of it.

The night of the seder, Eddie stayed in his room. I went to ask him to join us, as did Margie and a couple of others. Finally he came to the table, where he was quiet but friendly with everyone. Except me. He just ignored me.

It was one of those situations where everyone notices and tries to behave as if it isn't happening. I did too. I didn't know what else to do. Obviously I was at fault again.

He refused actually to seat himself at the table, but sat instead with his side to it, as if he weren't taking part but only visiting. At one point I couldn't help myself: I went over to him.

He was talking to someone next to him when I put my hands on his shoulders and leaned over close to his ear.

"Eddie, is everything okay?" I asked bleakly.

He brushed me away with his arm. "Just get outta here and leave me alone, will ya?!"

A few minutes later he left the table and went back to his room, which was a relief for everybody.

Things would get better. He'd go out on the road for a week or ten days and come back in a friendlier frame of mind. And when we went out with others, he could be very nice.

When I found out I was pregnant, and because there were many nights when I was alone, I wanted to get a house that wasn't so isolated. We leased a large, furnished four-bedroom, two-story brick house on North Maple Drive in Beverly Hills. It was the perfect place to start a family.

Then we bought our first home, a lovely English Tudor–style house with three bedrooms, in Beverly Hills. I loved it. Eddie and I moved in right away, furnishing it with items we borrowed from MGM.

Not long after Eddie and I finished our picture together, the studio loaned me out to Universal to make a film with Walter Brennan and Leslie Nielsen called *Tammy and the Bachelor,* with Ross Hunter producing.

CHAPTER 17

WHENEVER MIKE TODD WAS in town, we spent a lot of time with him and Evelyn Keyes. It was always fun to be with Mike and Evelyn because, for one thing, Eddie was always in a good mood.

Mike was just completing production of his greatest project, *Around the World in Eighty Days*. It would be his crowning achievement and it had cost millions, which he personally raised. He was the greatest promoter anybody ever knew. Mike did everything in a big way. He once hired Madison Square Garden and had a party for ten thousand and it was no big deal. Everything right down to the champagne and caviar was promoted too. Men and women just handed him their money. Utterly charming, brilliant, very handsome in an extremely masculine way. A strong face, square jaw, ruddy complexion, black hair—he was rugged and sensuous-looking. When he entered a room he took over. He had tremendous presence and magnetism. And yet he was not a polished man. His language was colorful and he could bombard any conversation with it. That was his style. He knew everybody all over the world, and everybody loved him from royalty on down.

Eddie emulated Mike. He wanted to be Mike Todd. He wanted to be that *in charge*. The more time they spent together, the more Eddie began to take on his ways. He started walking like Mike, and smoking the big cigars, and salting his language with some of Mike's choice words. Mike, as I said, respected Eddie's great success, and no doubt was flattered by Eddie's obvious admiration. Mike was old enough to be Eddie's father and yet he seemed very young, so they really were buddies.

In the early summer of that year, 1956, Mike and Evelyn had a barbecue one night at the house they shared in the Hollywood Hills. Among the guests were Elizabeth and Michael Wilding. We occasionally met the Wildings socially because Elizabeth and I were the same age and saw the same crowd. When Eddie first met Elizabeth, he was less than impressed. "She has skinny legs," he remarked to me that

152

night. "I could never go for someone like that." I have learned from that remark, many years later, that when your husband says that about a woman, she's the one to watch out for.

Elizabeth and I had known each other since age seventeen and the MGM schoolhouse. In those days, we had about as much in common as Salome and Peter Pan. I guess she liked me as much as she liked any girlfriend, but she usually turned to a man friend. After her horrendous marriage to Nicky Hilton, she turned to Stanley Donen. He was a friend, sympathetic, someone to talk to.

She and Michael Wilding had two little boys and lived in a sprawling modern house on a hilltop with a spectacular view of Benedict Canyon. All young Hollywood would be at their parties. Elizabeth was, understandably, always surrounded by men. Peter Lawford, Stanley, Michael, Roddy McDowall, and Monty Clift. By that time, it wasn't news to most of us that Michael and Elizabeth's marriage was in trouble. He had offered her a stable relationship after the nightmare of her first marriage. But Michael was a sweet, sensitive, gentle man and did not offer the passion and excitement that Elizabeth needed.

I didn't realize that night up at Mike and Evelyn's that something was beginning between Mike Todd and Elizabeth. Two or three weeks after that barbecue, Evelyn was out of the picture. Elizabeth filed for a legal separation from Michael Wilding and they were off and running.

Elizabeth was primed to meet a Mike Todd. He adored her and she worshiped him. Before Elizabeth, I had never seen Mike make a fuss over a woman, but she had every ingredient in a woman that he wanted—beauty, excitement, adventure and she was a big movie star. He showered her with gifts, treating her like a princess. I think he made Elizabeth feel more beautiful than she is, if that is possible. But theirs was a very volatile relationship.

The four of us would often go out together. One night not long after they'd started seeing each other, Eddie and I had them over to dinner. Mike was the kind of guy who would say anything—and I mean *anything*. It wasn't unlike him to look across the dinner table and say to Elizabeth, "I'd like to fuck you as soon as I finish this."

After dinner we were sitting in the den, when they started to badger each other. It became very verbal and seemed like a fight. I was shocked—after all, they were having a romance. Eddie, however, was amused and laughing about it. I wasn't.

All of a sudden, Mike leaned over toward Elizabeth and clobbered her, knocking her to the floor! He really hit her! Elizabeth screamed, walloped him right back, and from there they went right into a huge fight. He dragged her by her hair—while she was screaming and kicking at him—across the room into the foyer. I went running after him, jumping on his back to help Elizabeth. The two of them were slapping each other around. My heart was pounding. I was trying to pull Mike off, shouting at him to stop, and the next thing I knew they were wrestling on the floor, kissing and making up. Suddenly I'm like the cop in the wife-beating case, where the cop gets it. They both got mad at me for interfering.

"Hey, for Chrisake, knock it off, will ya!" Mike yelled at me.

"Oh, Debbie," Elizabeth said, getting up off the floor, her hair askew and her dress rumpled. "Don't be such a Girl Scout!"

"Don't worry about this broad, Debbie," Mike added, "she can take it." Now they were laughing.

They couldn't stop laughing. Elizabeth thought my trying to save her was hysterical.

I was furious. It was upsetting and I told them so. "If you have to do this, then do it in your own house, but not here." I thought somebody was going to get hurt. But I was wrong. Nobody got hurt. And they were like that during their entire relationship. They loved having a massive fight and then they would make up and make love.

After they left, Eddie was outraged with me. "They were just having a good time. Why couldn't you leave them alone?"

"Because I was afraid he was going to hurt her."

"That's ridiculous! They were just kidding around."

"A man slaps her onto the floor, then grabs her by the hair and pulls her out of the room and you call that kidding around?"

"What do you know about those things? They're just two people in love!"

I was really shaken up by the incident. I knew from his reaction that Eddie would have liked me to be more sexual and worldly.

I think it was the beginning of his being disenchanted. He didn't think I was funny. I wasn't good in bed. I didn't make good gefilte fish or good chopped liver. So what did he have? A cute little girl next door with a little turned-up nose. That was, in fact, all he actually ever said he wanted from me. The children, he said, better have your nose.

I don't remember the occasion that prompted her remark, but Elizabeth said to me again, sometime during that period, "When are you going to get over being a Girl Scout?"

"Never," I said. "I like being a Girl Scout."

"How boring. How *boring*," she retorted.

"How would you know, Elizabeth, you were never a Girl Scout."

"But I would never want to be," she added casually.

"But you wouldn't be allowed in the troop anyway, so it doesn't matter."

Elizabeth laughed at that. "Debbie, you're really so square, you're so square, it's impossible after all these years."

Nobody really likes being called square, even if they are. But compared to Elizabeth, there was no denying it. "We're very different, Elizabeth. But that doesn't mean I can't be me and you can't be you, so big deal."

"Well, I just don't believe it. Nobody can be a Girl Scout forever, Debbie."

"Why not?" I replied. "Two dollars a year and you can be a Girl Scout . . . forever."

But it bothered me when Elizabeth said that. She was always outspoken and I'm sure meant no offense, and I was never really afraid of anybody or felt that I had to prove myself. Yet, of all the women she knew at that time, she probably liked me the best, since she didn't have many close girlfriends.

It was fun and exciting to be around Mike and Elizabeth. They were having a great time in their lives, like two kids partying, hugging, loving, touching. With Eddie, I either felt humiliated or lost.

CHAPTER **18**

WHEN THE WEATHER TURNED cooler in Los Angeles, Eddie and I would go down to our little house in Palm Springs on the weekends. Eddie could play golf with his buddies and I could visit with friends. In late October of 1956, Margie and Bernie Rich had their first son at the hospital in Palm Springs. The day after Michael was born, I went to see them. When I was leaving the hospital, I suddenly felt ill. I sat down on the curb.

A man came up to me and said, "Is everything all right?"

All I could say was no.

Our family doctor from Burbank, Dr. Levy, happened to be in Palm Springs that weekend also. As soon as he saw me he knew I had begun labor. With Eddie driving and Dr. Levy in the front seat and me in the back, we practically flew back to Los Angeles.

On Sunday, October 21, 1956, our beautiful daughter, Carrie Frances Fisher was born. I breast-fed her and Eddie would sit with me, looking at mother and daughter like a proud papa. He loved the baby and he loved me. I felt that we had attained what was needed for a happy marriage—a family. Everything was going well for us. Eddie was doing his television show every Wednesday and Friday nights. He had a new hit record, "Cindy, Oh Cindy," and was making top money in the clubs. America's sweethearts had had a baby girl and it was news across the world. The day after she was born, RKO took out a huge ad in the trades promoting *Bundle of Joy* to theater owners as the "most prosperous holiday gift you ever had."

Things really hadn't changed, however. Within a couple of weeks Eddie was morose. He would get very bored and sit out by the pool for hours, ignoring me. In the last six weeks of my pregnancy he had been angry that he couldn't have sex with me. Was that still the problem? I had no idea.

About four months after Carrie was born, Eddie opened the Tropicana in Las Vegas. I went down for the opening. In those days, the show included Showgirls. They were tall Australian and English girls with elaborate headdresses that made them maybe six feet two—and no tops. As a gag, without telling Eddie, I got dressed up in one of their costumes—with a gold lamé top. When the lights came up, there were the mostly nude giantesses standing up on the huge catwalk—and me, all of five feet one and just about coming up to their waists! The audience screamed with laughter.

Eddie, surprised, looked up at me and laughed along with the audience. But backstage after the show he was furious.

"You shouldn't do things like that. It's showing off."

"It's not showing off. They loved it. We should do an act together. You sing great, so you sing and I kid you from the audience. They'd die laughing."

He couldn't do that. "You're trying to take the audience away from me!" he said and left the room.

He didn't talk to me for the rest of the night. I felt terrible. I wasn't trying to take anything away from him. I thought I was helping, adding some humor. It was only a ten-second gag.

The next day he completely ignored me. Finally I decided to confront him. Eddie was sitting in a chair, brooding, playing with his hundred-dollar chips. Eddie was a gambler. I went over to him and knelt down at his side, looking up at him.

"Eddie, I'm sorry about last night."

He just sat there saying nothing, like Bogart as Captain Queeg, playing with his chips.

"Eddie, please tell me why you're mad at me."

Without looking up, he shoved me away with his hand, knocking me onto the floor. "Don't bother me!" he snapped. "Leave me alone."

So I did. I got out of his way and I went back to Los Angeles.

I was very unhappy, but I didn't tell anyone. I felt we should have been happy. He wouldn't talk and I felt completely alienated from the world.

The November after Carrie was born, Elizabeth filed papers to get a California divorce from Michael Wilding. She and Mike Todd were always together now, but under California law it would be about a year before her final decree would come through and she could marry him. That December she and Mike were on a yacht in the Bahamas when she tripped and seriously hurt her back. Within a few days she had no feeling in one of her legs and they rushed her to a hospital in New York. It was there that they discovered she was pregnant.

Mike Todd didn't want anyone to know about the pregnancy until they were married, which he wanted to do immediately. Since California law wouldn't allow it, they were advised the best solution was to get a quickie Mexican divorce.

It happened almost overnight. Michael Wilding, the true gentleman, knowing she was going to have Mike Todd's child, obliged his wife. She, in turn, gave him their house in Benedict Canyon and everything else she had. We all flew down to Mexico. On the first of February the Wildings were granted a divorce in Acapulco and Michael flew back to Los Angeles.

We stayed at a villa in Acapulco. All day long on February 2 the trucks arrived with preparations for the wedding—a typical Mike Todd production. Thousands of white gladioli, bushels of white orchids, dozens of cases of champagne, crates of crab, barrels of baby lobsters, and pounds of the best caviar flown in from pre-Castro Havana. He had a mariachi band flown in from Mexico City and a jazz band flown in from New York City. With his friend the great Mexican comedian Cantinflas, he planned a fireworks display that cost tens of thousands of dollars.

The ceremony was to be private. Eddie was to be best man and I, matron of honor. While Mike was kept busy all day making the last-minute preparations, we sat by the swimming pool with Elizabeth, who was drinking champagne. Mike had wanted a rabbi to marry them but by midafternoon he had not succeeded in finding one, so he settled for the mayor of Acapulco to officiate at a civil service. After the sun went down, I went up to Elizabeth's room with her to wash and set her hair and help her get dressed because she had to wear a back brace after her surgery. Elizabeth wore a blue chiffon gown designed by Helen Rose, as well as Mike's wedding gift to her—an $80,000 diamond bracelet.

About nine o'clock, about an hour late, Elizabeth, carrying a bouquet of white orchids, was ready. Cantinflas and Mike carried her down to the terrace for the ceremony, with me following right behind. The mayor read the short service, Eddie sang "The Mexican Wedding Song," and then Cantinflas and Mike carried Elizabeth out to an enormous reception.

The next day Eddie and I flew back to Los Angeles and Elizabeth and Mike stayed in Acapulco to begin their honeymoon. Because of her spinal fusion, the doctors had considered it very dangerous for her to have a baby and had advised against it, but she wanted to have their love child.

By the time Carrie was six months old, Eddie was either not at home or not talking to me. One day I said, "Maybe you really need a place of your own. Then you can be by yourself and we won't get in your way."

"Maybe you're right," he said.

"I don't know what I can do to help you. What is it that you want, Eddie?" I asked.

He just looked at me. I didn't know where the reporters were getting their information, but there was speculation in the gossip columns. Did he want a divorce? Was that it?

I didn't believe in it. In my heart I was a Nazarene. I was brought up to think divorce was a sin. My mother and father had problems but they didn't dissolve the marriage over them. They survived for better or for worse and so could I. I never would have divorced. Ever. I had a child to think about now. We were a family. If he needed some space, then let him have some space.

"If you want to get away, maybe I can help you find a place. That way you can come home when you want."

I found a small house for him up in Laurel Canyon that was remote and private. We both went to look at it. Eddie was undecided.

CHAPTER 19

IN THE LATE SPRING, Eddie was going to London to play the Palladium and planned to meet up later with Elizabeth and Mike, who were on an extended honeymoon as well as publicizing *Around the World*. Eddie hadn't invited me but I wanted to go anyway.

Eddie was traveling with his small entourage: a secretary, at least one of the boys, as well as Dr. Needles. To ensure I'd have someone to talk to, I asked Jeanette Johnson. She was one of the few close friends I had who could afford to pay her own way and she had never been to Europe.

About a month before we left on our trip, *Tammy and the Bachelor* had opened to lukewarm reviews. It was not a spectacular success at the box office. The title song had been sung over the credits of the movie by the Ames Brothers, and I also sang it in the picture. My recording wasn't released until after the movie had come out, but unlike the picture, it took off right away. Seeing a big promotional possibility, Universal immediately pulled the picture for a few weeks until the record built momentum. A few days after we arrived in England, I got a wire from the United States informing me that "Tammy" was one of the Top Ten on the *Billboard* charts. Everyone was amazed because it was a sweet, simple little ballad in contrast to the hits by Elvis Presley, Jerry Lee Lewis, Paul Anka, and Buddy Holly.

From Eddie, there wasn't a word of congratulations or joy; not a momentary kick that his wife was on the charts. By then he had something like twenty-seven gold records, but now somehow I was a competitor.

It was a time when Elvis had taken all the crooners by surprise. No one expected rock and roll to last. The more Eddie thought about "Tammy," the more he talked about Elvis, who had also been signed by RCA. For years Eddie had been RCA's biggest recording star, until Elvis the Pelvis came along.

No one else quite saw it that way at the time, although maybe

Eddie was right to see the writing on the wall. In retrospect, his career probably peaked during or shortly after the Korean War. He continued to make hit records and to pull in big audiences. But after 1955, the screaming girls were chasing after this crazy guy with the guitar. It turned out to have been the phenomenon of "Debbie and Eddie" as much as anything else that had kept both Eddie Fisher and me big in the public eye.

As if that weren't bad enough, now it was Elvis, Paul Anka, Buddy Holly, Pat Boone, Billy Williams, and *Tammy*!! Within weeks "Tammy" was to become Number One and it remained there for almost three months. The record had such impact that when Universal re-released *Tammy and the Bachelor*, it grossed millions.

I was surprised by the record's success. I could be happy but I couldn't be glad. I had offended my husband without even trying.

Although no one ever talked about it, nor did I ever think about it, Eddie hadn't had a hit for a while and recording was *his* field. He was the one with the great voice in the family, not me. However, one of Eddie's great weaknesses was that he never realized he had any. Circumstances that didn't work out in his favor were always somebody else's fault.

Fortunately, having Jeanette traveling with us made the trip fun for me. She actually did go on to college and become a gym teacher at the very school we had attended. The international jet-set world of movies and show business was like going to another planet for her.

From London we all went to Paris, where one night we dined at Maxim's with Joe DiMaggio. Jeanette was in awe.

Then we went to Monte Carlo and then on to Rome. From Rome we went to the South of France to a villa Elizabeth and Mike had rented in Cap Ferrat. They were away on business and so Mike offered its use to us.

The villa, called La Fiorentina, was a spectacular, marble-floored mansion with gardens overlooking the Mediterranean.

The second day we were there, Elizabeth and Mike came back unexpectedly. I was a little concerned about Jeanette. Had I known they were going to be there I wouldn't have gone, if only because Mike and Jeanette were the opposite ends of the spectrum. If I was Peter Pan compared to Elizabeth, Jeanette was Little Bo-peep.

I could just imagine Mike saying something very off-color in front of Jeanette, and her turning beet red. In fact, I didn't have to imagine it. I knew inevitably he would; he didn't care what he said in front of anybody. It wasn't to be rude. That was his way.

The first thing I did when we heard they were coming back was to take Jeanette aside.

"He's a very unusual person," I told her. "Now whatever he says, or whatever he does," I advised, "don't even look embarrassed. Don't be anything."

Jeanette was unhip to be sure, but she wasn't dumb. She didn't know what to expect but she understood what I was talking about.

It was a good thing I warned her. She was given the bedroom across from Mike and Elizabeth's. He had been using the bathroom of that bedroom to hang his clothes. One late afternoon Jeanette was taking a bath when Mike walked in on her, wrapped only in a towel himself.

"Don't mind me," he said, "I just need something." Jeanette had not yet married and I have little doubt that was the only time since she was a baby that a man had come in while she was taking a bath.

Mike looked through his pants and suits for what he wanted and then sat down and started telling her about the birthday party he was planning for himself. Jeanette casually sat in her bathwater, completely unembarrassed, while Mike explained how he didn't like Gary Cooper's wife so he'd told Gary Cooper *not* to bring her to the party. To Jeanette everything he was doing and saying went so against her way of thinking that she found Mike interesting. And, surprisingly, because Jeanette knew something about fine art and Mike was interested in that, they had something to talk about. Which was a relief.

Being in the company of Mike Todd turned out to be an education for Jeanette. She learned something about accepting people for the way they are and not letting it bother her. Mike could always put anyone to the test. A group of us were sitting down by the pool one afternoon with Elizabeth and Mike. She was almost into her seventh month by then, and pouring out of her two-piece bathing suit. Mike, eight-inch Havana cigar in his mouth, had been entertaining us; suddenly he got up, walked over to Elizabeth, put his hand into her bathing suit, and started fondling her breast. Jeanette and I left. Eddie stayed for a while. He finally came up to the terrace. He enjoyed watching all of it. It was what he wanted that he didn't have with me.

This was not the sort of thing one observes while coaching the girls' soccer team at Glendale High, but Jeanette, to her credit, never turned so much as the slightest shade of pink. The rest of us were used to it. That was Mike and Elizabeth. Outrageously earthy, passionate, and flamboyant.

Besides, Elizabeth couldn't have been friendlier. She was very, very happy with her life. It was the happiest I've ever known her. She was pregnant with the baby she wanted, her back was finally healing after the operation, and they were still newlyweds, divinely in love; still slapping, still kissing, still making up. In the middle of fettuccine, they'd start having an argument, leave the table, and the next thing you'd hear is them going into this fabulous laughter on their way to the bedroom. They'd be gone an hour and a half and come back to finish their fettuccine cold.

After a few days at La Fiorentina, I made plans with Jeanette to go on to Spain and leave Eddie with Mike and Elizabeth and his much-needed space. The night before we were to leave, all of us had dinner together at the villa. It was a festive, partylike affair.

Neither Eddie nor I drank in those days, but at dinner I asked the butler to bring him a beer. Eddie was in a great mood whenever he was with the Todds, and the beer loosened him up more. He was acting as if I were actually his wife, even showing affection. After dinner, Jeanette went up to bed. The rest of us moved from the dinner table to the library. I ordered Eddie a second bottle of beer. The ice melted entirely.

He got drunk on two beers that night. Not only that, but he became very amorous. Elizabeth and Mike had put him in the mood, or he forgot whom he was with. It was a happy time with all of us entertaining each other with stories and jokes. Eventually they went off to make love and I turned to Eddie and said: "Why don't we do the same?" And so we did.

I had wanted another child as soon after Carrie as possible. I'd hoped she would have a brother who would be as close in age to her as I am to my brother, Bill. Bill was always my strength and my ally when I was growing up. He still is, to this day. I wanted Carrie to have that too.

At that stage of my marriage to Eddie, he wasn't interested in sleeping with me. There was less and less opportunity for me to get pregnant.

I just remember praying to God that night that I would be pregnant. We had had a good time and there weren't many of those. It was just right. And that was my son. That was luck. That was God.

I just knew when I left that I was pregnant. I couldn't have known, but I knew.

When I got home, I moved Eddie's things into the guest room so that he could have a room to himself until he found a little house he might want. This way he could get a taste of being on his own again. Once he had enough of it, he would see what he had with me and his children, however long that took.

Eddie stayed on in Europe for several weeks. One afternoon after he'd come back, I went shopping at Saks for crystal. I fainted in the store. Someone drove me home and called a doctor to come to the house to examine me. Eddie was called home from the golf course.

The doctor knew immediately. "You know what's wrong with Debbie, don't you?" he said to Eddie. "She's pregnant."

Eddie paled.

I don't remember what he said to the doctor but after he left, Eddie just stood by the window with his arms folded. I was lying in bed. I could see the tension in his face. He was very angry, standing there just staring out.

We were alone in the room. He turned to face me, his brown eyes black with rage.

"You're trying to ruin my career. You're trying to move me out, as if I've abandoned you, while you're pregnant! You're not going to get away with it!!"

I thought to myself, I'm going to have our child and all you're thinking about is how it's going to affect your career.

"No," I said, very even-tempered. "I never even wanted you to know I was pregnant. You just do whatever you want, Eddie. You go your way. I'll go mine. Everything will be fine."

"Look, I know what you're trying to do to me."

"Eddie, I'm not trying to do anything to you. This is my child. This is not yours. You didn't even want to make love to me. I had to get you drunk. So don't worry what Louella and Walter Winchell will say."

He looked at me stone-faced. "Well I'm not going anywhere. But you hate me so much you wanted to ruin my career, and it's not going to happen."

"Eddie, just go."

"You wanna give me a divorce, then just give me the divorce and get it over with."

"Eddie, I'm not going to give you a divorce but just go away. You're just making our lives miserable. I'm twenty-five years old. I have a career, a beautiful daughter, a successful husband, a lovely home, two cars, money in the bank, and I'm not happy. I want a second child and I'm going to have this second child. *This will make me happy!* I don't care what it makes you feel! So just go away and do whatever you want to do. Don't worry about us. We're not going anywhere!"

Eddie didn't respond. He left the room. It was the first time in months that I felt I was alive again. Telling him what I thought lifted years of weight off my shoulders. I knew I wasn't going to spend the rest of my life being miserable just because my husband was.

He did not move out. He had it in his mind that a separation for us would be bad for him. I didn't really want him to leave. I wanted us to work this out.

Eddie went downstairs and left the house. Several hours later he came back. I didn't know if I should be surprised or what. I asked him if he wanted to have dinner with me and Carrie, and to my surprise, he said yes.

He was very quiet all through dinner and I wasn't going to push it. Yet I could see that something had softened.

"Maybe you'll give me a son," he remarked from out of nowhere while I was feeding Carrie. I looked over at him, amazed at what I had just heard. He actually had a smile on his face.

I didn't even notice at first, maybe because I didn't expect it, but Eddie changed after that day. For the first time since Carrie was born he seemed like my husband and treated me like his wife. He came home to dinner. He was attentive. He was loving. He would kiss me and hold me. He would talk to me. There were no criticisms. It was like the bad spell really was over. Maybe he does love me, I thought.

I never knew why his attitude changed so much. All I knew was that I was happy about it. Maybe speaking up to him had made him feel better. I had never told him off before. There was no more talk of moving out. We needed a bigger house and found a white-brick, two-story, four-bedroom place on Conway Avenue in Holmby Hills. It was a spacious house with a large family room and a big bay window that overlooked a pool and a rose garden. We bought furniture and a station wagon. We were settling in, at last.

Eddie was very happy about becoming a father for the second time. He adored his baby daughter but still hoped for that son. MGM loaned me out again to Universal for *This Happy Feeling*, with Curt Jurgens and John Saxon, Blake Edwards directing and Ross Hunter producing. Almost a year had passed since making *Tammy*. In my seventh month I went to a baby shower with both Hedda and Louella. Among the guests was an also very pregnant Mrs. Ronald Reagan: 1958 was a bumper year for Hollywood babies. There were new Pecks, Ferrers, Stacks, Reagans, and Fishers.

Todd was born February 24, 1958. I had given Eddie a son. He was so thrilled. We named him Todd Emanuel—Emanuel after Manny Sacks, the recording executive who started Eddie on his record career. Mike and Elizabeth came to see the baby. Mike was thrilled to have our son named after him.

Todd came into this world smiling. With his birth, I felt somehow we had made it. For the first time in our marriage, I finally felt very happy and secure.

It was only for a moment. A little more than three weeks later fate dealt us all the wild card.

CHAPTER **20**

IT WAS GRAY AND MISTY, a chilly late-March morning. A Saturday; early, eight o'clock or so. I was sitting at my dressing table taking rollers out of my hair. Eddie was in New York, where he was going to sing a special version of "Around the World," written by Sammy Cahn for the Friars Club Roast of Mike the following week.

Frank, our Mexican houseman, who had once worked for Mike Todd, came rushing into my room, tears streaming down his face. "*Did you hear?! Did you hear?!*" he blurted out.

"Hear?"

"It's Mr. Todd! He was killed in a plane crash!"

My God! Mike! He can't be dead!

I reached over and turned on the small radio on the table. Mike's plane, *The Lucky Liz*, carrying Mike, his writer Art Cohn, and two pilots, had got ice on her wings, and in a storm over a mountain range in New Mexico, had crashed and exploded on the desert floor.

A grim chill jolted through me. Elizabeth! I thought; she's going to be destroyed. And what about the children!

What could I do to lessen her pain? Nothing. *But what could I do?!* That's all I could think of. I told Frank to get the car while I threw on some clothes.

It was about a ten-minute drive down Sunset Boulevard to their house on Schuyler Road in Beverly Hills. By the time I got there, the small hillside street was already jammed with cars. There were reporters and photographers all around. Everyone wanted a picture. I ran out of the car, up the steps, and into the house. Several people were already there including Kurt Frings, Elizabeth's agent, and his wife; her secretary, Richard Hanley; Sidney Guilaroff, Michael Wilding, and Rex Kennamer, Elizabeth's doctor.

Just as I walked into the house, I heard a shrieking scream from upstairs. Elizabeth appeared at the top of the staircase screaming, "No, no, it's not true! It's not true!"

I'll never forget her look of terror and anguish. I'll never forget that face—ashen, her violet eyes desperately sad, hair askew and wild—yet still incredibly beautiful, even in tragedy. And that piercing scream of agony after she called out Mike's name.

In her sheer white nightgown, she ran down the stairs in hysteria. I just stepped back as she ran by me and headed for the door, calling out Mike's name over and over. Rex and Dick Hanley got to the door just in time to stop her. Elizabeth collapsed in their arms, sobbing, "Why Mike? Why did it have to happen?" as the two men carried her back up to her bedroom.

Everyone in the room was deeply touched by her grief. Probably everyone was equally stunned. Mike Todd was bigger than life. He *was* life. He was Elizabeth's life. And now he was gone.

I didn't say anything to her. It was so awful I didn't know what to say.

The only thing I could do to help was to take Elizabeth's children home. The boys were three and five, just old enough and yet not old enough to understand.

Eddie flew back to Los Angeles and went right up to see Elizabeth. Eddie was perfect for her. He had been Mike Todd's best friend. He had slowly begun to pattern himself after Mike. He was almost as grief-stricken as she was. They could share that grief like no two other people. He was her only link to Mike. I knew that and I was glad that my husband could be of comfort to her. He was the next best thing.

Mike Todd's funeral was being held that following Tuesday, outside Chicago, where he came from. On Monday, on a private plane lent to Elizabeth by Howard Hughes, a group including her brother, Howard, Helen Rose, and Eddie, flew with Elizabeth to Illinois. I stayed at home with the children and Michael Wilding.

Michael was devastated for Elizabeth and very unhappy that she wouldn't let him try to console her. He spent the better part of the time, for more than a week, sitting at the bar in our playroom. He kept saying that eventually she would see him, she would see him. I sympathized but I also knew she never wanted to see him.

The two Wilding children stayed with us for about two weeks. Every day that he was in town, Eddie would go over to Elizabeth. Sometimes I'd go with him and sit downstairs while he read to Elizabeth from the hundreds of telegrams and letters she'd got from people all over the world. I wanted them to be alone to recover from their common loss.

He'd come home, shower, change, and go back. Elizabeth was in shock and pain. She needed him. She was also in the middle of making

Cat on a Hot Tin Roof when Mike died, so she had the additional pressure of the studio waiting for her to pull herself together. Within a couple of weeks, she was back on the set. But even after she finished the picture, she was still deeply depressed and inconsolable.

Eddie and I would beg her to go out to dinner with us—anything to lift her spirits and get her mind away from Mike. Just the three of us, to Trader Vic's or La Scala. When *Cat on a Hot Tin Roof* was released, Eddie and I took her to the premiere.

In June Eddie was playing the Tropicana in Vegas. Elizabeth came out for the weekend with Arthur Loew, Jr., Mike Todd, Jr., and a small group to see the opening show. Wearing some of her fantastic jewels that Mike had given her, she looked more stunning than ever, sitting there between Mr. and Mrs. Fisher.

When Eddie came back to Los Angeles in early August, I gave a thirtieth-birthday party for him at Romanoff's. Elizabeth was one of the twenty-five friends I invited, and the only one not to show. She claimed she didn't feel well. Elizabeth often had bouts of frail health, so I thought nothing of it.

The rumors began around that time. Elizabeth was spending a lot of time with Eddie. Or Debbie and Eddie. No one asked the logical question: Who could she date? She had just lost her husband, the love of her life. She'd always leaned on a man in difficult times. Eddie was helping her with the business of sorting out Mike Todd's estate. He was her support.

Besides, I knew what most people could never know: Eddie Fisher wasn't her type. She had just lost Mike Todd, an exciting, intensely passionate man. He was her equal. Eddie Fisher may have smoked the long cigars and done the swaggering and the rough talking, but it was only an imitation.

Eddie's attitude toward me and his children had never been better. He loved having a son. Unlike the way he was when Carrie was born, Eddie would often take Todd to the beach. Just as often he would also take Elizabeth with him, although I didn't know that then.

In mid-August, Eddie had to go to New York on business. Coincidentally, Elizabeth was in New York too. She had stopped off on her way to the South of France where she had rented a villa on the Riviera. Someone called me from New York and told me they had seen Elizabeth and Eddie out together at dinner. I said, "That's nice." And I meant it. Then there were a number of items in the columns about Eddie and Elizabeth going out dining and dancing in New York. The press drew the immediate conclusion that they were having a romance.

But I knew differently. He was showing her a good time. They were always in parties of four or more.

Eddie was due home toward the end of the month. He'd usually call me every day to check in and see how everyone was.

Almost a week passed after the day Eddie was due home. Three or four days passed when he didn't call. I was concerned but I wasn't really worried. There had been many times before when he didn't call for a few days. The press was now having a meal with Elizabeth and Eddie; everyone was calling me to confirm or deny. I refused to get into it. I told everyone exactly what I thought.

It all sounds naïve in retrospect because it was, but there was another side of it. I loved my husband. I never believed Elizabeth Taylor would want Eddie. He wasn't her type. I refused to believe that she, so bereaved over Mike, would ever want Eddie for anything other than comfort. The only quality Eddie had over Mike Todd was a voice, and I had never known music to be one of Elizabeth's big loves. But kissing him, or making love to him—as the ghost of Mike Todd—that just couldn't be, in my mind. It never would be. It was just publicity, all lies, and that's show business.

I'm slow at seeing what I don't want to believe. I can only say that now. To this day I believe they fell into it. But really fell into it. He, especially. She never loved Eddie.

At the time Mike died, I felt Eddie and I had made it. When I first started to read the rumors, when I first saw a picture of them together with the caption insinuating that they were lovers, I was offended. It's painful to read about your private life in the papers, knowing that strangers are reading about it too.

CHAPTER 21

EDDIE AND I had been invited to Edie Adams's house for dinner on a Friday night. But Eddie was still in New York, so I went alone. Dean and Jeanne Martin were there, along with quite a few of the regular crowd. There had been a big item in Walter Winchell that day or the day before about Eddie and Elizabeth having gone to Grossinger's for the weekend to dedicate a pool. Winchell had us practically divorced.

As I was turning the corner, walking from Edie's living room to the dining room, I overheard one guest say to another, "Debbie doesn't know, does she . . . ?" When they saw me the matter was dropped.

There was a definite feeling in the room. Something was different. I realized that no one asked me about Eddie. No one said, how's Eddie, or where's Eddie, or say hi to Eddie. Instead I overheard an occasional whisper or half-said remark.

I drove home from Edie's that night full of suspicion and distress. It had suddenly hit me. I thought to myself, how could she do that? How could she be that foolish? He really was with her. He really was with her right at that minute. I looked at the clock on the dashboard of the Continental. It was almost ten—about one o'clock in the morning New York time.

As soon as I got into the house I called Eddie's apartment at the Essex House. The phone rang and rang and rang. No answer. Everything goes late in New York, I thought to myself. I'd give him another hour. I couldn't get Eddie and Elizabeth out of my mind. It seemed clear.

I called again a little after eleven. Two o'clock in New York. My hands were ice-cold as if all the blood had gone out of my body. My stomach was thumping. The phone rang and rang and rang. No answer. I hung up, looking at the clock next to our bed: 11:10. I knew. I just knew.

Elizabeth, I figured, was at the Plaza because that's where MGM people always stayed. I placed the call.

"Good evening, the Plaza Hotel . . ."

"Elizabeth Taylor's suite, please . . ."

"Who's calling, please . . ."

"Debbie Reynolds . . ."

I stood there staring at the clock, not knowing what I was going to say when Elizabeth picked up the phone. I waited and waited. Two or three minutes, like hours, went by. The operator came back on the line. "I'm sorry but there is no answer in Elizabeth Taylor's suite . . ."

I put the phone down. I was sure he was there. I was sure of it. But he'd already covered his tracks with the Plaza Hotel switchboard. *How dare he* not take his wife's call! About ten minutes later, I placed the call again.

"Good evening, Plaza Hotel . . ."

"Long distance calling for Mr. Eddie Fisher," I said like a professional.

"Who shall I say is calling?" the hotel switchboard asked. Okay, Fisher, I thought, we're coming through.

"Mr. Dean Martin calling from Beverly Hills," I said like somebody's secretary.

"One moment, please," said the hotel switchboard.

Fifteen seconds later Eddie picked up the phone. "Well hiya, Dean, whatcha doin' calling me at this time of night?" he asked in a sleepy but jocular voice.

"It's not Dean, Eddie, it's Debbie."

There was dead silence. Then "Oh, shit . . ." Then the sleepy boy started to yell at me. "What the hell do you think you're doing calling me here at this time of night?! Goddamnit, you had no goddamn business calling me here!"

He was yelling at me?

"Just roll over, Eddie. I want to talk to Elizabeth."

I heard her say, rousing herself from her pillow, "Who is it, darling?"

"Tell her it's me. Put her on the phone, Eddie."

"Look," he started to explain weakly, "this is ridiculous. We're talking. I just dropped by."

"Eddie, it's getting close to three in the morning. You didn't just drop by. I woke you up."

"Goddamnit!" he yelled coast to coast, "we're not in bed. I'm just sitting here talking to her . . ."

"Tell her, Eddie. Tell her it's Debbie and I want to talk to her."

But he wouldn't. And he didn't. He just yelled at me. "Elizabeth and I are here and we are very much in love. I'll fly back to California tomorrow."

Suddenly I felt like I'd just had the wind knocked out of me. "Well, you don't have to bother!" I said and slammed down the phone.

I was numb. Blank. For a long time I just sat there on the edge of the bed, like in a vacuum. I felt very strange, as if I were alone on the top of a mountain; like floating in space.

It was the shock of it. Like: why? It's so silly. She doesn't love him. She'll never love him. What does she want him for? This is a joke. This is a scene from a bad movie. There's no way that Eddie Fisher is the one for her.

But there wasn't going to be any more denying it. It was no longer a secret. I was suddenly afraid of being alone. I didn't know if Eddie really was coming home the next day and I didn't want to be alone. I needed someone to stay with me.

I called my friend Camille Williams. Camille and I had known each other since high school. We continued to see a lot of each other, and so I knew she would understand. She was also still unmarried, so she could do it.

Camille said yes, she'd come to stay.

At seven o'clock in the morning the phone started ringing off the hook. Everyone wanted a statement. A statement about what? I played dumb. I wasn't going to talk to my husband through the press. By eight-thirty there were already a couple of dozen reporters and photographers sitting on the front lawn.

Camille drove up about nine o'clock and got the third degree before she could even get out of the car. Watching from the window the whole thing struck home with me.

How was I going to get rid of all those people milling around outside? How was Eddie going to come back into the house without the whole world watching? Eddie, so in love with Elizabeth. I didn't know what to do or what to say. So I prayed. I talked to my mother and to Camille and I prayed for the strength to get through this. I felt sick.

Eddie arrived from New York the following morning. He breezed into the house with his friend Joey Forman. They walked in like a couple of schoolkids. I was sitting in the den, waiting.

I was the first one to speak.

"Well, Eddie, this is just surprising to me that it's that serious."

He got a silly grin on his face. I was so angry I felt like hitting him. "What's going on?!" I demanded.

Eddie stammered for a second. "Well, I love her and I never loved you."

Just like that. Ho-hum.

Joey chimed in: "Yeah, that's right, he never loved you. He always told me that."

I said, "Joey, you shuttup. You *shuttup!*" I stood up, I was so angry. "In fact, you get out of my house!"

"I'm not leaving," Joey said defiantly.

"I don't want him to leave," Eddie added.

I was livid. "Oh, you always have to have your little support system, Eddie. Your little hanger-onners, your little mouthpieces. Why don't you speak your own piece?"

He looked at me very coldly, as he had done so many times before. "I can only tell you that I love her, I never loved you, and I want a divorce."

I sat down. "Oh. Well. I'll tell you what. You go off and be with her. She'll throw you out within a year and a half. And then we'll see if we can work it out. Because I'll never give you a divorce. We have two children. . . ."

"You're crazy," he said.

I was enraged at his attitude, just discarding us, as if we were unimportant because Elizabeth had beckoned. "She doesn't love you, Eddie. She'll never love you. You're not her type."

"Yes, she does," he snapped. "And I've never loved another woman in my life except Elizabeth," he said as if he were proud of himself.

"Then why don't you just get out? Now you've said all you should say. Just go and do what you want."

He and Joey turned to leave.

"We'll talk about it in a year and a half because you won't be with her!" I shouted after them.

Eddie and Joey left. I went to my room, closed the door, and sat on the bed so that I could cry alone.

I didn't know what would happen, but I wasn't going to just give up the marriage because he was having a high old time with the world's most beautiful woman. I hadn't asked him to marry me—on the third date—four years before. I hadn't pursued him. I didn't go and grab him by the whatsis and say "come on" to him.

I decided to call Elizabeth. She was staying at Arthur Loew's house. She wasn't in, so I left a message for her to call me. Eddie walked out the door and out of the problem. What was I going to go with a crowd of people standing on the doorstep?

My lawyer recommended we first see a marriage counselor. He gave me the name of a doctor at UCLA. I called Eddie about it. He didn't like the idea but finally agreed he'd go if we could go right away. I called the doctor and made arrangements for the following afternoon. The next day's paper had a quote from Elizabeth, who had just flown into town. She said any romance between her and Eddie was "just garbage," which I still think is a funny line, even more so in retrospect.

Eddie came to the house that afternoon. He had so much trouble getting to the front door that we realized we were going to have a problem leaving together, without being followed. UCLA was only about a mile from our house.

The marriage is falling apart but the problem is how to get out of the house unnoticed. Somebody got the bright idea of sending Camille out alone in the car. Meanwhile Eddie and I took off our shoes and ran barefoot through the back of our neighbor's property and down their driveway, where Camille, who had driven around the block, was waiting undetected.

I was looking for a way of keeping us married. I told myself that there had to be something I could do to keep us together. I would do something, say something, promise something, threaten something, anything to make Eddie stay. My children were not going to lose their father. I was not going to lose my husband.

Eddie couldn't have cared less. He made it very clear in Dr. Rose's office. He didn't care about me or the marriage. He only cared about Elizabeth. What about the children? Oh, they'll be fine.

We left the doctor's office together. Not speaking. I never once asked myself why I wanted to spend my life with someone who treated me half the time like a nonentity. I never saw it from that point of view because it was so obviously, to me, my failure. Elizabeth was the passion flower and I never offered him that. I actually thought being available and being subservient was enough. But it wasn't. He wanted to be Mike Todd. I couldn't give him that.

Camille was waiting in the car. There was no one else around. I got in the backseat, Eddie got in front. No one said anything. She turned the key to start the car. Nothing. She turned the key again. Nothing. Not even the whirring of the starter.

Oh, great. "The battery's dead."

"What should we do?" Camille asked.

Eddie was steaming. "Now whatta we gonna do?! Why didn't somebody take care of this?!"

Had I planned this too? Like Todd's conception? Was this my last big chance to keep him away from Elizabeth and ruin his career? With a dead battery? Eddie wouldn't have been surprised.

So there we were in the middle of the UCLA campus. There wasn't a phone booth in sight, or a taxi to hail, or even a student driving by on a bicycle to hitch a ride with. There was just us, one dead white Lincoln Continental Mark IV with Camille at the wheel; Debbie and Eddie and a mob of reporters waiting back on Conway Avenue for us to come out of the house.

We did the only thing we could do. We got out and pushed. The one lucky thing was that the car was headed in the right direction. Thank God the road was flat. With Eddie on one side, me on the other, and Camille steering, the three of us moved that boat off campus and onto Gayley Avenue. The whole absurd situation finally made us all crack up. Both of us exhausted from pushing tons of steel, Eddie and I had a good laugh until we reached the gas station. Then it wasn't funny again.

After we got the car started, we dropped Eddie off at Joey Forman's apartment and I went to the office of my lawyer, Frank Belcher, and called Howard Strickling, who handled all the press at MGM, to tell him that Eddie wanted a separation.

I should have felt relieved but I was numb. Howard immediately went over to the house and gave the reporters what they were waiting for.

"A separation exists between Eddie and Debbie. No further action is being taken at this time."

It was pandemonium when I got home that night. The next day, to get away from the crowd outside my living-room window, I took Carrie and went over to spend the day at Marge and Gower Champion's. Leaving the house that afternoon, I stopped at the side door to oblige the photographers with a picture. It became The Rejected Woman.

I'd pinned Todd's diaper pins on my blouse as I was rushing to leave, so that I wouldn't forget them. Strangely, those tiny diaper pins in the photographs seemed to catch everyone's eye. Some thought I planned that picture. Eddie made a point, after that, of putting down in public anything I said or did, with a remark like "She's playing the martyr thing."

When I got back to the house that afternoon, I learned Elizabeth had returned my call. But it really didn't matter anymore, so I never called her again.

My brother offered to move in with me for a while, and Camille was staying, so I wasn't going to be alone. My mother and father came over every day to be with the children. But the hard truth for me was that I was alone.

Of course, I wasn't exactly alone with a hundred strangers camping out on my front lawn—for weeks, as it happened. The press still didn't leave the house after MGM's statement or after they got a picture. What could I say to them? "He's not going to last with Elizabeth"? Should I have said that I felt sick to my stomach?

I sat in the window seat of our bedroom and prayed. I was doing a lot of praying. It was the only thing I was doing that I was certain was right. The press wanted a statement, so I wrote something out on a legal pad. I felt very tentative about saying anything. If Eddie ever heard it, and I knew he probably would, I wanted Eddie to know there was still room to work things out.

I went to the screen door to give the reporters my statement. "I am still in love with my husband. I am deeply shocked over what has happened. We have never been happier than we have been in the past year. Eddie is a great guy. Do not blame him for what had happened. The separation was not my idea."

The next day Joan Crawford called to console me and offered me and the children her house if we wanted to get away from the press. Lucille Ball called to see if I was all right. Cloris Leachman called, as well as family and old friends.

I didn't hear from anybody else after that. I only gradually realized the situation. Now it was going to be Eddie and Elizabeth as the hot couple. It took a long time to face that.

I had a constant pain in my stomach. I didn't feel like eating anything except popcorn and milk shakes. For the next few days I couldn't sleep. Camille would sit up with me till all hours while we listened to Frank Sinatra's love songs on the record player.

For me, if someone is taken from you by death, it's a sadness that never ends. But when Eddie left me for another woman, it seemed worse. I found myself missing him, asking myself why the marriage had ended this way, and why it had failed. Reminding myself that it had failed because of me; obviously I was not enough of a woman. Finally I had to admit that it was over, completely over. That was a hard admission for me to make.

To this day I find it very difficult to discuss my painful thoughts. I used my religion a lot in those terrible days. I'd talk out loud to Jesus. It helped. Had I found a brilliant doctor to go to, I might have been better off, but I didn't.

CHAPTER 22

EDDIE WANTED THE DIVORCE right away. I didn't. I wanted a separation, even a long one. I knew he was going off with Elizabeth. I was resigned to that. But they weren't. That wasn't enough. Neither wasted any time saying that I was robbing them of their happiness. It was Elizabeth who decided to tell the world that my husband hadn't been interested in me anyway, that his leaving home had nothing to do with her.

So there was huge pressure. You can actually feel pressure when Elizabeth Taylor tells the world that you're depriving her of a lover. I guess you can even feel Elizabeth should always have a lover, even if it's yours. The message was coming through the news media, but it really was Elizabeth and Eddie. She wanted to be married. I didn't blame her, so did I.

In the long run Elizabeth did me a big, big favor, but I felt she was very mean about me too. I knew that was her manner. She saw the man she wanted and nothing was going to stand in her way. Fine. She got the man she wanted. When she later met Richard Burton, I thought, there he is, the man for her—a type of strong, brilliant adventurer. Richard Burton was even better than Mike Todd because he had no rough edges. And he was an artist.

With all this going on, I did not feel like working. I didn't even feel like eating. Over that year and a half I dropped down to almost 90 pounds from my regular 102.

But they were waiting at the studio where we were filming *The Mating Game*. George Marshall, our director, would bring a blender onto the set and make me milk shakes.

The publicity impact of the separation was incredible. It was ongoing, getting bigger by the day. It was hotter news than our engagement and wedding. The whole world seemed to have an opinion about it.

I didn't want to have to depend on Eddie for money. He wasn't very dependable when it came to emotional matters, but financially he was very, very generous for years, to a number of people. He showered Elizabeth with baubles and real estate and the royal life-style. But he always had had a problem with my spending his money. So I got used to spending my own.

I felt that he should share the expense of raising Todd and Carrie; he owed his children that. But he wanted to pay alimony, not child support, in order to get his tax break. I wanted our property so Carrie and Todd would have a home. Other than that, I really didn't care what he took.

That Wednesday when he left the house, he left pretty much for good, taking only the clothes he had on his back. I sent everything over to him when he asked for it. But he never came by to see Carrie and Todd. I wasn't going to make a point of it because I didn't want them to notice. I wanted them to love their father, no matter how I felt. The reason they didn't see him, I explained—for years—was that he was out earning a living to support us.

In the first week of December, right after we finished *The Mating Game*, I gave in and filed for divorce. Between the work schedule and the interviews and my family life, I didn't have the energy to fight it. Christmas was coming and I wanted it to be beautiful for my children. With all the difficulties and problems, I had been blessed with friends like Camille and Rudy Render and my brother, as well as my mother and father, who were always there for me. Right after Eddie moved out, Bill moved into the family room in the cellar and stayed until I didn't need him. Despite the loss of their father, who came only once during that time to see them, the children were surrounded by loving family and friends. I was lucky.

On Thursday, February 19, I took a day off from the studio and with my lawyer and Camille as my witness, went to Superior Court in downtown Los Angeles. I took the witness stand at 8:45 A.M.

"You have alleged," my lawyer Frank Belcher began, "in your complaint that your husband has treated you in a cruel and inhuman manner. Will you tell the court just briefly, please, of what that treatment consisted?"

"Well, my husband became interested in another woman."

"When did this occur?"

"During the first part of September, which led to our separation on September ninth."

"As a result," Frank Belcher continued, "did your husband and the *other woman* receive a considerable amount of publicity and notoriety?"

"Yes. There was a great deal of publicity caused by this new interest."

"Their pictures appeared in the papers together?"

"Yes."

"And does this apparently continue down to the present time?"

"Yes."

"Did he ever discuss with you the matter of divorce?"

"Yes."

"What briefly did your husband tell you in this respect?"

"That he wished a divorce."

"What effect, Mrs. Fisher, has this course of conduct on the part of your husband had on you?"

"Well, to say the least, I was very distressed."

Then Camille testified the same, even more briefly. Eddie and I had signed a forty-eight-page settlement agreement at the beginning of the week. The judge approved it and a divorce decree was granted to "Mary Frances Reynolds and Edwin Jack Fisher," becoming final in one year.

The papers the next day blasted out the news in banner headlines: DEBBIE GETS MILLION DOLLAR SETTLEMENT. This was to consist of "$36,000 a year for the first two years," and "$30,000 after that until" I married or died.

CHAPTER 23

EDDIE MADE TWO PAYMENTS before we ran into problems. He was not happy, because Elizabeth and he wanted to get married. California divorce laws in those prehistoric days required a year's wait before the final decree. They didn't want to wait. They wanted me to agree to a Mexican or Nevada divorce.

I didn't feel like it. He got to walk away from our marriage and his family without any complications. I didn't see what difference a few more months would make to them. I was through giving, so I said no.

The movies must be one of the few businesses where personal pain makes you more valuable. MGM had all they could do to decide whom they'd loan me out to and for how much. Not that it caused a big increase in my salary. But I didn't mind. I was happy to be working.

Right after *The Mating Game*, I was loaned out to Twentieth Century-Fox to make *Say One for Me* with Bing Crosby and Bob Wagner. It was not a gratifying experience. Crosby was pleasant, but a man who kept to himself. Seeing RJ only reminded me of all the things that didn't work out. Our lives had changed drastically in the previous four years. He had met Natalie. I had other things to think about—like getting on with my life.

Immediately after I finished the picture at Fox, MGM put me to work in *It Started with a Kiss*, with Glenn Ford, shooting on location in Spain. When I was first told I'd be going to Europe, I was devastated. The idea of leaving Carrie and Todd, not seeing them and holding them and putting them to bed at night, was deeply upsetting. Fortunately, my mother and father moved into the house and took care of them.

I was miserable leaving California for Madrid. I didn't know one soul in Spain or on the picture, so the studio did allow me to take Camille along as a traveling companion.

It rained the first four days on the set. I sat in my trailer or slept. One day I heard a banging on the door.

"Oh-pen the door, I can't stand to be alone anymore. You must let me in and talk with me," said a woman with a sweet but thick foreign accent. I opened the door. It was Eva Gabor. She was in the picture and rained out too.

Eva and I became instant friends. I'm never at a loss for words but neither is Eva. There isn't much she won't say or ask. And I found her accent fascinating. After listening to her talk for about three days, I said to her, "You know dahling, it's a veddy, veddy interesting zing; you have a veddy un-uzjoo-wull voice."

And she said, "Oh really, dahling, how do I zound?"

"Chuss lakh me," I said in a dead-serious Hungarian accent.

She looked at me puzzled. "Are you zounding funeee?" she asked.

"I don't know, do you zink I em?"

"Let me listen," she said.

I spoke, impersonating her voice and inflection.

Finally she said, "You *doooo* zound *funneee*. You have an ac-cent."

"Yes, I dooo," I continued, "and zo doo you."

"Izzat how I zound? Well, I don't mind it, dahling, except you zound like Zsa Zsa."

Eva and I always had a great time together. She was very interested in my marriage with Eddie.

One afternoon we were visiting the Prado museum.

"Dahling, why did your marriage end to Eddie? Weren't you sexy?" she asked me.

I said, "No!"

"Well then, I much teach you." She pointed to a painting of a woman reclining on a chaise with a long string of pearls falling between her breasts.

"See how they disappear into her cleavage. . . ."

"So?" I asked innocently.

"Vy, dahling, pearls muss *always* fall between the bosom. The skin vill make them warm and lustrous. Then vhen he kisses you, he vill see how rich you are by the pearls. I suppose you have short pearls?" Eva asked.

"Yes."

"I *knoooo* it, dahling! I have a lot to teach you."

"But, Eva, you can't fall asleep with your earrings on! What if you slept on one and scratched yourself?"

"Ah, ziss is going to be a tough job, I can see that."

One afternoon she came rushing into my hotel room. "Dahling, my fiancé is here and I vant you to meet him." Right away. She wanted me to meet him right away.

We went down the hall to her hotel room. We walk in and he's not there. "Come with me, dahling," she said.

I followed her into the bathroom, where sitting in a tub full of water—without the bubbles—was her fiancé. She introduced him. "This is my darling," she said. I didn't know to what—or whom—she was referring.

Eva's approach to things, especially men and lovemaking, was eye-opening to me. It was very European, very open and candid and fun. I particularly noticed that nothing was thought of as sinful.

During a break in the shooting, we went to Paris for a few days. Eva bought clothes and I bought paintings. Years later when she was looking at one of them, she remarked that all the clothes from that trip had worn out and she had nothing left. "I should have listened to you for something, dahling," she said.

Glenn Ford, who was playing opposite me in the picture, was going through his divorce from Eleanor Powell. Just like Eva, Glenn and I hit it off immediately. We talked about the problems of a failed marriage. I listened a lot but I wasn't very sympathetic to the male side of the story at that point. We did share common frustrations and pain. It was silly for me, of all people, to be advising him but he wanted to hear it. That created a bond.

There came a time when Glenn began to think perhaps he was in love with me. I don't think he ever was. The press speculated about that too but that was mainly a fishing expedition—they were looking to prolong the Debbie-Eddie-Elizabeth soap opera. Glenn did ask me to marry him later on in our relationship. I didn't feel I wanted to fall in love with anyone.

Thirty years later, he is still like a best buddy; a friend I can talk to. We were never involved with each other physically. He calls me Ma and I call him Father.

Not long after we'd arrived in Spain, Camille was called away to London to dance in a show with Dan Dailey, whose partner had died suddenly.

I was alone, but not for long. Going to Spain turned out to be something I needed. I missed my babies terribly but I got to look at my life from a slightly different angle. I was having fun and I felt like having fun. It was different—and fascinating—the scenery, new people, new friends, and good times together.

The press followed me everywhere I went. One foray in a "car of tomorrow" in Madrid made the cover of *Life*. The press also served to remind me occasionally of the not-so-distant past. More and more frequently they wanted to know if I'd consent to a Mexican or Nevada divorce. I always said no.

I flew back to Los Angeles from Spain on April 2, 1959, the day after my twenty-seventh birthday. Forty or fifty reporters and photographers were waiting for me when I got off the plane, shouting questions. Eddie and Elizabeth had held a "news conference" the night before in Las Vegas in which they *asked* the press to ask me if I would consent to a "quickie" divorce.

"Elizabeth said that you were holding them back from happiness because they couldn't be together until your divorce is final," one reporter told me.

"Elizabeth said she was converting to Judaism and the only thing preventing their eternal happiness was you, Debbie," another said. "Do you have any comment?"

Elizabeth was giving him everything he wanted, even marrying him in a temple. I was the roadblock to his happiness.

This time I said yes. The longer it dragged on, the longer it would take for me to put it all behind me. That's it, I thought. They're both out of my life forever; I can start again.

After our divorce, Eddie never saw the children. He once called and asked to see them. I got them ready and he never showed. Carrie, just three years old, stood on the couch looking out the window for her daddy who never came. He missed the joy of seeing his children grow up. Connie Stevens also gave him two of the loveliest girls. All of his children stand by him to this day. Carrie has helped him out a number of times financially. Connie's been terrific with him. I'm not. He's a needy, dependent person. I don't know what to compare him to—he's like an elevator that can't find the floor.

I don't think Eddie ever knew who he was. Perhaps the drugs totally put him away.

He cut me to the quick and hurt me deeply. I felt, how dare he walk in and say "I never loved you anyway." Let him at least have respect for the mother of his children. But no, respect was something Eddie never considered.

In the end, all I had left from our marriage was the feeling that it was my failure. At the time, I spoke publicly in a generous and forgiving way. I wanted to feel that way, to be a bigger person. I was still young enough to think I could talk my way into feeling differently, but I didn't.

I hated him. I think I had to hate him before I could stop the love of him. You kill the love by hating.

He wanted to be a movie star. So he married one. Then left me for someone even bigger. Looking back many years later, I can see that Eddie wasn't that infatuated with Debbie Reynolds. I was not a woman of the world, or a passionate woman like Elizabeth. He was way over-matched with her but he didn't know that, and she didn't realize it at the time, probably because she was in despair.

He was a very difficult man and yet he married the most interesting women. Many times I've asked myself why any of us cared for him. Years ago, when Carrie was seventeen, she brought him to see me in London where I was appearing. I didn't even recognize him. He had had dental work. I made a point of being friendly and warm to him because it was long over. I found that the anger I'd felt for so long was gone. Instead I felt sorry for him. He looked like an old, beaten man.

CHAPTER 24

IN THE TEN MONTHS after Eddie left, I dated a bit, three men particularly—Glenn Ford, my old friend Bob Neal, and Walter Trautman, a businessman from New York. But none of it was serious. I wasn't interested in getting involved. The hurt was still fresh. I'd also been working nonstop: three pictures, one right after the other. Whatever time I had, I needed to spend with my children.

Camille remained the steady friend. When she came back from her stint with Dan Dailey in London, she stayed with me. Bill continued to stay too. My children had a family, even if they didn't have a father.

Judy Garland and Sid Luft lived two blocks away in a big house on Mapleton Drive. Many times, when Sid was away from the house, Judy would call me. I'd go up and visit after I'd put the kids to bed. She didn't like being alone. I understood; neither did I.

I had first met Judy in the early fifties right after she'd been dropped by MGM. Roger Edens put an act together for her and she debuted it at the Santa Monica Auditorium.

A large group of us from MGM went over in a bus to see the show. It was a big huge barn and Judy's talent filled the place. She was brilliant and great and she brought down the house. Everyone cried. She generated such joy and excitement. It was after seeing Judy that I knew I wanted one day to have an act.

By the time we were neighbors, her marriage to Sid Luft was in trouble. She complained to me that he didn't like her having friends around much of the time. Sid could be very domineering. There were times, she said, when he'd lock her in her room and tell her to dry out. She didn't understand. She didn't think she was that bad. His treatment only made her lonelier and more depressed.

When we would get together at Judy's, she would have her little drink. I didn't drink in those days. We would talk about music and her life and why she was not happy. We'd talk about MGM and Dr. Blank and the lot and working in the movies. She'd tell me about her problems in the business and counsel me on how I shouldn't put up with this and to be careful of that. Shoptalk for movie stars was what it was. She knew only too well the pitfalls of show business for a woman.

Judy was a great storyteller. She'd get up and sing and dance around the room. Then it was wonderful, and great fun. She loved performing; *loved* it. I'd get up and we'd both dance, like two kids in high school.

Liza, who was about ten at the time, would sit on the stairs listening to her mother. Slowly, she'd work her way down to just outside the room. If I happened to walk out of the room and see her, I'd take her up to bed. It might be ten or eleven—late for a little girl. Joey and Lorna, who were just toddlers, would already be asleep. Liza never wanted to go to sleep, however. She wanted to listen and to be around her mother.

Judy and I got together regularly for about two years—during and after Eddie. Eventually she and Sid separated and the house was auctioned. She lost everything.

After almost a year away from Eddie, I still felt withdrawn and isolated most of the time. Socializing seemed like an effort and I didn't really like going out in public. Camille and I would go to the movies in Westwood. Finally she persuaded me to give a party and come out of the shell. Thelma Ritter and her husband, Joe Moran, came; Karl Malden and his wife; Lucille Ball, Jack Lemmon.

During the time Eddie and I were breaking up, I also got more involved with the Thalians. The Thalians started out as a group of young Hollywood people who often partied together, including Hugh O'Brian, Huntz Hall, Nicky Blair, Margaret Whiting, Jack Haley, Jr., Gary Crosby, Natalie Wood, Bob Wagner, and David Wolper, to name just a few. It was a very interesting group of people, almost all in show business in one way or another.

Someone got the bright idea of turning one of the parties into a fund raiser for charity. Everyone would pay twenty or twenty-five dollars to attend. It was informal at first, but by the late 1950s, we'd named ourselves (after a charitable organization that had existed years before in the film industry) the Thalians—Thalia being the Greek goddess of the theater—and we made it our charter to raise money for children who were emotionally disturbed, abused, or from broken homes. All these years later, the services are also available to adults and to people with drug problems.

I had been inactive during the time I was married to Eddie. Margaret Whiting was president of the charity when I rejoined. She was going back to New York to live and so they needed a replacement and asked me. I said yes. In those days we had been raising about ten thousand a year. (Twenty-nine years later, I am still president, although Ruta Lee and a fine board of directors run the organization and keep it going. We now raise millions. We built our own clinic at Cedars-Sinai Hospital for seven million dollars.)

About that same time the Thalians were beginning to get into big fund raising. I was asked to meet with Harry Karl to solicit a donation. However, in this particular instance I wondered, why do I have to ask Harry Karl for money? He always gave every year anyway. Harry Karl, Conrad Hilton, Nick Schenck, Sidney Korshak, Al Hart, Alfred Bloomingdale, Armand Deutsch—all gave a thousand dollars each year to underwrite the Thalians' Ball.

But Harry Karl had a reputation. A shrewd businessman, shoe manufacturer, multimillionaire, he was probably the most freewheeling, high-spending habitué of Hollywood's café society.

Beautiful women, expensive restaurants, lavish tipping; the last of the big-time spenders, Harry literally came from rags to riches. In 1914 his mother, Rose, a Russian immigrant, had found him as an infant crying in a trash can, in the Hell's Kitchen section of Manhattan. Rose and her husband, Pincus, were childless and took the boy in as their own.

When Harry was still a toddler, the Karls, including an adopted daughter, Sara, moved to Los Angeles. A shoemaker by trade, Pincus started a shoe business, fashioning shoes for the Los Angeles Police Department. As an eight-year-old, after school, Harry worked for his father polishing shoes. By the time he was twelve, he was teaching his mother and father how to read and write English.

When Harry finished high school, his father sent him to law school. From law school he went right into the family business. Pincus Karl died in 1953, leaving the bulk of his estate—$7 million, shoe factories, and two hundred retail shoe outlets all over the western United States— to his beloved son.

By that time, Harry had already embarked on his extracurricular career as a high roller. Harry did work very hard with his father and after his father's death, at building up the business. Nevertheless, he had a natural appetite for the good life. He had been married three times. He was well known, even famous, for his two tempestuous marriages to Marie McDonald, a singer/actress who was known in the press as "The Body." He also divorced her twice. I'd met Marie in the early fifties when we both did USO work. She was a beautiful lady, about ten years older than I; of Irish-Italian background, with a great figure; one of the first of the blond bombshells. The first time I saw Harry, he was with Marie at a party. She was so gorgeous, I thought, what's she doing with him? Harry wasn't ugly, but his looks weren't among his strong points.

I later saw them together in Las Vegas. I was having dinner one night with Harry Cohn of Columbia Pictures and Jack Entratter, who owned the Desert Inn. At the next table Harry Karl and Marie were having dinner with two other men. Everyone was talking about the fact that Harry had just won $150,000 in the casino the night before.

Harry was also famous for his generous charitable contributions. The year before, 1958, he had given $250,000 to the City of Hope, a cancer-research charity in Los Angeles. That was an enormous gift, comparable to more than a couple of million in today's dollars. Zsa Zsa Gabor, who dated him, was quoted as saying she'd never marry Harry Karl "because he gives too much of his money away." By the time I'd met him, he'd given away millions to charity.

The time had come, someone figured, for the Thalians to get one of those big Harry Karl gifts. He was the easiest touch in town.

Jack Haley and I went to meet Harry for lunch at the Luau on Rodeo Drive. Steve Crane owned it. He was once married to Lana Turner and was Cheryl's father. Harry was friendly, soft-spoken, beautifully dressed, with impeccably combed prematurely gray hair, hazel eyes, and black horn-rimmed glasses. There was an aura of importance about him.

Although he was actually about forty-five, he looked—to my twenty-seven-year-old eyes—much older.

That afternoon, I asked him for a $5,000 donation. No problem; fine, it's all yours.

He asked me for a date. I said, I don't date, which was basically the truth.

Harry didn't take no for an answer. He persisted, calling me every day—just to say hello, sometimes asking me out and sometimes not. I must have been somewhat intrigued, because finally I said I'd have dinner with him—at my house with me and my parents. To my surprise, he agreed. I still thought, after one dinner, this man-about-town will be bored stiff and stop calling.

It didn't happen that way. Harry seemed to have a wonderful time. He adored my father. They talked baseball. Toward Mother he was charming and attentive.

There was something else too—although I wasn't conscious of it at the time. Harry thought everything I did or said was either the funniest or the most wonderful thing that ever happened. That was very refreshing after three years of Eddie's stony reproach. In fact, it was like having the sun come out again. Harry accepted me for myself; he even liked the way I was.

Nevertheless, I wasn't really interested—in Harry or anybody else. I had a little more than a month off before I was to start *The Gazebo*, another picture with Glenn Ford, also with George Marshall directing—my fourth picture in less than twelve months.

I rented a beautiful house on the ocean at Waikiki, for the four weeks, from Winthrop and Jeanette Rockefeller. I took my parents, the children, and a nurse. My single objective was to Get Away From It All.

The first week I slept. The second week the phone started ringing. Both Walter Trautman and Bob Neal had come over from the mainland and were calling me for dinner.

Then late one morning, the maid came in to tell me that Harry Karl was on the phone. He was staying at the Royal Hawaiian with his driver, his barber, and his barber's assistant!

Harry was the only man I'd ever met who had his hair combed every day. No matter where he went, he took his barber along. Tony Curtis later told me that he used the same barber as Harry Karl. Once when Tony was in Europe making a picture, he wanted to have this barber, Murray, brought over from Beverly Hills to cut his hair. But he couldn't get him. Harry Karl was also traveling through Europe at the same time, and the barber was with him.

Just before Harry had left for Hawaii, Murray made a bet with Leo Durocher, the manager of the Dodgers, that he could cut Harry Karl's hair without lifting a pair of scissors. Just before Murray left for the airport to make the flight to Hawaii, he put his arm in a cast and sling. Harry took one look at the arm and got very nervous about his daily cut.

"Don't worry, boss; I can do it lefty," Murray said.

Harry didn't like that idea. None of this "lefty" stuff. Instead, he had Murray hire an assistant who could do the actual cutting while he supervised.

So the very next morning Harry sat in the chair with a new barber while Murray stood behind him and told the assistant how to cut the boss' hair. This charade went on for two days. On the third day, over drinks, Murray took off the sling and slipped the cast off his arm and told the boss about the bet he'd won. Harry just thought that was the funniest thing.

*   *   *

I found all of this very amusing, but not enough to have dinner with the man. I did see both Bob Neal and Walter Trautman during the stay, but not Harry. He continued to call every day anyway.

Our stay in Hawaii was a perfect rest. I went right back to work as soon as we returned to Los Angeles. Harry's daily phone calls or flowers did not let up. After a few weeks of his asking, I made a date to meet him for cocktails—just cocktails—at the Polo Lounge.

He had the cocktails, I had a Coke. We weren't there five minutes when he pulled a gold cigarette case out of his vest pocket, opened it, set it before me, and asked if I'd like a cigarette. Since I didn't smoke in those days, normally I'd just wave it away. However, this time, inside the slender, shiny box was a gorgeous diamond clip, sitting there among a bunch of Winstons. I looked at Harry, whose eyes were on me, smiling, waiting for my reaction.

I put my hand over the case, closed it, and gently pushed it back at him. "No, thanks, I don't smoke."

It was that night, or not long after, that Harry first asked me to marry him. Eddie had asked me to marry him right away. So had Walter Trautman. I guessed that was how men did it.

My "no" didn't deter Harry. Nor was he discouraged by the fact that I wouldn't even make another date with him. He'd call anyway. And send flowers of course—bowers of flowers. Sometimes he'd send toys to Carrie and Todd. That impressed me, considering their own father never even called. Sometimes Harry would even invite my mother and father to dinner, without me. They went. And they loved him.

In early September, a Thursday, just before Labor Day weekend, Harry called and again asked me to marry him. He had to have an answer right away. I thought, this is silly; the man's crazy. I'd never even gone out with him—except for cocktails. I said no. I hardly knew him. He hardly knew me.

Three days later, on Sunday, I picked up the *Los Angeles Herald* and read that "Joan Cohn, the beautiful widow of movie mogul Harry Cohn," had married "Harry Karl, Hollywood's most philanthropic millionaire." Harry Karl *married* to Joan Cohn?! The man who for the previous three months had been asking me to marry him?!

I didn't know what to think. Obviously it was not a joke, although it seemed like one. I knew Joan, not well, but socially. She had started out in Hollywood as an aspiring actress who was signed to a contract with Columbia about the same time Rita Hayworth was. Legend had it that one day Harry Cohn, who owned the studio, called Joan into his office and told her that he had decided to make Hayworth a star and her his wife.

Now she was Mrs. Harry Karl. I had to laugh. I couldn't help but wonder *why* Harry had pursued me so intensely if he was planning on marrying her. I wasn't about to pick up the phone and ask him. It was all very odd, but no great personal loss; I wasn't in love, in any way, with Harry Karl.

Three weeks later Harry called me. I answered the phone. He told me that he and Joan had broken up.

"You and Joan should try to work it out. She's a lovely woman," I said and hung up on him.

The next time he called I was out.

The following day it was all over the papers. The gossip columnists had a ball with that one. The marriage had lasted a total of twenty-one days, and for her trouble, the fourth Mrs. Karl received $100,000 as a good-bye kiss.

Again, Harry kept calling. I was unavailable to come to the phone.

THERE WERE OTHER, more important, more pressing matters to deal with in my life. The year 1959 was my tenth at MGM. The separation and divorce from Eddie made me big box office. I had my forty-weeks-a-year contract and, theoretically, the alimony from Eddie, and that was it. I was living in a large house with a nurse and a cook and a big mortgage payment every month. I had been in the business long enough to know that a movie career has only a few good years. I had never taken a dramatic lesson in my life. I'd been taught to dance and to sing; I was a natural comedienne and I was "cute" and "adorable." I knew the limits better than anybody else. I had maybe four or five years left as a young leading lady. If I was lucky.

Money had never been an issue with me. But it was now. The checks from Eddie, which stopped after the second month because I wouldn't agree to a "quickie" divorce, just never resumed. I didn't want anything from him and I didn't want to *need* anything from him.

But what if two years down the road, after making its pile, the studio decided to drop me? I now had two kids to feed and educate and care for.

Eddie had made me aware, when we were first married, of my value to MGM. I tried then, at his urging, to renegotiate my contract but got nowhere. After almost three years of going along, I finally told them I was too frustrated to continue working under the old terms. I wanted to do television. I wanted to make records and do outside deals on my own. This time I told them that if I couldn't perform as a free human being, then I wouldn't perform at all, for anybody.

Harry had helped by introducing me to Irving Briskin, a business manager and producer who was a friend from the Friars Club. We worked out a new contract for four pictures at $2,000 a week. During the same period, I formed my own production company—Harman Productions, after my grandparents—and signed a three-year, $1 million deal with ABC, calling for one television special a year. I also signed a contract for five pictures—the first being *The Rat Race*—with producers Bill Perlberg and George Seaton, for a lot more money, plus 10 percent of the gross and story approval as well.

Irving and Harry had helped negotiate my deals with Perlberg/Seaton as well as ABC Television. For the first time I had men making business choices to my advantage and in the best interests of my career.

The Rat Race was going to be a departure for me. I had to play a young girl who has been in New York for five years trying to break into show business. To keep from starving, she models at whatever she can get daytimes, and at night works in a dance hall.

I decided I'd do some research on that kind of life before I started the picture. One night some publicity people from Paramount took me to a dance joint on West Forty-sixth Street in Manhattan. It was a seedy run-down place with a group of very voluptuous girls and a few dozen guys, mainly older men—a deadbeat-looking crew. They were polite but standoffish. I couldn't get to know them under the circumstances.

The next day I called a shop in Times Square and told them I needed something to wear in a dance joint. The one dress they sent up didn't look like much when I took it out of the box. But on, it was wild, a strapless number. I wore it, along with a blond wig like the one I'd be wearing in the picture.

That night, I went back to the "club." Without the extra company, the other girls got right into what I was doing, and offered advice.

"The first thing, honey, is to get noticed, to shock a man right out of his seat with what you're wearing . . . or not wearing," I was instructed by a beautiful black girl named Veronica.

The most important thing was to keep a guy dancing, because if a man became interested in one girl, he was apt to spend fifteen or twenty dollars on her in one night.

The only man I seemed to shock into showing interest was a little Italian deli owner named Joe.

Joe and I started dancing. He reeked of Parmesan and pepperoni. The top of his head came up to my nose. Almost instantly he was kissing my shoulder and saying "I go for you baby." It broke me up. Joe was not pleased but I couldn't help it.

When he left me on the side of the dance floor, Veronica sidled over and said, "That ain't it, kid."

Kid.

That same week, I was a guest on Jack Paar's *Tonight* show. Paar was *the* late night talk show in America. He was a very controversial host and everyone, all over the country, talked about his show the next day, sometimes even in headlines. The only way to succeed with him was to have something interesting to talk about, otherwise Paar took over.

I decided beforehand that I'd tell him about my brief career as a dance-hall hostess with Joe.

Paar listened intently and then asked me to show him. The two of us got out on the stage, dancing and clowning around, with me leading him. When we sat back down, he said, "Jeepers, you're strong. Were you that tough on Fisher?"

I didn't know what to say. I could feel the audience waiting, feel their anticipation. But I was suddenly dumbstruck. There were no jokes there for me. I felt as if anything I said would have been wrong.

My answer was to take a quick dive under Jack Paar's desk and pull him under with me. He disappeared from the camera's and the audience's view. All they saw was his handkerchief flying into the air with one of his shoes.

Immediately, huddled behind the desk, he began helping me. "Shall I take off my shirt?" he whispered.

"Don't bother," I said, unbuttoning a few buttons and pulling out the tails. By the time we stood up, the audience was also on their feet screaming with laughter and applause. I had been "tough" on the toughest guy on television.

I did what came naturally in any tight spot, emotional or physical: I made a joke. The next day there were headlines in the New York papers: DEBBIE STRIPTEASES PAAR.

And no one ever knew the answer to the original question, least of all me. Was I "that tough" on Eddie? Was that maybe another reason why he left? Was that another part of my failure in the marriage?

CHAPTER **26**

WEEKS WENT BY and Harry kept on calling but I wouldn't go to the phone. Then one day I got a call from a friend of his, a very powerful lawyer named Sidney Korshak.

"Won't you please take a call from Harry, Debbie? It's eating him up inside. He just wants the chance to talk to you."

"No, Sidney," I said, "I don't need this."

Just before Christmas Sidney Korshak called again, asking me "this one last time," if I'd see Harry Karl. I didn't want to see Harry Karl. I didn't care why he ran off and married Joan Cohn one weekend. But finally I said yes because I knew if I didn't, Sidney, or somebody else, would continue calling me.

Harry showed up the following afternoon in his chauffeur-driven Rolls-Royce with flowers for me and toys for Todd and Carrie.

It was very pleasant, although I still wanted to know why he was pursuing me. Finally, when we were alone in the den, I asked him why he would propose to me one day and marry Joan Cohn the next.

He looked at me very seriously. "I felt it was my last chance," he said. "I'm getting older and I know you are too young. I know you're too successful, too unreachable to ever love a man as unattractive, as old as me."

He caught me off guard. I didn't know what to say.

"I could give you and Carrie and Todd everything in the world, everything your heart could desire, but you've already made it quite clear money is not the issue. So," he sighed, "I had to face it: Why would you ever marry me?"

"You mean just because I said I wouldn't marry you, you married another woman twenty-four hours later?" That didn't make sense.

"It was the rebound, Debbie," he said. "I made a mistake; I admit it. But I was very upset."

He leaned across the couch, took my hand in his, and stared into my eyes. I remember thinking that he was so fastidiously dressed, even to the perfect, almost razor-sharp crease in his trousers. And he was considerably older. How could a man like that be a father to my children? If I needed a man, that was what I needed him for.

He didn't ask me out that afternoon. Instead he wanted to know if he could come by and visit again in a few days. He made it very clear what his intentions were, but he also made it very clear that he was not going to pressure me. He was going to accept everything on my terms.

Just before Thanksgiving that year, Harry and I went on our first real date. I took him to the ballet to see *Swan Lake*. That night when he arrived at the house to pick me up, he presented me with two small velvet boxes. In one was the most beautiful pearl pin in the shape of a swan with a neck of diamonds. Inside the other was a matching set of earrings. He had had them made just for the night at the ballet with me. I couldn't help but be very touched by the specialness of his gesture. He even stayed awake through the ballet.

Harry was willing to go and do anything I wanted to do. After our date at the ballet, he never made a plan without asking me—always with the understanding that I'd join him only if I wanted. If I didn't, fine.

Although he was not handsome, I soon saw enormous attractiveness in his dignity and manners. He was very, very kind and gentle and sweet with everyone. I really appreciated that after living with a man who was never any of those things unless he wanted something.

CHAPTER 27

For my fourth film commitment to MGM under the new contract, I was loaned out to Twentieth Century-Fox to do a comedy-western called *The Second Time Around* with Andy Griffith and Thelma Ritter.

Thelma and I hit it off immediately. You didn't dare turn your back on her in a scene because she would figure out how to steal it, no matter what. She wasn't mean about it. She just knew a million ways to be funny.

In the picture, I played a ranch hand on Thelma's ranch. We were shooting a scene in which I had a speech and Thelma was supposed to be fixing some shoes in the background. The director, Vince Sherman, called "action" and I began my lines.

I was just a minute into the scene when I heard, behind me, "Hm-mmm-rrrrr-hmmmmm-rrrr . . ."

It was so loud, I had to stop. I turned around. Thelma had this shoe on a metal shoe block, preparing to put on its sole. She had nails in her mouth and the hammer was going. The camera had stopped, yet she was still into it—spitting nails and banging on the shoes—doing a full monologue with her business, à la Marcel Marceau.

Oblivious to everything and everyone around, she didn't notice that I was staring at her. She just kept tearing into her piece of business.

Finally, my hands on my hips, in exasperation, I yelled: *"Thelma!"*

She looked up, not a flicker of a reaction. "Whaaat?!" she said with her flat New York *a*. "Why'd ya stop? The scene was goin' great."

"There is no scene if you're doing all that, Thelma," I said.

"What's the matter?" she said, "can't ya compete, kid? Can't ya *compete*?!"

"Not with that, Thelma. That's not fair."

Thelma shrugged and did Thelma Ritter-rolling-her-eyes. "Awww . . . jealous young stars!"

She never cracked a smile.

Andy Griffith was the male lead in the picture. There was a scene where he had to ride a horse onto Thelma's ranch: Thelma and I were waiting on the porch for him to arrive. He came around the corner on a big black horse.

I had thought Andy was a rider until I saw him come bouncing along in the saddle like two hundred pounds of jelly wrapped in bucksuede. Not only that, but it was the kind of bouncing that could hurt a man, and it was hurting him. He'd forgotten to wear an athletic supporter. We could hear him muttering under his breath, "Son of a bitch! *Oooooh! Ooooh!* Son of a *bitch!*"

Andy reached the porch, brought the horse to a halt, and then, just as he was about to dismount, he took one final bounce in the saddle, let out a loud yelp, lost his footing, and slid violently off the horse onto the ground.

"*Sonuvabitch!*" he shouted, writing in agony on the ground, holding his groin. "That damned black, damned . . .

Vince told Andy to go into his trailer and put on a supporter because they had to do another take.

About fifteen minutes later, Andy returned, got on the horse, and we started over.

Thelma and I stood on the porch, waiting; biting our tongues.

Once again, our hero came lumbering around the corner of his black beauty—still bouncing away. He reached the porch, halted the animal, prepared to dismount—when one foot slipped out of the stirrup and bam! he fell out of the saddle and onto the ground again.

"*Sonuvabitch!!*" This time Andy wasn't hurting, he was mad.

We did another take. He went out; we stood there waiting. He bounced in, stopped; accidentally slipped out of the stirrup and boom! once again, off the horse!

I didn't think we'd ever be able to stop laughing.

Andy got it on the fourth take.

At the end of filming, I gave a cast-crew party. Everybody got an individual present. For Andy, I raided the prop shop at Fox—and stole a real—stuffed—Palomino horse. "A little something you can practice on," I said when they rolled it into the party and right up to Andy.

He loved it so much he wanted to take it home that night. The only way he could figure out to transport it was to anchor it to the top of his station wagon, which he did.

Driving down the Freeway to his home in the Valley, he got stopped by the California Highway Patrol. They wanted to know where he got that horse and where he was going with it. Only a fool or a thief would drive around with a dead horse on the top of his car.

Andy had had a few drinks at the party. "Listen," he protested to the cops, "this horse here is my friend. Roy Rogers stuffed Trigger, so I stuffed this. It's my pet horse."

They let him go. Andy loved taking the horse with him when he went to a party.

Juliet Prowse, who was under contract to Twentieth Century-Fox, also had a small role in the picture. She and Frank Sinatra were having their mad love affair and were engaged. Frank wanted her to quit her career when they got married. She had already told him that she didn't want to.

She and I discussed the dilemma one day over lunch.

"Forget your career," I advised, "and take a year off. At the end of a year, he'll want you to go back to work because you'll drive him so crazy dancing around the house. But it'll be his decision. You have to say yes," I insisted.

"Oh, no," she said. And of course, she never did give in. Many years later we were talking about that little discussion.

"I wish I'd listened to you," Juliet laughed in retrospect. A little too late. He advised me, I advised her, and we all missed.

In May 1960, they premiered *The Rat Race*. Harry took me to the opening. The afternoon before, the florist delivered four dozen roses wrapped in a mink stole.

When I finished *The Second Time Around*, I flew down to Miami for a few days rest at the home of my friend Phyllis Pollack and her husband, Albert, who owned the Thunderbird Hotel. I first met them on my honeymoon with Eddie. Mother and Daddy stayed with Carrie and Todd. Harry visited the children every day and had dinner a couple of nights with my parents. The fourth day I was in Florida, two crates of oranges arrived for me from California. Each orange was wrapped in tissue with pictures of Carrie and Todd printed on them. Enclosed was a note from Harry: "California misses you. Come home soon. I love you, Harry." I was so touched, and suddenly feeling homesick for my babies, I felt like getting on the next plane.

There were still other men calling me. But I liked Harry. He was solid and fatherly and loving. He didn't come on with me, but at the same time he was sexual.

One night over dinner he said, "So, Debbie, when are you going to set the date?"

I knew what he meant, of course. I had been divorced from Eddie for a year. It was beginning to occur to me that I might be bringing up my children without a "father" in the house. The possibility scared me.

Eddie would never be that for us. I felt my children needed that image. I needed it too.

"What makes you think you'd like being married to me, Harry?" I asked.

"How can you ask me that?" he protested. "I love you. I love Toddie and Carrie like they're my own. . . ."

"I don't need a husband, Harry. I need a father for my children, and how could you ever be their father? They'd muss up your sports jacket."

Harry saw the kids only when they came to say good-night to him, or when the nurse was looking after them. He never even helped them eat an ice-cream cone. He was too well dressed ever to go in for that sort of thing.

He said I was wrong; that all I had to do was try him out to see.

I thought seriously about it after that. He had many things going for him. He was a lawyer. He was sensitive and generous and yet not pushy. He was a very rich man, which is impressive to anybody. He advised me well in business. And I was: eighteen years younger, perfect figure, a movie star with two beautiful children. I would get "security," and he would get the cover of *Photoplay*.

The summer before, I had rented a beach house in Malibu, and I decided to do it again this year—for June, July, and August. It was a big house with four bedrooms and a guest suite. I hired a French couple to clean and cook and of course we had the nurse.

It was a perfect time to find out just how serious Harry was about my children. I invited him to move into the guest suite and share the parenting with me. He agreed. Todd always got up at 5:00 A.M. and wanted to play. I'd take him down to Harry's bedroom and put him on Harry's stomach. I thought, if he doesn't mind being awakened by Todd, then maybe he can love him.

We all lived together. Harry and I did not live intimately, although no one believed that. Early in the morning Todd and Carrie would automatically go down to "Howwy," while Mommy slept in until nine. He would take them out walking on the beach, coming back with sand all over him. He went swimming in the pool with them, mussing up his hair, letting it get wet. In the afternoon he'd sometimes take them to get ice-cream cones, which inevitably got all over his perfectly pressed silk shirts, but I never heard one word of complaint about any of it. He even went days without a haircut.

His friends were shocked. They couldn't believe it was Harry. I could see he wasn't exactly the beachcombing type—he'd go out in the sand in his velvet slippers monogrammed in gold with "H.K." He never let on what I learned years later—that he really didn't like the beach at all. He was intent on letting me see that he could be a father to my children. And he was succeeding. Before the summer was out "Howwy" was becoming "Daddy Howwy" to Todd and Carrie. He passed all the tests.

Since the beginning of the year there had been speculation in the gossip columns and fan magazines about marriage for me and Harry.

In the late summer, about the same time the children and I moved from the beach back to the house on Conway, Hedda Hopper made it her business to advise me. In public. In a letter, which she published in *Modern Screen* magazine. It ran under the headline: A letter to Debbie: Please Don't Make Another Mistake—Harry Karl Has Already Made Four.

The article contained all half-truths and innuendo. It was also obvious from which direction the innuendos were coming—Marie McDonald.

Getting to know Harry, I had also got to know a little more about Marie and the problems she could create for him. Two years before, in 1958, after she and Harry had divorced for the second time, she disappeared one night from her home in Encino and turned up twenty-four hours later 150 miles out in the middle of the desert, bedraggled and bruised. She accused Harry of hiring two men to kidnap her. The story was splashed in newspapers across the country. She later admitted she had lied; it was a publicity stunt.

I knew their marriages had been extremely stormy. Marie was well known to be a very mercurial woman and a hard liver who drank and drugged and moved in the fast lane. Despite that, she had custody of their three children, Harrison, Dede, and Tina, who was born the same year I had Carrie. Harrison and Dede had been adopted during Harry and Marie's first marriage. Tina came several years later, and was the reason why Harry remarried Marie. Her second divorce settlement from Harry was considered to be one of the most generous on record in Hollywood—$50,000 a year for twenty years whether or not she remarried, plus child support. Somehow, for Marie, that was never enough.

I would have overlooked Hedda's public letter if she had not made a statement to a mutual acquaintance that not only was Harry "old and unattractive, but he was Jewish." That really made me angry. I wasn't going to call her or write her, I was going to tell her to her face.

The day the story was repeated to me, I got in my car and I drove over to her office. Hollywood's second-most-powerful gossip columnist worked from a simple little office on the second floor of an old building at Hollywood and Vine.

I didn't warn her I was coming. I had no appointment; I just walked in and told her assistant I wanted to see her.

Hedda knew exactly why I was there. She walked out of her office (wearing a hat) and tried to calm me down.

"Dear, I'm very busy and I know why you're angry anyway," she started out.

I wasn't going to be ignored. "First of all, Hedda, you don't tell the world what to do. You're not the Almighty!"

"Now, dear," she sniffed, "just calm yourself. I simply told you you should not marry Harry Karl."

"The trouble with you, Hedda, is that you're anti-Semitic and you hate it that you're not a movie star!" I shouted at her, knowing that Hedda had started out in the business as an actress in silents. With that, her secretary and her assistant both cleared out of the room. It was well known that she felt she should have had more of a career.

Hedda turned on her heel and walked back into her office, as if she weren't interested. But I was close behind, reading her the riot act.

"Who do you think you are?" I demanded. "How dare you!"

Hedda stopped in her tracks. She turned to face me, eyebrows raised, looking down her nose. "And I am *not* anti-Semitic. Many of my friends are Jewish!"

"You know what I mean, Hedda Hopper!" I blasted at her. "I am not going to have you dictate to me. I am not going to have you tell me what to do with my life!"

Raising her voice a decibel above mine, she shouted: "Well, little lady, I'm telling you *you're going to make the same mistake as I did with Hopper!* The old fart! He'll just do you in, dear, do you in." She sat down in the chair behind her desk.

I was insulted. "Harry Karl is not Mr. Hopper. And even if he is, that's my business and not yours! So don't tell me what to do!"

"Why don't you marry Glenn?" she asked. "He's wonderful. He's rich too. And you take such a good picture together." That was the crux of it. Hedda liked me. She wanted me to marry someone handsome and Hollywood.

"But I don't love Glenn. And I don't think our lives would work that well together," I tried to reason with her.

"Sit down, dear," she said, as if she had finished discussing it.

I sat down.

"Is it all over now?" she asked.

"Is *what* all over now?" I thought she was talking about me and Harry.

"Have you said it?!" she replied.

"Well," I said, "are you off my back? Are you off his back? Will you stop calling Harry 'that old Jew'? Will you stop writing about us?"

"Look, darling, I couldn't care less to write about how you're going to just blow your life," she said haughtily.

"Fine," I said. "Then will you stop?"

"Yes yes yes yes yes yes. Yes, I will," she said. "Are we still friends now?" she asked with a smile and a lilt in her voice that she used when she wanted to ingratiate.

I didn't answer right away. She waited patiently. I sat there looking at this woman, behind her desk in that pink *hat* and veil—the biggest thing in the room, covered with enormous silk flowers; the matching pink dress, like a society matron with just a dash of show biz. I had to laugh.

"You're so bad, Hedda," I said shaking my head. "You're such a bitch."

"Yes I am, dear," she smiled proudly. "And you'll soon learn."

Hedda kept her word. She never wrote anything unkind about Harry again. We remained good friends. She came to every birthday party Carrie and Todd had.

But she never got over it either. To the day she died she never liked Harry. She also died before he and I ended, so I never did have to hear her mouth off about it again. Had she lived, I can hear her saying, "I told you so, I told you so."

Hedda wasn't the only one. When I first started seeing Harry, after his divorce from Joan Cohn, I went down to Acapulco to make a cameo appearance in a picture called *Pepe* that George Sidney was directing with Cantinflas as the star. Because it was a short trip, with all expenses paid, I invited my father and Jeanette Johnson to come along as my guests.

George Sidney's wife, Lillian Burns, who had been my acting coach in the early years at MGM, was also in Acapulco with her husband. They were staying in a large house with a pool. One day she invited Jeanette and me over for lunch and a swim.

Since I first met her and worked with her at MGM, Lillian and I had been friends. In the years that have followed, Lillian has become my closest friend, adviser, acting coach, and mentor. Back then we had the kind of friendship you might have with a teacher you respect and admire. And Lillian is very much the teacher.

So it was difficult that day, before lunch, sitting around the pool, when Lillian confronted me.

"You really can't be serious about marrying Harry Karl, can you, Debbie?" she asked in that slow, deliberate, and theatrical tone.

I didn't know what to say. You don't question her authority; it's implicit in the voice.

"Well?" she said, waiting for my answer, which wasn't forthcoming. "This will be his fifth marriage, Debbie. You don't think they ended for no reason, do you?"

"I think I know what I'm doing, Lillian," I offered quietly and somewhat meekly.

"Look at who he married before—Marie McDonald; look at the kind of woman she was."

"Marie had a lot of problems," I conceded, "but they weren't Harry's fault."

"She drank, drugged, slept around. That's the kind of woman he married—twice to her!"

"He married her the second time because of the baby."

"Fourth marriage, Joan Cohn," she continued. "At least she was smart. She got out, and with a hundred thousand dollars and a couple of furs."

I felt I was trying to come up with the right answer in twenty-five words or less. She wasn't just making conversation; she was serious.

"He gambles, darling! He's a gambler!" she said.

"All I can tell you, Lillian, is that he's very nice to me. And I feel I need a man who will take care of me; a man to whom I am the most important thing in his life."

"Well, you won't be," she said with a certain sadness that she gets in her voice when something doesn't seem right. "It'll be his gambling, and you won't be. You're not going to change him."

What did Harry's gambling have to do with anything? In the six or seven years since his father's death, Harry had doubled and almost tripled his fortune. I felt this time I had to marry the wise old owl.

The truth was, although I never confided it to anybody, including Lillian, for the first time in my life I felt lonely and frightened. I had a big career and I knew not one thing about business. I had children to bring up. I felt I was in a very exposed position. Harry was older and urbane and wealthy and thoughtful. I wasn't deeply attracted to him physically. But I wasn't unattracted to him either, because he was so kind and loving and companionable.

Harry was my harbor. He would make me safe.

I was still a child and immature about men. I was aware of that. But how was I going to change it? With Harry, I was going with my mind and not my emotions. I thought that was being very grown-up; the way to avoid a lot of problems. I knew it was. I'd seen examples of women who married for the same reasons and the marriages worked.

When I got back to my hotel in Acapulco that afternoon, there were waiting, as there were the day before, and would be the day after that, fresh flowers and a Special Delivery letter from Harry in Los Angeles.

Hello Baby Doll:
   I love you. I adore you. I miss you and time stops when you are away from me. I can't take it. It is as I told your mother—I didn't think I had the capacity anymore to want and give of myself in love. The morning starts as I open my eyes and my thoughts are all of you. This is the way it will always be. I only hope you feel the same and that I am everything you want. If so, what a great life it will be for us! . . .
   I am leaving to look at houses and lots which gives me a close feeling as it represents something for us and the children. You're my whole life now, my happiness, my health and peace of mind are in your hands. I love you more than anything in the world.
                                                                Harry

Every day, four, five, sometimes six handwritten pages. I may have been escaping from reality, I won't deny that. I didn't want to love. I wanted someone to love me more, so that I could be in control; so that everything could go my way.

CHAPTER 28

By THE END OF that summer in Malibu, I knew we were going to be married. The final decree of his divorce from Joan Cohn was about to come through. But I was taping my first television special for ABC that October. As soon as that was finished, I was starting *The Pleasure of His Company* with Fred Astaire and Lilli Palmer. It was my second picture for Perlberg/Seaton, with George Seaton directing this time.

We didn't keep it a secret. When I told Lillian that the marriage was definite, she shook her head and said, "If you're going to marry Harry Karl, be sure your diamonds are bigger than Marie's." Harry gave me a seventeen-carat pear-shaped diamond ring for our engagement. It was bigger than Marie's.

Harry had recently completed a very large house near the top of the hill in Trousdale, with a magnificent view of the city. But I wanted the children to live on a street with neighbors, where there were other children. I wanted them to be able to ride their bikes and go to a school nearby. I'd bought a house mainly for the lot, behind the Beverly Hills Hotel, and was thinking of tearing down the old house and building a new one. We also considered adding on to the house on Conway, which was definitely too small, because I wanted to have more children.

Harry also had a beautiful five-bedroom house on two acres in Palm Springs. It had a pool and a panoramic view of the mountains. He had a live-in couple who cooked and took care of the house.

I wanted to be married before Christmas so that the children could have a real family holiday. Edith Head had designed a wedding dress for me before I went to work on *The Pleasure of His Company*. Mother wanted to make it for me: ankle-length in pale-blue organza. She started right away, in late September, knowing Harry and I would probably decide at the last minute.

We decided about a week before Thanksgiving. I told my children and my parents.

On a Monday morning when I wasn't going to be on camera, we

went over to the courthouse in Glendale to get the license to avoid the possibility of running into any reporters.

It was to be a small, candlelight wedding at 9:30 in the evening on the Friday after Thanksgiving. Harry was Jewish, and I, of course, was Protestant, but he agreed to a nonsectarian, double-ring ceremony performed by the Reverend John Mills of the Little Brown Church in the Valley, who would be reading from my late Grandpa Harman's Bible. Once again, Jeanette Johnson was my maid of honor, and Harry's brother-in-law, Saul Pollock, was best man. We were married at Saul and Sara's house.

I was in the middle of shooting and had to work that day. We invited twenty guests including my parents, my brother, and Grandma Harman; Harry's mother and stepfather, and his daughter from his first marriage, Judy. After the ceremony, there was wedding cake, champagne, and a buffet.

For a girl who always dreamed of a big traditional wedding, I didn't get any closer to it the second time around. At about 11:00 P.M., we got into Harry's Rolls and made the two-hour drive down to Palm Springs for the weekend. I was due back on the set the following Monday. Our plan was to take a monthlong honeymoon in Jamaica with the children after the New Year.

We had a wonderful group on *The Pleasure of His Company*. I learned a great deal working with such consummate professionals as Lilli Palmer, Fred Astaire, and Charlie Ruggles, who played my grandfather. Charlie and I became fast friends. I called him Grandpa.

Fred was a joy to work with. He was a very quiet man, sweet and friendly, and of course, always dressed in that famous Astaire style. It had been almost ten years since he had rescued a distressed little girl from the rehearsal-hall floor at MGM. In *The Pleasure of His Company*, he played my father and we had a small dance section to do. At first I was afraid that I wouldn't follow him correctly. However, with Fred, you couldn't *not* follow because he led you. Even a klutz could look great with Fred Astaire.

Harry and I had come back from our weekend "honeymoon" to the house on Conway. Suddenly the tiny driveway was occupied by Harry's limousine with chauffeur, the Rolls, my Continental, and my station wagon. The children would adjust to Harry, but it was obvious from the first day that the house wouldn't.

Harry had vanity. He was fastidious so I knew he was vain.

He was a man who owned two hundred pairs of shoes, dozens of suits, sports jackets, and trousers; not to mention thousands of accessory items like socks and underwear.

He had hundreds of shirts, all custom-made. He sent them to New York to be laundered. When the package was unwrapped, the shirts had to be repressed to get out the wrinkles caused in continental air transit. If there was even the tiniest piece of thread or a stitch out of place, back to New York it went.

There wasn't room for all of his things at the house, so he kept a suite at the Beverly Hills Hotel just to hold his clothes until we solved our living situation.

Harry spent over an hour getting ready every morning. Murray the barber came at six-thirty or seven. He would shave Harry, then wash, cut, and blow-dry his hair. Harry also had a very thin moustache that Murray kept shaped. I used to darken one side a bit with an eyebrow pencil because it was a little gray.

I loved preening him. He was a rich man who wanted to look handsome and the attention made him happy. I was just being the wife I had always wanted to be. I had his slippers by his chair when he came home. I had the glass iced, the olive or the onion, the vermouth. I had his bath drawn and his robe laid out and that's the way I wanted it. He said to me, "You take care of the uptown, and I'll take care of the downtown." In other words, he'd take care of business and I'd take care of the home.

He loved Carrie and Todd. The first weeks of our marriage, Carrie, who was four and used to sleeping with her mother, wanted to sleep with us. So she did; right in the middle, until she got used to Harry and then she went back to her own room.

Nobody snored as loudly as Harry. It often made me think of the story Judy Garland had told me about her marriage to Vincente Minnelli. Vincente snored loudly too. At one point in their marriage they were working on a picture together. Vincente would fall right to sleep, snoring up a storm. Judy would lie there, exhausted, yet wide awake because of the noise Vincente made. Finally one night, she sat up in frustration, hit him on the nose, and broke it! Only because I was a drop-dead sleeper did I survive.

In January 1961 we all went on a honeymoon—my mother and father, the children, the nurse, Harry and I. I had been to Jamaica ten years before with Carleton Carpenter, and in my memory it was the most wonderful place. Harry and I went two days ahead of everyone else, to a hotel in Montego Bay. The place was teeming with bugs. Lizards and bugs. Harry was bitten up terribly. I was up with him all the first night, putting lotion on his bites. Finally he looked at me, pained, and said: "Do we have to stay here, baby doll?"

He was so uncomfortable, I couldn't say no. So that dream was over. We went back to Miami to my friend Phyllis Pollack's hotel, where everyone joined us.

Just before we left for our honeymoon, Harry found us a new house on Greenway Drive in Beverly Hills. It was a very modern split-level overlooking the golf course of the Los Angeles Country Club. The exterior, which Carrie always said looked like a post office, was blocks of rough marble. I had wanted an English-style country house. But I knew Harry liked showy, modern homes. It was a beautiful neighborhood, and the children could ride their bikes to school, all on sidewalks, without having to cross one street. I would never be crazy about the house, but we had compromised and both got something we wanted. I felt very good about that. The price was $545,000. Harry put up $200,000. I sold my house on Conway for $145,00 and gave Harry the money toward the new house, leaving us a $200,000 mortgage.

The house had ten thousand square feet of living space that occupied the entire second level—a huge master suite with his and her sitting rooms, dressing rooms, and bathrooms. There were two additional bedrooms for Carrie and Todd, an enormous living room with a fireplace, dining room, library, kitchen, laundry, and two maid's rooms.

Behind the house was a terrace and three swimming pools—built on a slight hillside—an upper pool with a waterfall into the next and then into the last, which was L-shaped and deeper.

Harry had a decorator he'd used before. He'd given her carte blanche, unlimited funds, and the request that it be ready in two weeks. Well, not quite two weeks, but she was good: The house was ready in two months. She'd bought the silver, the crystal, the rugs, the vases, right down to the safety pins in a little jar.

But I wanted our house to reflect our personalities—not hers. I love to collect antiques, painting, and sculpture. The house had a great deal of glass and two small atriums. The ceilings were twelve feet high and the double doors of the living room, dining room, and den slid into the wall, giving the effect of an enormous living space.

We made very few changes in the original house, except to convert the carport into a projection room.

The master bedroom was a comfortably large room, about thirty by forty. One wall was sliding-glass doors, which led to a balcony overlooking the Los Angeles Country Club—the club that Eddie "could never" belong to (neither, as it happened, could Harry Karl). As in the rooms downstairs, the bedroom doors slid into the wall, creating spaciousness. On either side of the bedroom were the dressing rooms, bathrooms, and sitting rooms. My bath was done in rose-colored Italian marble with a wall of mirrors and two crystal chandeliers. Off the bath was a huge walk-in closet with a fourteen-foot ceiling and two tiers for hanging clothes, as well as a fur storage.

Harry had a suite of closets, a bath, a gym room with the white-marble barber's chair, a steam room (in which we also installed a ballet barre), and a sitting room.

With the Greenway house, we finally had room for all Harry's clothes. I had a lot of clothes but nowhere near what Harry had. There was a huge closet for his shoes. He had dozens of alligator shoes, dozens of velvet slippers, dozens of slip-ons. There were drawers for his hundreds of shirts, organized by color. Drawers for underwear, for handkerchiefs, for scarves, for neckties. There was a drawer for black socks, a drawer for blue socks, a drawer for brown socks. I would straighten the drawers all the time. Harry was fanatically well organized and used to being waited on. I liked helping make this possible, catering to him really. I took very good care of him; that was what a good wife did.

Nearly every night he would come home with a gift. His idea of a simple little gift was a beautiful $2,000 Rolex wristwatch with a cover of diamonds in the shape of a flower and a band of tiny strands of braided gold, with a diamond clasp. Or a $5,000 Gucci purse. Twice a week he would bring me a pair of earrings. He loved jewelry and he had a good eye for it. He often bought it for himself too—cuff links, tie clips, rings, watches, belt buckles, cigarette boxes. But the gift giving never stopped.

He ordered me a custom-made Rolls-Royce on a trip we made to England. A coupe, British racing green, shorter than most, with the old-fashioned headlights. It took a year to be delivered, and when it arrived, it was just another on the very long list of his lavish and thoughtful gifts. Harry was very generous to everyone—his ex-wives, charities, his six thousand employees, who one year received a 40 percent across-the-board raise. He was always sharing the wealth. I liked and respected that about him.

Once, when I was married to Eddie, I sent his business manager the bill for three pairs of shoes I had bought—not expensive ones, but the standard size 2. The business manager sent it back with a note informing me that I should pay for them since I could also deduct the cost from my income tax because I was an actress! With Harry it was: "Honey, can I buy this?" "How much is it?" "Thirteen thousand." "Yes." Harry, I saw this Meissen vase today, this Renoir, this eighteenth-century bergère. "Buy it." Harry had never collected paintings or *objets*, but he loved beautiful things.

CHAPTER 29

LIFE WITH HARRY WAS very well organized and very affluent; his life-style required it. We had a Chinese couple who were the cook and butler, a maid, a woman who cleaned; a laundress who came in every day, the nurse for Carrie and Todd, and of course, Harry's chauffeur. I had never been in charge of a staff before. At first thought the idea was awesome. How to organize them all? I decided to set up a Caper Chart, just the way we learned in Girl Scouts. Each person knew exactly what they had to do and on what day they had to do it.

The first year, we saw mainly his friends. They were basically an older crowd of businesspeople who belonged to the Friars and to Hillcrest. I found myself out of the conversation lots of times, although I didn't mind. I enjoyed the way they knew how to function in life. They were all very nice to me. I probably liked the men better. I was younger than most of the women and we didn't have very much in common.

We entertained a lot of Harry's business associates. I loved planning the evenings down to the smallest detail, reading all the books on china, silver, crystal—setting the perfect table for the perfect menu. We had violinists to accompany a pianist at cocktails. The Dom Pérignon flowed and the caviar was served up in sterling-silver buckets.

I was, and still am, a fussybritches, worrying about everything being perfect, running around with the staff right up till the last minute. Then I know it's all fine, with everything done right. After dinner we have a band and dance, with people entertaining. Then I'm a guest, as far as I'm concerned; eat, drink and be merry. I always entertain at my parties—sit on the piano, stand on the piano, sing and clown.

We gave an anniversary party for Marge and Gower Champion, and a wedding reception for Jack and Felicia Lemmon. My old friend Jerry Wunderlich from MGM designed it all in yellow and white, with lemons as centerpieces. Everybody came. At Marge and Gower's party, Gower dove from the roof into the pool. Lana Turner rhumbaed with Ricardo Montalban and Jennifer Jones sat on the floor taking it all in.

211

I had my first glass of wine when I was twenty-eight. A couple of years after that, Harry introduced me to vodka and 7-Up, which I liked because I couldn't taste the liquor.

Anything I earned automatically went to Irving Briskin, who managed it with Harry. That was our deal; he'd "take care of the downtown," and I'd "take care of the uptown." I never had an allowance. If I needed money, Harry would hand me a hundred-dollar bill. We lived in a dream world, the kind of world that exists only among the very rich.

A few months before we were married, when I was making *The Second Time Around* at Fox, I got a call one day on the lot from Henry Hathaway, asking me to have lunch. Henry Hathaway started out in the film business as a child actor in 1908. He directed his first full-length feature, a western, in 1932. Since that time, he had directed dozens of pictures including *The Lives of a Bengal Lancer*, *The Trail of the Lonesome Pine*, *The House on 92nd Street*, *Niagara*, and *The Desert Fox*.

I'd never met him although, of course, I'd heard of him. Before the lunch I asked a few friends, including Glenn Ford, what he was like. Well. The stories were unreal. How awful he was! Like Hitchcock. And he was especially horrendous to women!

So. We met for lunch at the Fox commissary. He was handsome, ruddy-faced, tall, silver-haired and fatherly, although brusque. He told me he wanted me to play the part of a seventeen-year-old girl named Lillith in an epic he was doing in the Cinerama process at MGM. It was called *How The West Was Won*. I listened intently as he described the part. I knew that at twenty-nine, I could play younger roles, but a teenager? Furthermore, although he was most polite with me, I could see that behind that gruff exterior could lie a temper.

Finally, when he was finished talking about the part, I said, "It's very kind of you to want me for this picture, Mr. Hathaway, but I couldn't possibly work for you."

"Why not?" he asked.

"Well, because I hear you're the toughest director living."

He scowled slightly. "That's ridiculous, kid. Who the hell told you that? I'm not tough at all."

"Well, Mr. Hathaway, I don't want to say who said that, but I'm the kind of person that if you yelled at me, I'd faint; and you'd have to cut shooting . . ."

"Now wait a minute . . ." he interrupted.

"And so it's better if you get somebody else . . ."

"Wait a minute!" he interrupted again, coming on like Cagney. "Who the hell said I'm tough?! I treat my actors and actresses like kings and queens!"

"That's not what I heard. I heard you just tear them down and rip them up and . . ."

Hathaway was red-faced, boiling. "Now wait! What the hell is this anyway? Listen, kid, I'm telling ya ya gotta take this picture! I want you for that part!"

"I don't think it's a good idea for me, Mr. Hathaway."

He stood up and banged the table. "You're doin' this picture and I don't give a shit what the hell you say! And I won't ever yell at you, ya hear?!"

I was surprised he didn't add, ". . . you little bitch!"

I was doing the picture.

Hathaway went off scouting locations not long after that. I never saw him again until the following May 1961 when I arrived on location in Paducah, Kentucky.

I went from the plane right into my costume, makeup, and wig. I walked onto the stage and Hathaway says, loud and gruff, "Yer late!!"

I stopped and turned, facing him. "Don't yell at me," I said, as if to remind him of our conversation that day in the commissary.

"I'M NOT YELLING!! GET YER ASS OVER THERE!" he said, yelling every word.

I pretended I didn't notice. "May I ask what scene we are shooting?"

"DON'T ASK QUESTIONS. JUST WALK FROM THAT HILL OVER THERE AND LOOK OUT THERE," he said, pointing.

"What am I looking at?" I asked.

"WHO THE HELL CARES?" he snapped. "JUST LOOK!"

"Mr. Hathaway," I said, "I don't shoot a scene like that."

"Look, kid, I don't have time for this shit. Now walk over there and look out there and I'm going to roll it. ROLL IT!"

So I walk up to the notch and look out. I don't know what I'm looking at but I try to look wistful. I figure "wistful" will work.

"PRINT!" he yells. "That was great."

"Now may I ask what that was?"

"Read your script! DON'T YOU READ YOUR DAMNED SCRIPT?"

"You're yelling at me," I reminded him.

"I'M NOT YELLING," he said, "THIS IS HOW I TALK. NOW GET OFF THE SET. IT'S NOT YOUR SCENE."

This was how it went. A couple of days later he started in **again**.

"Don't yell at me, Mr. Hathaway, because I'll faint," I warned him politely.

We began the scene and he broke in, yelling and cussing at me.

So I fainted. Pretending, of course. I collapsed and fell on the ground, limp as a dishrag, eyes closed.

"What the shii. . . ! !" Hathaway bellowed. "What? What the hell is that?"

The crew, who believed it, were all rushing around me, slapping my wrists, lifting my head, trying to revive me.

"WHAT THE HELL IS SHE DOING?"

"She fainted, Mr. Hathaway," someone replied meekly.

"SHE DIDNT FAINT. SHE'S FAKING!" He came over and nudge my lifeless body with his foot. "GET UP!" he shouted, furious.

I wouldn't. He nudged me again. He was really going nuts. "She's faking! Get up, goddamnit! Com'on, kid!"

But I wouldn't and I didn't. I kept my eyes closed, which was very hard because they'd put smelling salts to my nose. Then three men lifted me up to carry me off the set.

Hathaway was wild. "YOU KNOW YOU'RE FAKING! Look at the sun! It's leaving. I could get this shot. . . ." He was following us off the set. "I didn't yell at you for Chrisake!" he explained.

Eyes still shut tight; no response.

"I didn't yell at you, goddamnit! I know you're faking."

Nothing from me. They were just about to lift me into my trailer.

"You're making fun of me, aren't ya?" he said. "Okay, I apologize! I won't yell, okay?! Now will you wake up?!"

I opened my eyes wide. "Okay," I said.

He looked at me hard. He looked as if he didn't know if he should laugh or yell. "You little bitch," he muttered.

A few minutes later we got the shot and Hathaway calmed down.

He did it one more time the next day and I immediately fell to the ground.

"STOP THIS!" he shrieked.

Finally he started to laugh and it became a joke. I'd say, "I'm going to faint, Mr. Hathaway," and he'd say, "Okay, okay, I apologize."

How the West Was Won had a great cast including Karl Malden, Jimmy Stewart, Robert Preston, Gregory Peck, Henry Fonda, Lee J. Cobb, Carolyn Jones, George Peppard, Richard Widmark, and three women, all of whom became my friends: Agnes Moorehead, Thelma Ritter, and Carroll Baker. I'd known or worked with all three before, but it was the months of location that brought us together; we became comrades.

I took Carrie and Todd and their nurse, Dottie Wolfe, to Paducah with me. Harry would come for long weekends, or a few days at a time.

The location was an island in the middle of the river that was uninhabited because it was under water part of the year. It was also a haven for all kinds of lovely creatures like snakes and spiders. But Hathaway wanted it because it was authentic. He also wanted the actors to get the feel of what the pioneers had to go through. We got it.

Carroll Baker and Jimmy Stewart had to shoot a love scene under a old oak tree on that same island. Carroll put her arms around Jimmy, reached up to kiss him, and just as she was about to, she saw a long, black, slivery water moccasin baring its fangs and forked tongue, four feet from her face.

She was so stunned that when she first opened her mouth to scream, nothing came out. Jimmy, not knowing what she was seeing, thought she'd opened her mouth to kiss him. So he obligingly kissed her. But just as he did, Carroll pulled away from him, a scream ripping out of her face.

"THE SNAKE!" she screamed and ran away from him.

For the briefest moment Jimmy thought that his approach was evidently so macho that Carroll was just overreacting.

Then Henry yelled: "SNAKE! CUT!" and sent a crew after the doomed reptile. They killed the snake, and Jimmy and Carroll (who was still shaking) resumed their clinch.

There were a lot of action shots that were dangerous and even terrifying. Thelma and I shared several. We had a scene where we were driving the covered wagon with six horses in front of us. There's no way that a woman can hold six horses back unless she's raised with them or is the strongest woman on earth.

We were in Telluride, Colorado, near the Black Canyon. Hathaway had set up this spectacular "stampede" shot. Thelma and I were playing two "pioneer women." I was holding the reins and she was sitting in the seat beside me. The cameras were rolling.

Thelma and I were galloping along on the wagon seat, bouncing around, hitting our heads, when she started getting nervous.

"Son of a bitch!" she yelled over the din. "Stop those horses!"

"Sure, Thelma," I yelled back, "tell me something else!"

"Holy shit," Thelma screamed. She had a gift for the English language.

Hathaway wanted a stampede and he got one. We were heading at increasing speed across the desert floor toward what is called the Dallas Divide, which is a cliff that is part of the Black Canyon! It was really happening.

"Son of a bitch!" Thelma continued yelling.

At that point the cliff was about half a mile away. No matter how hard we tried, we couldn't slow the horses. I didn't know what to do. "Maybe we'll survive if we jump," I yelled to Thelma.

She yelled back, *"Jump?!* Jump?! What the hell, we'll be killed if we jump!"

"KILLED?! We'll be killed if we go over, so I'm taking my chances. I'm breaking every bone in my body!" I shouted.

I could see Thelma was getting prepared to do the same. We had to figure out how long to wait before jumping, so they could get the shot. It never occurred to Hathaway that we might be killed. We wouldn't dare die. It was not allowed on Hathaway's set.

Finally, just as we were a few hundred yards from the edge, moving along to our end, the head wrangler told Hathaway that he had to come in after us. The director wouldn't let him go and wouldn't let him go until the last minute. Then they rode up and pulled those horses so hard I thought they were going to break their necks!

Another time, on the Gunnison River in Oregon, Thelma and I were on a wagon again and supposed to float across the river to the other side. Hathaway had rigged it so that the wagon would fall over in the middle of the river and we would swim to the other side. This was in the rapids! And the water! They had to break the ice near the shore for us to swim into it! Not only that, but Thelma and I were wearing long skirts and petticoats. I took one look at the situation and decided to have a word with the director.

"Henry, I don't think we can make it to the other side in those rapids."

"It's just a short swim," he said. "You can make it."

"But those are rapids!" I pointed.

"I'll have frogmen under the water. You won't drown."

It so happened that while shooting a rapids scene up in Oregon, one that this was being matched to, two stuntmen had drowned.

"Henry, I don't think I wanna do this."

"What does that *mean*, you don't wanna do this?"

Luckily I had worked with Gene Kelly before this or I would never have had the kind of discipline to go through with it. I was now going to walk on water for this director.

Thelma wasn't disturbed. "Aw, com'on, Debbie, we can do it."

"Thelma," I said, "I'm a good swimmer, but are you a good swimmer? You're from New York. Where'd you learn to swim?"

She shrugged. "I can hardly swim, but he said there's frogmen.

We'll make it. You gotta have guts, kid. That's what the movie's all about." And she went over to get into the wagon.

I went to talk to the frogmen. "How is Miss Ritter going to make it across these rapids?" I asked.

The man was very reassuring. "We're gonna swim up underneath her and suspend her body. We'll do the same for you, Debbie—guide you across because the camera won't see us under you."

Oh. Okay.

It took about three hours to set up the shot because there were eight wagons going into the water. This was a major production. And a major risk.

We got into the wagons. Hathaway called, "ROLL IT!" and with a great lurch, down the mountain we went.

"Hang on!" I screamed at Thelma, while holding on to my side for dear life.

We smashed into the freezing cold water. The impact was so great that the wagon just splintered, broke up, and we were thrown out. Luckily it didn't land on top of us. It just went flying down the rapids. And so did Thelma and I.

The water took my breath away. I thought my eyes were going to fall out of my head. Plus, we had on those petticoats.

I tried to swim toward the other side, paddling frantically, being pulled helplessly downstream by the current, hitting all kinds of rocks, my hands ripped and bleeding. And there was *nobody* under me!

I could also see there was no one under Thelma, who was no more than three feet away from me at first. She was going "Ooo-ahh-glurg-glurk," and going under. I couldn't do anything to help her; I was fighting, as it was, to get to shore, well aware of the fact that Hathaway had not yelled "Cut." When I finally heard it, I was hundreds of yards downstream, so far down that we were off camera.

Fortunately, up ahead of me, I saw that two frogmen had got Thelma. I continued bouncing over rocks and boulders like a piece of Styrofoam, when finally a guy grabbed me.

They took us into the trailer to try and warm us up. I looked over and saw that Thelma was worse than I—all cut up; her hair all matted. Someone handed me a shot of brandy and told me to gulp it down. I did, but it stung my insides like a torch. I thought I was going to throw up.

Hathaway came into the trailer to see us. He loved it.

"You girls looked great! Just great!" he said.

I was cussing at him. Thelma was cussing at him. "You son of a bitch! We could have drowned," she said.

"Well, you didn't, you made it, didn't ya? Gotta believe in Hathaway," he said with a grin on his face.

I felt like slugging him but I still barely had the strength to breathe. "I could kill you, you bastard!"

The next day they had to get a shot of me emerging soaked from having swum across the river. I was standing at the river's edge when Hathaway came over to me.

"I think you should be sexier in this scene," he said.

"In what way do you wish?" I asked.

"Usually when a woman gets wet and cold, her nipples stand out."

"Oh, really, Mr. Hathaway? Well, all I can say is I'm very cold and this is the best my body can do."

"Don't worry," he said. He turned to one of his assistants. "Get some oil and put it on her nipples. That'll make them stand out."

"Now," he said to me, the oiling completed, "the only other thing is you should get more water in your petticoat."

He could see I wasn't delighted, but that didn't faze him. So I dipped myself deeper into the river, making a tub full of water with the front of my long skirt.

"There," he said, satisfied. "How do you feel?" he asked, a sly Hathaway glint in his eye.

"Fine," I replied nonchalantly. "Just wonderful, thank you, Mr. Hathaway."

Whereupon I lifted the "wetter" petticoat full of water and splashed it all over the front of him.

He jumped back and yelped in shock.

"How does it feel?" I asked with a big smile on my face.

"Son of a bitch!" he muttered, moving far enough away from me to avoid getting it again.

He was tough, but I loved him. Hathaway, it turned out, liked me so much, he kept enlarging my part. I'd say, "Henry, I don't want to do any more stuff."

"I'll tell you what yer gonna do. I'm writing you into the last segment. You're going to be an old lady, that's how I'm tying the whole thing together."

Eight months later, I was still working on the picture. "Henry! It'll be a year before I'm finished!"

"That's the end of that," he scowled. "You're doin it."

"Yessir."

He went back to that part of the country a few years later to make *True Grit*. He loved it there. He was a real character, such a funny, wonderful man.

Between shots, or during breaks, everyone had his own way of waiting. Many times on location, because of the elements or the shot, we'd sit around together, amusing each other with stories.

One day, in Kentucky, it was rainy. With the Cinerama process, it was necessary to have perfectly clear light because it was shot from both sides and the front. So we had to wait for the sun.

We were in deep woods by a stream, with the bugs and the water mocassins, sitting way up off the ground in our chairs, the girls with their skirts and petticoats pulled up far from the ground, telling jokes; the stuntmen, me, Karl, Agnes, Thelma, and Carroll.

After about two hours of storytelling and laughing, like kids at camp, waiting for the rain to stop, we were tapped. It got very quiet for a moment.

Jimmy Stewart, who had been off to the side, reading, closed his book and looked over at us.

"Ah-ah-ahr ya all outa . . . sto-ries?" he asked, in that immortal stammer of his.

"Uh, yeah, Jimmy, we don't have any more to . . ."

He got off his chair and pulled it closer to the group.

"Ah-ah-ahr . . . well, ah-ah-ja-ever hear of the sto-ry about this man who-who-who-uh was walking his . . . dawg . . . down the street, and he meets this . . . uh . . . friend, and he says . . . uh . . . he's walking his dawg and the friend says: 'Say, uh-wha-t kind of dawg is that?'

"Well, he says, 'Uh, this is a Mexican Spitz!'

"He says, 'Wuh-wuh-well, I've never-never heard of a Mexican Spitz.'

"The other man says, 'Waal, that's my dawg; and that's what it is.'

"And the first man scratches his head and says, 'Waal, I don't think that that's a Meh-xican Spitz.'

"'Waal, yeah, that's what it is.'

"And then the li'l dawg looks up at the disbelieving man and the dawg . . . he-he-he says: 'Seen-yore!'"

At which point a little drop of white spittle fell from between Jimmy Stewart's lips onto the pages of his open book, which he then quietly closed.

"Seen-yore."

We all fell off our chairs and laughed for half an hour.

In early February 1962, just a few weeks from completing *How the West Was Won*, we learned that I was going to have a baby in September.

We finished shooting in March and the following day I reported to work on *My Six Loves*, which was being directed by Gower Champion at Paramount. The cast, including David Jansen, Cliff Robertson, Eileen Heckart, Max Showalter, Mary McCarty, and Alice Pearce, were all very funny people. We had a million laughs on the picture; it was like a great big party. Alice Pearce and I became good friends and remained so until her untimely death.

By the time we completed *My Six Loves*, I had been working for one year straight without a break. Harry, who had to go to Europe on business, decided we should also take a few weeks' vacation there.

A couple of years before I married Harry, I had met the French Baron Edmond de Rothschild at an Israel-bond rally. A charming man, very continental and effusive, he had graciously invited me to "let him know" the next time I was going to be in Paris.

I sent a cable to the baron telling him that we were coming to Paris and that we would love to take him and his wife to dinner. Two days later I received a cable from *monsieur le baron* telling me that he would be very honored to give a party for us at his residence. Frankly, I thought that was wonderful, and immediately wired back our acceptance.

The baron's house—what the French call an *hôtel particulier*—was an enormous cream-colored eighteenth-century palace with a slate roof, approached through huge iron gates, into a courtyard to a circular drive and a porte cochere. There were liveried footmen standing on the front step, two to open the doors and help us from the car.

Another footman announced us as we walked into the entrance gallery. That was something even Harry hadn't thought of for our house. There were violins playing and guests milling about the big marble room. A woman, who introduced herself as the baron's secretary, explained to us that the baron would be a little late. She took us around and introduced us to each guest.

The party, followed by the violins, moved into a large drawing room with walls of gilded hand-carved boiserie, hung with tapestries and paintings, furnished with spectacular French antiques. A few minutes later, a door flew open from a smaller room, and the baron, pulling on a jacket, speaking English in a French accent, rushed up to me.

"Oh, Debbeeee, eet's so wonderful to see you! You look so beautiful, and oh my goodness—you are pregnant. You are like me!"

I wasn't quite sure what he meant but it amused me and so I played along. "Oh, I didn't know you were pregnant. That's wonderful! Congratulations."

"Oh, yes," he said. "I am so excited because for any moment I am going to be a father. I am so hoping that it will be a boy. If I get a boy, I think I will marry her."

"Oh," I said, "that would be nice too." Evidently there already was a baroness but she was pretty much out of the picture. Baron Edmond then told me how the mother-to-be was this beautiful young girl he had first seen one day when he was riding in his car and she was crossing the street. He followed her and courted and wooed her, but couldn't marry because he already had a wife—always a good reason. (As a matter of fact, he was soon divorced and shortly thereafter took a new wife.)

There were four tables of ten set in the stately dining room. Each table had two waiters to serve. I was seated at the baron's table, on his right, and Harry was placed at another table.

For the main course, a huge fish was served on a tray. Being the guest of honor, I was served first. However, I had never read in any of my many books how to begin cutting into this fish. It was probably salmon, but I only remember it seemed like the biggest fish ever. I thought, well, I'll just hit it in the middle. I figured who wants the head and who wants the tail?

Then came another dish on a tray—small potatoes in a white cream sauce. Just as I was serving myself, the bowl the potatoes were in suddenly slid off its tray, pouring them all over me, down my bosom, over the baby, in my lap, and all over the floor!

Edmond was aghast. It could go without saying that I was a little surprised too. The butler, in terror, ran off for some towels. Edmond immediately started retrieving the potatoes from my bosom, apologizing profusely. He was a natural at potato picking.

"It's all right, Edmond, I'll have the potatoes later—cold."

The butler returned with towels. I was a little embarrassed about the mess, but Edmond, the perfect host, was so happy to be reaching for the potatoes that for the rest of the night he talked of nothing else. When the baby was born, he said, I should name him *petite pomme*.

Harry and I spent the next few days in Paris shopping for antiques and art for our new home, including a small Renoir that I bought for our bedroom. From Paris we traveled to Venice and then to Rome, where we were going to see Pier Angeli whom I hadn't seen since she moved back to Italy a few years before.

Pier and I were the same age—thirty. It had taken us both, coincidentally, that long to find a stable combination of marriage, family, and career in our lives. The pain and disaster of our first marriages were completely forgotten those two days Pier and I visited in Rome.

Harry and I had a suite at the glorious Excelsior in Rome. While I visited with Pier, he made a quick trip to Spain to a shoe factory that he owned with a partner. The second night he was gone, I woke up with the start. The baby! I put my hands over the child. Something was wrong. I had some staining, but nothing major. There was no pain. But the baby had dropped about three inches. My stomach had gone down and had got very soft all of a sudden. There was no movement.

I knew immediately. It was dead. The baby was dead.

Harry came back to Rome the following afternoon. I told him. He looked at me as if I were crazy.

"What're you talking about? You look fine, darling," he said.

"I am fine. But the baby's not."

"Then we should get you to the best doctor in Rome. Call Pier. She must know the best."

If I didn't want to see an Italian doctor, then he wanted us to get on the next plane for California. But we had been planning to go on to Florence for a few days. Harry had some business matters to attend to there. I didn't feel that great, but I knew there was nothing anybody could do.

So we went to Florence, with me feeling progressively queasier. Why I didn't go right home, I'll never know. I could have aborted on the street. Perhaps I was wishing I would.

When we were returned to California four days later, I immediately went to see Dr. Levy.

That baby was dead. Nothing could be done. In 1962 a woman couldn't just get an abortion in her seventh month of pregnancy. She had to carry the fetus until it aborted itself, which for me meant the entire nine months. And to perform a cesarian under the circumstances would have risked my life.

So I had to walk around with my dead child inside me and not tell anybody. People would look at me and say: "You look fabulous. What are you going to name the baby?"

I'd say, "Well, I don't know."

It was devastating. After just a few days of that I realized that the best thing for me and my health was to stay home.

CHAPTER 30

ONE DAY IN EARLY AUGUST, the phone rang. It was a man I knew from the Bel Air Presbyterian Church, who worked at Twentieth Century-Fox Studios.

"Debbie," he said, "I just had a very strange phone call from Dr. Billy Graham.

"He said he was in prayer last night and was given a vision—that Marilyn Monroe was going to die . . . and it wasn't her time. He wanted to know if you would go see Marilyn."

"But I don't really know Marilyn," I said, which was true. I'd met her several times but I was never part of her crowd.

I knew Dr. Graham, but why this phone call came to me, I couldn't understand. Besides, I went on to explain to the caller, I wasn't in any condition to leave the house.

Marilyn had been fired from a picture at Fox not long before. In those days any star who stopped things from going the studio's way was disciplined. Marilyn was very depressed and no one seemed to be able to console her.

"Dr. Graham said that someone who is close to her must tell her about his vision," the man from the church repeated.

What friends of Marilyn did I know? Who could I tell that she would listen to? Finally I thought of someone who cared and understood. I called Sidney Guilaroff. He had done Marilyn's hair, as he had done Garbo's and Taylor's at MGM. Sidney knew everyone and all their secrets and was totally trustworthy.

Sidney agreed to go see her the next day. As usual, there were people there—a woman publicist and a few hangers-on—drinking with her and trying to cheer her up.

He called me afterward to tell me that he couldn't get to see Marilyn alone to talk to her.

"Sidney," I said, "you have to go back. This is very important. This is a possible death." Sidney was not one ever to meddle in anyone's privacy. But like a lot of people who knew her, he regarded Marilyn's condition as very delicate.

So he went back again the next day. He called me late that afternoon. "Debbie, I cannot get through to her. All those people are there and I will not sit with them, waiting for nothing."

We would have to find another way, I thought to myself.

That was on Friday. The following Sunday morning Harry woke me to tell me. Marilyn had "committed suicide" the night before.

I was beside myself with the feeling of guilt that I had failed in my task. We could have done something, *anything* that might have at least helped her through one more terrible night alone.

About a week or ten days later, I received a phone call from Dr. Graham, who, like millions of us, was greatly upset about Marilyn's death. He told me that in his vision there were a lot of Hollywood people whose lives were in jeopardy. He suggested that if I could arrange a meeting at my house with people in the entertainment industry, he would like to come and talk to them.

A few days later I gave birth to a girl child without life. I still don't want to remember it. An autopsy was performed in an attempt to learn what was wrong. But there was nothing wrong. Not with the child and not me. It was a one-time-in-a-million matter. Harry, who was deeply disappointed, had to bury the body. I never knew where he buried her. I never wanted to know.

Two weeks later Dr. Billy Graham came to our house to speak to about forty of us, including some of Hollywood's biggest stars. Marilyn was still very much on people's minds. There was a lot of hurt and pain expressed—people trying desperately to find their way in life. The session went on for about three hours, which amazed even Dr. Graham. He said he had to do it because he felt guilt-ridden.

Now we know, of course, that Marilyn couldn't really have talked to anybody about her problems. Everybody used her. Men wanted to take her to bed. She was a gentle, childlike girl who was always looking for that white knight on the white horse. She lived in a total dream world. And why not? What sex symbol is happy? Of course she walked into the path of disaster, which shows you how gullible she could be. She was so easily taken in because she wanted so much to be loved— such a sad life—such a tragic ending. Her legend lives on. Just how did Marilyn die?

All those weeks of that summer are still just a series of horrible memories.

23. Eddie and I with Dean and Jeanne Martin in front of the entrance constructed for the engagement party Eddie Cantor gave us at the Beverly Hills Hotel, 1954

24. RJ and I at my engagement party at the Beverly Hills Hotel

25. Eddie and I in London, where he went to sing for the queen, 1954

26. Eddie pressing his finger into the arm of Max (Dr. Needles) Jacobsen. I was smiling on the outside but I didn't get the joke.

27. I, Jeanette Johnson, and Eddie on our wedding day. A girl's best friend hugs a girl's first husband. Little did Jeanette know she'd be lining up for two more.

28. *Above*, the bride and groom, with best man Milton Blackstone (forcing the smile), and attendant Jeanette Johnson, Grossinger's, 1955

29. *Right*, always there for me: Daddy, Billy, and Mother on my wedding day at Jennie Grossinger's, 1955

30. On our honeymoon, Miami Beach, on my twenty-fourth birthday, 1956

31. The bride and groom back in L.A.

32. The Todd wedding, February 1957. I was Elizabeth's attendant and Eddie was best man.

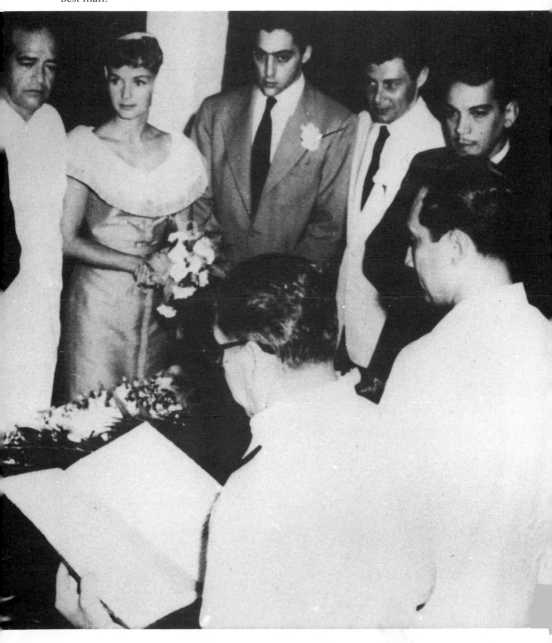

33. America's Sweethearts, now married and not as sweet

34. Elizabeth's first public appearance after Mike's death. She attended Eddie's opening in Las Vegas, June 1958.

35. Miss Davis and I on the set of *The Catered Affair*, MGM, 1956

36. *Tammy and the Bachelor,*
Universal Pictures, 1957

37. *Below,* recording "Tammy." Eddie
was not thrilled.

38. Rudy Render and I
with Jerry Fielding

39. *Right*, with Camille Williams and
the man she married, Jerry Fielding, a
top TV and film composer-conductor.
I did an album with Jerry. Everyone
was trying to keep me busy after Eddie
left.

41. Arriving in New York from Europe. Reporters asked if I would give Eddie a quickie Mexican divorce.

42. Carrie at two years and Todd at four months

40. *Left*, on the MGM back lot with Carrie and Todd during the making of *The Mating Game* with Tony Randall

43. With Bob Neal after Eddie and I broke up

44. Hedda Hopper said, "Why don't you marry Glenn? You look so good together."

45. Harry and I at our new home on Greenway Drive, Beverly Hills, 1962

46. *Left*, Carrie and Todd,
ages five and three

47. *Below*, a happy family at last, with
Harry Karl, 1962

*   *   *

The picture that caused the most controversy in Hollywood that year was MGM's remake of *Mutiny on the Bounty* with Marlon Brando playing Fletcher Christian. It had gone millions over budget, changed locations, scripts, directors, with even the main stars, Brando and Richard Harris, rumored to be fighting and threatening to quit. Every day the Beverly Hills–Bel Air rumor circuits were feeding on the latest gossip from Tahiti, where the picture was filming.

It was also a perfect picture for a charity premiere. I went over to MGM to ask if the Thalians could have it. The answer was no.

I didn't like the word *no*. If I could get to Marlon Brando, I knew he'd help me because it was for a children's charity. But I was too chicken to call on him myself. I was in awe of his talent and there were a million stories about his outrageous conduct and behavior. However, I wanted that premiere for the Thalians, and Marlon and I did have a mutual friend, Jerry Wunderlich.

I called Jerry and he invited me to lunch at the studio commissary. Marlon happened to be on the lot that day also. After lunch Jerry and I walked over to his dressing room. We could see Marlon sitting inside dressed in the white breeches he wears in the picture, talking to one of the stuntmen on the film.

Jerry knocked on the door and poked his head in. "Marlon, I'd like you to meet my best friend, Debbie Reynolds."

"I'm gonna meet Tammy?" he asked with a sly grin. "Sure, Jer," he said with a wave of a hand. "Com'on in, Debbie Reynolds."

I've never been nervous about an opening, a film, or anybody anywhere—other than when I met Gable—and years later, Hepburn. But now I was. I had my little speech memorized, and all my books with the programs listing all the donors. I was the pitch lady.

I walked into the small trailer, very basic, with a sofa, a makeup table and mirror, and a padded, backless stool. Marlon was sitting there, his legs apart in a very relaxed, Napoleonic, sexual manner. He never rose, never stood up. I sat down on the little stool across from him. The stuntman got up and excused himself while Jerry sat on the steps in the doorway.

"Are you Tammy?" he asked, in his slow, mumbled accent.

"No, I'm Debbie."

"No, you're Tammy," he said.

He sat there all askew while I sat there very primly, legs together and back straight. He was putting me on; and I knew it. But I was so busy trying to figure out how to match wits with him—and get over my discomfort—that I had to go along.

Marlon looked at me for a moment, as if he were studying me.

"Uh . . . why do you want to see me?" he asked, cocking his head to one side.

"Well, Mr. Brando . . ."

"Call me Marlon . . ."

"Marlon . . . I would like to obtain this picture *Mutiny on the Bounty* . . ."

"Why? It stinks."

I said, continuing my pitch, "It's very popular and everybody's talking about it . . ."

"Yeah, I can understand why. The gossip. The stupidity of MGM. I can understand that."

"I would like it for a premiere to *raise-money-for-children*," I said very, very quickly. I could see that that got to him.

"Oh. For children?"

"Yessir. It's for children. It's a charity." I handed a book over to him. He took it, and flipped through it.

Then he looked at me again, taking it all in. "I say, uh . . . how many carats is that diamond?" Out of the blue.

I told him.

"You should trade it in," he said, "for a smaller, better one. It's a little yellow."

I hadn't noticed. "Well," I said, "who cares? That's shoe business."

He laughed at that. "So, uh . . . how come I didn't know you were married?"

I didn't know what to say. "Well . . ."

"I thought it was over with that guy, that Eddie, the singer . . ."

"It is . . ."

"Then how come you . . . uh, got married after that? Who is this guy with the shoe biz?"

"His name is Harry Karl and he sells shoes."

"Why would anybody want to do that?"

"His father had the business and my husband inherited it."

"Ah. He's rich."

"Yes, he's rich."

"Then that's why you married him, huh?"

"No, that's not why I married him."

"That's gotta be why because I saw a picture of him . . . he's not pretty."

I didn't know how I was going to get him back to talking about the premiere. "Well, I'm not here to discuss my marriage."

Marlon continued to be amused. "Yeah, well I wanna talk about it. So I'm gonna talk about it. Why would you marry a guy like that?"

With that, Jerry got up and excused himself, which made me doubly nervous. My heart was pounding.

"Mr. Brando . . ."

"Marlon . . ."

". . . I would just like to discuss this premiere . . ."

"Who gives a shit."

"I do," I said. "It's for the children."

"I know, I know . . . it's for charity. So whadda you want from me?"

"I want you to let the Thalians have the premiere to raise money." Finally.

"I don't care," he replied. "I'm not going to the premiere. I don't like MGM. I don't like the picture. I barely feel like finishing it, but I'm stuck, so I'm here."

"But it's for charity!"

"It's for charity, it's for charity," he repeated my words as if he couldn't have cared less. "Look," he said, leaning forward, looking very serious, "I'll tell you what. You go upstairs and tell them . . . they've asked me if I would come to the premiere. I told them never. And I mean never. But I'll tell you what. I like you. You go up there and tell 'em the only way I'll come is if you get the picture for your children. Otherwise, I don't come."

Everyone was making bets that Marlon Brando wouldn't show.

It was the hottest ticket in town. We planned a big cocktail party before the premiere. Bart Lytton, the banking tycoon, set up a huge tent in the parking lot of his bank. Jerry Wunderlich decorated it with a Tahitian theme. We hired Tahitian musicians and Tahitian dancers, and buses, which we also decorated, to transport everyone from the tent to the Egyptian Theatre for the picture and then back again for a supper.

The day before the premiere, Brando's wife, Movita, called me again.

"Marlon says he doesn't think he can make it because he doesn't have a tux," she said.

"Then tell him to wear a sweater. Tell him to come any way he wants."

"Well, Debbie, I don't know . . ." she said, doubtfully.

"He has to be there, Movita, or else we lose the whole premiere for the children."

We sent a limousine for the Brandos that night. Everyone was sure he wouldn't be there. However, they arrived. A little late. He was dressed in black tie. The press went nuts. I rushed out to greet him. He came in, stopping for a television interview and a radio interview. He couldn't have been nicer to everyone. Just as we were walking into the tent, he said, "Ehhh . . . here's something for the kids," and he pulled out a check for $5,000, co-signed Movita Brando and Marlon Brando. I hadn't asked him for the money.

Later, at the premiere, Lana Turner was sitting near him and turned to say, "Hi, Marlon."

He looked at her with a tiny scowl. "Do I know you?" he asked, giving her a hard time.

She turned around in a huff. Marlon laughed. He put everybody on that night. After the screening, he came back to the party and stayed late, and had a wonderful time. The Thalians raised $200,000, thanks to Marlon.

I heard later from Jerry Wunderlich that Marlon had had a great time at the party and was very pleased that we'd raised so much money. I never saw him after that until one day a few years later when he called. He had been to Biafra in North Africa and photographed the starving children. It just killed him. He wanted me to give a party to raise money.

"You know all the rich people. You have a big house. I can't do this. I don't know how. I want you to invite everybody rich."

"Everybody?" I repeated.

"No, no, just the very rich. We'll ask them to give some money. Okay, Debbie?"

"Okay, Marlon. I'll do it."

He gave me a date. With Jerry Wunderlich's help, I made up a list of fourteen couples, with the dinner catered by Chasen's.

Marlon showed up in a white turtleneck sweater, looking so gorgeous—very slim and handsome and Roman. After dinner he ran a film of the children. Speaking very slowly, in his low, way-low voice, he mesmerized the guests with his tragic stories. When the film was over, he asked for money and everybody gave. He was very charming to everyone, thanking them graciously, and thanking me. Then he left. And I never heard from him again.

CHAPTER **31**

MARLON WAS INDIRECTLY responsible for a new dia-
mond Harry gave me that fall. A blue diamond. Twenty-one carats of
blue diamond; $200,000 worth. I'd mentioned Marlon's remark about
the first diamond being "a little yellow." Apparently "a little yellow" was
like saying Harry gave less than the best.

That fall I had signed to do *Mary Mary*, the screen version of Jean
Kerr's long-running comedy that starred Barbara Bel Geddes and Barry
Nelson on Broadway. From a professional standpoint, it seemed like a
good career move. It was going to be an important picture, with a big
budget, produced by Jack Warner himself, who would be paying me a
big salary and a percentage of the gross.

But when the time came to do it, I felt indifferent. Despite the rest
after losing the baby, I was still tired and rather depressed. I didn't have
to work if I didn't want to. Harry and I wanted a bigger family. For the
first time in my adult life, I felt secure.

It was when I first went to work on the script for *Mary Mary* that I
came to the realization that I was not really a good actress. I knew I had
the potential, but not the training. I'd conveniently avoided facing that
fact. I wasn't serious. I did cute and adorable and called it acting. At age
thirty, it was time to get out or get in. My first thought was to get out.

I went to see Jack Warner and told him.

"You can do it, kid," he said.

"No, Mr. Warner, I want out."

"But you're the star of the picture," he argued.

"But I'm not good enough," I protested. "I'm not right for this part;
I'm just not good enough."

"Look, kid," he said, "I'm paying you three hundred and fifty thousand dollars! You think maybe Jack Warner doesn't know what he's
doing? You were making seventy-five bucks a week when you first came
over to my studio. Now it's ten percent of the gross. You think I'd waste

all that dough on you if I didn't think you could do it? I *know* what you can do!"

I didn't care what he was paying me. How was that going to make a difference? I was now the very rich Mrs. Harry Karl.

"I'll give you the biggest, best trailer on the lot," he added, as if he thought I was just negotiating, which I wasn't.

"Listen, kid, you'll be great" were Mr. Warner's parting words to me that day. He meant it and believed it. The problem was I didn't believe it.

When I decided not to fight him, the role became a challenge, because the truth was I didn't know how to approach it.

I went home and called Lillian Burns Sidney. If she'd work with me, I thought to myself, I'd learn how to do it. Lillian was much more than a drama coach; she was really a director. It was no accident that all those years at MGM, she'd sit down with the producer, the director, and even the writer of a new picture before she went to work with the actors.

Her input and influence were legendary. When she was at MGM, unlike most of Mr. Mayer's executives, Lillian was never afraid to express her views—in no uncertain terms. And Mr. Mayer was never afraid of hearing them.

She was also famous with the actors and the directors for being tough; a taskmaster. She had a great talent for reading a script and knowing whether or not it would play. Many people can read a scene and tell you if something's wrong and even what it is. But Lillian could always take it one step further. She knew how to fix it. That's genius.

When Mr. Mayer was in his final power struggle with the Loew's bosses in New York, he hired Dore Schary to be production chief. Lillian marched right into his office and told the King of Hollywood what she thought.

"Now you've done it; you've ruined everything," she said.

"Why? What's wrong with Dore Schary?"

"Nothing's wrong with Dore Schary except he only likes 'message pictures.' No musicals, no comedies, no adventures. Just messages. They won't have need for anybody around here. Even you! You'll see." She was right, of course.

Within a year Mr. Mayer was gone, and Lillian went over to Columbia to work as the executive assistant to Harry Cohn—a position that had never existed before. Harry Cohn wanted her because he knew she was a valued asset of Mr. Mayer's, and Harry Cohn wanted anyone Mayer valued. He figured it was good for business.

After Harry Cohn's death, Lillian, who had been in the business for more than thirty-five years, was offered a production deal by the studio. Her agent, Abe Lastfogel, and her husband persuaded her she could be more helpful working on George's pictures, and so she turned Columbia down.

When I first met Lillian in those early "university" days of MGM, I avoided learning anything from her. Instead of her being my drama coach in those early years, we became friends.

When she agreed to work with me on *Mary Mary* I called my agent to make arrangements with Jack Warner to pay her for her services. A few days later I got into my Rolls and drove that mile and a half from the house on Greenway to Lillian and George's.

I couldn't really imagine how anyone, even Lillian, could teach me to act. I remember wondering what she could do to teach me. I figured she'd act out the scene and I would mimic her.

I told her my idea, first thing.

"Oh, no," she said, very slowly turning her head from side to side. "That's not acting, darling. If you want to *learn* to act, then you'll have to act yourself."

Lillian always read a script aloud for the first time. You can't know how something is going to play if you don't hear the words, she'd say. But when she read it, she'd act out all the parts. Then she'd read it a second time, again acting out all the parts, but this time with some differences. Then she'd read the scene again and ask me about my character. "Who is she? Who is this character?"

"No," she'd say, "that's simply the beginning." Then she'd begin to point out what I missed. "Don't you see this, Debbie?" and she'd go on up a whole other avenue that I'd missed and that she'd got right away.

She worked with me right through the entire picture. Days I wasn't shooting, I'd go up to her house and work out the next scenes. Days I was shooting, I'd come home, have dinner with Harry and the children; put the children to bed, and then drive up to Tower Road and work for five or six hours on the following scenes.

She was, and still is to this day, an unrelenting teacher who digs and digs and digs into a part and demands the same of her students. Her criticisms can seem devastating at times because she goes right to the heart of the problem of a performance as she does with a script. There was no avoiding a difficult part by making with the jokes.

As a natural mimic, I have always observed the way people walk and move their hands. But as one who did not laugh out loud or cry easily in front of others, I had to learn the technique for doing those things on cue. I had to learn how to take everything I felt and use it. I was not in

control of my craft until I was thirty, and only then because of this
genius teacher, from whom I am still fortunate enough to be learning
today.

Not long after I finished working on *Mary Mary*, Harry and I went
to New York for business and shopping, and to see some Broadway
shows. One of the hot tickets was Meredith Willson's musical, *The Unsinkable Molly Brown*. I ran into Marge Champion, who asked me if I'd
seen it. When I told her I hadn't, she said, "You know, Debbie, you
really should because they're planning on making the movie and you're
very right for it."

So I went to see it. I loved the role and Marge was right; it was
perfect for me.

I started campaigning for it as soon as I got back to California.
MGM was doing it and Larry Weingarten was producing, with Chuck
Walters directing. I called Larry.

"Well, actually, Debbie," Larry started in, "we're trying to get
Shirley MacLaine and Robert Goulet for the picture. We don't know if
we can get Shirley because Hal Wallis has got her under contract. But
we'll certainly keep you in mind." Which meant they intended to get
Shirley for the role.

I contacted Bob O'Brien, who was president of the studio, and Bob
Weitman, who was production chief. But I got nowhere. I had Wilt's
brother, Al Melnick, then my agent, go sit outside Larry Weingarten's
office until Larry would see him about me. Al told Larry that I would
do a "test" for the part. No. I said I'd do it for no salary. No. They
wanted Shirley. Chuck Walters, the picture's director, wanted Shirley.

"You see, Debbie, you're just not the right type in their eyes; that's
why they want Shirley." I knew exactly what they meant. There's a
number in the show where Molly, in an Old West saloon, sings "Belly
Up to the Bar, Boys." They could see Shirley doing that, but not
Tammy. They were wrong. I knew I was so right for the role. My voice
was right—a low, full sound. Molly was a really gutsy yet sensitive,
vulnerable girl; and I could play it that way. I *was* Molly Brown and I
intended to prove it.

That's what I thought. They finally had Shirley signed, so I was just
wasting my time and energy.

Coincidentally, around that same time, I had been booked to do a
nightclub act in Las Vegas. For years Jack Entratter, who owned the
Sands in Las Vegas, had been after me to do an act for his hotel. There
was always a reason why I couldn't—either a picture, or more often and

more important, because I didn't like being away from my babies. But in 1962, Rudy Render had gone to see a run-through of Mitzi Gaynor's act. He came back raving. He wanted me to do one. The children were now old enough to go anywhere I went—and had even gone on location. Harry went to Sidney Korshak, who was the lawyer for the Riviera Hotel, and Sidney arranged a booking.

Meanwhile, two weeks into the New Year, 1963, Harry and I were given very special good news: I was pregnant again, with the baby expected in late summer.

We knew I wouldn't be able to do much after late April, so we set the booking in Vegas for early March. I went to work with Bob Sidney, a choreographer, and with Rudy. Willie Kovan, my wonderful tap teacher at MGM, came in to work with me on some of my songs. Camille Williams's husband, Jerry Fielding, did the musical arrangements, and Jerry Wunderlich, the sets. I hired writers, four male singer/dancers, and Michael Woulfe, who had also done the clothes for *Susan Slept Here*, to do my costumes.

We put the act together in about two weeks, then took several more weeks—which seemed like months, looking back on it—to rehearse it. I would work with Bob during the day and then at night, after I'd put the children to sleep, Rudy and I would go into the music room at Greenway and work on the songs. When Rudy and I worked alone together, it was like playtime—sheer pleasure. He was a master at vocal layouts and knew how to get me to be creative in my performance. The day I walked out of the last rehearsal, I was ready. I knew everything backward and forward.

I opened with "I Want to Be Happy," and finished the act in a clown outfit singing "Make 'Em Laugh," and for an encore, I closed the show with the quiet, sweet "Tammy." It was basically song and dance and comic impressions—something I did all the time for friends, but never before for the public.

In early March, we took the act to the Shamrock Hotel in Houston. Bob Sidney liked to try out at the Shamrock because it was lucky for him.

He was right. Opening night was a smash. From Houston we went on to Vegas to a solid week of what *Variety* called "boffo" business in the big Versailles Room at the Riviera. Opening night brought a big crowd from Hollywood, including Jack Benny and Red Skelton, who came backstage afterward to give me their praise and their critiques. But the response was tremendous, and the impressions just killed 'em. I loved it! The Riviera was so pleased that they asked me to come back for two weeks following my engagement at the Eden Roc in Miami.

Back in Vegas, I played the two weeks. I loved playing to a live audience. I had, in effect, made a new career for myself, as a live performer, with an image at least slightly more womanly and less cute.

The two weeks at the Riviera was the last of my commitments until after the baby was born. In fact, although there were always film possibilities under discussion, I had no further contractual obligations beyond the third month of my pregnancy. It was never determined what had gone wrong the year before, but I wasn't going to let anything create problems this time if I could help it.

I was surprised when I got a call one day from Al Melnick, telling me that Hal Wallis would not release Shirley MacLaine from her contract in order to do *The Unsinkable Molly Brown*. Which meant that if MGM used Shirley in the picture, it risked a lawsuit with Hal Wallis; so now they wanted me. Would I still be interested? Of course! Except that I was already "booked" until the late fall. Al, however, had already discussed that with Larry Weingarten and MGM. They were willing to wait. They were also willing to pay me considerably less than they were going to pay Shirley, knowing that I, the rich Mrs. Harry Karl, would have done this one for nothing.

A few days later Shirley called me, outraged.

"Hello, Shirley."

"Debbie, what is this shit about *Molly Brown*? I mean, the role is mine. I signed for it and now I hear that you undercut my price and now I'm out?!"

"That's not exactly the story, Shirley . . ."

"Yes, it is. You undercut my price. Larry Weingarten told me you'd do it for nothing. . . ."

"Number one, Shirley, you're in a lawsuit and it's not up to me to make MGM's decisions. . . ."

"That's not the point. I can work out the lawsuit."

"Then you'd best call MGM. I have nothing to do with this, Shirley. What do you want me to do, turn it down?"

"They gave it to you because you'd do it for nothing!"

"Look, Shirley," I tried to reason with her, "I'm sorry you don't have it and I'm thrilled that I do. But I'm not in a lawsuit right now, so I can do it. And I didn't undercut your price. I don't know your price and I'm not going to tell you mine.

"But also, Shirley, this might be my last film and I'm sure you're going on to make many great films."

She didn't even hear that, but it was true. Shirley was a leading actress. She was also a much more "in" actress in Hollywood than I ever was. The times were changing and they were just right for her. It was obvious that her film career had many more years left than mine. I was like Doris Day and Donna Reed: cute, cute, cute—the ruination of careers.

Before the contracts were signed, Chuck Walters, who was going to direct the picture, came to the house to visit me. It was a terrible rainy day in Los Angeles. The streets of Beverly Hills were flooded and Chuck drove all the way in from Malibu. His coming to see me in that kind of weather made me a little nervous. Although I had been told I had the part, I knew Chuck didn't want me; he wanted Shirley.

Chuck had directed me and Frank Sinatra several years before in *The Tender Trap*. He started out in the business as a dancer and choreographer. I had been an admirer of his long before that, when he staged Judy Garland's first club act.

We visited for a while, and then he said, "Debbie, I wish you'd turn this part down. Because you're totally wrong for it."

"I'm not going to turn it down," I replied. "It was my dream to play this part long before Shirley was even up for it."

"Well, you can't do it, you know," he countered. "You're much too short for the role."

I started to laugh inside. I was reminded of a story Helen Hayes told. When she was up for *Victoria Regina*, they told her, "Miss Hayes, you know we'd love you to read for this role, but you're a little too short for the part." She said, "How short is the part?" She got the job.

"I'm too short for the part, Chuck?" I asked, smiling. "How short is the part?"

He stared at me and then started to laugh. "That's very funny, Debbie."

I told him the Helen Hayes story. "It's possible, Chuck," I said, "that you could be wrong."

CHAPTER 32

IN LATE MAY of that year, Harry and I went off to Europe for a couple of weeks. My mind has long since blocked the memory, so I don't recall the details of where and exactly when, but, like a recurring nightmare, it happened again: the baby. I woke up in the night, and the baby had *dropped a couple of inches*! I couldn't believe it, but I knew it; the baby was dead.

I wanted to scream. Was this some kind of damnation, I remember asking myself. Had I done something to deserve this? Why did this have to happen to me again?! What is wrong with *me*? I kept asking myself. What had I done wrong?!

Harry was in a daze about it. We flew back to Los Angeles the next day and I checked right into St. Joseph's Hospital in Burbank. Again the doctors told me I would have to carry the child until the ninth month. But this time I refused. Finally, three doctors had a meeting and decided I could have an abortion, thank you very much.

The question was: How? What do you do? Poison. They put acid in your veins. It blows you up like a blimp and forces every factor out of your body; that's how.

Okay. All I remember about it is my mother and a nun who was the nurse in my room with me. I held on to them, my hands pulsating in theirs, in labor for fourteen hours. And finally, this thing, this piece of dead matter, came out of me. In a sac. Had the sac burst, I would have died of peritonitis.

A boy. It was a boy. Harry buried him, as he had buried the girl. I don't know where because I wouldn't acknowledge it. I refused. I had really felt that baby would be born healthy. The doctors all told me it could never *never* happen again. Never. So I was confident. We were confident. But we were wrong.

A few days later, Harry came in the station wagon with Carrie and Todd to take me home. Still too sick even to sit up, I lay on a blanket in the back of the car, explaining to my intensely curious children that

God had decided Mommy shouldn't have a baby because she had been feeling sick.

During that summer when I was recuperating, Jacqueline Kennedy gave birth to their third child, Patrick Bouvier Kennedy, who died a few days later. I felt just terrible for her. I sat down and wrote her a six-page letter. I spent days on wording it just right so that I wouldn't sound foolish. It was probably the silliest thing I ever did but I needed to do it. It was one of the few ways I found to express the tragedy I felt for her, and for myself.

The doctors still did not know what had caused the two stillbirths. I had always been healthy. The drug I was given to induce labor, however, really bloated me and remained in my system for quite some time. I continued to feel very weak and ill. One night, shortly before I was to begin shooting *Molly Brown*, Larry Weingarten and his wife, Dr. Jessie Marmorston, came to dinner. During the course of the meal, I was so overcome with fatigue that I had to go upstairs to lie down. Jessie came upstairs to my room and looked in on me.

She took my pulse and then my temperature. "I don't want you to go to rehearsals tomorrow. I want you to stay in bed and take some tests."

The next day she sent over a nurse, who put me through a series of tests. The following day the results came back: My whole system was so down that I had nothing—no estrogen, no vitamins, no minerals, no anything. Four doctors who went over the tests and analyzed them, without knowing the patient, guessed my biological age to be that of an ailing woman between sixty-five and seventy-five.

Following the death of the first child, and then the second, I had nothing left in my system. Somehow, through the years, by my third and fourth pregnancies, I hadn't rebuilt any of my strength. My body was allowing me to survive, but the child couldn't. That was finally the explanation for why the children died.

By the time the test results came back, I really thought I was going to die. I couldn't take four steps. I had already begun strenuous rehearsals for a strenuous film. Lillian and I had begun working on the part and we'd work until two or three in the morning.

Jessie Marmorston put me on shots every day. Estrogen, female hormones; all kinds of different things, for the next six months. She saved my life.

I went to work preparing for *Molly Brown* in late August. During the day there were rehearsals for the musical numbers. I'd be home in time for dinner with Harry and the children at six o'clock, then put the children to bed and drive up to Lillian's. I wanted to be completely prepared by the time we began shooting. I didn't expect to get any direction from Chuck Walters and I didn't.

Lillian was my director, with the exception of the choreography. She worked every line and every moment of the picture with me. When I went to work on the "Ain't Down Yet" number, Lillian went and got a pail and a broom from her kitchen. With the bucket on my head and the broom over my shoulder, I paraded around her living room, going through the song, line by line.

There was no detail in a performance that Lillian didn't attend to. When she worked, she could be brutally critical because she always had her eye on the finished product. Many a night I would leave exhausted, even at times with a raging headache, but it didn't matter: She had so much, and I learned.

In October, I packed up Carrie, Todd, and Dottie Wolfe, and we flew out to Telluride, Colorado, to begin shooting. The location was freezing cold, icy and muddy, exactly what the real Molly Brown came from.

From the beginning, Chuck Walters would approach my scenes voicing his doubts.

"Now this is a very difficult scene, Debbie; a very strong scene. I don't know how you're going to do it."

"I can do it, Chuck. Don't worry about it."

Every day it was the same dialogue.

I'd say, "Just roll the camera and I'll play it."

After four weeks in Colorado, we came home and he was starting to treat me a little nicer.

Then there was a big party scene with Mrs. McGraw when Molly goes next door to her house. She climbs through the hedges and says: "Howww-deee. My name is Mrs. J. J. Brown and I live next door," and we crash the society party.

Chuck said, "I don't know how you're going to do this scene, Debbie. It's the hardest one of all."

"Look, Chuck," I said, "Just don't worry about it. Obviously I know what I'm doing. Just roll the camera."

Then the rushes started coming in and we could see the film. One morning, Chuck came over to me on the set and gave me a kiss. "Well, you're right," he said, "you're not too short for the part."

"You're a very tough customer, Chuck; very hard to convince."

From then on, he worked very hard with me, helping me add to the role. But it took a long time to win him over.

We shot the bulk of the script first, with the musical numbers coming afterward. The schedule kept being cut back because MGM was shooting *Dr. Zhivago* in Europe and it was running way over budget. MGM kept cutting our budget to add on to *Zhivago*. Eventually they'd cut it by almost a million dollars. Some of the scenes, particularly the "sinking of the *Titanic*," were less effective than they should have been, because of the cuts.

Chuck was then worried about the dance numbers because the dancers had worked for two months on them and I'd had only two or three days to rehearse my part.

When it came time to shoot the "He's My Friend" number, Chuck came into my dressing room to talk to me about it.

"It's so tough, Debbie, I think we should cut it; I don't know how you can learn it."

"I have to learn it. I'm going to learn them all. It won't be a great musical if we don't have the numbers. Maybe you could shoot it in one take."

Chuck came up with the idea of filming that number with two cameras, something that had never been done in film. He shot the same way they filmed Spencer Tracy's great monologue in *Judgment at Nuremberg*, shooting it one time only.

It was a seven-minute number. All three of us collapsed at the end of it. Grover Dale played one boy and Gus Triconis, who later married Goldie Hawn, played the other. One of the boys fainted and had to be revived with ice. But we didn't have to do it again.

I never worked so hard physically on a movie as I did on *Molly Brown*. Harry would come to Colorado to visit for a few days at a time. My mother came up to stay and fell in love with the country. She and Daddy ended up building a small house on the mountainside, which they used for almost the next twenty years.

Right after *Molly Brown*, I was offered *Goodbye Charlie*, which Vincente Minnelli was directing with Walter Matthau and Tony Curtis over at Twentieth Century-Fox.

Lillian was against my taking the part from the beginning. Her objection was that it was a one-joke story—a man dies and comes back to the same situation, with the heart and mind of a man but reincarnated as a woman. It turned out Lillian was right, but I wanted to work with Vincente Minnelli, so I said yes.

Lillian and I worked like dogs preparing for the picture. One particularly memorable scene for me, eight or nine minutes long, took place in a kitchen. Tony Curtis came in and said good morning and then I took over, making his breakfast. Because there was so much to do in the scene, I didn't want to look at anything, as if it were really my kitchen. To prepare, I had my father build me an exact replica of the studio kitchen set in the basement of my house. I remembered my lessons from Bette Davis about props.

When it came to the actual shoot, I was already working with so many props, my hands full of the coffee and orange juice and eggs, that I didn't know what to do with the toast. Agnes Moorehead, meanwhile, was on another set at Fox making *Hush Hush Sweet Charlotte* with Davis. So I called her.

Agnes came down in a housedress, with a turban around her head, a little handkerchief, and stage blood all over her from the murder she'd just committed in the picture.

"Watch this rehearsal," I said.

She watched me go through the whole business, still not knowing what to do with the toast. After the scene, I walked over to Agnes and she said, "Put it in your mouth."

Well, of course. So I stuck it in my mouth and continued my dialogue with a mouthful of toast. It worked out wonderfully. Agnes saw what to do with a problem, just as Lillian did.

CHAPTER **33**

I FIRST KNEW AGNES during my early at MGM, but we didn't become friends until the making of *How the West Was Won*. When I first met her, I thought she was very serious.

Which was true. But she loved fun people. Getting to know her, I thought she was quite brilliant. She carried herself with great poise and dignity. Perfectly groomed, often in a dress or suit of lavender or pink (or gray with lavender or pink accessories), she had beautiful auburn hair.

She was a very ambitious actress. Acting was her life. In the 1950s she did her own one-woman show with which she toured America. It was ever a source of pain and disappointment to her that in Hollywood she was mainly cast in roles supporting women whose talent rarely matched hers. Nevertheless, she was totally dedicated and worked very hard on any role that was given her. Nominated eight or nine times for an Academy Award, she never won, which I know greatly disappointed her.

Agnes liked Harry a lot and he liked her. They had met on the set of *How the West Was Won*. They were the same age and shared a generational respect for courtesy and dignity. We were neighbors—she lived only a block and a half from us over on Roxbury Drive—so we often had her to dinner, sometimes two or three times a week.

Agnes had been married three times, but never successfully. Each marriage seemed to end with her losing more of her assets than she had in the previous one. Harry was always trying to find her a man who would protect her and love her, although he never succeeded.

Agnes was always taking time from her work to do something charitable, giving readings and entertaining. At one hospital for children, she met a set of twins, a girl and a boy named Sean. They were from a family who had more children than they could support. The little boy was in worse shape than the girl. His eyes were crossed and he was almost dying from malnutrition. Agnes asked if she could take the boy back to California, which was agreed upon.

Agnes was a strict disciplinarian. She expected that from everybody around her, including the little boy.

Sean reached the teen years in the mid-1960s, and like the other kids, he wanted to let his hair grow long. But Agnes said, "If you grow your hair long, I will not have you in the house."

That was a line he probably heard many times: "As long as you're in my house you'll behave as I say." So he ran away. He was gone about three weeks. When he came home—starving—he had long hair. Agnes said to him, "I'll take you in if you cut your hair, but otherwise no."

Sean cut his hair and stayed. But he was very unhappy about the rule and it created an ongoing duel of wills. She wasn't going to bend and he wasn't going to bend. Then she found beer cans in his room. Well. There was a big problem with that. Then one day she told me she found a dismantled gun in the room. By then he was about seventeen. She knew he was very angry at her, and finding a gun made her afraid of something drastic. She confronted him about it and he denied it.

"You do have a gun," she said, and she took him upstairs to the drawer where it was. With that, she told him to leave.

And Sean left. Never to come back.

I don't think Agnes meant to be unloving. In her heart of hearts I don't think she knew what she was doing. As a friend—and she had many—she was loyal and loving. She cared very much for other actors who were struggling or might have had personal difficulties. More than once, she took an actor in need into her home. None of us ever doubted her sincerity. She just had a thing about what she wanted her child to be and he had to *be* that whether he liked it or not. When he wasn't, he had to leave.

CHAPTER 34

FROM THE TIME I WAS an eleven- and twelve-year-old and went with my friend Jeanette and her parents to their beach house in Balboa, I'd always dreamed of having a house on the ocean. I was talking about this one day on the set of *Molly Brown* with Chuck Walters, who told me he had a lot—just a slice of land really, 35-feet wide and 120-feet deep on Carbon Beach in Malibu that he'd be willing to sell. Chuck already had a house at the beach. It also happened that I owned a Facel Vega that Chuck coveted. The car was worth about thirty thousand. So we made a deal: For the Facel Vega and thirty thousand cash, Chuck sold me the lot.

Late that spring, with the money I made from *Molly Brown*, we began construction on a $150,000 beach house with five bedrooms up and down. The children and I loved our beach house.

That fall, with *Goodbye Charlie* and *Molly Brown* completed, Harry and I decided on a European trip just to get away and rest. We flew to New York in the first week in October for a few days' shopping, staying at the Regency Hotel, with reservations to sail on the seventh on the *Queen Elizabeth*.

The night before embarking, I got a call from a columnist telling me that Elizabeth Taylor and Richard Burton were going to be on the same ship.

I put the phone down and told Harry. We'd planned to go by boat so that we could have peace and quiet. I knew what having Elizabeth and Burton on board would mean. "Look," I said to Harry, "let's either fly over or forget this trip."

"No," he said. "It's a big ship. We won't even see them."

I thought about it for a few minutes. "I suppose you're right," I said, agreeing to the original plan.

I hadn't seen or spoken to Elizabeth since right after Mike Todd died six years before. I had no desire or reason to, although I certainly didn't bear a grudge after what seemed like a lifetime. What concerned me was the press who were then following the Burtons around and reporting on them practically every time they went to the bathroom. I knew that if they saw Elizabeth and me together, all the old coals would be raked over again. I didn't want that.

Harry called Cunard and made arrangements for us to pre-board the ship the following morning in order to avoid "the traffic." We got up very early, had breakfast, and started for the lobby to wait for our car. We were traveling light—I had one hanging bag, a flat bag, and one for my makeup; Harry had two suitcases. The elevator opened and there was the lobby, jammed with at least ten bellhops, more than a hundred pieces of matching tapestry luggage, bird cages, animal cages; and a half dozen members of what was obviously the Taylor/Burton entourage, including Richard Hanley, whom I hadn't seen since the day I took the Wilding boys home from the Todd house on Schuyler Drive.

Outside the hotel there was a cadre of reporters checking out the half dozen station wagons being filled with the Taylor/Burton luggage.

"Hey, Debbie," one of them shouted, "did you know Taylor and Burton were going to be on the same ship as you and your husband?"

"Are we?" I answered blithely. "Isn't that ironic."

After we were aboard ship and in our suite, I was told by one of the stewards that there were at least ten reporters and photographers making the crossing also.

I looked at Harry. He looked at me. "I told you," I said. "They're not going to let us get away from this."

There were six suites in first class on the *Queen Elizabeth*. Harry and I had one, and it turned out, Elizabeth and Richard and their family and entourage of eleven had the other five. After Harry and I were unpacked, undressed, and relaxed, I decided to send Elizabeth a note saying, let's have cocktails, say hello, and get this over with. After all this time, what difference did it make?

Evidently Elizabeth was thinking similarly: Our notes crossed in the hallway. We made a date for that evening. Elizabeth and Richard were to come to our suite.

Harry was so excited he spent longer getting ready than I did. The Dom Pérignon was chilled and the caviar and canapés laid out on the ship's silver trays. A few minutes before nine the stateroom buzzer rang. Harry answered, and there they were—Elizabeth looking as radiant and gorgeous as ever and Richard looking handsome and very amused by the whole thing. I think Elizabeth was as nervous as I, in that we both really wanted to be friendly and forget about it. There was nervous giggling. Elizabeth said, "Well, isn't this the silliest?" And I said, "It's just totally ridiculous." Harry poured the Dom Pérignon. Elizabeth held up her glass of champagne and said, "Just look how you lucked out and how I lucked out! Who the hell cares about Eddie?"

We all cracked up, drank to that one, and that's all anyone ever said about Eddie. I could see Richard was having a grand time with the situation, watching us two girls meeting again after all those years and all that publicity. He had a wonderful, dry, cryptic way, as the English often do. No one was funnier and more tongue-in-cheek than Richard Burton.

We talked about the press and how we were going to get rid of them. Elizabeth suggested that we take care of it by all having dinner together—in the dining room.

So when the Dom Pérignon was finished, the four of us went down to eat.

We walked into the dining room, which was jammed by that time, everyone in the middle of their meal, and a hush went about the room. Forks and spoons stopped in midair. Nobody spoke a word. Across the room a potted palm was literally moving across the floor, barely disguising a photographer who was not supposed to be there. Reporters were milling about—also off limits—while other photographers were maneuvering behind post and pillar, cameras coming out from underneath tables, clicking away. The four of us stood there, like stately heads, staring them all down until the maître d' ushered us to our table. By that time we were all feeling no pain and laughing at Richard's witty asides.

We ordered. Elizabeth's favorite at that time was pasta and boiled potatoes; a diet she wasn't on. And champagne for all. People were standing up to get a look, commenting to each other on what they were seeing. Halfway through dinner, Elizabeth said, "You know, I have to go to the ladies' room and I don't dare go by myself."

"Oh, Elizabeth, I'll go with you," I said.

So we got up and left the table, and with that, twenty-five other women got up and followed us. They all tried to walk into the powder room with us. There was a line halfway across the lobby.

I said to Elizabeth, "You go first and I'll hold your bag."

Elizabeth went into the bathroom and while I was waiting outside the door, one woman tapped me on the shoulder, and said in a loud whisper: "How can you even talk to that woman?!"

Behind her another woman spoke up: "Yeah, we've never forgiven her and we never will!"

Behind the second woman a third woman piped up: "Do you think she'd sign my autograph book?"

"Oh, she's really very nice," I said. "And she has a divine husband."

Just then Elizabeth came out. I gave her her purse and mine to hold, and I went in. I never knew what they said to her.

We all disembarked at Southampton, just in time to see what a field day the international press was having with our shipboard "reunion." Elizabeth and Richard, of course, went on to fascinate and amuse the paparazzi and reporters who'd taken up permanent residence outside their various doorsteps across the world. Harry and I had ten peaceful, lovely days in France and Italy and then a relaxing, far quieter sail back to the United States on the S.S. *France.*

I was happy for Elizabeth. More than five years had passed since Eddie left me for her. It was like another lifetime. Both she and I found real happiness in our lives away from him. The thought gave me just a little pleasure too.

I'd gone from being a girl who never really thought about what she wanted from life to a woman in her thirties who *had* what she wanted. For the first time, I actually felt very attractive. I had a wise and devoted husband, and two beautiful children to whom he was a loving, patient father. I was earning a million dollars a year. We were living a fascinating social life, and we lacked for nothing. In the early days of television, MGM had a slogan it used in all of its advertising: "Movies are better than ever." This was one of those movies. Only this one was going to play forever.

CHAPTER **35**

By 1964, the Thalians had raised their first million toward the building of a free clinic at Cedars-Sinai Hospital. Probably because of it, that December, I was one of twelve women honored by the *Los Angeles Times* as "Women of the Year." I was truly thrilled and proud to have been recognized, alongside successful businesswomen, educators, doctors, and philanthropists. Los Angeles was really my hometown. It was local girl makes good.

Harry and I had no real problems in our life except, on rare occasions, Marie, who had been Harry's second and fourth wives. Harry said very little about her, although I knew she could be a very volatile woman.

Harry felt he had been manipulated into the second marriage. They had been divorced for years. One day they ran into each other in Paris and spent the night together. Two or three months later, she announced that she was with child—Harry's child, she said.

Harry didn't believe her. *After one night?!* I could believe her of course; I had Todd. But Marie had never got pregnant during their first marriage—both their children, Dede and Harrison (Bo), had been adopted. Furthermore, Harry knew that there always were other men in her life.

Marie insisted: Harry was the father. Finally, to give the baby a name, they married for the second time. Tina Marie Karl was born a few months later, a month before Carrie.

In the second divorce, Marie received a bigger alimony—$50,000 a year for herself, whether she married or not, as well as child support— $7,000 a year for each of the three children, plus medical expenses. Despite the fact that she still worked an act in clubs, including Vegas, Harry's contribution was never enough. And she could make Harry's life miserable when he balked at her demands. She made it very difficult for him to see the children. They were taught to hate their father. As a result, he never did see them. Carrie and Todd became his children.

Our only contact with her was over the phone or through her lawyer. Harrison, who went to a military academy in nearby Westwood, came around about once a month for dinner. Harrison was a handsome boy, even more handsome in his school uniform. Dede, however, never came to the house; and I had never laid eyes on Tina.

Then, on the afternoon of Christmas Eve, 1964, Marie showed up at the door, unexpected and unannounced, with eight-year-old Tina in tow. I was home alone.

Her hair in rollers covered by a scarf, and looking frumpy, Marie was still beautiful. She had kept her famous figure, whence came the name "The Body." But there was puffiness around her eyes, her lipstick was a little too thick, her mascara was working overtime. The edges had begun to fray.

I tried to be really nice. We'd known each other long before I met Harry. She was cordial with me, but nervous, talking a mile a minute. We sat in the living room—a very beautiful room—all done in off-white carpet, with soft apricot pillows and antiques. One wall was huge sliding glass doors overlooking the terrace, the pools, and the golf course in the distance. There was an oversized Christmas tree that I had decorated myself, with Rudy's help, hanging every light, surrounded by hundreds of Christmas gifts that overflowed out into the entrance hallway. It was an expensive home and it looked it.

Christmas was very special at our house. After those childhood years in Burbank with a neighbor's shrub for a tree, once I could afford it, I went all out. I wanted my children to have something magical and unforgettable.

The little girl sat on the edge of her mother's chair, never leaving her side, very withdrawn, hanging her head, eyes blinking continually as if she had a nervous tic. Unlike her mother, she was not attractive. Occasionally she'd peer out from under her eyebrows to sneak a look around the room, sometimes stealing a glance at me—her Daddy's wife. I was fascinated to see that Harry's child—the child he claimed wasn't his—looked just like him.

I had no idea why Marie had come unless it was to complain that Harry should give Tina more allowance per week. I told her that Eddie never sent me any money and yet I gave the children an allowance of fifty cents a week. So, since Harry sent her plenty of money, why couldn't she?

"Well, I'm not going to," she said. "If you're a fool, you're a fool. I want him to come and hand it to her."

"A man who doesn't live with his children is not going to come every week and hand a child fifty cents, Marie."

They stayed a couple of hours, Marie and I just chatting about this and that. Then, just as suddenly as she came, she had to leave, and they left.

When Harry came home and I told him Marie had been there, he was upset that I had let her in.

"I can't believe she behaved herself!" he said. "You should never have let her in." He was obviously upset. "Now she'll be back—and just like the last time: when you least expect it."

That didn't matter to me. I didn't have anything against Marie. I just wanted to make the situation easier for Harry. She did call a few times after that visit, but as it would happen, I never would see Marie again.

CHAPTER 36

THE UNSINKABLE MOLLY BROWN was the holiday show at Radio City Music Hall in New York, and in its ten-week run, established record grosses for the famous showcase theater. The film brought me an Academy Award nomination for Best Actress in 1965 and overnight I was the number-two box-office draw in the world for that year. I put my hands and feet in the wet cement outside Grauman's Chinese in Hollywood, and at Cape Canaveral, Florida, Gus Grissom and John Young lifted off to outer space for the third manned space flight ever in a capsule christened *The Molly Brown*. I was playing the Eden Roc in Miami when the sensational space flight occurred. After their triumphal return to earth—in those days astronauts were the national heroes—Grissom and Young and their wives came down to Miami as my guests to see the show. My life was so rich and rewarding; every new day was exciting.

I got to know Mary Pickford through the Thalians, when she and Buddy Rogers were the grand marshals for a big circus party we staged.

She called me up and asked in that tiny, quiet, little-girl voice, "Debbie, this is Mary. Should I wear my emeralds or my rubies?"

Not the dress; the jewelry. She dressed around her jewelry. "Wear your emeralds," I said.

"Oh, good; yes. And I'll wear my white dress. That'll be pretty, won't it, Debbie?"

"Yes, Mary, you'll look beautiful."

"Oh, do you think so, Debbie?" she asked, like a child uncertain.

And she did look beautiful. She and Buddy looked divine riding in a carriage all around the Shrine Auditorium where the Ringling Brothers circus was appearing. It was a party of stars, but little Mary in her emeralds and white dress, the first movie star that ever was, was the thrill of the evening, and she basked in all her glory.

By then, Mary had already withdrawn from public life. Sometimes

I'd go up to Pickfair to pay a visit. One day the butler asked me if I'd speak to her over the intercom.

"Debbie, how are you, dear?"

"I'm fine, thank you, Mary. How are you?"

"Ooh, it was so sweet of you to come and see me, but I don't look right. I can't fix myself," said the tiny voice over the wire.

"I understand, Mary. When I'm alone in the house, I can look in a way that I'd never let anybody see."

"Oh, thank you, Debbie."

We'd have our little chat, me on the intercom in the entrance hall of this great house full of glamorous memories; its mistress exiled to her grand but solitary boudoir, her house phone the only contact with the outside world.

She had a barn on the property where she'd stored all of her costumes and memorabilia as well as much of Douglas Fairbanks's and some of Chaplin's. Buddy Rogers would let me look. After her death it was all auctioned. I bought a number of things including about thirty of her dresses, a wig of her little blond curls, her makeup kit, as well as Douglas Fairbanks's "Zorro" costume, hat, and sword.

Buddy Rogers was very good to Mary, but it must have been lonely for him too. He traveled a lot for charity, and did his act. Buddy protected his wife from the clamoring photographers who were just curious to know what America's Sweetheart looked like in her eighth decade. He dispensed their names jointly with goodwill on many charities, and opened their famous house to fund-raising events, while Mary withdrew into the darkness.

CHAPTER **37**

AFTER THE BOX-OFFICE SUCCESS of *Molly Brown*, I was offered a lot of pictures. I was always conscious of trying to keep my work as close to home as possible. I could take Carrie and Todd with me when I went on the road with the act. I could rent an apartment or a house in Las Vegas and we'd still have a family life. A film on location is not always as accommodating, and as the children were beginning to grow up, I wanted to be there the way my mother was for me and my brother.

I chose *The Singing Nun*, about Sister Sourire, the songwriter/ singer who became a recording star while belonging to a Belgian convent, because it gave me a chance to work with Greer Garson and with Agnes again.

Hayes Goetz, my producer, even agreed to give me Wednesday afternoons off so that I could be the leader of Carrie's Girl Scout troop. I felt it was instilling a sense of tradition and stability that I got as a kid, although I'm not sure what Carrie felt. She was growing up in a very different world from the one I grew up in. That was reason enough, I thought, for me to be there. Days when shooting schedules didn't allow me time to change out of my costume, I'd show up in the full nun's habit. The kids loved it but there were a couple of other mothers who didn't recognize me and thought I was either a real nun or a nut.

With Harry, I had succeeded in giving Carrie and Todd a father and giving them a sense of solid family we wouldn't have had if I were on my own. Also, my mother and father still lived in the little house in Burbank and the children saw them all the time. Harry also had a daughter, Judy, from his first marriage, whom we saw quite a bit. Judy was only a few years younger than I, and more like a friend than a stepdaughter. And then there was Mama Karl.

Rose Karl was an angel, a simple woman who never took on any of the affectations of the wealth her husband accumulated in their lifetime. She remained in the same little bungalow they had shared on Orlando Street in West Hollywood, where Harry and his sister were brought up. After Pincus Karl died, Rose was so lonely.

After living alone for a few years, one day she drove her Cadillac—the company Cadillac—up to Harry's office, put the keys on the desk, and said, "I don't want to drive anymore or live at the house where I'm lonely."

"What do you want, Mama?" Harry asked.

"I want to go back and live at the hotel where I went on the honeymoon with your father."

Harry told me about it that night when he came home from the office. I thought that was sweet, and offered to take Mama Karl to the hotel—called the Cadillac—which was on the beach down in Venice.

The next day I drove her down to visit the hotel. I took one look at the place and thought she'd lost her marbles. A four-story stucco building, paint peeling and faded, it looked like an old seaside apartment house. It was not plush.

We walked into this building with the carpets fraying and mismatched, a beat-up old piano, some wooden chairs, and a couple of worn leather sofas. There was a TV chained to the wall—because it was a pretty rough neighborhood in those days.

The place was owned by Mr. Gross, a man about Mama's age, and the clientele were all older, retired people. He showed us a little apartment for Mama. The elevator would take only two people at a time. It stopped with a lurch and a loud, grating noise, on the top floor. We got out into a dark, narrow hallway lighted by a naked bulb dangling from the ceiling. It smelled dank and damp because it was right on the beach.

Mr. Gross led us down the passage, its paint peeling, to an apartment that faced the water. He opened the door, which filled up half the living room. He opened another door, which took up half the bedroom. The rent was $125 a month. Mama loved it. She had one of the few apartments with a private bath.

Her kitchen was the little utility kind—in a closet. But it made her think of those joyous early days with Pincus Karl; she wanted it.

It needed a little work, to say the least. She told me she could spend $700 putting it into shape. She just picked out the carpet and then said: "You do it." Mother made drapes for her. Dad fixed the radiator and built a cover for it. We replaced all the doors inside the apartment as well as her little stove and refrigerator. Because she was on the top floor, the roof leaked right into her apartment. So we reroofed the hotel. The final cost ran into the thousands, but I told Mama it only cost the $700 she felt she could spend.

The Cadillac Hotel turned out to be a haven for Mama and many other people. Mr. Gross was like a Jewish saint. He never raised the rent. Every night he served coffee and snacks. Some people would play pinochle while one of the men would play the piano and sing for the group. Mr. Gross created a family where everyone looked after each other. If they were feeling ill, he'd take their temperature. If they needed to see a doctor, he'd drive them.

Mama Karl became especially fond of Mr. Gross and also another older man named Phil. Phil had a face so ugly it was beautiful. He had only two teeth and only one hand. Once a week I'd have a driver go down to the beach and bring the three up to Greenway for dinner. They'd spend every holiday—Yom Kippur, Thanksgiving, Christmas— with us. Once, when I was playing the Cocoanut Grove, we hired buses and brought everybody in the hotel down as Mama's guests—eighty of them. Some people came in wheelchairs and a couple of them had oxygen tanks. Several ordered two dinners each and put the second one in their purse to take home. Everybody got smashed and had a ball.

After that, we gave a birthday party every October 15 at the Hillcrest Country Club for Mama Karl and for my father. She'd invite all her friends from the Cadillac Hotel and Daddy would invite his pals from the railroad and from Burbank. We'd have a hundred people, a band, a buffet, and a huge cake. Everyone had a wonderful time.

CHAPTER 38

ON THE MORNING OF October 22, the day after Carrie's ninth birthday, a friend called to tell me the news they'd just heard on the radio: Marie McDonald was found dead in her bedroom. She was forty-three.

The first thing I thought to myself was to get the children and bring them home so I drove right over to Hidden Hills in the Valley.

The house was surrounded by reporters, police cars, curious neighbors, and a hearse. It looked as if there was death inside. The sheriff was questioning Marie's husband, Don Taylor, in the bedroom, no more than eight feet away from where the body, covered with a sheet, lay on the floor.

The room was a mess. Beside her unmade bed was an end cabinet full of prescription drugs, syringes, needles, and assorted paraphernalia. Marie, it turned out, was addicted to Demerol. So was her husband. Was he the one who shot her up? The sheriff's men were wanting to know. Inferences of murder were in the air.

I found the three children at the table in the kitchen, as if someone had told them to sit there and wait. I told them to get their things, that they were coming home with me. One of the cops told me I couldn't take them; that they were witnesses to the death. I knew a little about juvenile law from when I made *Susan Slept Here.*

"You can't hold them. They're juveniles," I informed him. "I'm taking them home to their father's house."

As soon as we were in the car, I told them not to worry, that they would have a good home with their father and me.

Tina asked if she could call me "Mother."

"That's all right," I said, considering the horrendous situation she was in. "I will be your mother from now on."

I really knew nothing about Harry's children, about what I was taking on. We never knew until Bo came to live with us that his mother used to beat the boy, digging her diamond ring into his back so deeply that it scarred.

Dede, who was sixteen and in private school, didn't want to come with me. Her mother had drummed it into her head that her father was hateful. Until she went away to school, Dede had been, from a very early age, the nurse/maid for Marie. Until Tina was sent away to school, Dede was also nurse and mother to her.

The children had been living in a house of violence. Marie and her husband fought all the time, in drugged, drunken brawls. There was a plate-glass window in the master bedroom that had been broken and replaced a dozen times because Marie had flung something through it in a fit of anger. Once during an argument she cut herself on the shards of glass, splattering the furniture and wiping the walls with her blood, almost bleeding to death before the paramedics got there to save her.

These three children were being rescued from that—a madhouse of total abuse and neglect—to a house where a voice was never raised except in laughter or a song.

As soon as we got back to Greenway that afternoon, I called Harry, who was in London on a business trip.

"Well," I said, "that's that. You took my children; I'll take yours."

"I don't want them," he shot back.

"What?"

"Who said they're mine; they're not mine."

"They're not your children?" I asked. "You didn't sign the papers to adopt them? Two adopted children and one of your own blood?!"

"How do I know she's mine?" he snapped.

"What are you talking about, Harry?" I was shocked. It was his daughter. She looked like him!

He groaned. "Whatever you do, Debbie, I don't want them in our home."

"Then where are they supposed to go, Harry? They're all underage."

"Look, Debbie, I'm very happy with you and the children and I don't want anything to change it. That will change it completely. Put 'em in a school. I don't want them there."

I couldn't listen to Harry on this one. He just didn't want his serene life interrupted.

Marie, it turned out, had died because there was air in the needle that injected her. Her husband was facing murder charges. Two days later, in the same house, he gave himself an overdose and died. That was the end of that chapter; there was no turning back for anybody.

As big as the Greenway house was, it really couldn't accommodate three more children. Despite its size, there were only three bedrooms—

the master suite and Carrie's and Todd's. I emptied out the larger of the maid's rooms off the kitchen and placed Tina in there. Bo would sleep in Harry's sitting room, and I put Dede on a daybed in the living room.

The crowd was temporary. Both Dede and Bo went back to boarding school, which Dede especially preferred. Tina was another story.

She was a sad, desolate child, clinging like an animal, always longing to be loved yet endlessly demanding. Always nervous, perhaps the most abused and neglected of Harry and Marie's children, she was tragic.

My reaction was to want her and love her and make her well. I felt I could give her a stable home and the love she hadn't had; I could do that for all of Harry's children.

Coincidentally, and fortunately, Marie had taken her children to the same pediatrician as I—Dr. Wile. Marie, being a drug addict, had given birth to an addicted baby—Tina. The first six months of her life, Tina had remained in the hospital in withdrawal, and under lighting conditions that impaired her sight—hence the blinking and twitching. When she went home, it was to a mother who mostly drank, shot up, and partied all night and slept all day. Marie's bedroom was off limits to the children. Her actual presence was often made known only by her screaming, glass-shattering arguments and fistfights with boyfriends.

"You'll always have a problem with her," the doctor said to me about Tina. He told me he had other children who were born addicts, all of whom showed similar, difficult traits—particularly nervousness and agitated personalities.

I disagreed. I'm so stubborn I think I can save anybody. Besides, at the time I had been very active in the emotionally disturbed children's program at the state hospital in Camarillo, and through the Thalians I was around children with emotional problems. I thought a lot of patience, effort, and love could cure Tina. To me the most important factor was love.

From the moment I brought her home, she wouldn't leave my side. She wanted to be with me exclusively. This would leave time for nobody else, and I had two children who were quite used to their mother's attention.

If anybody came to see me, she'd act as an animal would. We were having company one night for dinner. Just before they were to arrive, Tina left a puddle in the foyer, in front of the door. I was shocked and upset by the desperate behavior, but she couldn't help it; she just panicked as would a frightened animal.

I cleaned up and took her to her room and explained that company was coming. "That doesn't mean we are going to leave you. We're going to be right in the house." She calmed down for a moment.

I could see it wasn't going to be easy. Whenever anyone else was getting my attention—the other children, Harry, business or dinner guests—Tina wanted it. When we had company, she wanted me to help her with her homework. If I didn't help her, she wouldn't do it. When I left the house without her, she'd get hysterical.

Not having been raised with Carrie and Todd, she had nothing in common with them. They would play together for a while but they'd always get into a fight. Tina didn't know how to play. It was like taking a newborn puppy and trying to teach it in a very short period of time what had gone untaught for nine years.

Her reaction to the situation was to get attention to keep attention. She'd be sick, throw up, fight, cry. When I started shooting *The Singing Nun*, I took her on the set with me every day.

I had always been interested in disturbed children. I knew from experience that Tina was definitely a disturbed child. The physical and behavioral symptoms were obvious. Whatever light there was in her life came from her older sister, Dede, who was her surrogate mother.

As a family, we ate together every night at six. Tina was not used to this. She was nervous and fidgety in her chair. The first time I gave her a salad with bacon bits on it, she chewed on them for a moment, and then without fanfare, sprayed her mouthful all over the table.

Everybody stopped eating and gawked. My patience and compassion were being tested, as they would be hundreds of times to come.

"You mustn't spit your food on the table, Tina."

"I don't like this," she whined.

Harry, who said nothing, was visibly irritated.

"That's all right," I said to him. "She doesn't like bacon bits. We didn't know that."

The next time the other children had a salad with bacon bits and Tina had one without.

"How come they're having bacon?" the child protested.

"Because you said you didn't want it, Tina."

"Well, I want it now!" she demanded.

The next time she was given bacon bits. Again she spewed them all over the table in front of herself.

No matter what I did, it was going to be wrong. So I had to punish her by making her eat alone in her room.

The next day I'd bring her to the table with the family and it would start all over again.

Harry said nothing until he asked if he could have his dinner up-stairs on a tray. The table had gone from peaceful to the fights of all time. After a while my children didn't want to eat with her either. So she and I ate alone in her room many, many nights, for months and months.

"You love them more than me." It was always that. No matter what I did, I was always going to have to prove my love.

"That's not true, Tina," I would say. "But you must try a little harder to join in."

Eventually Tina began to learn manners at dinner. It was going to be one step at a time.

At times, it was a difficult adjustment for all of us. If she didn't want to go to bed, or to do her homework, or to finish a meal, she'd try to run from the house to get away. It was a good thing I was in great physical shape for I'd often have to chase her, grab her, and hold her to the ground until she stopped screaming.

Day after day after day; week after week, month after month after year after year.

Before long, it became a competition with Carrie. Whatever Carrie wanted, Tina wanted too. If Carrie learned a certain piece on the piano, Tina would learn it too. She would take some favorite thing of Carrie's and when I found it in her room, she would deny doing it. It was as if she did it only so that she would be caught, always to get the attention.

Of course, she naturally wanted her father's love. She'd always wanted to have her daddy. Then when she came to live with her daddy, he turned her away. Carrie and Todd would climb up in his lap. Tina would go over to him, reach her arms up, and Harry would ignore her. I would pick her up and put her in his lap. He'd let her sit there for a minute or two, and then he'd move his knees as if to let her down.

After the children had gone to sleep, I'd talk to him about it. But it was the same old story: he didn't believe she was his daughter and he didn't want her. It was heartbreaking to watch, but he wouldn't budge.

And, like her father, Tina wouldn't budge either. She had been raised in a home where there was a lot of hitting. Her stepfather Don once in a fit of temper picked up the pet dog and choked it to death in front of her horrified eyes. So for the first two years she was with me, I would hug her and kiss her, hold her and rock her except in extreme situations, in which case I would give her an old-fashioned spanking. Whatever I had to give, she wanted; and then she wanted more.

She and Harrison would fight—fistfighting. She would taunt him until he slugged her. Of course he was twice her age and twice her size. I couldn't physically stop him. The only thing I could do was reprimand him.

But once in a fury, Tina would never back off anyway. It was as if she went into another personality. One day during a screaming argument, she bit him on the shoulder, hard enough to draw blood. Outraged from the pain, Harrison went after her. Pandemonium set in.

When I realized what had happened, I was outraged too. It seemed as if there was no end to this arguing.

Instinctively, I grabbed her by the arm and bit her. Hard. She screamed and cried hysterically. I had become Nurse Ratchett in *Cuckoo's Nest*. Marie's madhouse was my madhouse and now we were all confined.

But my reaction worked. I could talk to her through the tears and get through to her. She understood the violent discipline far better than I did.

She and Harrison would still occasionally fight, but she never bit again.

Harry was no help. Everyone I knew, even the doctors, advised me to put her in a clinic. "You can't help her," they said. "It's not your problem."

But I still believed I could. I thought she could get better. If she stayed at home, in a real home; if she had a center, we'd be able to overcome. I thought it was that simple.

CHAPTER 39

ALL OF THIS UPHEAVAL was taking its toll on our marriage. My husband now preferred taking his meals alone and that made a difference, however subtle. It seemed that I was over here in the middle of the children's lives; and he was over there, with his Scotch on the rocks and his television—which my father had wired for earphones so that nothing could disturb Harry.

I wasn't completely left out. We still went to premieres and parties together, and for weekends in Palm Springs. He spent as much time with me as he could whenever I worked out of town.

I always made a point of having his cocktail ready when he came home at night. Now I would join him and have one too. That had become our time together. To talk about our day. But not the children. He didn't want to know about them.

After I lost the second child, the doctor advised that it would be dangerous for me to get pregnant again. That frightened Harry. The first thing he did was have a vasectomy.

He also withdrew mentally. There was less intimacy. In the beginning, I attributed it to the tragedy of our loss as well as Harry's fear for my life.

About the time his children came to live with us, however, his sexual attraction to me was nil; gone. I thought of it as something that was changing, something that was temporary. There were kisses on the cheek, a peck on the lips, but there were no longer sexual intimacies— an embrace, a caress.

Of course, after several years of marriage, intimate sexual habits naturally change. I knew that. So I tried not to notice. I pushed down the loneliness—and my confusion—by submerging myself in the children and their problems—which were now monumental—and my work and anything else I could do to keep the blinders on.

In early 1966, Norman Lear called me about a role in a picture he had written and was directing, which Bud Yorkin was producing, called

Divorce American Style. I'd heard about it and knew there was a part that was not only right for me but also something more akin to who I was—a married American housewife in her mid-thirties whose marriage is threatened. Dramatically it was a good film for me.

Norman was a tough man to do business with at the start. He knew I wanted it.

"You know, Debbie, I'm not sure you're up to the part," he very bluntly said to me over the phone one day. That was Norman's way of negotiating: We want you but are you worth the money?

"You know," he said, "there are other actresses who could do the part who are interested," he continued.

"Then why are you even talking to me?" I asked.

"Well . . . You could be good . . . and we'd like your name . . . if we can get it at the right price."

So that was it. He wanted me but he didn't want to pay the going price for an actress who'd been nominated the year before. He got me.

I loved working with that cast. It was a chance to work with Van Johnson, who was a big star when I first went to MGM. And Jason Robards, and Dick Van Dyke.

Going to work was an enormous relief. It felt like being let out of school. Jason Robards was leasing a house out at the beach in Malibu. On Friday nights, Dick Van Dyke and I would take him home in my car, with my guard Zink driving.

Both Jason and Dick were drinking in those days. I'd have my nightly cocktail with Harry, but that was about it. But we'd get to the house, and Jason would ask us all in for one drink. Once inside, he'd put a record on the phonograph and the entertainment began. Jason is a frustrated musical-comedy star. He'd put on the Broadway cast album of *Mame*, don a straw hat, and with his cane, dance all over the house singing all the songs. He was such fun.

Dick and Jason reminded me of the times with Clifton Webb and Noel Coward. Everything they did was clever and witty. By now we were all drinking.

By two or three in the morning, the party would wind down. Jason would offer us a place to sleep. We'd thank him and decline; then, after a rowdy round of good-nights, Zink would drive me and Dick back to Beverly Hills.

We finished shooting at the end of June. That summer I took the children to the beach. Harry came down maybe three times.

When the summer was over, I decided it might be good for just the two of us to get away by ourselves and get reacquainted, so to speak. I chose Acapulco because it had always been a very romantic place to me. We booked a suite for three weeks at the Acapulco Towers.

I never liked the idea of being away from the children for any length of time, but I felt Harry and I needed time alone together.

Mother and Daddy moved in to take care of the children. They didn't know then that there was trouble. No one knew because I told no one.

One early evening in Acapulco, I had just got out of the shower and was about to dress for dinner. Harry was sitting out on the terrace having his cocktail. There was a beautiful sunset on the horizon with the lights in the hills surrounding the bay beginning to twinkle in the dusk.

The time was right to make a move. I'd never done this sort of thing before. I took off my robe, threw it on the bed, and—stark naked—I sauntered out onto the balcony and sat down on Harry's lap.

He put his arm around my waist and looked up at me with a smile. "Have a drink, baby; they're wonderful," he said.

I took a sip of his drink, and sat back in his arms.

And that was it. Nothing else. He said nothing and he did nothing. I sat there for several moments, feeling more self-conscious by the second. Several lifetimes passed by. I never looked better in my life and I loved him. And he loved me, so why wouldn't it happen?

But it didn't. I found it fascinating that he could do just that—an arm around my waist, and nothing more.

Finally I got up—nothing was said—and I went back into the room to get dressed. Was I humiliated? Embarrassed? Hurt? Angry? I didn't know. I only knew another question mark had been added.

The next day, I asked him why he hadn't made love to me in almost two years?

He told me he had an infection.

"An infection?"

"Yeah, you know, a kind of infection men get."

Several years before, when we were first married, one of Harry's good friends, whom we'll call Sam, had a mistress who was a famous actress. Sam's wife, Mabel, never seemed to go anywhere with him. She was always "home in bed with a migraine." I asked Harry one night why she was ill all the time.

"Well, you know he isn't able to really be with her," Harry explained. "They've been married a long time and he's not really attracted to her anymore."

"But that's dreadful, Harry. You mean they never make love?"

"Uh-huh," Harry nodded.

"How does he get away with it?" I asked.

"Well, he tells her he has this 'infection.'"

So when Harry Karl told me he had an "infection" that day in Acapulco, I looked at him blankly and asked, "So what am I? Another Mabel?"

"Of course not, Debbie."

He wouldn't discuss it any further.

That's when I started having insomnia and migraine headaches too. Something was very wrong. Any woman knows, if her husband doesn't touch her for more than six months, one year, two years, three years, there's a definite problem.

I didn't really think it was another woman. Harry was always home at six o'clock every night. He went to the office, to the Friars Club, and home. I could always get him on the phone. When would he be seeing "her"?

"I thought of private detectives. I thought of a marriage counselor. But all of that meant letting someone else in on the problem and I didn't want to do that.

Besides, the real failure, I felt, had been—once again was—me. I had failed my husband, somehow. I didn't know how, but I knew I must have; and I did not know what to do about that.

It was completely over after that. I was never touched, ever again. Except in bed, watching television, he would hold my hand.

Ironically, we started to spend a great deal of time in the bedroom. We'd eat dinner in bed, watch TV. The children were invited in and soon they even moved in. Todd adopted the couch on one side of the room and Carrie and Tina slept on the love seat at the foot of the bed. When they had friends over, they camped out in the bedroom too! Harry didn't mind. Their presence helped us avoid any discussion.

I wanted to avoid any confrontation. That allowed me the privilege of thinking maybe things would just get better. I was trying to figure things out. But all that came up was this overwhelming feeling of rejection. *For the second time!*

Sometimes I would get so mad, I didn't want to talk to him. Everything was a question.

It wasn't really so much the sex—or lack thereof. I'd married a man who, I thought, would be all comforting, a best friend; the wise old owl. I don't believe that love has to be all sexuality. I think of it as respect and friendship. Comfort and sharing—that's what was major to me.

However, the reality was, I was a young woman in my thirties. I needed to be touched and kissed. I'm not saying all the time, but certainly occasionally. When there was nothing, I had to question that too.

Many nights I just didn't want to go to bed for fear he'd wake up and I would have to talk to him. People would come to dinner and I would beg them not to leave. I ran an open house, saying please stay; please stay. Helplessly, desperately seeking companionship.

That's when I started to drink. I'd put the children to bed. Then I'd come downstairs and mix myself a vodka and ginger ale. Nice and sweet to cover up the taste of liquor.

Rudy Render, my devoted friend, would stay night after night till one and two in the morning—for years—just to keep me company. Rudy and I would sing and play and have a good time. Some nights I would get in the car and drive up to visit Agnes or Lillian. I would have been lost without those three friends. I don't want to give the wrong impression: I wasn't morose all the time. I always put on a good front.

CHAPTER 40

AFTER *Divorce American Style* there were no film offers, but I hardly noticed. My career was busier than ever. I had six months of club dates in Las Vegas, Lake Tahoe, and Reno, as well as Eden Roc in Miami, along with a contract for two television specials for ABC.

The Las Vegas Riviera booked me for the first time for six weeks over the Christmas and New Year's holidays, which are traditionally a slow time in the casino business. At $80,000 a week, they were banking on my bringing in business. The whole family could spend the holidays together in Las Vegas.

That Christmas I wanted to buy cars for my brother and for Rudy. They were going to cost about $13,000 in total. One early afternoon, I went to the cage in the hotel and asked if I could have the cash and debit it to my salary.

"I'm sorry, Miss Reynolds, but I am not authorized to give you credit," the man in the cage politely told me. I was quite surprised. They had always advanced me cash in the past.

"Is there a new policy?" I asked. "I'm sure it's all right."

"No, ma'am. It's just that Mr. Karl has already exceeded your salary in the casino."

"Oh," I said, "well, thank you. I'm sorry to bother you. I'll just have to get it from my husband, I guess," and I walked away.

I wasn't surprised that Harry used my salary to gamble because he had done that in the past, although never all of it—which in this case was almost half a million dollars. It did annoy me that he had done that, considering that I still had three weeks left on the engagement, with all the salaries of the company and the musicians to pay.

Later that afternoon, I asked him about it. He was annoyed too.

"I'm sorry, Debbie," Harry said. "It was a mistake for me to go against your salary, but they shouldn't have done that! They knew they could have asked me for it," he said, adding that he would take care of everything. In those days I had a small checking account, but my salaries always went to the office. Harry had a secretary, Ida, who paid all the bills. The cars were purchased; the company was paid and I forgot about it.

After Vegas, we went to the Continental Room in Houston. Harry, who had flown back to California to look after his own business, surprised me at the opening-night show with *forty* dozen red and yellow roses sent to the stage. From Houston we flew to Miami for a two-week booking.

From Florida we flew to New York to publicize *Divorce American Style,* and then returned to California. I had five weeks off and then did the act for the first time at Harrah's in Lake Tahoe. That was the beginning of a long, long friendship with Harrah's. Twenty-seven years later, Holmes Hendrickson and Doug Bushhausen are still booking me into Tahoe and Reno.

In the first five months of 1967, I spent almost fourteen weeks on the road doing my act.

By now I was actually thinking about retiring from films—or doing maybe a picture a year. I could always do the act and have the rest of the time for my family.

CHAPTER 41

FOR MY THIRTY-FIFTH BIRTHDAY Harry gave me a bracelet of thirty-six diamonds from Cartier. It was beautiful, but I needed a different kind of gift—a kiss, or even a touch of the hand.

There was genuine affection in his gifts. I didn't doubt that. However, although diamonds may be forever, it would have been more meaningful and reassuring if he'd made love to me. But I didn't expect it. The scene was set, so I suppose I wasn't disappointed.

In early June, we were invited by President and Mrs. Johnson to a state dinner at the White House for the British Prime Minister Harold Wilson and Mrs. Wilson. Janis Paige, (who came with her husband, songwriter Ray Gilbert) and I were the only actors represented at the occasion. I've met every president since Truman and I've been invited to dine at state dinners several times, but it's not something you ever take for granted.

Meanwhile back at Greenway, Dede, age seventeen, who was graduating from high school, announced that she was getting married. Oddly enough, Harry, who took no interest in his children, objected. She was too young, he said, and I agreed. But the truth was she hated Harry and had no use for me, so it didn't really matter what we thought.

She was going to do it anyway, so why not give her a nice wedding and send her off with love and blessings. Harry soon came around.

It was one thing we could do for her that she'd always cherish and remember.

The young people picked a date in August. It was going to be a traditional wedding at the Roman Catholic Church in Beverly Hills— since Marie had brought the children up in her faith—with a reception at Hillcrest.

There was much to do and plan. One late July afternoon, I happened to be in town working on details, when the doorbell rang.

I opened the door and there was a man wearing a trench coat and hat, with a pipe in his mouth. Before I spoke, he introduced himself.

"Mrs. Karl, my name is James Smith and I'm with the Federal Bureau of Investigation."

A man says he's from the FBI and you think he's either joking or got the wrong house.

He said, "I'd like to discuss a problem with you; may I come in?"

After checking his credentials, I said, "Certainly," and led him into my formal living room.

He gazed out at the pool with the three tiers of waterfall into waterfall into waterfall, overlooking the links of the Los Angeles Country Club.

I sat down. He sat down.

"I'd like to ask you a few questions about Mr. Karl."

That caught me off guard. *Harry?*

Outwardly I remained very cool. "I don't understand."

"Are you aware your husband gambles?"

"Of course. A lot of people gamble. I work in Las Vegas, Mr. Smith."

"He gambles very heavily," the FBI man continued as if I might not have known, "losing thirty, forty, or fifty thousand dollars in a day, every day. Did you know that?"

"No."

"But he has for years. Why wouldn't you know it?"

I didn't really believe the man. "I don't consider that any of my business, or yours," I replied. "It's his money, not mine."

"Well," he said, "it is definitely my business because your husband is being ripped off and he doesn't know it."

I don't know why, but the man annoyed me.

"Are you aware," he went on, "that Mr. Karl regularly goes to a friend's house and plays cards?"

"Yes," I replied, aware enough to know exactly who he meant.

"And that he plays cards at the Friars Club?"

"Well, I know that. They all play cards at the Friars."

"Then you didn't know, Mrs. Karl, that they're being cheated?"

"At the Friars?? I think someone's given you the wrong information, Mr. Smith. Do you know who belongs to the Friars? Jack Benny! Dean Martin! George Burns!" I said.

"We know that, ma'am," he said, continuing. "But we have just broken into a scam that the club is experiencing."

"Well, I can tell you my husband never cheated anybody." The whole thing sounded preposterous.

"Mr. Karl wasn't cheating. He was being cheated."

"Look," I said, "I don't know anything about gambling. I don't gamble and I'm averse to gambling. But you should know Mr. Karl is a very wealthy man. He has his own money and he can do with it what he pleases."

"Does your husband own a ten-thousand-dollar bill?" he continued.

"As a matter of fact, he does," I answered. "Why would you ask?"

"Because I have it," he said. "He just paid someone this ten-thousand-dollar bill. Do you know where he got it?"

I knew Harry had a ten-thousand-dollar bill only because as a joke one night in a restaurant he tipped the cocktail waitress with it. She walked away beaming because she thought she'd been given a hundred. When she realized what it was, she almost fainted. She showed it to the maître d', who brought it back to the table.

"Oh, I'm so sorry," said Harry. "I have so many."

Harry thought it was very amusing and gave the girl a hundred to keep. Several other people thought it was amusing too. I thought it was rude and ostentatious.

"I have no idea where my husband got it, Mr. Smith. But he was left a fortune by his father, who went through the Crash and didn't believe in banks. Maybe he cashed hundreds for thousands and thousands for one; I don't know."

"Maybe," the FBI man said. "All I know is he lost it. In one card game. And he paid off with it, plus a lot of other cash and a couple of mortgages with your signature on them, Mrs. Karl. That's why I'm here."

"I really don't know what that means," I said very honestly.

He showed me the mortgages. I looked at them, having no idea what exactly they were or why this man had them. I'd signed a lot of papers in my lifetime—contracts, agreements, et cetera. I rarely ever read them. That's why I paid lawyers and agents. That's what I trusted Harry to do. He knew about everything I put my pen to, and I resented this man's questioning.

I didn't really believe him. The whole thing sounded ridiculous. Who in his right mind would lose that kind of money day after day after day? Should I call my lawyer? I excused myself for a moment and called Harry at the Friars Club, where he always was at that time of day.

I knew the Friars well. It was a private men's club of successful, rich lawyers, businessmen, and entertainers—in Beverly Hills. Harry was a founding member. The club always contributed to the Thalians. During our fund raising, in fact, I used to take the children over and sell thousands of dollars' worth of raffle tickets in their garage. These rich men were very charitable.

"Harry, there's an agent here from the FBI, asking me all kinds of questions."

"What kind of questions?" I could hear panic in his voice.

"About you and card games and the Friars."

"Get rid of him. Don't talk to him."

"I'm trying not to," I said, "but it's rather difficult. He wanted to know if I knew about the ten-thousand-dollar bill."

"Don't talk about anything and try to get him out of the house. I'll be home soon, but make sure he's gone."

I put the phone down. Something was wrong.

I went back into the other room.

"Mr. Smith, I'm afraid there's nothing else I can tell you. Except that I know, whatever the problem is, my husband has done nothing wrong. He's a very honest man."

"I don't doubt that he is," he answered. "But we'd like to talk to him anyway." Then he thanked me for my time and left.

When Harry came home, we discussed the matter, but only briefly. His attitude was the same as the time in Vegas when the cage wouldn't give me an advance to buy the cars. It was all a big mistake, a big misunderstanding.

"Where is your ten-thousand-dollar bill, by the way?" I asked. "Are we in trouble?"

"Of course not. I have millions," he said, brushing over the first question.

The FBI came back to the house three or four times after that. Finally Harry was served with a subpoena and had to testify before the grand jury.

Then it all broke—but really broke. In headlines. The scam was a fact. And certain people were being cheated, including Tony Martin and Harry Karl and others. Harry was the biggest loser of them all. Harry had to admit that he'd lost hundreds of thousands of dollars at the card table. He never knew he was being cheated. None of the losers knew. They thought they were playing cards and just losing. The friend who had the card games at his house finally squealed. He was a loser too, although he must have known he was being cheated if he could squeal about it. He got immunity. One man went to jail.

After it all came out, I asked Harry about it.

"Harry, how could you lose hundreds of thousands of dollars there and keep going back?"

Without giving it a thought, he said, "It's mine to lose."

"You're right," I said, never questioning further. He was right, and I thought no more about it, until later on, when I was forced to. It was impossible to believe that someone could lose forty or fifty thousand a day for *years*. That's a lot of shoes and slippers. When I was married to Eddie, he and Mike Todd and Dean Martin and some of the other boys would have their card games and even lose thousands. But not every day. It was an occasional thing. Besides, they were all earning big money and the card game was a way to have fun. I suppose it was for Harry too. I hope so, because it was never fun for me.

CHAPTER 42

FROM THE MOMENT I BROUGHT Harry's children home, our life changed irrevocably.

My little theory about the hug and the kiss was way off. When Tina flung herself into a tantrum, it was Jekyll and Hyde time. We were dealing with hysteria. It was always the hit that made the impression. And there was always something to provoke it. Whatever she did, she'd say Carrie did it. Carrie's things would continually disappear—rings, clothes . . . We'd always find them and there would always be retribution.

Everybody told me to give her up. But how do you do that? That's something about me, something in my nature. I cannot accept failure. In most cases, I feel deeply that I can *do* it. And in most cases I've done it. Maybe it's my desire to think I'm needed. But in the case of Tina, it was more than that. It was a case of how do you not care when you care?

Harry had married what was the perfect situation for him. Then it took on the pain of life and he couldn't handle it. And by the way, neither could I, although I was bound and determined to try. Harry didn't want anything but wonderful and pretty—Rolls-Royces, Beverly Hills houses, a movie star and Tammy rolled into one for a wife, with two gorgeous children at her side. Problems undercut his perfect life and he found it very confusing and difficult to accept the trauma.

All of this was self-evident now that I think back on it. But I didn't want to see it. I preferred keeping my life busy with the routine and the schedules. I've always had a million things going at one time. There were the children, the Girl Scouts, the houses, the Thalians, traveling with the act, television appearances, personal appearances at Karl Shoe Stores, not to mention our social life which was as active as we wished it to be.

So we pretended, or at least I did, that we still had the perfect life:

health, wealth, marriage, family, and togetherness. That's what I wanted, and Harry did too.

I still did my bit as his wife, making sure that the house was run smoothly. I still oversaw his wardrobe, often giving a quick press to his shirts as they came back from the laundry in New York. I still occasionally straightened his socks and underwear drawers, so that everything was in perfect order.

CHAPTER 43

FOR YEARS MY AGENTS HAD been trying to talk me into doing television. I wasn't easily persuaded. Friends who had done it—Donna Reed, Lucy Arnaz, Eva Gabor, Hope Lange—all said the same thing about it: "You'll have no personal life. It's constant around-the-clock work. You can't please your audience every week. You can't get good scripts."

Then my agents came to me with a "fabulous" deal from NBC: a comedy series, giving me 50 percent ownership, $25,000 a week, a guarantee of a second year no matter what the first year's ratings were, an NBC-financed film of my choosing, which I would star in, plus 50 percent ownership in a future series in which I would not appear. The man who'd created *I Love Lucy*, Jess Oppenheimer, would create and run my show and would own the other 50 percent. I would even have the right to pick my own sponsor. I told NBC that I wanted an all-American sponsor like Coke or General Foods or Wesson Oil.

When they told me the sponsor would be American Tobacco, I said nothing doing—no cigarette commercials. I was against smoking. Harry smoked three packs a day. I had to learn to smoke for *The Rat Race* and it took me two months to break the habit. I started again for *Mary Mary* and it took two years to quit. To this day I am an on-again off-again smoker. I think it is a vile habit and I didn't want to look as if I were endorsing it.

No problem. I was a Star then, a movie star, which in television was spelled H-O-T! When they want you they want you and you can make your own terms. My agents came back and told me that American Tobacco was now American *Brands* and that they had many other products, such as Mott's applesauce and Hunt Foods. That was fine. I signed a deal that guaranteed I would have fifty-four shows in the can.

I wanted to shoot it at MGM. NBC rebuilt a whole sound stage for me with a separate entrance gate on Washington Boulevard. We had Harry Stradling, Sr., the great cameraman, with a three-camera setup and a wonderful crew. We were going to have a live audience and a production schedule that allowed me to have Wednesday afternoons for the girls' Brownie troop as well as the weekends with my children. Tom Bosley, Don Chastain, and Pat Smith were signed as regular cast members. Jess Oppenheimer delivered a light, clean, very funny situation comedy.

In the spring we went to work, and with nine shows in the can, broke for the summer. On Tuesday night, September 16, 1969, at 8:00 P.M., Harry and I and the children settled down in the bedroom to watch the debut of *The Debbie Reynolds Show*.

The first thing we saw, of course, was the commercial: *Pall Mall cigarettes*!! For a moment I thought it was a mistake, left over from the previous half hour. But then I knew. There was more smoke on the screen than in the San Francisco fire. I had been lied to and I was livid. How dare they?!

Harry, the businessman and obviously the more practical in that situation, tried to pacify me. I called Mort Werner, the NBC vice-president in charge of programming, to vent my anger. He couldn't be reached. I called Lillian Sidney, who agreed with Harry.

"But, darling," Lillian counseled maternally, "you smoke cigarettes *yourself*! You can't dictate to the network about the sponsor! They'll cancel you in a minute!"

"They can't cancel me, Lillian," I said. "I have a two-year contract, pay or play," meaning they pay you even if the show doesn't air.

I wasn't listening to Lillian. I was the big star and I was very headstrong. Liquor advertising had already been banned from television and it was only going to be a matter of months before the surgeon general would ban cigarette advertising. Since mine was a family show, I couldn't see why they had to do it on my half hour.

I called Bill Barron, my press agent from Jim Mahoney and Associates. Bill saw it my way and he advised me to push the issue and hold the network and sponsor to the original agreement.

Wednesday morning I sent a wire to Mort Werner at NBC, which read in part:

I was shocked to discover that the initial commercial aired during the premiere of my new television series was devoted to a nationally advertised brand of cigarette. I feel that my representatives and I fully outlined my personal feelings concerning cigarette advertising and clearly stated my position in advising everyone concerned that I will not be party to such commercials which I consider directly opposed to health and well-being. This gesture is a complete breach of my agreement with NBC and I hereby tender notice that I will cease production with the completion of Thursday's shooting day.

The wire made every paper in the country; even headlines in some. The show was so highly touted that a lot of the press thought I'd done it as one more publicity gimmick. The boys at American Brands knew better and they were furious. So were the boys at NBC. "She can't tell us what we're going to spend our advertising dollars on," American Brands told NBC.

"You can't tell them what they're going to spend their advertising dollars on," NBC told Debbie Reynolds.

Oh, really? said Miss Crusade, Miss Girl Scout. I actually thought I could. After all, I had a contract.

Wednesday afternoon a meeting convened between me and the network and my agents in the living room at Greenway. The network wanted me to give American Brands a waiver which was the same thing as giving them a release from my contract. My agents convinced me that by doing that I would be showing good faith to the network because otherwise American Brands was going to pull *all* of its advertising—which amounted to tens of millions of dollars—from the network.

So I signed the waiver and American Brands was released from its two-year option on the show.

American Brands dropped the show like that, which left NBC holding a big-budget sitcom minus tens of thousands of dollars in weekly commercial fees.

What I had done, unwittingly of course, on the advice of my agents and the network, was to release not only the sponsor but also NBC from its contractual obligations. It never occurred to me that my own agents would advise me against my own interests, considering their commission. However, I was wrong. Debbie Reynolds was involved in a power play with American Brands, Inc., and Debbie Reynolds could do nothing but lose.

After the first thirteen shows were completed, NBC, whose executives had stated verbally that they would continue with a new sponsor, pulled the show. I had their word but I didn't have it on paper. I don't do those things anymore. If I had just shut my mouth and paid attention to my work, instead of taking a stand against smoking, I might have been a very rich woman today. There was enough going on in my personal life to justify my rage, but typically I wouldn't confront that. It was far, far easier for me to vent my anger at two major American corporations and the largest talent agency in the world. It was also the stupidest mistake of my entire career.

CHAPTER 44

IT WAS THAT SAME YEAR that MGM, already in deep financial trouble, hired a former television executive to head the studio and take them out of the sea of red ink. His solution was to *sell* the studio! The back lot—hundreds of acres where thousands of dreams for hundreds of millions of people had been created before the cameras for almost fifty years—was going to be sold. The costume and sets departments—the most lavish and complete in the entire film industry—were going up on the auction block!

It broke my heart to think that they were going to just get rid of everything. Harry and I got together with Al Hart, who was head of City National Bank, to discuss buying the back lot. My idea was to turn it into a Disneyland-type amusement park. This included the Andy Hardy Street, the Showboat Lake, the Esther Williams Swimming Pools, and dozens of other magical locations.

Al Hart offered to raise five million dollars for the real estate. For some reason, the farsighted geniuses who were now running MGM couldn't see why anybody would want to tour a studio back lot. They had to leave it to Lew Wasserman and Al Dorskind at Universal to show them several years later. Instead it was sold to a real-estate developer for about the same price we were offering, and today that once magical place is wall-to-wall-condos, hundreds of them.

I took out an ad in the *Hollywood Reporter* asking people to contribute to a fund to buy the costumes and props. The response was overwhelming, but just when it looked like we'd pull it off, the new MGM president decided he couldn't wait and he sold the whole collection to an auction company.

Nevertheless, when the auction took place, I was there. Harry was behind me 100 percent, although for the first time in our marriage, he told me we'd have to take a short-term loan because everything was "tied up" temporarily because of "investments." Well, I thought, he still has his four hundred shoe stores and I still have my contracts with

NBC. So I went to the bank and borrowed $180,000. I bought hundreds of costumes—Garbo's, Gable's, Garland's, Gardner's, Astaire's, Fairbanks's, Crawford's, Kelly's, Mae West's. I bought furniture and props from Academy Award–winning films—*The Good Earth, Showboat, Singin' in the Rain, Meet Me in St. Louis,* and many other pictures.

I would have bought everything they were selling if I had had the money. My ultimate dream was to have a Hollywood museum.

Actually bringing a Hollywood museum to fruition is something that has, up to now, been an impossible task. In 1969, movies were considered commonplace and hardly "art." Television was fast replacing films. I was simply the fanatic collector of kitsch. Each successive attempt we've made to either raise money or obtain land has become embedded in local politics and/or financial problems. It still is a dream of mine.

In the meantime, the whole lot of MGM memorabilia went into a warehouse and I went back to finish filming what turned out to be the last episodes of my short-lived television series.

Things weren't going so well at home, although everything was all bright smiles and flashbulbs on the outside. I would rarely stop to notice if I could possibly avoid it. Whenever I had a spare moment, I'd find something to do, even if it came down to cleaning my closets or Harry's drawers on a Saturday afternoon.

I was doing that one afternoon, that same autumn, when I came face to face with a reality I couldn't avoid. I was straightening Harry's underwear when I found, tucked away underneath, little pieces of paper with handwritten numbers on them: $200, $300, $400, $600. There must have been more than a dozen.

Later, when Harry came home from Hillcrest, and we were having our cocktails, I asked him about them.

"Oh, that's cash I get every week," he said casually.

"I don't know what that means," I said, "cash every week."

"Cash from Irving, that he gives me every week. Do you need any?"

I was still confused. Since Irving Briskin was *my* business manager, why was he giving *Harry* cash every week? I used to get $25 a week from Irving—pin money. Sometimes I'd ask him for $50 or $100. Yet he—my business manager, whom Harry had hired—was giving him cash.

"You know, Debbie, it's cash—something he can take off the top of some deals—cash, honey. That you don't have to report."

Cash. Off the books. I knew what that meant although I didn't understand what that had to do with my investments. But then I didn't keep track of my investments. Harry did. I signed tax returns and didn't know what they were. Everyone had power of attorney. Harry, his secretary, Ida, Irving, even Al Hart at City National Bank had power of attorney over my money.

Irving had bought a hospital in Santa Monica. I knew that. He'd also put some of my money into a video machine called Scopitone, which turned out to be about twenty-five years ahead of its time, but I didn't know that. As far as I knew, it was doing well. Once there were a couple of apartment houses on Wilshire Boulevard in Westwood that I wanted to buy, but when I mentioned them to Harry and Irving they were not impressed. They did not consider me a businesswoman, so obviously I didn't know.

Not long after that, Rod Taylor told me he was looking for a business manager and I recommended Irving Briskin to him. He went to see him.

After the meeting, the same day, Rod called me on the phone and said, "Debbie, that guy is a jerk! He wants twenty-five percent!"

"Twenty-five percent for what?" I dumbly asked.

"Twenty-five percent of your income for managing it! That's outrageous!"

That was the first I'd heard of the 25 percent. I told Harry about Rod's meeting.

"Is that true?" I asked. "Because if it is, that's ridiculous."

"Well, that's what he gets, Debbie. He's a business manager and producer."

"Producer of what? I haven't made a picture that he's been involved with in years."

"He's always looking for projects for you, honey," Harry said blithely.

"I don't care what he's doing. I'm not paying him twenty-five percent."

"Well, you have been all these years, so why should you stop now?"

I looked at Harry, sitting in the chair across from me, sipping his Scotch. Was I crazy? He wasn't upset, or disturbed, or even the slightest bit concerned. He was always cavalier about his own money. There had been instances in his own business when, quite by accident, he discovered that key salesmen and executives had been stealing goods and money and it was almost impossible for him to bring himself to stop them. Now he was doing the same thing with my money, and I wasn't going to let it go on.

*   *   *

When Irving Briskin settled with me a few months later, I got $300,000 in government bonds. In the 1960s, I had given him and Harry every cent I had made—nearly $10 million. The hospital in Santa Monica was his, it turned out, not mine, not Harry's. The Scopitone machine was so far ahead of its time no one bought it. I did spend some of my money at times—buying antiques or paintings or gifts. I didn't mind sharing what I had with Harry because he was my husband. But only $300,000 *out of $10 million*?!

All those little pieces of paper I'd found were not money that Irving had made off the books. It was my money that I'd earned and paid the taxes on. I felt raided and raped. To this day it still shocks me. It's not a unique Hollywood story. Doris Day's husband and business manager robbed her of millions and she never knew until her husband died. How can a husband do such a thing to his own wife?

Money has never been the most important thing to me in life, although I like luxury as much as the next person. I love my memorabilia and my antiques but I have never coveted anything. So when all of this came out in the open, I was angry, but I was not destroyed. I was thirty-seven—still a young woman. But time has made it worse because as I get older I realize that it was my youth, my working years, my sweat and energy, that they helped themselves to—all of it just dissipated as if I never even mattered to them.

Well, I was the one who did it. I gave the responsibility to Harry and I never thought about it. Harry was going to take care of it: "You take care of the uptown; I'll take care of the downtown." Of course, there is no such thing. In marriage, you're in the middle of it and you're never out of it. But for almost ten years I believed him.

CHAPTER **45**

AT THAT POINT in our marriage, almost everything that could go wrong had gone wrong. Harry's gambling had created problems far beyond anything I'd ever dreamed. He was now losing large sums of money to the kind of people who don't send a collection agency around when you're overdue.

I didn't know what I was going to do. If I left him, where would I go? I had the children to think about. Mine and his. Bo had dropped out of school and didn't know what he wanted to do with his life. Tina was organized and supervised but her life was every inch as difficult as when she first came to live with us. She remained a willful, volatile child with infinite needs. Now, as she approached puberty and adolescence, it was surely not going to magically ease up. Neither child could count on their father. Fortunately I could always work; we could depend on that.

In the spring of 1970 Harry came to me for money. This had never happened before. Of course, before he automatically got everything I made. However, after Irving Briskin was gone, that all changed. And as it happened, I wasn't working, so nothing was coming in from my end.

All I had was the bonds I bought when I settled with Irving— $300,000. Harry said it would only be used as collateral against a loan he needed for the business.

I should have known something like this was coming. For weeks he had been very depressed. Harry was one of those people who just took to his bed when he couldn't handle something.

"Harry, what shows when the ostrich sticks his head in the sand?" I asked him one day, sitting on the edge of the bed. "Because that's what you're doing. You have to get up."

"Debbie . . . please . . ." he said, "I feel like I'm going down."

I·looked at this man whom I'd married to be my "protector," this

282

great big man, eighteen years my senior, lying there on our oversized bed, in a sea of custom-made sheets, overcome by his circumstances, like a half-drowned dog. I felt tremendous anger mixed with pity and sorrow. How did we get to this place? I kept asking myself. We, who started out with *everything*!

Yet somehow in my gut I knew it was happening, I knew that it was bad, and that I was going to be killed.

That afternoon, I walked down to the bank in Beverly Hills where I met Harry's secretary, Ida. I got the bonds out of the safe-deposit box and she took them over to his bank. I was nauseated the whole time.

When I came home I threw up and then sat there in the bathroom sobbing. Harry came in.

"I shouldn't have given you this money," I blurted out.

"I know," he said very quietly.

"But I did," I said, unable to look at him.

"But I had to have it, Debbie."

"I know," I said, "but it's every dime I have. What if you fail us?"

"I won't."

"I think you're going to. I think it's all so awful." And I just sobbed on, uncontrollably. I felt so sick, I couldn't talk. Harry left the room and I went to bed for the rest of the day.

CHAPTER 46

TWO YEARS BEFORE, I was talking about retiring. Now I had go to work. For one thing there was the loan I'd taken to buy the MGM memorabilia.

There were no bookings on the horizon. I hadn't worked Vegas in more than two years and there were no movie or television offers coming my way. My only alternative was to put together a new act and take it on the road. I went to the bank and borrowed another $140,000. You could do that if you were Debbie Reynolds the movie star married to the rich Mr. Harry Karl, whose money seemed to grow on trees. No Beverly Hills banker would think otherwise, or even suspect that I was the tree where Harry Karl grew his money.

The New Debbie Reynolds Show featured Rip Taylor, a group of ten singers called The Unusual We, and five hefty girls called The Weight Wotchers. ("Weight Watchers" wasn't too happy about that but there was nothing they could do about it.) I had a new act with wonderful new numbers choreographed by Ron Lewis.

Carrie and Todd went with me. Carrie made her professional debut singing "I've Got Love," from the musical *Purlie*, and "Bridge over Troubled Water" (she got a standing ovation almost every night). I sang her a number by Harry Belafonte called "Where Are You Going, My Little One?" It was a wonderful moment when she sat on a stool next to me. Then Todd, who played the guitar, did a number with me and Carrie. I was so proud of my children. I sang, danced, played the tuba, and did impressions. And I made a new friend, Rip Taylor.

Besides the cast, the company included a lighting director; a sound man, Rudy; one drummer; my hairdresser, Pinky; and two in wardrobe—one of whom was my mother. The family was still together, even on the road.

We were thirty-two on the bus-and-truck tour from July through late September, all over the United States.

In Valley Forge on closing night, my truck with all the props and costumes ran into an electric pole and cut the lines down for the show opening the next night. It wasn't my fault, but the producer, Lee Guber, blamed me and wouldn't pay us for the engagement. I had to sue for the money and it took six months to get it. My payroll was $30,000 a week, in addition to the costs of traveling from place to place. I needed money for the gas, the chicken dinners, and the motels.

I called Harry and asked him for some money from what I'd loaned him. He said he didn't have it because it was "still collateral" against his loan at the bank.

I was so angry I called to find out if the bonds were still there. They were not. They weren't collateral. They never had been. They had been *pledged* against the loan, and later called. When I told Harry, he said he'd give me a note, which he did—a piece of paper that I had until the day he died. It was just paper. I still needed cash to meet the payroll.

One night in Toledo I came down with the flu. It had been coming on for weeks. I'd get very dizzy and my arms would go numb. Then just before I was to go on, my arms suddenly went dead. I felt so ill I lay down on the floor. When I did that, I couldn't breathe.

"I'm dying," I thought. "I know I'm dying! Grandma Reynolds had a stroke at thirty-nine and here I am, thirty-eight, and it's my turn." I terrified myself with that thought.

Meanwhile, I knew Mother was thinking the same thing—which made me even more nervous. By the time the doctor arrived I was hyperventilating. He wanted to give me something and put me to bed.

"You can't leave me," I said to the doctor. "I'm going to die tonight." I didn't want to die in some broken-down motel and I didn't want to go to the hospital.

It was like going nuts. I missed the show, of course. The doctor was so upset and worried after all my pleading that he took me and Mother home with him for the night.

By morning, like a miracle, I was feeling fine, although I was exhausted and traumatized by the whole experience. The doctor recommended several weeks of complete peace and quiet—an impossible request at that moment in my life.

The quick "recovery" didn't calm the fears I was carrying around inside. With all my other problems, I felt I now had the worst one—death—stalking me. I worried about the children and who would take care of them.

Several weeks later, in Westbury, Long Island, it happened again:

dizzy, nauseated, arms go dead. I lay there on the floor hyperventilating.

Again they called a doctor who gave me a shot and put me in bed. Again I was told it wasn't a stroke; that I wasn't dying. The next morning, just like Toledo, I felt fine.

But it wasn't just a simple case of exhaustion, the new doctor said. He suggested that I go into New York for neurological tests. *Neurological tests?!*

"Do you think it's a tumor?" I asked nervously. "Do you think I'm going to have a stroke?"

"No."

"Then why neurological tests?"

He explained that it appeared that I might have suffered what they call "transglobal amnesia." He thought we should find out to be sure.

I didn't agree. My intuition told me it wasn't my brain. But I still felt that something was putting me down and out.

"I'm going to call Jeane Dixon," I told Mother when we got back to the motel. "She'll know everything about me. I know she will." I had always been an admirer of her abilities.

Mother thought I'd totally gone off my rocker. I felt certain Jeane could tell me what was wrong, and specifically if I was dying. That afternoon I called her in Washington.

She told me she would see me if I could make it down there the following day. I said I could. We made an appointment for lunch at a Washington restaurant.

I had never met Jeane Dixon. She was a tiny woman, with a sweet, ethereal face and big, wide, compassionate eyes. It immediately felt comforting to be in her company.

I told her what had happened, that I was afraid I was going to die.

"Well, I've been praying very, very hard," she said in her soft, melodic voice. "Your life is very difficult now . . . but you're in no danger health-wise. Just great stress. Your body is telling you that; that's what's happening. But I'm so . . . sorry about your husband."

I hadn't said anything about Harry. "What about . . . my husband?" I asked.

"Well . . . I'm sorry about the divorce."

"But we're not divorced."

"Oh . . . that's it . . . but you will be. And you have papers all around you. Mortgages, contracts. Have you signed all these papers?" she asked quizzically.

"I'm not sure." I wasn't sure what she was talking about. Rarely, if ever, did I know what I was signing.

"There will be a divorce," she said very quietly. "Everything will be lost and you will move to a new location. But you must rest, Debbie. Please rest. You won't die."

Hearing about a divorce disturbed me, but any kind of problem was minor compared to her news that I was going to live.

"You won't be out of your troubles for at least ten years," she continued.

Ten years?! This was 1970. I'd be almost fifty!

I asked about Harry's health.

"He is not ill. There is no 'infection.'"

I had said nothing to her about Harry's "infection."

"But there are many women in his life," she continued, as if I had known that. "He doesn't love any of them. He loves only you. But you will be destroyed if you don't leave him."

I was floored.

"But you will always have a career and you will always be able to depend on it." That didn't sound like much solace. But she spoke with such quiet confidence that it never occurred to me *not* to believe her.

I left Jeane Dixon that day in a completely different frame of mind. It wasn't imminent death that I had to worry about. It was all the things I'd been trying not to look at. But I felt stronger. Somehow I could work it out.

I couldn't get over what she said about Harry and the "many women." When? Was he taking them to the Friars and Hillcrest with him? Was it when I was on the road? The only women I saw around him were the manicurists. That was a possibility. But in the house? With all the rest of us there? I couldn't believe that about him.

The tour was over in late September. We'd made enough money to pay off the loans for the memorabilia and to finance the act, and that was it. I had some time off until we were playing the act in Tahoe in late October. When I got back to California, I enrolled Tina in a boarding school in Ojai. She was now fourteen and still very much in need of supervision and attention. But it was a lovely boarding school, with beautiful facilities, and only an hour and a half from Los Angeles.

She hated the idea of being sent away from home. It was one more example to her of how I didn't love her. I felt bad but there was no alternative. All our lives were being challenged and torn apart at that time.

Whatever changes were coming, I knew I'd have to be on the road a lot just to keep up with my financial obligations. If I had to leave Todd or Carrie with Harry and the staff, they would be all right. Todd, who was only two when Harry and I were married, adored his stepfather, and Harry was very good to Carrie.

CHAPTER 47

JEANE DIXON'S WORDS were still very much on my mind. But if Harry had been fooling around with other women all this time, why would he admit it just because I asked him? I decided to ask his closest friend outside of Los Angeles, Gregory Peters. Harry and Gregory were partners in a shoe factory in Spain.

I got myself booked on a television show being shot in London, *Kopykats*, with Rich Little, Frank Gorshen, and Fred Travilena. The show paid for my tickets to England and gave me an excuse to go see Gregory in Spain without Harry knowing. Carrie came with me.

When I finished the show, Carrie and I flew to Madrid, where I'd reserved a suite at the Palace Hotel. I called Gregory and asked him to dinner.

I always sensed that he was a good friend to me, too. I needed to talk to a friend who was not going to tell his wife, or even worse, a columnist. I also didn't want Harry to know what I was doing.

As soon as Gregory arrived, we sat down at the dinner table and I started.

My hands were ice-cold and my insides were shaking. "Gregory, you know, I'm very unhappy. My life has been very difficult for the past five or six years. I know you can help me."

He sat there, patiently waiting.

"You have to tell the truth," I said. "Gregory, when Harry travels with you, does he see other women?"

Hesitantly, haltingly, it came out. "Yes."

"What sort of women? A regular woman? Does he have a mistress? Was it one?" It was important to me to know that.

"No," he answered.

"Not one other woman?"

"No, Debbie. Just releases. Many women. Not even affairs," he said. Gregory knew that I was very unsophisticated about the ways of men. He explained things clearly and concisely for me.

288

I sat there eating nothing. He was so nervous, he never stopped.

So, Debbie . . . I was thinking to myself, Harry wanted it and bought it. Perfect wife, two children, three beautiful homes; a wife who never made less than half a million a year and usually a million and a half a year—which she gave to him; and he had his ladies on the side. What a perfect system, I thought. It made me sick.

I wanted to know everything Gregory could tell me. I'm sure he could see that I was trying to ask my questions in an orderly fashion, all the while thinking I was going to faint.

Gregory talked while he ate. He told me that Harry owed him $1.7 million. He had borrowed more than his half share in the business from Gregory. He told me about their trips to Las Vegas together when Harry lost hundreds of thousands of dollars, sometimes in a night.

I certainly did not understand the magnitude. I did not understand that my husband, who had $21 million when I married him, had blown almost all of it and almost all of mine. The enormity would take time to comprehend.

It was mostly the women that I wanted to know about. The girls, young girls, the manicurists, everybody there for one reason only—to perform one act. It was the culmination of what I had avoided. I never wanted to face the fact that my second marriage, which I had convinced myself was so perfect, was a disaster.

It was the rejection I felt again. I had actually thought, after Eddie, that marrying an older, more stable man like Harry, would make my marriage safe in that area. Certainly I was not the hottest ticket in town, but I was knowledgeable enough about sex to be a dutiful wife. I never rejected my husband. He was not a man who had a quick arousal, so there was a good deal of time spent on foreplay on his behalf. Not on mine. That was, I felt, part of my duty. I did not find that offensive or something I couldn't perform. After the second baby's death, Harry was truly concerned about me. But many women?! It was like having the bottom drop out.

Gregory stayed for four or five hours. I kept thinking, "I want to escape. I don't want to be put there again."

I said nothing to Carrie that night when I went to bed, although I was sure she suspected something. She had known nothing of my unhappiness before this. The children had never heard us argue or raise our voices.

Leaving Spain for Los Angeles was the hardest part of all. Harry always met me at the airport whenever I went away. I didn't want to see him and I knew he'd be standing there with his great white shock of hair, smiling.

By the time the plane put down at LAX, I was hysterical.

"Mother, you have to stop crying," Carrie said, almost pleading.

"I can't stop crying," I tried to explain.

"We've got to get off the plane," she said.

"I don't want to get off!" And I couldn't stop crying.

I sat in my seat for about fifteen minutes after the plane had emptied. That's when Carrie found out about my problems. Naturally she was very concerned and upset for me.

Finally we disembarked. As we entered the terminal, there he was. Mr. Strength. Mr. Take-Care-Of-Me, standing there like the Devil. I hated him. I just hated him and I didn't know what to do or say. I had to let him kiss me. I turned my cheek. Then he embraced Carrie.

He never noticed a thing. We got into the limousine and drove off to our big house in Beverly Hills. He talked but I didn't say anything. How was I going to find a way to tell him?

I went back to the socks. The drawers. One of the drawers had a false back with another compartment behind it, to hide valuables in. I'm not a snoop, but this was my life I was looking for.

There they were—more little bits of notes like the ones Irving Briskin had given him. Only this time it was girls. "Mary Jane, Motor Inn Lodge," with the number. Or "Vivian Lawrence," whatever, and the number. All these names and numbers.

I still didn't confront him. I didn't want him to touch me; even to hold my hand. I told him his snoring bothered me so much he had to sleep in his sitting room. Although his snoring had never bothered me before, he believed me and went.

I didn't want the marriage to end, even after all this. Yet I couldn't stand being with him. I had that deep-rooted mentality of not wanting to dissolve a marriage. To do so meant failure and would ultimately be my failure.

"You know in fact he does love you," I'd tell myself. "He's just . . . humiliated you."

"You know in fact you could stay married," I would reason. "But in a fashion that is unacceptable."

I didn't fool around. I didn't have lovers all those years, even though I felt frustrated. I wanted to be touched, I wanted to be held. I wanted to be loved.

CHAPTER 48

THE NBC DEAL had included a guarantee of two pictures for which NBC was obligated to put up half the money. They couldn't cancel that. The summer before, a director named Curtis Harrington had come to me with a book called *Best of Friends.*

I really loved the book. It took place in the 1930s and involved two women whose sons had committed a murder together. The boys were both convicted and sent to prison. The mothers, having met in the courtroom, standing by their sons and defending them, became "best of friends." Both women had lived in small rural communities all their lives, both tragic lives. After their boys were sentenced to prison, the two women decided to move away. So they went to Hollywood to make a new life together. They rented a little duplex where one taught dancing, for which the other played the piano, in the studio below. The second woman, it turned out, was psychopathic, with lesbian undertones. The dancing teacher met a man and started dating. The other woman became very jealous of the relationship, eventually went insane, and in the end killed her friend.

It was a drama with musical numbers; a lot of interesting elements. NBC put up $750,000 and Marty Ransohoff and Filmways matched it, with Curtis Harrington directing, and George Edwards producing. I was cast in the role of the dancing teacher—naturally.

Shelley Winters played the role of the psychopathic friend. Shelley and I had never worked together but had known each other in the fifties. She was always unpredictable, but so rowdy you knew she was doing it on purpose. Shelley liked to shock and I always thought that was amusing.

Dennis Weaver, Agnes, and Michael MacLiammoir were also signed. The picture was scheduled to go into production in October. I didn't make a salary but I was going to own 50 percent of the movie, and it was not an expensive picture, so there was a chance that eventually I'd make some money.

I loved the title *Best of Friends*, but Otto Preminger had just made a picture called *Such Good Friends*, and he felt the titles were too close. He took the matter to arbitration with the MPAA and the producers gave in. Our screenwriter, Henry Farrell, had also written *Whatever Happened to Baby Jane?* That was a box-office smash, so someone creative decided to call our picture *What's the Matter with Helen?*, which I hated.

In retrospect, if I were naming the picture, I'd probably call it "Shelley or Die," because that's what it soon became.

Shelley Winters is wildly bananas. I'll say that from here to China, because she is. It's not that she's not funny, provocative, and all those other things, but when she's working on a film, she's unpredictable, to say the least. I called her "Killer" on the set. To this day I call her Killer. She gets so into the role she becomes it. In this case she was playing a murderess.

When we first got together to read the script, she said, "My psychiatrist told me not to do this picture because it would probably flip me over the edge."

I looked at her. Never having worked with her, I didn't realize that whatever Shelley says is the truth for her at that moment; not an act. That's Shelley.

It started out very well because she liked rehearsing. She can be quite brilliant. We got along fine, although Shelley likes all the attention.

She lived on my route to the studio, so every morning, I'd pick her up. One morning just before dawn, as I was driving along Santa Monica Boulevard, I saw a woman in my headlights, in the middle of the road, trying to wave down a car. As I got closer I noticed it was Shelley, hitchhiking, in her nightgown, looking like she'd just rolled out of bed, with her piano practice board under her arm.

It was a sight that gave me a pause.

"Shelley, why aren't you waiting at your house?" I asked.

"Because I thought I was late."

Okay. I said no more.

Prior to the shoot you always test the clothes. Our designer was a very talented man named Morton Haack, who'd also done *Molly Brown* and was very good with people who had fitting problems. I had a problem with being very short and Shelley had a problem with weight. I'd lost a lot of weight and was down to 104 for the film. However, I wasn't unhappy about the loss because it meant I wouldn't have to wear any undergarments, as women in the Thirties tended not to do. I had wanted to affect that Harlow look for the picture. We'd even hired Sidney Guilaroff, who did Harlow, to do the hair.

Shelley and I had just put on the first of our costumes for Morton, when she, in a sudden fit, started ripping her clothes off.

"You're designing badly," she yelled at Morton, who was just a little less stunned than I by the outburst. "You're trying to make Debbie look better than me."

"No," he retorted, "I'm just trying to dress you properly for your character."

"Well, you're making her look skinny and *me look fat*."

"Shelley," Morton said impatiently, "you *are* fat! Have you ever looked?!"

A huge fight ensued. Before it was over, she had ripped off every last piece of her clothing, torn it up, and walked off the set, wearing not a stitch. She refused, after that, to wear anything made by Morton. Eventually he quit and went back to London.

"I'll never dress another actress as long as I live," he told me before he left. "I'll never design again." And he never did. Fortunately, his family had left him wealthy.

Shelley was always talking about losing weight.

"I'm going to lose twenty pounds on this picture. I'm going to start tomorrow," she'd say. In the next breath she'd order potatoes with her lunch. When lunch came, she'd take a taste of the potatoes. "I wish I hadn't tasted these, they're good." A half hour later, she'd be asking what's for dessert. She'd eat pasta for lunch with wine; brownies, cookies, and desserts all day. It was one of her heaviest times. It was also perfect for the part.

One day she got angry at me for being too thin. She accused me of doing it on purpose. But it was right for how I saw the role. The two women were dowdy farm girls, and when they moved to Hollywood, boom, my character changes and her character stays the same.

She was so angry she slammed into her dressing room. Soon everything was flying out through the door of the trailer at me—lamps, pillows, clothes, her Bible, her chocolate-chip cookies—everything that wasn't nailed down. Then she started kicking and banging on the open door, all the while yelling and cursing, to the point of incoherence, about me and how thin I was. She knocked the door right off the hinges while the entire crew stood there agape.

*   *   *

Shelley is the first one to tell you she is a Method actress. I am not. But I thought we could work together because I had worked with Carroll Baker and other actresses who were trained at Strasberg's Actors Studio.

It's so much fun when you do a scene together where one takes the low line and one takes the high line and you set each other up and build to a climax. It can be exhilarating and exciting. You can go any-place with it if you're together.

I soon found out that was not possible with Shelley. She *is* her Method. She acts completely without anybody else. You're there and if you can live through it, you can meet the challenge. But it's a back-breaker.

She had also decided she needed music to put her in the mood. Puccini. Wagner. A grip carried around a record player wherever Shelley went. She had him play music nonstop. Soon it was driving me nuts. Try remembering lines with a loudspeaker blaring Brünnhilde in your ear.

"I play music to affect the emotional memory," she said.

I didn't know whether to slug her or kick the record player. One day we were shooting a tough scene where I had most of the lines. Shelley would have an "Oh dear," and then I'd have another five pages. In the background the dirges were going right up until they'd say "Roll it."

"Shelley," I said, "that music is making this scene very difficult for me."

"Debbie, this is the only way I can work. I've won two Academy Awards, you know." She was always throwing that up to me.

Meanwhile I'm trying to think of my lines and all I can hear in my head is this oom-pah-pah, oom-pah-pah with marching feet.

When Curtis Harrington asked her if she could lower the sound a bit, all she could say was: "You take time to load the cameras, so why can't you take time to load the actors?"

She had the habit of constantly changing her lines *during* the scene. If you don't know that's what's coming, it is very difficult. When Shelley first did this, Curtis Harrington very diplomatically stopped ev-erything and read her the correct lines.

"I don't learn words; I learn thoughts," she snapped. And she went on doing it her way.

I've been known to break tension by clowning or making a joke. One day while we were waiting for the lighting to be set up, I was horsing around and telling jokes with the crew and everyone was having a good laugh.

Unnoticed by anyone, Shelley had left the set. A few minutes later the production manager took Curtis Harrington aside to tell him that Shelley was in her trailer taking off her costume because she wasn't going to work anymore that day.

"But why?" Curtis asked.

"Because she can't do her job when people are laughing," he was told.

Curtis rushed over to Shelley's trailer to talk to her.

"I just can't," she said, slowly shaking her head over the crisis. "I just can't. . . ."

"But Shelley," he said, "just stop and listen for a moment."

She did. The set outside her trailer was silent.

"You see," Curtis said, "no one's laughing now."

It was true. No one ever laughs if they think production might be shut down for even a day.

Finally she relented.

A few minutes later Curtis came over to my trailer and gave me the news: No More Laughing On The Set. I understood. No clowns allowed; only divas.

It was always like this, day after day. One obstacle after another after another. Finally one day I just couldn't stand it. I stopped the scene, rushed over to the wall, ripped the fire hose out of its case and turned it on her.

"*SHUTTUP SHELLEY!*" I screamed.

We had some of the biggest battles of my life. I loved the picture and hated the work.

Weekends away from the camera didn't help because I was so unhappy. I'd go down to the house in Palm Springs, just to get away. Once there, I could go off for long afternoon drives by myself.

During those lonely days, I often thought of my old friend Bob Neal, whom I'd dated back before I met Eddie. He had had a lavish house there, and we had had wonderful times together. Bob loved show business, the parties and the people. Twice he had proposed, and twice I'd turned him down, thinking he was not right for me.

One of those Saturdays I drove through the area where his house was located, just to see if I still remembered the place. But the flora and bushes lining the streets had grown so much taller, and the azaleas had grown wild over the adobe and brick walls surrounding the houses. I had no idea which house was his.

I wondered what it would be like to see Bob again. We'd lost contact over the years. I didn't know if he'd married, or even if he still had a place in Palm Springs.

I called his sister to ask about him. He was still a bachelor, she told me, and he still had the house. "I'm sure he'd love to see you, Debbie."

The next day was a beautiful, sun-drenched afternoon. I decided to pay a surprise call on my old friend. As my car turned the corner onto his block, I felt dizzy with nervousness. I drove by the house a couple of times before I could bring myself to stop.

I checked my lipstick in the rearview mirror. I checked my eyes, my hair. I was so young I didn't need to check anything, but I didn't know that.

Finally I got out and walked up to the house. I quickly pushed the doorbell before I could change my mind.

I had never called upon a man friend in all my years of marriages. But I needed to look into the face of somebody who had once cared so much, a man who once found me attractive.

A tall, distinguished-looking black butler answered the door.

"Is Mr. Neal in?" I asked.

"I will see," he said. "Would you please wait?"

No sooner had he closed the door when a wave of embarrassment washed over me.

I turned and ran down the walk. Just as I opened the car door, I heard my old friend's voice.

"Mary *Frances*!! Well, what do you know about that?"

I looked up, happy to see his dear, handsome face.

"What fun to see you!" he said. "Come on in and have a drink."

He led me into the house. I entered his world once again—a house more beautiful than I remembered. How quiet and safe it felt.

We spent the next few hours reminiscing. We talked about his life and what he had been doing. His free-spirited personality was exactly the same, reminding me of how, at seventeen, I was frightened by his fast and crazy-wild ways. Wild to Mary Frances.

So many memories flooded my mind that afternoon that it was difficult to tear myself away—to get back to my husband who was hell-bent on destroying our lives. My heart was aching by the time I got up to leave.

Bob walked me to my car and when I got inside, he leaned in through the window, brushing my lips with his, and said good-bye.

I drove away, hardly able to see the curves in the road through the tears—tears for what I didn't have; tears for what could have been; tears for what was gone forever.

Three weeks into the shooting of *Helen*, I just couldn't take anymore. I wanted to replace Shelley. As a producer, I had some say.

Geraldine Page was ready to come in. Then it was pointed out to me that we had so much footage already, replacing her would put the picture $400,000 over budget.

So she stayed and bedlam prevailed. Then I got another one of my hyperventilation attacks on the set. I just fell down. Not one thing could move. They called the paramedics and an ambulance. My brother, Bill, who was my makeup man, sat at my side.

Bill held me in his arms while I sobbed. Everyone on the set was nonplussed. Bill was devastated by what was happening to me. It was the first time my brother and I ever shared a moment like that. I will never forget it. I was so starved just to have someone's arms around me. Curtis Harrington later told me they were afraid I was in such bad shape that they'd have to close down production.

Shelley was upset too. But for different reasons, as well. "Don't you die, Debbie," she kept yelling. "Don't you dare!"

The ambulance came and they put me in it.

They shut the door, with Shelley banging on the windows as they drove me away. "Don't you dare DIE, Debbie! They'll blame me! It's not my fault!"

I was in the ambulance and she was still in her part: the psycho.

I got over my attack rather quickly; production was not shut down. We were getting close to the end. Thank God.

I gave a party for the cast and crew at the end of the picture. Shelley came, her joyful self, just as happy as if nothing had happened. She brought a handsome young man. We all had dinner and afterward sat around talking about the whole experience. I started telling stories on Shelley—about the operatic records and ripping the door off the hinges, et cetera.

With every story Shelley would say, "Oh, I didn't do that, Debbie. You really have such an imagination."

And then the crew would chime with "Yeah, Shelley, you really did. You did do that, Shelley, you did that."

"Well, I certainly didn't mean it, Debbie," she said. "You know I love you."

Throughout the shooting, Shelley always complained that the cameraman made me look better. It was because I had used an eyelight for my scenes—a little bullet lamp that sits on a tripod by the camera, that gives your eyes an extra bit of light to make them stand out. At the party, as a farewell gift I gave her my eyelight so that she "would always look beautiful like Debbie."

Well, she loved it and was full of laughs and gratitude. She left the party taking the eyelight, her chocolate-chip cookies, a glass of wine, and her boyfriend, happy as could be that she'd look good in her next picture.

I swore that I'd never talk to her again. But I didn't keep that promise for long. *What's the Matter with Helen?* opened to good reviews. Shelley said to me, "The only reason you received any notices at all was because I drove you so crazy that you became good."

"You drove me so crazy I almost died," I said. "You're neurotic."

"You have to be neurotic, Debbie, to make a part work for you," she instructed me.

I must say I'm very fond of Shelley today. I don't think anyone in her life knows what's going to happen next, including Shelley, although she may plan the scenes, because her life is full of them.

The film was not a box-office success, although after seeing it more than fifteen years later, I still regard it as one of my best films and some of my best work. With all the crises, Shelley's performance was possibly one of the best in her illustrious career. However, United Artists, which released the picture, never got behind it.

CHAPTER 49

IT WAS DURING THAT TIME that Harry came home one day with a paper for me to sign.

"What's this?" I asked, looking at it, wondering what he'd tell me after all those years when I'd sign anything without so much as a question.

"It's just a continuing mortgage for the beach house, like a renewal," he said casually while pouring himself a drink.

The beach house belonged to me. It wasn't held jointly. I didn't even know it had a mortgage on it. I'd bought the land and built the house with the money I made on *Molly Brown*.

I looked at the paper for a few more minutes. Harry sipped his drink and waited. He must have wondered what I was thinking. I'd never taken so long to sign anything before.

Finally I put it down on the coffee table. "I won't sign it."

He was taken aback. He set down his drink. "But you have to," he said.

"No. I don't have to do anything." I got up out of my chair to leave the room. "And I won't."

It festered inside me. Why would he do it? That's what went on in my mind over and over. I had faults, flaws, shortcomings, hang-ups, but all in all I was a pretty terrific wife. I gave everything I had to give. So why would he do it?

I told Agnes my problems. She listened patiently. I could spend hours talking, and I could cry with Agnes, but her advice was always stoic. Go back to him. You can work it out. She thought what he had done was terrible, but she liked him. I understood. You couldn't not like Harry, on an everyday basis.

I could cry with Lillian but there was nothing she could say, except "I told you so," which she didn't do. Lillian's own marriage was far from perfect at that time too.

Carrie came to know after seeing Gregory in Spain. Even then, I didn't discuss it. She now knew that Harry and I had problems. He has a gambling problem. There are debts. It's very bad. I'm not sure how I'm going to handle this.

That was it. No discussions. She listened, and she asked questions. "Why, Mother?" Carrie always wanted to know "why" from the time she began to speak. Her first word was "hi" and her second word was "why."

I didn't want Carrie to be upset—although looking back, how could she not be? I didn't want her to feel sorry for me. I didn't want her to feel the way I did as a young girl when my mother would cry on the back step and tell me how lonely she was because my father paid no attention to her. I knew Carrie couldn't *do* anything to change things. I didn't want to burden her with the anguish young people can so easily feel about their parents' problems.

One afternoon right after the New Year in 1971, she handed me a note pad. "Read this," she said, and walked away. From the time she learned how to spell and write, Carrie was always putting things down on paper—little stories, rhymes, poems. The talent was evident from the beginning and I was awed and dazzled by it. I knew then that she would one day have a career as a writer. Anything she gave me to read was a joy to behold. I was so proud of her.

I sat down in my dressing room to read what looked like an essay.

Sacrifice for love is "noble"—is healthy—is reasonable . . .

it began. An essay on "personal sacrifice," I thought, smiling to myself; how fascinating . . .

Sacrifice for sacrifice's sake only gains your own depletion.
    It doesn't matter. There was no love. It's not romantic. NO. AMEN. It's not worth it. NO. He's not worth it . . ."

I realized this was written for me, to me . . .

If it could matter—if anything you gave him could bring his self-respect back, then YES.
    But he doesn't want help. He only wants what he cannot have. And he cannot have that because he made it eventually impossible.
    You owe no debt. He did himself in. He wanted to lose. And

your giving to him is a waste. Sacrifice to him is a waste. He is VERY happy being unhappy. He doesn't want to be happy because he screwed it up. We were the "ideal family." Nothing wrong. He ruined it. He lied. He deceived. He somehow chose this state. He could get out. He could work. He WON'T. Not CAN'T. WON'T. And that's not your problem.

That's why I hate him. If he loved me, if he loved us, he never would have fucked it up. It was only him. He did it.

I AM CORRECT NOT IRRATIONAL OR EMOTIONAL JUST ACCURATE AND ANGRY. YOU HAVE A LOT TO GIVE AND DON'T GIVE IT TO THOSE WHO COULDN'T GIVE A SHIT.

He will never love you for what you give him from now on. Because you don't give it out of love, you give it out of guilt. He's only taking advantage of you. He'll use the hard earned money you give him for his whores, gambling, masseuses and vanity. He gave up. YES. So why contribute?

Giving to Harry is banging your head against a wall. Giving to Harry doesn't matter. Your guilt is unfounded. Learn to act out of love. Stop doing things you "should" do. Do what you want to do. If you want to give, at least give to someone it makes happy. Giving to Harry makes no one happy. ACT out of love. There's nothing you "should" do. There's no such word. Only do things that make you and other people happy. Both you and Harry are miserable, so why drag it out? It only makes all of us unhappy. Todd and I included. There must be ends to things. Everything ends. Even this essay.

"Both you and Harry are miserable. . . . It only makes us un-happy. . . . Todd and I . . ."

I sat there, staring at the pages I'd read.

. . . I AM CORRECT NOT IRRATIONAL OR EMOTIONAL JUST ACCURATE AND ANGRY . . .

Her large loopy letters, the open, innocent penmanship of a bright child, filled the small pages with a powerful impact. It dawned on me. I was almost forty years old: My fourteen-year-old daughter was living in reality and I was living in a nursery rhyme. The dish ran away with the spoon.

How sad for her. I had not been able to protect her from it. Watching me when he came home every night. Seeing him kiss me on the cheek. Seeing me turn the other way. Knowing that the women who came to the house daily, supposedly to cut his hair or nails, were in fact performing sexual favors. This was the home I found for my children.

Carrie was right. We had had the "ideal life." Harry still treated all of us as if nothing had happened. It was as if to him, nothing had. I knew in my gut I had to get out of it. I didn't want it and at the same time, couldn't imagine my life without it.

I signed a new Vegas contract in 1971—my first in almost five years—with Howard Hughes's Summa Corporation, a two-year contract to play the Desert Inn, guaranteeing me almost half a million a year. "The Million Dollar Baby" they called me; "one of the town's most lucrative contracts," crowed one of the columnists. Not as lucrative as it sounds when you finish paying everybody—two dancers, nine singers, arrangements, accompanist, conductor, orchestra, lighting, sound, wardrobe, and hairdresser. Then don't forget Uncle Sam. But I wasn't complaining; I was delighted. It came in the nick of time.

We started putting the act together in January. The first gig was scheduled for four weeks beginning March 11.

The whole company flew to Vegas a few days before, to rehearse. Harry was coming down for opening night. I got him his own room.

Late on the afternoon of opening night, I was just about to leave when Harry barged in. This was the first I'd seen him since he'd arrived. He was very agitated.

"Why do I have my own room?" he asked, looking flustered and embarrassed, like a fifty-eight-year-old, white-haired little boy.

"Because you snore and you keep me awake," I said lamely, but quickly.

"That's an excuse," he shot back.

I turned to leave the room. "I have to go now, and put my costume on," I said, closing the door behind me. I knew he had no argument with that.

I was standing in front of the elevator when he came out into the hallway, and started walking toward me.

"You're trying to *humiliate* me," he yelled.

It was the first time in our entire relationship that he had raised his voice to me. "You're trying to embarrass me. You want them to think that I don't sleep with my wife!"

"Well," I said, "you don't."

Those were the strongest words I'd ever had with him.

Just at that moment, as if it had been written in a script, the elevator arrived. I strode in and the doors closed behind me.

Back in the suite after the show, Harry was waiting. "You're angry at me about something."

Angry was too nice a word. "See this ring," I said, pointing to my twenty-one-carat diamond. "This doesn't mean anything! *This*," I said, pointing to the wedding band, "is the important one."

He looked at me, staring, and said nothing.

"I just can't sleep in the same bed with you, that's all." I turned around and went back to taking off my makeup.

He sat there, saying not a word. A few minutes went by. He got up, got some more ice for his glass, poured himself another Scotch, and took a drink.

"You're right, Debbie. I do snore too loud. We're really all right. This is just a change in our marriage."

"You don't want to sleep with me anyway, so . . ." I added.

But he didn't pick up on it. He said nothing. I dropped it. I didn't care anymore.

A few minutes later he gave me a peck on the cheek, told me he was going to go to bed, and left. I knew he wasn't going to bed. He was going to gamble; gamble at least some of my salary.

But I didn't discuss it. The money. The women. What could I say? Don't do that or else! Or else what? I simply had to find a way out of the mess without destroying everyone's life. It would take time, I told myself, but I'd find a way.

CHAPTER 50

THE FIRST TIME I MET Warren Beatty I was sitting underneath a hair dryer at MGM. It must have been about 1960 because I remember I was between husbands.

I was reading a book and suddenly the lid went up. This gorgeous young man wearing horn-rimmed glasses was smiling down at me.

"I've always wanted to meet you," he said.

I had already heard of him, Shirley MacLaine's brother.

"My name is Warren Beatty."

He'd already had a string of heartbreaks. Joan Collins, Leslie, Natalie; I can't remember the order.

He pulled a chair up, sat on it with the back in front of himself, like a schoolboy, his face no more than twelve inches from mine.

I was sitting there, no makeup, my hair up, embarrassed. He was adorable, it was true, totally adorable. It was the boyish charm that got to you. Plus the talk among the girls that he was the greatest lover ever, that he satisfied women until he was bored with them.

We chatted. He asked me if I'd like to have dinner with him.

"No."

"Why?"

"Because. I don't feel we're compatible."

"But why?" He looked amused and slightly hurt.

"Because. You're not my type."

He just kept looking at me.

". . . You're a very forward young man," I added.

"Age has nothing to do with it," he stated.

I thought of Leslie, who left her family for him, and then he left her.

"No, thank you," I said.

And that was the story of Debbie and Warren.

More than ten years had passed since that day, when one afternoon Carrie went on an interview for a part in Warren Beatty's new picture *Shampoo*. She came home with a script, very excited. They wanted her.

"In the story, I'm supposed to have an affair with Warren," she said, starry-eyed.

Wait a minute, I was thinking to myself. Warren. Leslie, Joan, Natalie, and who knew how many others. And now my own daughter? Carrie? At seventeen?

I was all for Carrie having an acting career. When she was four and five years old, she was performing little "plays" in her closet for her mommy and her brother. When I first did my act in Vegas, she learned every step and every line. It all came very naturally to her, and I assumed that she'd one day have a career.

But did she have to start it with Warren Beatty as her lover, on film, that is?

I sat down to read her script with an open mind. My eyes came to an abrupt halt: Her first line ever on screen, her first time ever on screen, would be: "Wanna fuck?"

This was a problem. I knew how much the part meant to her. She wouldn't have been fazed by the language, I was sure.

"I hardly think you'll be pleased later on, Carrie."

She was not pleased, at that very moment, with her mother. She looked at me blankly. "Mother, I say 'fuck' every day, so it's no big deal to me."

"That's a very special word," I added tactfully.

She changed her approach. "Oh, Mother, please let me do it. It's a wonderful part and it's going to be a wonderful picture."

Carrie was always a determined and expressive child. There had been a stage she went through when one of her teachers in school would call her "Debbie." This often happens with stars and their children, who end up feeling they have to fight for their identity. And Carrie always had an identity.

Carrie and I had reached that phase where there is not a lot of communication. But I felt very shut out. I didn't like it, although I knew she had to go through it, just as when the script for *Shampoo* came up, I knew it was important for her to do something on her own, and not as Debbie's daughter.

It was the language in the script that got to me. That and Warren worried me. Here she was, barely a teenager. Now he's going to be *Uncle* Warren?

Carrie told Warren I objected to her using the "F" word. He called me and asked if he could talk to me. Sure, I said.

"I don't like the wordage," I told him. "Maybe it would be all right if she said something different," I conceded.

Warren behaved patiently with me. "What would you suggest, Debbie? How about 'screw'?"

"Okay," I said, "how about it?"

"Because it won't work for the script. Fuck is fuck."

"Well . . . maybe it isn't just the word, Warren. Maybe that's not what's bothering me. You know Carrie is very mature for her age, but she's still really just a child . . ."

"You're being ridiculous and Victorian," he said.

"That's what I am."

"No, you're not; and she isn't, and you can't hold her back. She's anxious to do this and she'll be damned good. I promise you I'll never be anything to her but her uncle and the producer."

He finally persuaded me. He'd be the producer and her uncle. And it was a great part in a great script. When it came to shooting time, he picked her up every morning and returned her every evening.

I was wide-awake at 6:00 A.M. the first morning Warren came to the house for Carrie. There he was, at the door, tousled hair and all.

He knew what I was thinking as I watched my child go out into the world. "I promise you, Debbie, I will not touch her. If I tell you that's the truth, that's the truth."

Fine. Fine. I found it hard to believe, but he kept his word! He never made a play and Carrie made her motion-picture debut with a brilliant performance in a brilliant comedy.

I always tried to do everything in my power to give my children a semblance of a "normal" life. But growing up in Beverly Hills with your mother in the entertainment business is a far cry from 1034 Evergreen Street, Burbank, no matter how you look at it. My daughter was a more sophisticated child than I had been. Fortunately, she had the same sense of right and wrong for herself that I did when I was her age. I never had to worry about Carrie just as my mother never had to worry about me.

For Tina—and for me with Tina—it was different; and not so simple. Neither time nor patience made life easier for Tina. There were no rules that she'd adhere to. And there was no stopping her.

She was obsessed with the idea that Carrie got more than she did. More of everything. When she didn't like her school clothes, she simply took herself down to Theodore, an expensive boutique on Rodeo Drive, and charged a whole wardrobe. It never occurred to her to either ask or inform me. For her sixteenth birthday she wanted a Porsche. So I bought her one. Not a new one, but a nice one. When it broke down once on some hillside road, she got out and just left it there, where it remained until we sent someone for it.

She hated the private school we'd sent her to. She was always threatening to run away but she hated being away from home more.

I didn't want her to come home every weekend because I couldn't always be there.

When I tried to explain *why*, she would fly into a rage: I didn't want her, I never loved her; I didn't care. She was wrong. I did care.

But she won. She was out. She was home. My problem was I wouldn't be home much now, so there would be no controlling her. When I was home, I could lay down the law. She had to be in by a certain time and I had to know where she was going. But unless I followed her, how could I ever be sure?

Once she was back living at home, she found a new group of friends, people who took her to parties. Parties in the early 1970s in Beverly Hills always meant drugs. Sex and drugs. I had long before warned Tina about her special problem with drugs, because she had been born an addict. Many, many times I tried to impress on her what Dr. Wile had told me about addicted infants: Their systems are hypersensitive to addictive drugs.

She didn't care. She was growing up and wanted to go out at night. One night I discovered she was leaving at eleven o'clock.

"Where are you going at this hour, Tina?"

"I'm going to a party."

"With whom?"

"With myself."

"At eleven o'clock at night, going as a single girl to a party? No."

"I'm meeting a lot of people there." She named a few.

"That's all the more reason why you're not going out. You have a date, you have a date. You're invited, you're invited. But you're not going alone up to someone's door."

"Well, I'm going," she shrugged coldly.

Well, she wasn't going, as far as I was concerned. It was no small confrontation that night. I had to physically tackle her to stop her.

She found other methods. One early evening she left, telling me that she was going to stay overnight with a girlfriend. The following day, by late afternoon, she hadn't returned home. About dinnertime, the doorbell rang. I was sitting in the den with Harry.

The butler came in and said, "There's a man at the door with Tina."

A man? With Tina? I went to the door—and standing there was a man, a skinny little character with glasses, like Wally Cox, holding my stepdaughter in his arms. She was completely unconscious, ashen; out like a light.

"I brought her home," he said casually, as if he were delivering pizza.

I was shocked and angry at the sight. If it's never happened before, it doesn't occur to you when your child tells you she is going to spend the night with a friend, that she's going to come back almost a corpse, a leftover from a drug-induced free-for-all.

But somehow I knew what had happened. I hated the delivery boy.

"Would you mind carrying her in, since you carried her out?" I said, barely stifling my fury.

He took her into the living room and put her on a couch.

"What did you give her?" I asked. "What has she had? We have to know."

He looked at me, his eyeballs dilating. "Well, I have to go now. That's the way it goes, babe." And out the door he went.

It gave me chills to look at her, her clothes wrinkled and stained— looking dead, like a bag of bones.

I took her hand and slapped it for a reaction. Nothing. I tapped her cheek. "Tina. Tina. Wake up."

Nothing. She was completely out. But she was breathing.

I called the doctor. I wanted to call the police, but that would have meant calling the world.

Before the doctor arrived, Tina awakened. She lifted her head, and still disoriented, looked around. Then she vomited all over herself. We sat her up, and she threw up again. With every breath she heaved, more would come up. She went on and on and on.

The doctor came.

"Definitely drugs," he said. "The child is very ill. It's too late to pump her stomach."

There was nothing he or anyone else could do but wait until she got rid of whatever she had ingested.

We put her in her room and I took care of her. For three days, Tina threw up green bile. It turned out she had been to a party at a Beverly Hills mansion. The host gave parties swarming with young starlets and sexually enthusiastic older men, including many celebrities. Drugs, booze, and mind obliteration was the name of the game.

My hope was that this would teach Tina a lesson, making it clear how she could have lost her life. It was only a hope, and not a realistic one. But I had no alternative. I was in no position to stop working to stay home and keep an eye on her. I couldn't handcuff her to the bed or lock her away as I've read some parents have done.

I sent her to a psychiatrist, thinking perhaps the counseling would help. She went, but she wouldn't talk to him. Her mother, she said, had always told her *never* talk to a psychiatrist. It was just throwing money away. Money that we didn't have anymore.

CHAPTER **51**

By 1970–71 HARRY KARL was dead broke. It didn't look as if he was broke, with his three hundred shoe stores, the factory in Spain, the three fully staffed houses, the shirts flying to New York, the Rollses, and the wife working the theaters across the nation. Who would think Harry Karl was broke?

Even I had a hard time believing it. Where did twenty-one million dollars go?!

Where you throw it, that's where.

I think it finally hit home, once and for all, the night I went into the wall safe in his den to get out my emeralds. Every piece of jewelry I kept there, including my diamond cross, was missing. Hundreds of thousands of dollars' worth of jewels and Harry had hocked it all.

I just stared. Had I put them someplace else and forgotten? Were they really *gone*?!

I didn't waste any time asking where and why. And Harry, unflappable as usual, told me "we" needed the money.

Oh.

Since he still had the business, and since many times over the years he had received offers to sell it, obviously the time had now come.

Hartfield-Zodys, the department-store chain, and its chairman, a very nice man named Abe Marks, made the offer. It came to about five million in cash and stock.

Part of the deal was that Debbie Reynolds would do television commercials for Zodys. For nothing. They had originally wanted exclusivity, but I wasn't about to do that. I was only willing to get Harry out of the hole. Or so I thought at the time.

There were all kinds of papers for me to sign. It was a merger and, as Mrs. Harry Karl, I was a principal. What I had yet to learn was that I didn't own anything. I was equity. It was like my first contract at Warners—the options were all theirs.

310

Karl Shoes had millions in outstanding debts to the State Street Bank of Boston. Because Harry had owned Karl Shoes outright, he had been able to *personally* borrow those millions, using the company as collateral. When Hartfield-Zodys assumed control, it did not assume the debt. That was Harry's, and the State Street Bank of Boston now owned him. Everybody thought he was richer because he sold for millions. But it wasn't his money anymore.

It was about that same time that Harry Rigby, the Broadway producer who'd been responsible for the spectacular revival of *No No Nanette,* called me about doing a revival of the 1919 musical *Irene.* I hadn't been on a stage in a legit show since *Best Foot Forward* with Joan Bennett in St. Louis in 1950. I had never been on Broadway.

Harry Rigby was one of the all-time Broadway characters. Tall, bony, almost anorexic-looking, with fine gray hair, he had a high, nasal voice in a range somewhere between a flute and Phyllis Diller. His conversation was full of dramatic gestures. *Irene* represented more than money to Harry. This was going to be the all-time Broadway hit! Harry lived, ate, and slept the theater.

They all laughed at him when he first came up with the idea of reviving *Nanette* and, what's more, starring Ruby Keeler, who hadn't set foot on a stage in almost forty years. They thought he was crazy. And he was. But it was creative crazy and the show, of course, turned out to be a smash.

I knew I had to go somewhere; there weren't any films coming my way. So I told Harry to send the script to Lillian. If she thought it was right for me, I'd do it.

Harry flew out to California and met with her, spelling out his plans. Among other things, he said he was after Sir John Gielgud, one of the world's greatest Shakespearean actors, to direct the show.

Lillian read the script and listened to Harry's ideas.

"It'll take some doing, but I *think* it could work, Debbie," she said.

That was all I had to hear. It was like the last lifeboat; I just grabbed.

Harry was jubilant. He called Sir John, who happened to be in California at the time, and asked if he would come over to the house to meet me. I was awed by the thought of working with the great Gielgud.

When we met I was even more awed that he recalled meeting me at MGM almost twenty-five years before.

He had been making *Julius Caesar,* and I was just a kid they were trying to figure out what to do with. George Cukor was directing a test of me and asked if Sir John could talk to little Mary Frances about

Shakespeare, which she had never read, let alone acted. I listened raptly, I'm sure, and forgot it all shortly thereafter. When you don't know, you forget foolishly.

In the music room at Greenway that afternoon, with Rudy accompanying me on the piano, I sang Sir John several songs from the show. He was a great audience. He agreed on the spot to direct. Harry Rigby had succeeded in bringing together the never-imagined theatrical combination of Debbie Reynolds and Sir John Gielgud.

Irene, I knew, was going to be my ticket out of the marriage. I would take Carrie out of school and put her in the show, so that she could be with me. I'd leave Todd with my brother until he finished his school year. And then I would make the separation legal. Tina would live at home with her father until the house was sold. She would then have to go to school. In the meantime, I'd pay the mortgages, pay the help, pay the gardeners, and pay for the food and expenses at Greenway. Carrie and I would stay in hotels until the show opened. Then I would rent a house or apartment in New York and send for Todd.

The show was slated to begin rehearsals in New York the last week in October, with a tryout in Toronto the end of November, then on to Philadelphia and an opening in New York in January 1973.

I asked Bill if Todd could stay with him and his family. He would have a stable home life with an uncle and an aunt and not be raised by a stepfather whose time at home was spent in bed watching television with a set of earphones planted on his head.

When Bill asked his wife if Todd could stay, she said no. Todd, in her view, was a totally spoiled Beverly Hills kid and therefore would be a bad influence on her children. Her decision came as a real blow to me and my brother. It was bad enough that I had to take Carrie out of school. That was basically the end of her formal education.

My children were spoiled in the sense that I gave them wonderful toys. But neither was difficult or a disciplinary problem. Todd was, in fact, one of the most agreeable, children I've ever known. When he was two, his four-year-old sister hit him over the head with a plastic baseball bat and knocked him out. When he came to he was smiling.

So Todd would have to stay with Harry until the show opened on Broadway. At least, I rationalized, Harry was good to Todd, Bo, and Tina. Mary Douglas French, the housekeeper who'd been with me ten years, would also be there. He'd have his friends and his things and his own room. I'd have to settle for that.

CHAPTER **52**

THE DAY BEFORE I WAS to leave for New York, I was running around the bedroom and dressing room getting myself packed and organized. Harry was on the bed, sitting up, dressed only in a silk shirt and his boxer shorts. He was sucking on a Popsicle, earphones on his head, watching Hepburn and Bogart in *The African Queen*.

I went over and sat down next to Harry, who was riveted to the tube, his lips barely ever leaving the cherry-flavored ice.

"Watch this scene, dear, it's fabulous," he said without looking away.

I pulled the plugs out of the earphones.

"Harry," I said, "I've told you for a week now—tomorrow I am leaving to do this play . . ."

"Yes, I know," he said, plugging the phones back in. "But watch these two—they're tremendous in this scene."

I spoke louder. "You know, we really have to talk about this. Because I don't know when I'm coming back. If at all."

"Fine. Whatever you want to do," he said, glued to the TV.

I couldn't believe he'd heard me.

I spoke a little louder. "Harry, you really have to understand something. I might not be back. I might get a separation."

"Whatever you want to do is fine."

He was better at ignoring facts than I was. He was an ostrich.

I finally stopped talking. I kissed him on the cheek, got up, and left him with his movie. Bogart and Hepburn were on the boat, going down the river, heading for the rapids, And I was on my way out the door.

The first day of rehearsal was in New York in the cold and creaky old Broadway Arts Studio, on October 23, 1972. The producers turned it into a media event. Sir John Gielgud comes to Broadway to direct a revival musical with a stellar cast including Ruth Warrick, Patsy Kelly, Billy De Wolfe, and Monte Markham as my leading man.

313

Billy De Wolfe and I sang "They Go Wild, Simply Wild, over Me" for the television cameras. The press applauded and the air was full of that sweet smell of success.

Sir John was an enthusiastic director. He had staged both plays and operas in Europe but this was his first time out with a musical comedy. However, with Sir John in one place directing the book part of the show and Peter Gennaro in another separately staging the musical numbers, the finished product had an ominously patched-together quality.

There was a new script reworked by Harry Rigby and Hugh Wheeler, but it still failed to pull together smoothly. Harry, for all his enthusiasm and effusiveness, was not a strong producer, much less a writer. Shtick was his metier. His way was to ignore things until they couldn't be ignored. Then he'd criticize the script by telling the writer, "That stinks" or "That's bad." You can't say that to a writer and expect good results.

Only a few weeks into rehearsals, Billy De Wolfe's health was failing badly and he had to leave the show. The press saw his leaving as one of the first signs of a show in trouble, implying the health issue was an excuse, but Billy died not long after.

Peter Gennaro's dances were good, and the costumes and sets were good, but Sir John was having difficulty with the pacing of a musical. Without direction, my instinct for handling the problem as an actress was to add to my performance by playing to the audience almost the way I would in a club—playing for laughs. What developed was a very slow-moving show with a series of big production numbers. It wasn't working.

Five weeks after rehearsals began, on November 27, *Irene* opened in Toronto at the Royal Alexandra Theatre. It was chaos. One local critic liked it and the other hated it. The trade reviews recognized the commercial possibilities but were less than wild about it.

Opening night, the leading man started in on his song—which was "You Made Me Love You"—eight bars late, and sang against the music. It was awful. One of the all-time great pop standards and you couldn't even recognize it coming out of his mouth. So I stopped the orchestra, and said to the boys in the pit, "This is a fabulous song, when we do it right. So why don't we start over again."

We did just that.

Well. After the show the leading man spent forty-five minutes reading me the riot act in my dressing room.

"You're not an actress. You can't act your way out of a paper bag! How *dare* you stop a play? How *dare* you!!

"You were singing in the wrong key," I explained. "Eight bars ahead. And you never knew the difference."

He continued raging and I just sat there and let him go on. Harry Rigby, our producer, meanwhile, was sitting on the floor playing Chinese checkers with my hairdresser. He wouldn't discuss it.

The leading man kept right on telling me off. Finally I'd had it.

"I wonder if you've read one thing in your contract," I said. "I have the right to fire the leading man."

His face changed. He didn't know that.

"Well, I don't need this," he snarled. "I can quit."

"I hear the California air's wonderful this time of year," I said. In other words, go if you want.

He stayed.

It was all a big mess. Everyone knew it. We started making changes. A new opening number. A new finale. Drop this song, add that. Move this scene, cut that. Another new opening number; another new finale. *Nothing* worked. Everyone was insane with exhaustion.

Our fourth week in Toronto, on a Sunday night, I developed a sore throat. By Monday morning I felt fine but couldn't talk. Janie Sell, who was my understudy, but who also had her own part in the show, wasn't prepared to go on for me. The theater owner refused to call off the performance because, he claimed, he had several hundred people coming all the way from Buffalo, in a snowstorm, on a special theater tour.

Well, I thought, the show must go on. Sir John decided that he would stand out on the stage and read my lines, and the lyrics of my songs, while I would do my dancing. We had guts! It was less than successful. The next day the newspapers made a small international incident out of it.

The following day I recovered but I was beginning to feel as if I had been drafted for a war. The only thing that saved us was that we were doing capacity business every night with a fifteen-dollar top, a very expensive theater ticket in 1972.

The opening in Philadelphia was even worse than in Canada if that was possible. The critics skewered the show. Harry Rigby was now apoplectic with rage at Sir John. Every train from New York seemed to bring down some possible new director.

I was on the phone to Joe Stein, who wrote *Fiddler on the Roof*, talking him into coming in and rewriting the script. Joe had his own problems—his wife was dying of cancer.

Todd called me from California one morning.

"Mother, I don't want to bother you, but there's no food in the house."

Harry, I assumed, was giving Mary money for food. That was our arrangement. Mary got on the phone. She hadn't had money for food in more than two weeks. I wired them a check for $600 for shopping, but the whole thing made me all the more uneasy about Todd's situation.

I was miserable and I was tired. I'd gone from a 112 to 97 pounds, exasperated and crying all the time because the show was in such chaos.

And it had to be a success!!

I felt like my life was wrecked. It was Christmastime and my son was in California. The script was a disaster; the staging was off. I knew they were trying to replace Sir John, but who could be sure what the next director would do?

I had an idea. I called Gower Champion in Malibu. If anybody was a miracle-worker, it was Gower.

I told him our long, sad tale. He had some time, so he said he would come to Philadelphia and look at everything. I was ecstatic, although not all the producers were.

CHAPTER **53**

PATSY KELLY CAME INTO my dressing room one night after the show.

"You know the show's a dud, don't you?" she asked after a sip of gin.

"I know."

"Well, we gotta fix it."

"I know that, Patsy."

"But how the hell do you fix it?"

"I called Gower Champion and he said he'd take over the show."

"Well, that's great!" she said, and promptly passed out.

She looked like I felt. She had only had a couple of drinks, but she was blotto from stress and overwork—not before or during the show, but right after. Bob O'Connell, my wardrobe man, put her in a wheel-chair. Then he and I and my hairdresser, Pinky, wheeled Patsy to her room, undressed her, and put her to bed. She was out. Sometimes I envied her.

The three of us went back to my room. We were sitting there, dis-cussing the problems of the show, exhilarated that Gower was coming in, hopeful that disaster would be staved off, when suddenly, out in the hallway, we heard a loud crash and a woman screaming.

We ran out the door and before us in the elevator, door wide open, was Patsy, lying stark naked on the floor, partially covered by dozens of hors d'oeuvres, small sandwiches, pickles, cheese, and crackers.

"I've been raped," she was yelling.

"How could you be raped?" I asked. "You were out like a light, in bed, all alone, just a few minutes ago."

She lifted her head off the floor and looked around. "Well, I dunno," she stammered. "I got on the elevator and this waiter came . . . and he raped me!"

What had happened was some waiter had been waiting for the ele-vator (at four in the morning) with a large tray of food. The door opened and Patsy was standing there in all her glory. She fainted at the sight of him, and fell to the floor. He screamed, spilled the hors d'oeuvres all over her, and fled.

O'Connell, Pinky, and I became Patsy's guardians. Every night we'd have to take care of her because she'd get upset about something. It gave her an excuse to have a drink, and Patsy was a notoriously big drinker. Every night was a new experience with Patsy, and a hysterical diversion from our backstage worries.

Despite all the problems with the show the box office was booming. People were lined up every morning and the theater was packed every night. By that time the show had become hot copy on both coasts. A show in trouble, *big* trouble; rumors flying, most of them untrue. *Irene* had already become the most expensive show in the history of Broadway—$750,000—and was getting more expensive every day.

The producers let Sir John go. A sensitive, gifted man, after all of his hard efforts, he'd become the fall guy. The night he was leaving he came to my dressing room, and leaning against the door with tears in his eyes, he said: "I've been told to go, Debbie. They want me to leave. This has never happened before. It's all so unfair."

They had treated this great talent in such an insensitive way.

Joe Stein came through for us with a better script. The first thing Gower did was to extend the out-of-town tryouts for an additional four weeks in Washington, D.C., and postpone the New York opening to March 13, after two weeks of previews. New songs were added. Some songs were dropped. A new opening number, a new finale. Dialogue was being revised daily.

From the time in Toronto, I had wanted Lillian to coach me for the part, but for personal reasons, she couldn't leave California. Finally, on our first Tuesday night in Washington, she and George showed up at the performance. Backstage afterward, I could tell by the look on her face that she had a few thoughts.

"This is not Vegas," she said. "There's a proscenium arch between you and the audience this time. You can't go out to them. You must take the audience in and make them follow you."

That night she and George came back to my hotel. He fell asleep on the couch while Lillian and I went to work. We were up until 4:00 A.M. The next day was Wednesday—with matinee and evening performances. Lillian stayed over one more night, working with me until the early morning hours.

We opened in Washington less than a month after President Nixon's second inauguration. The president was already besieged by the oncoming Watergate scandal and he rarely made public appearances. On the afternoon of February 22, however, we learned that Mr. and Mrs. Nixon and their daughter Tricia were coming to that night's performance, along with dozens of Secret Service agents. It was the first time the president had attended the theater in the five years that he'd been in office.

After the show, the Nixons came backstage to say hello. He gave the show a rave and predicted it would be a big hit when it reached New York. His "review" made every newspaper, including some in Europe, and was reported on every television news show, giving *Irene* the kind of publicity money cannot buy.

By the time we finished our Washington tryout, *Irene* had done almost $1.5 million in record out-of-town business, and was going into New York with $1.5 million in advance ticket sales.

Harry and I still did not have a legal separation. He was planning on coming to New York for the opening. I had rented a townhouse but I didn't want Harry to stay with me. Now that we were going to be settled, it was time for Todd to come East to join Carrie and Pinky, who were staying with me.

I was afraid Harry might just want to remain in New York for a while, so I invited Mama Karl to come along for the opening too. I booked a suite at the Plaza for her and Harry, using the excuse with him that his mother was too old to stay alone.

Harry was very upset. "All my friends will know," he said.

"Tell them you're there because of your mother, if anybody asks. Besides, you know, I'm staying. I'm not coming home."

Harry said nothing, as if it didn't register.

"I'm not coming home to our marriage," I said again. "You have failed us."

"Aw com'on, Debbie, you know I love you. You know it's all going to work out okay."

It was as if he had a block. He'd cost me years of my life that I could not get back. That I was broke and forty and fighting for a new career on Broadway—where they would rather say good-bye to anyone from Hollywood than hello—was something that never seemed to cross Harry's mind.

We took *Irene* into New York on the first of March for the two weeks of previews at the brand-new Minskoff Theatre at Broadway and Forty-fifth Street. The night before opening we learned that the show had been given four Tony Award nominations: myself for best actress in a musical, Patsy Kelly for best supporting actress in a musical, George S. Irving for best supporting actor in a musical, and Peter Gennaro for his choreography. It was the first time in the history of the Tonys that nominations had been made before a show opened.

Irene finally opened on March 13, 1973, to decent reviews and a glittering after-the-show champagne party. The following morning there was a ticket line around the block. The show had been saved by Gower.

CHAPTER 54

FOR MY NEW HOME away from home at the Minskoff, the producers flew in Jerry Wunderlich, who designed a two-room dressing room for me, with grass-green carpets, walls covered with green and white trellis paper, and couches and chairs of white wicker. They even furnished daily bowls of fresh white daisies for the white coffee table. There was a limousine to take me to and from the theater, and as the star of the biggest hit musical on Broadway, I had invitations for every spare moment. The five months on the road paid off. I had proved to myself that I could do something I had never done before. I was forty-one and going strong. I felt that God was shining down on me, giving me a new direction in life.

Yet the truth was I felt tired and lonely. I was glad that Harry had gone back to California. I was happy to have my children with me; and I have always been very lucky to have the company of good friends like Rudy and Pinky working for me. But the homelife that I'd had with Harry for the past thirteen years was gone, over, finished. All that was left were just pieces of memories, debts, and casualties. No amount of public acclaim could heal such a hurt. Onstage, with the hair and the makeup, I looked fine. Offstage I was drinking too much and I looked like the victim of a war. Which I was.

The only way I thought I'd get through it was to keep imagining a five-year plan. I'd tell myself I was at the beginning of the tunnel, but if I could just get to the middle, I'd see the light at the end. Carrie said to me one day, "You're the only mother I know who works right through a nervous breakdown."

The breaking up of our family affected everyone. When I left California to go into rehearsals for *Irene*, Todd turned the back of the house into a Western town. He banged, he hammered, and instead of crying over the separation from his mother and sister, he took every bit of anger and frustration out by building.

When he came to New York, he took me by the hand and never let go for six months. When I came home from the theater at midnight, he'd still be awake, just waiting for me.

One Saturday night, about a month after we'd opened, I came home about 12:30. I had done a matinee that day, so I was very tired; so tired that I didn't take my usual bath. I didn't even take my makeup off. Instead I took off my clothes, put on a robe, and went into Todd's room.

He was watching A *Place in the Sun* with Shelley Winters and Montgomery Clift. Monty was drowning Shelley. I sat down on the sofa and was watching with Todd, who was casually fidgeting with a gun that looked like a prop I'd bought a few years before at the MGM auction.

Jokingly he pointed the gun at my head.

"Don't ever do that, dear; you don't point a gun at someone."

Then, still casually kidding around, he pointed it at our poodle, Killer.

Really annoyed, I said, "Todd, don't ever point a gun."

"Oh, it's nothing, Mom," he said.

A commercial came on the TV, with people tap-dancing. Todd said, "I'd love to learn how to tap dance."

I explained to him how much fun it was, but how difficult it was to learn. "You know you have to have loose knees and loose legs if you really want to be good."

At that moment, he casually pointed the gun at his knee, pulled the trigger, and it went off. Blood was spurting in the air, as if the kneecap had been blown away. He looked at it. I looked at it. His jovial face went from white to yellow.

I tore up a sheet and tied a tourniquet. There was a huge hole in his leg. He was just lying back staring at it. I was alone in New York City. I knew no hospital. I had no doctor. It was one in the morning and blood was all over everything. Frantically I dialed the operator.

I was crying into the telephone. I wanted to find a taxi to a hospital somewhere. "My son is bleeding to death! He's going to lose his leg!"

The operator must have thought I was some kind of drugged person, because she hung up.

Then I remembered I had an answering service. I called them. "Look," I said, "something terrible has happened. . . . My son has shot himself!"

The girl said, "Listen, call me tomorrow, you'll feel better."

"No!" I said, "I'm serious. I must know the name of a hospital!!"

The girl at the answering service started to cry. I was crying. "Please! Get me a cab! Hurry!"

I got off the phone to attend to the tourniquet, remembering to release it every twenty seconds so as not to cut off circulation in the leg.

I was running from Todd to the window and back again to Todd.

The doorbell rang. I ran down to let the driver in. He looked at me and said, "Oh, my God, it's Korea!"

I thought he meant I looked like I'd been in the war. Later he explained he'd seen me in Korea almost twenty-five years before.

He came upstairs with me. I was in a robe with only my makeup base on. I'd taken off my eyelashes. Big pieces of my hair were sprayed red for the wig I wore in the show. I looked like an Elsa Lanchester reject. I put on slippers and a brown dress with big white buttons. I left a note for Pinky and Carrie, who'd gone out to a disco: "Todd shot himself, I've gone to the hospital."

The driver threw Todd over his back—a fireman's hold—and carried him down to the landing. The two of us put him in the cab and we quickly drove to New York Hospital six blocks away. Meanwhile, I had to keep releasing the tourniquet, which got blood all over the cab.

At the hospital, the cabbie never left our side. There was no one in Emergency except a young resident, who proceeded to clean the wound. I was certain that Todd would have to have surgery. The doctor went off to report the accident.

"Mother, that's quite a mess, isn't it?" Todd said, staring at it.

"Yes, dear, you'll not tap-dance in the near future."

"We'll just sew it up," the doctor said when he came back.

"You can't sew it up. Just patch it until we get a surgeon," I said.

Then I called Jerry and Maggie Minskoff. They came down, thank God.

Maggie, who was a nurse, took one look at it and said, "Don't sew it up. The wound needs more cleaning."

"Right," I said, "but we don't have a doctor."

The Minskoffs called their doctor.

Then six cops showed up on the scene.

"You the owner of the gun?" one of them asked gruffly.

"Yes."

"We have to place you under arrest," another one said.

Under arrest?

It was two-thirty in the morning. Was this some horrible dream?

"I didn't shoot the gun!" I said. "It's not even a real gun. It's not even my gun. It's my son's. Or my husband's. It's a prop!"

"It doesn't matter, lady," another cop said. "You're the adult. He's the child and you're under arrest."

"This is silly. What if people are being murdered now, while you're arresting me?" I asked.

No response.

"You're arresting me?! Tammy?! You're arresting Tammy while the rest of the world's up for rape?!"

"Sorry, ma'am, the law's the law," one of them said.

I wasn't going to just leave my child and go with them. I put up enough of an argument that they let me see Todd to his room and sign the papers so that they could perform surgery in the morning.

Then I was taken off to the precinct. It was three o'clock in the morning. In my little brown dress, house slippers, I looked as awful as one can look at that time of night after sweating through two shows, major dance numbers and all.

At the precinct, the joint was jumping. They took me to a room where they were booking hookers.

That section was so busy, they ran out of ink for fingerprinting before they got to me. So they took me to the men's section with the rapists and the male hookers. There were fewer than in the women's section. Everyone was yelling "Hey baby, over here. You can sleep with me in my bunk." "Great, thanks a lot!" What a night.

I was allowed one phone call, so I called Pinky at home. "I'm in jail and Todd's in the hospital because he almost blew his leg off."

The police decided to release me since they didn't have Todd's gun, the murder weapon. At six o'clock on Sunday morning, the cops took me home.

Picasso died that day, but the picture of Todd in the hospital bed bumped him off the front page of the New York *Daily News*.

Eddie Fisher, who was lying on some beach down in Jamaica, heard about it and called. It was the only time Eddie ever called.

"What did you do to my son?" he demanded to know.

"Why would you care?"

"Because I love my son," he defended.

"Eddie," I said, "you don't even know your son." And I hung up the phone. I don't think I'd ever been more angry at him.

The following night the police got the gun. Todd, they found, unbeknownst to any of us, had a small arsenal. So I had to go back to the precinct. The same cabdriver drove us. Carrie and Killer, our poodle, came with me. The three of us sat for two hours on a wooden bench in the station house.

Because I couldn't be there, I sent Pinky to the hospital to be with Todd. They wouldn't let her in because she wasn't family. So she went outside, sneaked in through a service entrance, and stayed with Todd after he came out of surgery. I knew with Pinky there that he'd be all right. I didn't know where we—Carrie, the dog, and I—were going to land. I had to be arraigned—for possession of an unlicensed firearm. After the arraignment, I was released—fortunately—since it was now Tuesday and I had a show to do that night.

We had a happy ending. Todd didn't hit his kneecap or the main muscle. The surgery was successful in cleaning out the wound.

The cabdriver whom I'd met in Korea never left my side. Five years later, when I was in New York and had called for a cab, incredibly this same guy showed up.

"Remember me?" he asked.

"No," I said, truthfully.

"Remember this?" he said, pulling out the rags we'd used that night for Todd's leg, as well as the pictures that had been in the papers.

I'll never forget that. I went to church over that. He was a real hero.

CHAPTER **55**

TODD RECOVERED. I'd put him in a professional children's school in New York, which he hated. It was all creative children—ballet dancers, pianists, actors—not for Todd. Todd liked to build things. He liked to take pictures with his movie camera; he played with guns, et cetera. The boys didn't like him and he didn't like the boys.

One afternoon I came home and he was sitting on the floor of his bedroom with a redhead—long beautiful red curly hair—with their backs to me. I said, "Oh, hi, honey, how are ya, dear? Introduce me to your girlfriend."

A boy turned around. Hair down to his shoulders. Richard Friedlander. He was fifteen, a year older than Todd. I was embarrassed and Richard was insulted, and that was our meeting.

Like Todd, Richard didn't feel he had much in common with most of the other boys in the school, and so they grabbed on to each other.

Richard was a little rebellious. His parents were having a hard time with him and he didn't want to live with them. He stayed with us for one weekend and, after that, moved in.

I became his adopted mother. Richard never finished school. He traveled with me and took extension courses. He learned to do my sound when he was seventeen and eighteen, studying with my sound man.

Todd hated the road and later went back to school, and Richard stayed on and became a top sound technician. He and Todd are still good friends and he's a wonderful adopted son.

Once I knew *Irene* was a hit, I felt strong enough to hire a lawyer and start separation proceedings. I was not going to go down with that ship. I'd already played that scene in *Molly Brown*. In the late spring of 1973 my lawyer informed Harry over the phone, and he didn't believe it. He blamed everyone but us.

The following September, after almost thirteen years of marriage, we were divorced. This preceded the settlement, which was going to be complicated because of our various properties. Also there were other surprises in store. Until the legal division of property, I agreed to let Harry stay in the house on Greenway with me paying the upkeep and expenses, so Tina and Bo would have a home. When I finished *Irene* and returned to California, he would vacate.

In the midst of all this, I wrote out a check for $37 for the repair of a faucet in the New York house and it bounced. I was stunned since I was then making $15,000 a week, all of which was being managed by the Los Angeles office of one of the largest, most prestigious accounting firms in the world.

After my experience with Irving Briskin, I was careful to choose from the bluest of the blue bloods. My caution didn't matter a damn. A woman who was managing my account for the firm absconded with *all* the money—$160,000! I'd send my check in each week and she'd take it. She stole everything I'd made since I left California to go into *Irene*, every single dime that I was out there killing myself for three afternoons and six nights a week. She just forged my name and helped herself.

When I found out, I thought, "You are just up for grabs. You might as well go sit in the middle of the street, hire somebody with a gun, and say 'Shoot me.'" I was so angry, I thought I was going to have a stroke.

To make matters worse, the prestigious accounting firm stood behind its employee. I had to hire teams of people just to find where the money went. It took months to get the information out of the banks. Then I had to sue the firm to get my money back. They finally paid me back through their insurance company. The woman never even went to jail.

After I separated from Harry, I dated a couple of men—one was a really nice man named Jim Travis, who was in the advertising business in New York. Jim was a terrific, very funny man, very bright, and separated from his wife. We'd go out to dinner on my night off, and always had a great time.

Then one matinee, Bob Fallon, whom I'd known in California, came backstage after seeing the show. I was so excited to see a friend from home. Bob, a tall, good-looking man, had been married for years to Marie Wilson, a wonderful comedienne, until her untimely death in the late 1960s. I had known Marie through the Presbyterian Church in Hollywood. They were always at every charity function.

He was living and working in New York now. He asked me out to dinner, and from that we began to date occasionally. Very slowly a relationship developed.

It was comfortable. He knew everyone I knew. He loved show business and movies and knew everything I knew about them. He loved to dance. He was attentive and amusing, the perfect companion—don't ask too much, don't expect too much.

Our friendship lifted me from the empty, cursed area that I was in—feeling abandoned and disillusioned. I felt like a woman again. I actually found myself caring about how I looked. I wanted to go out to dinner instead of going home and eating popcorn with the children and drinking wine every night. Being with him absolutely put light into my life.

CHAPTER **56**

AGNES MOOREHEAD, COINCIDENTALLY, was starring in *Gigi* on Broadway at the same time I was doing *Irene*. She had had surgery on her hip before leaving California to do the show. She hadn't been feeling too well after the operation, complaining from time to time about having a bad stomach. I didn't think anything of it because she was still eating her chocolates like crazy, and otherwise she seemed all right. You don't take a play on the road if you're not feeling well.

She'd asked me before she left California to be executor of her will and of course I said yes. I didn't think anything about it. To me it was just Agnes putting her house in order.

On Sundays in New York, I'd pick up Agnes at the Uris Theatre after the matinee and she'd come to my townhouse to have dinner. She ate nothing but mashed potatoes, and when I asked her why, she'd say her stomach was upset.

On New Year's Eve 1973, Agnes and I gave a party together for the casts of *Gigi* and *Irene* upstairs at Minskoff, overlooking Times Square. It was great fun. Agnes had a grand time.

I still had eight weeks of nightclub commitments with the Summa Corporation that I had to fulfill in 1974. My contract with *Irene* gave me control over who played my role while I was away from it. I chose Janie Powell, who, I felt, could prove it on Broadway (and she did)— the fans loved her.

We returned to Beverly Hills in early February. Todd would stay in the Greenway house and Carrie and I would stay in Agnes's house until Harry vacated.

The day I arrived, there were dozens of cars up and down Greenway Drive. At number 813, the cars jammed the driveway. I walked into a party of hundreds of strangers lying about all over the house. Tina was entertaining a bunch of people she'd never seen before.

I took one look at the crowd and blew my top. "OUT! OUT!" I yelled. "Either get out or I'm calling the police."

329

Tina showed up from out of the mob. "You can't throw them out," she screamed—her first words to me since I'd left a year ago.

"They're out. OUT!"

Upstairs lying on the bed, watching TV with his earphones on, as if he'd never moved while I'd been gone, was Harry.

"What's going on?" I wanted to know.

He looked at me. "Oh, you're back, darling," he said as if nothing had ever happened.

"What is happening here, Harry?"

"What?" he asked dumbfounded. "Everything's fine."

"Fine? Nothing's fine. Why don't you get up out of bed and have a look?!"

He didn't want to do it.

It had become a flophouse. Nobody even knew anybody's name.

To any stranger who might walk in, the house looked as lovely and serene as it always had. It had been well maintained. But it had also been used and cleaned out. Everybody had been in my room. They'd broken the locks and gone into my closets. My furs were gone. My antique silver was gone. Anything of value just disappeared—camera equipment, plates that had been given to me by Mamie and Ike Eisenhower. They'd taken everything, mentally, spiritually, and financially. There were no words to express how it felt. I suppose I was lucky the furniture was still there.

Back in the bedroom, Harry said, "Why are you so upset?"

"You don't understand what's happening here," I said. "There are strangers all over the house. Do you know that?!"

"Well, they seem like nice kids," Harry answered.

"You're insane," I said. "You've died. You just haven't rolled over."

I threw Tina's boyfriend out that day, cleaned up the house, and went back to Agnes's. They were all leaving very soon, I'd decided.

The next day I got Tina an apartment, a lovely one in Beverly Hills, with a big living room, kitchen, and bedroom. I furnished it for her and she loved it.

She was eighteen years old. "Now, Tina," I said on the day she moved in, "get your life together. You're on your own here. You're a young girl, but you can do it." I prayed it would work.

Harry got himself an apartment in Century City right near Hillcrest. Judy came over so that I could coach her on how to take care of her father. I explained about pressing his shirts and cutting cotton squares and putting out oil for his hemorrhoids.

"You take care of *this*?!" she looked at me aghast. "All of this; even the *squares*?"

"You have to, because he has a problem with that, Judy. It's not anything to be embarrassed about." Then I moved to the shoes. "This is how you shine the shoes. . . ."

"I'm not going to do any of that," she said curtly.

"Well, that's what he will expect. He's used to it."

Judy thought about it for a minute, picked up the scissors reluctantly, then the cotton pads, and started cutting.

Jerry Wunderlich had been in New York during this time. He called me a few days after I'd gotten Harry out of Greenway and moved in myself.

He'd just taken Agnes to the train. She was going back to the Mayo Clinic in Minnesota.

"Maybe we should go with her," I said, alarmed at the developments.

"No," he said, "she didn't even want me to tell you."

I reached her by phone at the hospital. "Well, you see, I've been quite ill, Debbie," was all she'd tell me.

I talked to her every day after that, for about three weeks. Her condition got worse and worse. I could tell just by the sound of her voice. Something was very, very wrong.

"Agnes, I'm flying in," I finally said one day.

"Oh, no, dear, I don't want you to see me like this."

"Like what?"

"I've lost all my hair from the chemotherapy."

"What chemotherapy?!"

"Well, Debbie, it's over," she said abruptly. "I'm dying. Pray for me."

Those were her final words to me.

She died two days later. My brilliant, witty, intelligent friend— funny as can be, a great teacher, a great actress, a great friend. And now she was gone forever from my life.

I just didn't believe it.

Her last wish was that there be no funeral. The burial had been arranged by her in advance. She had the crypt with the fence around it, where her father was buried, on their farm in Ohio.

A few weeks later Agnes's mother came in to Los Angeles from Ohio for the reading of the will. I'd never met her before. She didn't look a bit like Agnes. She was an amazing lady, ninety-four years old, with not an ounce of senility. She'd never wanted to live in Hollywood and Agnes certainly wasn't going to live in Ohio. The two women, being strong individuals, could never have lived together.

"Mother will be all right," Agnes had said long before, when discussing her will. "She'll have my house but she'll never want to live in it. You'll sell it and it'll bring a lot of money for her. You can put the money in bonds. And with my residuals from *Bewitched*, she'll have so much money, she'll never need a thing."

Agnes's lawyer was a man I find hard even to think about, whom she'd met about a year before. When it came time for the reading of the will, he informed me that Agnes had left him everything.

"I don't believe that," I said to him over the phone.

"I'll send you a copy," he replied.

And so he did.

There was, indeed, a new will, changing the earlier one, with Agnes's signature on the last page. The first and last pages read the same. I was still the executor. The middle pages were all different.

Her mother was left the furniture in the house. Elizabeth Montgomery was left a piece of jewelry. In the original will, she had left me a sapphire ring, which, she'd often told me, she wanted me to have. That wasn't in the new will.

The lawyer got everything else—the house, the stocks, the residuals.

I learned from talking to Mrs. Moorehead that he had been at the hospital frequently right up to the end of her life.

The lawyer was not crazy about me. What he seemed to want was for me to disappear. I wanted Mrs. Moorehead to contest the will. But she was an elderly woman in her nineties. I worried that the stress of going to court would affect her health.

The next surprise was that there was nothing in the safe-deposit box, yet Agnes told me she kept jewelry there. I had given her some beautiful antique watches because she loved them. Harry and I had given her some antique gold earrings. Her pearls weren't there. The diamond heart that she always wore wasn't there. Just the sunburst pin that she'd left to Elizabeth Montgomery. Nothing else.

Everyone who knew Agnes was shocked. Someone who didn't know her intimated to me one day that the lawyer had been Agnes's lover. I absolutely didn't believe it. Agnes, by that time in her life, was a woman without emotional involvements. She'd said, "I'll never love again. I married three men and each one killed me." She started all over again after each marriage, saving and saving. Agnes wouldn't allow her life to be disturbed again emotionally after the last marriage. I was

Agnes's closest friend. I knew everything that went on in her life. The next innuendo was that she and I were lovers. Then of course there were stories that I was after Agnes's money.

I finally resigned myself to the fact that Mrs. Moorehead wasn't going to get what was coming to her. She and I went over to the house on Roxbury Drive to go through Agnes's clothes. The lawyer called to tell me that she couldn't take anything other than what had been bequeathed.

"She'll take what she wants," I said.

"I'll sue you," he warned.

"Then come over and do it now," I replied. "Come over here and tell her mother to her face that she can't have her daughter's portrait." I hung up.

We held an auction of the furniture. I called all Agnes's friends and sold them as much as I could. Mrs. Moorehead realized only $30,000 from the sale of the furniture.

Once the estate was settled, the lawyer sold the house for more than $1 million.

I was never able to reach her son after Agnes died.

I felt very sad for the boy, who was then in his twenties. Without a family, or knowledge of his family. His twin sister had become the adopted daughter of one of Hollywood's richest, most prominent families. Yet he didn't even know she existed. Nor does she know she has a brother.

How ironic it was that Agnes, who had lived so frugally all her life, had accumulated an estate that hardly even benefited her own mother. Harry and I had once given her a case of wine. When she died, there was one bottle gone from that case. "It's too good to drink," she'd say about it. Then a relative stranger came into her life and ended up with everything she'd worked so hard to keep.

A few weeks later when I was playing Vegas, Jerry Wunderlich came down, along with Ross Hunter. After the show we had sort of a wake, talking about Agnes, crying and wondering how it all turned out so badly.

I was awakened later that night by a deep chill in my room. It was as if the temperature had suddenly dropped fifteen degrees. I opened my eyes and Agnes was standing at the end of the bed. She was wearing a gray suit and her hair was all up in red curls. She looked at me and said, "Talk to thy father."

I sat up and instantly she was gone. I said to myself, "Am I mad? Am I going crazy? This can't be happening." I started to sob.

I turned on the light and wrote down the words on a pad. "Talk to thy father." Frantic, I called Jerry Wunderlich.

"Jerry, you won't believe what has just happened." I told him the story.

"Are you drinking?!"

"No. I was asleep."

I never repeated the story again because I didn't fully believe it myself. Talk to God? "Talk to thy Father"? Talk to my father? At the time, I immediately started praying. I wondered if I'd strayed too much from my religion. Was that it? I've never forgotten the words and I've never gotten over them.

I feel Agnes's spirit all the time. Sometimes I'll ask Agnes what she thinks about something and I'll get messages in reply. I know I'm not nuts. I'm a sane woman, but those little moments sometimes seem very real.

CHAPTER 57

NOT LONG AFTER Harry moved out of Greenway, we met there to discuss the divorce settlement. Harry was represented by Arthur Crowley, the famous divorce lawyer.

We all sat down in the living room. Harry was, as usual, immaculate in a suit and a tie, and now walking with a cane. He told us what he wanted.

Everything, they said, should be split down the middle. That included Harry's debts; to the State Street Bank of Boston alone, this was more than a million dollars. There were millions in other debts, including the $1.7 million he owed Gregory Peters. He owed suppliers, manufacturers, individuals, and if we didn't file joint bankruptcy, half the debt was mine.

I didn't want to file for bankruptcy. I grew up in a world where it was a disgrace to go bankrupt. It was the last stop before the gutter. Nowadays it's fashionable. A little more than ten years ago, and forever before that, it wasn't.

Harry also wanted *one half* of my earnings from *Irene*, as well as the 10 percent agent's fee on my other earnings, plus a settlement of $25,000 a year for five years. Either that, or he would be my agent and I would pay him 10 percent of all my future earnings.

I was already paying $10,000 a week toward my half of "our" debts, those millions that Harry borrowed to cover his gambling losses.

Demanding half of what I made in *Irene* really disgusted me.

"Why do you think you should have half?" I asked.

"Because we really weren't separated at the time," he answered.

I sat there looking at this distinguished man whom I had once loved. Now he was behaving like a procurer who thought he deserved half my earnings even after I'd left him. It was so greedy.

His friends never would have believed any of this. Such a nice guy, Harry. Always tipped a hundred-dollar bill. Even when he was broke, he'd tip ten, twenty, fifty dollars. He just borrowed from his friends and hocked his jewels. A close friend, knowing how much jewelry he'd lost, and how much he liked it, gave him a beautiful pair of cufflinks. They were pawned too.

My green Rolls, it turned out, wasn't mine. It belonged to the company, and in the merger he bought it from Hartfield for $8,000, then turned around and sold it for $18,000.

"I'm paying off half your debts to the bank, Harry. You are certainly entitled to half the expense of supporting your son and your daughter. And half the cost of the mortgages and the cars. Otherwise, you have had enough."

I was very calm. I never yelled. My share was almost two million dollars in *debts*. There was a small amount left from the sale of the Palm Springs house, which I put in a trust for Todd and Carrie. I refinanced the Malibu house and then rented it out to pay the mortgage. Gregory Peters and the bank got the Greenway house for $480,000. (It recently sold for $7 million.) When I was working I got to pay the State Street Bank $10,000 a week until half of that debt was paid off. The sculptures were sold, the paintings, the silver; the twenty-one-carat diamond that cost $200,000 went for $75,000; everything was sold. They wanted me to sell my memorabilia too, but I refused. That year I bought a small condo in Las Vegas and became a legal resident of Nevada.

Suddenly, for the first time since I was sixteen years old, I didn't even have a car. Or a home. Bob Fallon found me a 1968 Chevy for $1,500 to replace the Rolls. No matter how many times I washed it, it seemed, the birds always managed to cover it with their droppings. We ended up calling it the bird-turd car. It was a perfect car to express how I felt about my situation. After all, why should my car be any different from my life?

CHAPTER **58**

FORTUNATELY IN 1974 there was work. Vegas, Tahoe, Reno. In July, we took the new act to London to play the Palladium. Everyone went: my parents, Todd, Carrie, Rudy, Richard Landers; my conductor; nine dancers, three singers.

It was my first European stage appearance, playing two shows nightly for three weeks. It was the first time a Vegas act played the Palladium. We were sold out around the block.

Carrie made her solo starring debut. Born with a great voice, she absolutely killed the audience; brilliant and wonderful in her Edith Piaf way—the opposite of me. I was there with the beads on, singing and dancing and chattering away. Carrie walked out, quiet as could be, belted out a song and killed 'em. When she finished, they gave her a standing ovation. I cried in the wings.

The reviews read: "Debbie Reynolds is the gold of vaudeville. She has presented us with her daughter Carrie Fisher— the platinum of vaudeville." What a beginning! She was launched and on her way.

However, every night before she went on, Carrie was a wreck, almost throwing up. I'd spend the two hours before each show giving her glasses of water, calming her, and getting her dressed.

This was not, she would say, what she wanted from life. It was all too much. She wanted to go to school, study acting, and become an actress.

I had wanted Carrie to be a singer because she has such a beautiful voice. I did not want her to wind up a forty-two-year-old singer-dancer from Hollywood, looking for a job wherever she could find it. So when she told me she was going to audition for an appointment to the Central School of Dramatic Arts in London I was pleased. She had dropped out of high school when we went to New York for *Irene*. She did extension courses for a while but never got her diploma. She needed an education; she needed training.

Central rarely takes Americans. Carrie prepared two scenes for her audition. She went down there on her own, did them, was asked to return, did them again, and eventually was "appointed," as they say, to the school.

On her way back to California she decided, I guess, that that was all too easy.

I had only about a week in Los Angeles before I was due back in New York to rehearse the National Company of *Irene*, which was opening in Chicago for three weeks in September. I would be away from home, and on the road, for almost three months. There were a million things to plan and organize.

"You have your reservations, dear, and everything's set," I remember saying to her about the upcoming move to London.

"I'm not going," she said in a very blasé tone. "I've decided to stay home."

"Oh?" I looked at her, surprised and disturbed. There was that sober determination in her eyes.

"You are *going*," I said. "What you did by getting into Central was something every actress dreams of."

"I don't want that. I want to stay in Los Angeles and decide what I want to do."

"No," I said. "You have no training and no education. Two years in school and you will be trained. You won't be an old lady when you finish. You'll be nineteen. Then you can do anything you want."

She was furious and we locked horns. We, who had never disagreed. It was the first time in our lives where Mother said "No." But she had such an abundance of talent that it made me become very strong. She was not going to be allowed to stay home and hum around Beverly Hills.

I left California certain she would soon be on her way to London. Two nights before her flight, she called, reiterating that she wasn't going.

Now there were three thousand miles between us. I couldn't physically put her on the plane. But I was adamant.

"No. You're going to do this or you're going to have to support yourself."

We fought for about six hours. Finally, about midnight, New York time, we both hung up exhausted. But Carrie never went to bed. She wasn't finished with the argument and she wasn't giving in. Instead, she went to LAX, got on the red-eye and flew to New York.

She showed up at my hotel at seven o'clock the next morning.

I hadn't changed my mind. We confronted each other in a battle royal, mother and daughter at each other. I remained very firm and hard.

"You are seventeen! Not eighteen! Not twenty-one! You auditioned for Central. You were accepted. Now, you will attend."

I knew she understood what I was saying. It was very hard to talk to her that way. Perhaps if long ago I had said no, it might have been easier now. But Carrie and I were always buddies. I was never the boss.

It was such a difficult time for all of us, but I felt she must do it. I would not back off. She did as I told her, and hated me for making her do it. When she left for London, I knew our relationship would never be the same. I felt sick. I'd lost my little girl. She was so angry that I wondered if we would ever be friends again.

Nothing would ever be the same for any of us after the Harry Karl marriage broke up. All of us were refugees from Harry—me, Todd, Carrie, Tina, and Bo. Carrie and I were driven apart by it. She had seen her mother, for the first time, collapse under the stress. She'd seen her mother—who always handled everything—suddenly wanting to take a drink and sit in the corner by herself. She didn't respect me anymore.

Perhaps I was subconsciously pushing her into adulthood so that she could help me deal with the problem. But it was too much for her as it was too much for me.

CHAPTER **59**

IN ITS FOURTEEN MONTHS on Broadway, *Irene* had grossed almost $7.5 million and broken all box-office records. When we opened in Chicago, the show set new all-time-record grosses of more than a quarter of a million dollars for ten performances. The Windy City was having rough weather that autumn—cold, gale-force winds and torrents of rain. None of it kept the theatergoers from *Irene*. To show my gratitude for their attendance on one stormy night, I went out for my final bow in a yellow slicker and sang "Singin' in the Rain" for them. It brought down the house, and it was a truly thrilling moment for me.

By the time the show moved to Dallas, I'd met a psychic named Greta Alexander, who gave me a reading one afternoon.

"You have a daughter . . . who's not your daughter," she said curiously, not knowing what she was saying. "I see a death. . . ." she continued.

"A death?! She's very young!" I said, half concerned, half disbelieving.

"There is death around this young girl," she repeated very quietly.

I wasn't quite sure what to make of her warning. Had she meant the drug overdose of two years before? Had she meant the time Tina totaled her car? Tina had had a horrendous accident on Wilshire and Westwood boulevards a few months before where she wrapped her car around a cement bench at a bus stop. Tina, however, had miraculously walked away from that accident, which occurred in an almost traffic-free intersection. She had no memory as to what caused the accident.

Could that have been the "death" Greta the psychic had seen around the young girl?

A few days later, Tina happened to call me in Dallas from Los Angeles. "Mother, I'd love to come visit," she said.

On the third day of her visit, at four o'clock in the morning, I was awakened by a phone call from Bo.

"We got a problem, Debbie," I heard his voice say right off. "There's a dead body in Tina's apartment."

I was half conscious.

"What is that, Harrison?" I asked, not sure that I'd heard it right.

"Debbie, in Tina's apartment: There's a *dead* person." He sounded as incredulous as I was.

Meanwhile, I was thinking, it's not Tina. She's in the next room.

"Wait a minute, would you?" I said, and shuffled into the bathroom to throw some water on my face. I'd had many things in my life: opening nights, birth pains, detectives at the door. But never a "dead person."

"You want to repeat that again, Harrison?" I said, back at the phone.

"They found a dead girl in Tina's apartment. She must have been dead for about four or five days. They don't know who she is because the body's very decomposed. All I could find out was they know Tina was there a few days ago, and that she left."

"Wait a minute, Bo," I said. "Tina's in the next room sleeping. Let me ask her what's going on. I'll call you back."

I hung up the phone and went into Tina's room.

She was sleeping like a rock. I nudged her. "Tina," I said, poking her shoulder gently. "Tina, wake up."

After a few seconds she opened her eyes. "Huh. . . ?" she said, looking at me.

"Tina. In your apartment, when you left, was there a friend?"

"Huh. . . ?" she repeated as if in a stupor.

"Tina, you'd better wake up because I want the truth on this. The Beverly Hills police are looking for you."

"They are?" she said, sitting up. "Jesus!"

Had this child murdered somebody? Had she had a fight and accidentally killed somebody?

"What happened?" I demanded impatiently.

"Mother, I don't know," she said, pleading in her voice.

I had no time for those answers. "They've established the day you left, Tina. And they know you came to visit me on the day they found the body. Now *who* is this person?!"

"I didn't do anything," she pleaded. "I don't know . . ."

"You couldn't take care of it? You couldn't have called the police?"

"But I didn't know what to do!" she protested. Obviously she knew about it.

"So you left her lying there?"

"I just didn't know . . ."

"Who was she, Tina?"

"I'm not sure . . ."

"*Tina.* . . !"

"She was just a friend. . . ."

"What happened?"

"There was a party. . . ."

"And?"

"I can't say."

"You have to say. We're talking district attorneys now, Tina. We're talking reporters and courtrooms and murder trials!"

She was sitting on the edge of her bed.

"I wasn't there! I wasn't even home. I was in Paris. London. They were using the apartment. . . ."

"Were there drugs?"

"Yes, I guess so. I wasn't there."

I believed her, but I was furious that she hadn't told me about it right away. Instead she had been using me as a cover.

"So you left to visit me. How kind. How sweet. Now you must go back home and face it."

The victim was a beautiful young aspiring actress, no more than twenty years old. She'd come to Hollywood and ended up spending all her time with the young son of one of the industry's most powerful men. As a favor to that boy, Tina let the girl stay in her apartment while she was away. There had been a party, with drugs. A needle containing a lethal dose was administered. When everyone realized that the girl had been given too much, they left her. Alone. To die. Real humanitarians, these people.

Tina, who had arrived back in Los Angeles a couple of days later, had been warned by her "friends" that something had "happened" to the girl in her apartment. She went to the building, and instead of entering the apartment—which was on the first floor—she looked in the window and saw the corpse, black from decomposition. She then went immediately to the nearest phone booth and placed a call to Mother.

I hired a lawyer for Tina, and a painting contractor to paint the stench of death out of the apartment. The matter of the dead girl was handled very quietly. By whoever handles those things. There were no headlines and no scandal. Soon after, the story disappeared altogether; and everybody got off. Tina never needed the lawyer, for in the end no one was held responsible. It just went away.

*   *   *

By the age of eighteen, Tina had spent as much time with me as she had with her real mother. I was the only parent she could turn to for whatever she wanted or needed. She understood that too; and like a lot of children can be with a parent, she held me responsible for whatever made her unhappy. I didn't like it, but I could never lose sight of the fact that I was her only connection to a family.

After nine years, I was not naïve enough to expect she'd change her ways. The most I could now do was to encourage her to make a stable life for herself. I could support her and pay for any schooling she might pursue, and also stick by her if and when she got into trouble.

CHAPTER 60

IN NOVEMBER, I came back to Los Angeles to be honored at the Thalians Ball, and to open in *Irene*. Almost three years had passed since I'd left. Now I was returning with a hit show. The opening-night audience was filled with all the old friends from MGM and the Thalians, as well as hundreds of people I'd known or worked with over the past twenty-five years. When I came out for my final bow, they gave me a standing ovation that went on for five minutes. I was very moved by their reception. I'd come home to the toughest audience, and they liked me. It's the highest compliment of them all, for a performer to be liked by his or her peers. You can live on that for a long, long time.

I was going to need something to live on, soon after that. It's interesting that in a divorce or bankruptcy in Hollywood, with a few exceptions, everyone becomes an ostrich. Like the divorce with Eddie, no one called—not to offer help, much less to ask me to dinner. People seemed to disappear. I never talked about my financial problems. Who would have believed me anyway? I was working all the time. And no one could believe that Harry Karl was broke.

Harry's sister, Sarah, being a business partner, lost everything too. She thought that Harry had spent his fortune buying me presents. Only after I sent her all the papers detailing my debts did she understand.

Mama Rose Karl had given her son all she had left, $30,000, so I took care of her rent and expenses and visited her every week. I never told her about Harry and me until long after it was over.

When she was dying, I called Harry.

"You know Mama's dying; you have to come."

"Debbie, I'm not feeling well today."

"I don't care, get over here. Your mother's dying."

"I can't, Debbie," he said. "I've got a bad back."

A bad back?

When I went back to her room, she was in a coma. I sat down by the bed, alone with her. Mr. Gross and Sarah were in the other room.

A few minutes later, she opened her eyes slightly. I put my hand on hers.

She turned her head to look at me. "You know I have to die now."

"I know," I said. "Try and breathe deeply for a few minutes, Mama." Slowly, she tried to inhale. She had no energy left after more than ninety years in this life.

"I have to go now," she said.

A few minutes later she was gone.

Harry never came.

We had been told we could live at Greenway until the bank sold the house and Gregory Peters got some of the money I owed him. Three or four months after I'd come back from touring in *Irene,* it was sold.

I was given three days to vacate. Fifteen years in a house and three days to get out. When Julie Andrews and Blake Edwards bought the house a few years later, they opened the safe in the downstairs storage room and found all kinds of papers of mine that I'd left. They found a hidden closet full of linens, which they returned.

Todd and Zink, my guard for many years, moved me.

Over a period of two weeks, when I knew Greenway was going to sell, I had looked around furiously for a house to rent. I wanted Beverly Hills so that Todd could finish high school there. Most of the houses were renting for $3,500, $4,000 a month. I couldn't afford that.

I finally found a place on Oakhurst Drive for $1,500 a month. I hated it, but I figured I could paint and wallpaper to brighten it up.

I was rehearsing a new act the day we were moving. It was just about dusk when I got over to the new house. I felt that coldly blank feeling that comes with turning your back on a whole way of life, knowing it's gone and still not believing it.

Walking from the car up to the front door, halfway up the walk, I remembered I'd forgotten to bring my new costumes in. I went back and opened the trunk of the car. As I was taking my things out of it, a very well-dressed man walked up to me from behind, put a gun to my forehead, and said: "Get in the house."

I thought he was kidding. It was the kind of thing you only see on television; not on some quiet, sedate, tree-lined street in Beverly Hills.

"What is this, a joke?" I said, half laughing. "Who sent you?"

Just at that moment Bob Fallon drove up, got out of his car, and walked up to us. Oh, I thought to myself, Bob's in on the joke.

"Is there any problem?" he asked the man with the gun.

The guy turned around, with the gun on both of us. I was still kind of chuckling about it. It was so real and unreal—like maybe a scene out of *Candid Camera*.

Bob looked at the gun, looked at the guy, and said, "This isn't funny, Debbie. It's not a joke."

Then the guy said, "Go in the house."

So we walked into the house, with him right behind us. In the front hallway, the man ordered us to get on our knees. In the meantime, another man appeared from outside. He had a longer gun.

"Where's the money?" he said.

"You can see we're just moving in," I said. There were boxes everywhere. "There's no money here."

"This is a rich house!" he said. "In a rich neighborhood," he growled.

Then, with his friend still covering us, he went into the kitchen, saw Mary, grabbed her, and pulled her into the hallway with us. Mary, who had a towel in her hand, threw it over her face, fell to the floor, and started screaming:

"I don't see nuthin'! I don't see nuthin'! Don't kill me, please don't kill me!"

The sight of Mary, crouched on the floor, screaming out from under a towel, was hilarious. But by then I knew laughing was too risky. And the man, who happened to be the same skin color as Mary, said, "We ain't killing you, sister." Then he looked right at me like: "But I'm killing you. You're going."

I didn't have my towel, so I couldn't throw it over my face. This man was very handsome—and I couldn't help noticing he looked like Johnny Mathis.

Fallon, seeing me look at him, kept grumbling under his breath: "Don't look at 'em, don't look at 'em!"

"Where's your jewelry?" the man with the longer gun asked.

"I don't have any jewelry," I said. "There's nothing here! We're just moving in."

Then they wanted all the cash. "Give us your cash!"

Bob had about two hundred dollars on him. And Mary had about a hundred and sixty I'd given her for groceries, so they turned that over.

The other guy ran upstairs and found a bunch of junk jewelry that I used in my Zsa Zsa and Mae West imitations. He brought that downstairs, triumphant.

"That's just *fake!*" I said. "You don't want that."

"It *looks* good," he said, giving me a suspicious eye.

"I'm telling you, it's fake," I advised.

Then they wanted me to dump out my purse, where I happened to
have my good pearls, a diamond clasp, and some jade jewelry. So I
poured it all on the floor. Lipstick, cigarettes, lighter, keys, Kleenex,
wallet, and the jewelry.

The first guy took one look at that and said, "And that's probably
junk jewelry too!"

"Yes!!" I said.

He believed me! thank God; and thus I was allowed to keep the little
that Harry Karl and the banks couldn't get their hands on.

When the men decided they'd got all there was to get, we were told
to go into the bathroom. With the guns pointed at us at all times, we
were very compliant. All of us thought for sure they would then shoot
us through the door. It was only reasonable—I'd seen their faces.

It was a tiny guest bathroom under the hallway stairs, almost like a
narrow closet. Bob had Mary climb up on the toilet and stand up close
to the wall. I pressed myself against the other wall and, sweating beads,
we waited for the bullets, praying.

Ten minutes went by; nothing. Had they left? We couldn't tell.
Twenty minutes; nothing. Thirty, forty, an hour passed. All that time,
we stood there stiff with fright, afraid if we opened the door they would
be standing there and shoot us, which was not very likely, of course.
Finally we opened it a crack, all of us shaking like leaves.

They were gone. They'd taken the cash and left.

Everyone was a wreck. Mary got out the brandy and we all had a
drink. We couldn't believe it; we'd moved into our new home only
hours before, and we were still alive.

"It just goes to show you," Mary said, "even when you're on a real
good roll, you can still get rolled." The three of us had a good laugh.

A few minutes later Todd and Zink showed up.

"I can't believe it," Zink said, "the one time I leave you for a half an
hour and you're held up." Of course, had Zink been there, it might
have been dangerous. He always carried a gun and probably would have
pulled it out. All of us might have been killed.

Bob Fallon and I were now seeing a lot of each other. I had also
been dating Stuart Davis, a nice banker, who was completely the opposite of Bob. His friends were bankers and businessmen with very nice
wives. I liked them, but I didn't feel it was a world for me. It was too
foreign to my life.

Bob Fallon, on the other hand, was Show Biz. He had a bravado
about him. He stepped out from the norm, in my eyes. Nothing sur-

prised him. He was willing to take chances. He was very different and I liked that.

When I left New York, he left New York and came back to Los Angeles where he'd always had a house.

Our friendship did not grow beyond that for quite some time. When I knew we both wanted more, I discussed it with Carrie and Todd. I wanted to make sure it would feel all right to them if a man stayed overnight with me.

He was the first man who ever really made love to me. Not Harry, not Eddie, but Bob taught me what it was like to feel a true climax of lovemaking. I had never had that. He was a very experienced and unselfish lover.

It was school for me. Kindergarten, intermediate, high school, and college. He taught me about physical love and sexual accomplishment. How you can have real satisfaction of the flesh, which I had never experienced. I thought the man had this wonderful, seemingly satisfied feeling, and the woman just sort of went through the motions. Bob taught me that joy in making love was for the woman to be totally satisfied.

We didn't move in together. I felt Marie's spirit very strongly in his house. He'd kept everything the same way after she died. I persuaded him to redo the place, and worked with him on planning the changes. Only then would I feel truly comfortable in the house if I was ever going to stay over.

After more than a year Bob asked me if I would go only with him, and not with other men. It wasn't a marriage proposal. I didn't want to marry and neither did he. It was a wonderful companionship.

He was used to being taken care of. Marie obviously had done that. I fit right into that mold. I looked after him, as I would a husband. I got very involved with the redecorating of his house, helping him as if it were my own. I gave him total loyalty and total caring, because that's what I do. He wasn't a man interested in money. He had simple tastes—his house, his cars, his boat. He had a wonderful son, Greg. He enjoyed life.

Some of the people close to me didn't care for his style. He was very sure of himself, very macho, and in many ways, he took over. He was never rude to anyone, but he could be bossy. But he was never unpleasant to anyone, and I didn't object because I felt he needed his identity around me.

Eventually I let him negotiate deals for me. He'd handled Marie Wilson's career very well for many years. He knew deals and he knew packaging the product. It's very hard for a man to date a successful performer and not be involved in her career. It's very hard for women, successful women, to have anyone do that. I would never want my man to feel that he's being put down. All the strong women I know make that concession. The man's the man and should feel like the man, so let him be. I don't want to usurp his malehood in any way. I don't want to be a man.

Bob also never took advantage of me financially. He was a producer but actually made most of his money in redoing houses.

CHAPTER **61**

MEANWHILE, over in London, Carrie was having a great time. She never called and never wrote. I called her. And worried myself to death.

"Hello, Carrie."

"Hello." Curt. Short. Angry. Don't bother. You made me come here. I'll do what I want. I'm doing what you said. You said to be here and learn. I'm learning. Stay out of my life. Don't call me; I'll call you.

It was always like that. Like that, or nothing. Sometimes she was not available to come to the phone. I felt rejected and terrible about the separation, but I hoped no matter how much she disliked me in the future, she would be happy and look back on it as the right thing for her to have done.

I went to London to visit for two weeks, staying with her. She was not thrilled to see Mother. One night she and her flatmate had a party and invited the entire cast of *King Lear*. Just prior to the guests' arrival, Carrie told me that it would be better if I would stay in my room. The party was for young actors and actresses and I didn't know any of her friends.

I took my bottle of wine and retreated. Well, it's Carrie's party and not Debbie Reynolds's daughter's party, I told myself. She didn't much like anything about my being there.

"I don't want to be here," she'd said more than once. "You're making me stay here, Mother, to be an actress. You got what you wanted."

No matter what, I wasn't going to let her out of her commitment. And no matter what, she wasn't going to let me out of hurting over it.

After the two weeks, I finally had to concede and withdraw; she'd won. She had treated me with either outright hostility or total disregard.

I flew back to California thinking, "I'll never do that again," and sat myself down for a good heart to heart. The separation between Carrie and Debbie was, in a way, permanent. She had had a taste of her own identity and Mother's was never going to get in her way again. It pained me but I knew it was right.

I never went, never called, and never wrote again. She was in London for almost a year. Carrie doesn't remember this. When she returned to the States, she stayed for a while in New York with Joan Hackett. Hackett was a wonderful mother-replacement in my daughter's life. She was vital and stimulating. She was bright and clever. She loved to read and constantly encouraged Carrie to do the same. Carrie turned totally to Hackett and completely away from me.

It was a great happening for Carrie, an older woman mentor, not unlike my relationships with Agnes and with Lillian. I felt very lucky that she had Hackett although I felt jealous too, because Hackett was everything I wanted to be to my daughter.

I did some TV. Bob Hope, Dean Martin, a guest on a game show like the *Hollywood Squares*, but for almost five years I made my living on the road. The act, *Irene*, the act, *Irene*, the act; Reno, Tahoe, Houston, Dallas, Miami, Valley Forge, Westbury, Salt Lake City, Phoenix, Atlanta, and anywhere else I could get a booking.

The act is a routine, just like going to work every day. I eat every day at 4:00 in the afternoon. The latest I can eat is 4:30. If the show starts at 7:30 or 8:00, I have to be there at 6:00, which means I have to leave the hotel by 5:30 or 5:45 at the latest.

Once in my dressing room, first I steam my throat with a vaporizer. A little salt makes the steam come out very strongly, warming the vocal cords and opening the throat. Then I vocalize for up to an hour, to warm up, to a tape that has been prepared by my vocal coach over the years. I've read that many opera stars vocalize in the shower. Men can do that without affecting their hair. Women cannot, although I've usually just washed my hair and it's still drying in a towel.

After thirty minutes over a vaporizer, I've naturally given myself a facial. Halfway through the vocalizing, I cease the steaming and lie down on the floor to do some exercises for my back (which is very bad), my legs, and my waist.

At the end of vocalizing and exercises, I sit down at the stupid makeup table where I begin to try to reverse the ravages of aging.

It takes a full half hour just to put on the makeup base. I'm so light-skinned I need a darker base, or else from the audience, I'll look as if I have no eyes and lips. Everything has to be four times more than what you are, emphasizing all the features. It takes me about a half hour just to put that on. The rouge, the shadowing, the base, the powder; that's the hard part.

By that time my hair is dry and I've finished my vocalizing. I then put on my "impressions" tape cassette. As I'm in the final stages of makeup, my hairdresser (Kelly Muldoon, who's been with me for the past eight years) is putting rollers in my hair and I'm practicing the sounds of the different people I impersonate.

Every night the impressions have to be brought forward in my mind, like a computer with information. No matter how many years I have done something, I always bring it right to the front of my mind before a performance. I don't have to practice Zsa Zsa and Eva Gabor every night. I have their voices down. But I do Dr. Ruth and Dolly Parton and Streisand. I do everything in their key and register. I have to be exactly like them—tone, dialect, placement; that's impersonation.

After the hair is down, I put on the body makeup, covering my neck and chest. All the skin that is exposed must be the same blend, including the hands, which mustn't look white against the face. Male performers wear pancake and females usually wear facial makeup. Men often don't bother with meticulous makeup. They hate it and apply the pancake with a seafoam sponge. Then they're off and running.

From the moment I arrive in my dressing room, right through the two hours before the show, I'm busy. Someone always drops in—the sound man, the lighting man. There are always little problems that require immediate attention.

I don't ever like to be late for my work. In my personal life I'm always fifteen or twenty minutes late—or even more. Because I usually have to live so closely by the clock, I don't like to when I'm not working. Onstage, you can't be late. Even in movies you can be, although it's really not forgivable. But onstage, the audience has been seated, the orchestra's in the pit, and everyone is waiting.

Ours is a small company these days—no more than ten or twelve of us. All acts need a road manager. Just getting transportation lined up for so many people is a gargantuan task. Everywhere you go you have to be met with buses for the crew and trucks for the luggage when you get off the plane. Kelly Muldoon and a travel bureau handle my arrangements. Stephanie, who is my wardrobe woman, packs the show costumes. Joey, my conductor, is in charge of the music. Kelly's in charge of the wigs and hair supplies as well as a million other things.

My staff people often have another person they work for—another

48. Mr. Hathaway telling me everything I need to know about *How the West Was Won*

49. Thelma and I getting ready to go over a cliff for Hathaway in *How the West Was Won*, on location in Colorado, 1962

50. Mugging around on the *Unsinkable Molly Brown* set

51. Grover Dale, Gus Triconis, and I dancing to "He's My Friend," *The Unsinkable Molly Brown*, MGM, 1963

52. "Belly Up to the Bar, Boys" from *The Unsinkable Molly Brown*

53. Happy at Greenway before life took on so many serious changes

54. With Barry Nelson in *Mary, Mary*, Warner Brothers, 1963

55. *Right*, brother Bill and I on the set of *What's the Matter with Helen?*

56. The Burtons and the Karls at the Thalians ball. Richard was the master of ceremonies that year.

57. With Fred Astaire

58. With Frank Sinatra

59. With Shirley MacLaine

60. With my beloved friend Agnes Moorehead during the filming of *The Singing Nun*. I still miss her every day.

61. Carrie and I onstage. "Where Are You Going, My Little One, My Little One," 1971.

62. *Below,* onstage with Carrie and Todd, *The Debbie Reynolds Show* at the Westbury Music Fair, 1971

63. *Irene,* New York, 1973

64. Sir John Gielgud and I in rehearsals for *Irene*, 1973

65. Patsy Kelly taken in my dressing room at the Minskoff with my poodle Killer and his brother during the run of *Irene*

66. Bob Fallon and I at the party just after the opening of *Irene* at the Shubert Theatre in Los Angeles, December 1974

67. Carrie and Todd on her twenty-fifth birthday, October 21, 1981

68. Doing my stuff at the Desert Inn, Las Vegas, 1978

69. Bob O'Connell taken at Ouray, Colorado. When he gave me this picture he said, "For a sensitive guy, do I look tough enough?" Pancho Villa couldn't have done it any better.

70. *Below*, Richard and I the night we met in Reno, 1984

star. They try to arrange the dates so that they work fairly steadily. They never pay for their rooms or their fare. That's a big nut every week, especially considering that I still have Mary, who's been with me for almost thirty years, and Margie, who was my stand-in through the sixties and has worked for me ever since.

Most of my staff have been with me for quite a few years. Stephanie has been with me for eight years. (Before that my mother and brother traveled with me for fifteen years.) Rudy Render was my conductor and pianist for twenty-two years.

I'm on the road on the average of thirty to forty weeks a year. Life there goes by the opposite clock from most people's. When I finish performing—anywhere from 11:30 P.M. to 2:00 A.M., I'm wound up and still bursting with energy. I can't go back to my hotel room and just go to sleep. If I'm playing Vegas or Reno or Tahoe, where there are other clubs, people get together in each other's dressing rooms and hotel suites. There's always at least a small group over at Debbie's. Food and drinks are ordered up and the talk begins—and can go till dawn sometimes.

I don't usually like to go out after the show, unless it's a special occasion. About six or seven years ago, in Vegas, there was a late-night birthday party for Tom Jones. I didn't want to go but Liberace talked me into it by telling me he'd pick me up.

Lee showed up driving himself in his big white limousine. He was all in white with his diamonds and I was all in black, so we were a perfect combination. The party was held in the lounge of one of the big hotels.

I was never so shocked as by the way the women behaved around Tom Jones. It was so blatant and obvious. They just pushed themselves on him—girls, women, maybe married, maybe whatever, visiting Vegas—they all came up to our table.

Tom has to have two bodyguards. Lee had one. Show people need cushions against someone who might be improper. It isn't being snooty or standoffish. It's just that they like to have a good time after work like anybody else. When you're famous, people feel they know you and therefore would like to visit with you. With someone like Tom Jones, this can be a really big problem because they also want to go to bed with him.

I never had a problem like that, of course, but I saw it with Elvis and with Eddie Fisher. The availability of women is staggering. I once worked with a star who had a different woman every night. Different type, different figure, different color hair. He had no particular choice or taste. It was extraordinary. I became fascinated with what was going to turn up after the show: the monkey? the donkey? or what?

Without the staff and the friends in the other shows, it's a lonely life, moving from hotel room to hotel room. There have been times when I've been touring for two or three months nonstop, and come home only to wake up in my own bed wondering where I was.

CHAPTER **62**

IN 1975, Carrie came back to Los Angeles where she interviewed for and got a part in *Star Wars*. Joan Hackett was in town also. One day Carrie told me Joan was having sort of a bad time; that she was low on money, hadn't been working, and really had no place to go.

"Invite her to stay here," I said. No one should be without a place to stay.

So Joan moved into Carrie's room until I went back out on tour, when she could move into my room. Joan didn't just stay there, she occupied the territory. With her and Richard Friedlander, Carrie, Todd, Mary—and I—and Killer the dog, it was one big family. Carrie and I were still not on the best of terms, but it didn't matter. She'd done her schooling and she was going to make *Star Wars*, which would change her life professionally and personally just as *Singin' in the Rain* had done to mine.

As much as things had improved since my divorce from Harry, with the debt still hanging like a looming black cloud over my head, the reminder was always there. I was earning hundreds of thousands of dollars a year and saw it all go either to the tax man or to some bank debt, for year after year. Knowing that I still had to earn the money to meet the payments had got to be one of the ultimate stress tests.

How lucky Harry had been with the way things turned out. Everybody else got burned, shorted, or destroyed. Anything he finally had in the end was because of me and Abe Marks from Hartfield-Zodys. Merging with Karl Shoes was practically the end of Hartfield's.

When we made our divorce settlement I never demanded he sell his membership in Hillcrest, which was worth about $50,000, to help pay off the debts, because it provided him with the company of his old friends. But for me, it seemed like one last straw. One day Todd, Carrie, and I were driving home from Santa Monica. We were coming up Motor Avenue toward Pico and Twentieth Century-Fox Studios when the Chevy broke down. We also happened to be across the street from Hillcrest.

I walked over to the club to phone for a repair truck. When I saw the doorman, I told him why I was there.

"I'm sorry," he said very coolly, "we cannot allow you since you are not a member."

"But I just want to use the phone. My car broke down. . . ."

"I'm sorry, Mr. Karl's inside," he stated officiously.

I could feel myself stiffen, outraged. Another slap; here we go again.

"I don't want to say hello to Mr. Karl." I tried to sound reasonable. "I just want to use your phone booth."

"I'm sorry, but Mr. Karl . . ."

"I don't want to use him for the telephone," I cracked. "Put a dime in his mouth, I wouldn't get the number . . ."

The man wouldn't let me in. For sixteen years that man couldn't bow and scrape low enough when I walked by. Not that I ever expected or liked anybody to bow and scrape—that was just the type he was. Now I wasn't even allowed to use the phone!

I started to cry; I couldn't stop myself. When I got back to the car, Carrie and Todd were upset that I was upset.

We had to walk several blocks to find a public phone. I couldn't get over the irony. He kept the membership while I had his losses.

Feuer and Martin, the Broadway producers, came to me that year about doing a revival of Irving Berlin's *Annie Get Your Gun*, which Ethel Merman originally had done on Broadway, and which Betty Hutton did in the movie.

It was a short engagement—seven weeks in San Francisco, six weeks in Los Angeles. The producers had wanted to take it on to Broadway, but Ethel Merman, who originated the role, was still living and I thought I'd be severely compared to her. I have a light voice; she had a great big voice. Also, I didn't want to do a play in New York for a while. I wanted to be able to go home. I wouldn't be out of town for long, which appealed to me. They offered me all the creative choices, including naming the director.

I asked Gower Champion and luckily he said he would do it.

One day after rehearsals, I was sitting in my office when the phone rang. My secretary came in and said, "Debbie, there's a phone call for you. Mr. Berlin's on the phone."

I said, "I don't know a Mr. Berlin."

She said, "Irving Berlin?"

"Well, everybody knows that Berlin." I hadn't thought of him. He was well into his eighties and hadn't made a public appearance in years. I picked up the phone and said hello, and sure enough, it was Irving Berlin.

"Hello, Debbie . . ."

"I'm delighted to hear from you, Mr. Berlin."

"I want you to do *Annie Get Your Gun* and I want you to bring it to Broadway because I can't travel. So you'll have to bring it to me."

"Well, Mr. Berlin," I said, "it was Ethel's show and I feel we'll be killed in New York being compared to her."

"No," he said, "you'll have to come."

Not long after, we were rehearsing the show for its opening in San Francisco when it was pointed out the lyrics for "I'm an Indian Too," with their references to "baggy pants" and "runny noses," were outdated and likely to alienate people, especially those, like Marlon Brando, who campaigned for American Indian causes. Instead of taking the song out of the show, it occurred to me to ask Irving Berlin if he might write some new lyrics.

So I called this extraordinary man, who'd written his first hit song in 1903, and explained the problem to him. He was eighty-seven then.

"That's a very good point, Debbie," he said. "What was okay in 1948 when the show opened might not be right today, so I'll have them for you tomorrow."

Tomorrow? I wondered if I'd heard him right. But sure enough, the next day we had the new lyrics. He had written them overnight, and it was a show-stopping number.

Our version of *Annie Get Your Gun*, with its updated lyrics, was a great production, and very successful. After our tour, we were booked for an additional three months in the summer of 1976, playing the civic auditoriums in the West. We never did take it into New York, however, and Irving Berlin never did get to see me in the show.

During those years, Lillian became progressively more important to my life, and I to hers. Not long after *Irene* opened, Lillian's husband divorced her.

They had been married for more than thirty years and in many ways it had been a very close marriage. Closer than most people's because Lillian—besides maintaining her responsibilities and powerful position at MGM, and after that, at Columbia Pictures—had always worked with her husband helping him develop his films.

Lillian had a breakdown. She was uncontrollably despondent and took to her bed; so sickened that she had to have a nurse in attendance.

After that she wouldn't see anyone. She never unpacked or left the apartment for more than a year. She just lived with her belongings in crates and her broken memories.

I could talk to her on the phone during those days, especially at night after the show. She still wouldn't allow anyone to see her. Only after I went and sat in the hallway and sent a message that I was not going to leave until she would see me, did she finally let me in.

I looked at all the cartons and started unpacking. Lillian began to realize she had to start living again. We found her a larger, nicer apartment in the same building. Sidney Guilaroff, his friend Michael, Margie, and I moved her in.

At that point, she got a little interested and wanted to buy a rug for her new home. That meant to me that she was recovering. She found some of her things in an antique shop and had to buy them for the second time.

It was a very bitter, angry divorce; and it was very sad for both of them. To this day, she is still suffering, at least financially, and he's fine. Her problem, I suppose, was that she couldn't believe that he'd left her. It was even more painful because it divided them and their friends, after a marriage that had been rich in friends.

There were some who stayed by her. There were also some of us girls from MGM whom she'd stood by, such as Donna Reed, myself, and Janet Leigh. We were the children Lillian never had.

After her divorce, knowing that she often had a hard time sleeping, I would call her after my show, no matter where I was. These long late-night calls really brought us to the relationship we have today. She is my second mother, my teacher, and my adviser. She always expects the best, and I admire that. And she is a compassionate friend and counselor when I need it.

It's a rare thing, in my business, to have a close friendship that lasts for years. We all have separate careers and everyone is so busy. You move, you travel. You don't make a lot of friends along the way, you make acquaintances. Your best friends are your suitcases and when the suitcases wear out, you're left with nothing but new ones. The road is a lonely life. We see the maids and the bellmen more than we do friends. After twenty years of being away, you find your friends have long stopped calling.

However, I still remember my friends as friends, even though I haven't seen them in years. In my mind, I still think of them as close.

I always made a point of calling Joan Crawford in her later years when she lived in New York. She had befriended me in the early fifties when I was at MGM. She remembered all the holidays and the birthdays. She was one of the first to call and offer consolation when Eddie left. It wasn't a close friendship. It was superficial in that respect, but it was consistent and it endured.

Joan loved the business. She was a movie star and an actress. She never gave up her career. Her career gave her up.

Some movie stars cannot go on the stage. They like the camera. They know a camera like nobody else. Lana, Ava, Joan. It's a wonderful craft to know but it doesn't transfer to the stage; that's a whole other technique. When Joan couldn't get film roles, she had a huge void in her life. Her children were gone, and Alfred, who was young enough that he could have lived with her in her old age, died in his late fifties.

I never knew the bad side of her. She was always very sweet and kind to me. We did share the same masseuse, Nancy Gianno, for many years. When Nancy would come over and massage me, she'd tell me how Joan was. Just as, I'm sure, she did with Joan. Sometimes stories about the children would come up. One day Joan was in a bad mood and made the boy sit on a stool and remain there. Nancy was proud of the fact that she'd persuaded Joan to let the boy get down off the stool. There were also a few inklings of her drinking, but I never saw her drunk.

When she married Mr. Steele she was very happy. Whenever I'd go to New York, we'd have lunch at "21" and she wore a big hat. Everybody stared. She always had a certain table on the second floor, on a corner so that everyone who walked by would see Joan. And she loved that attention.

In 1976, I was in New York to attend a fund-raising cocktail party for the Thalians being given by Marty Kimmel, a wealthy New Yorker—who was once married to Gloria DeHaven—in his penthouse apartment. I called Joan and invited her.

She arrived, wearing a beautiful black taffeta dress, her hair done up and looking great except for her eyelashes. She wore rather thick ones, and obviously because she couldn't really see very well anymore without glasses, she had put them on above her own.

I happened to greet her at the door. Before she had a chance to say hello to anyone, I told her I wanted to show her something in the bedroom.

As soon as the door was closed behind us, I said to Joan, "I know you won't mind my saying this, but let me just fix your eyelashes because . . ."

I put the adhesive on, glued her own up to them, and then rebrushed them with mascara. She thanked me.

We went back into the living room. She looked terrific. She posed for pictures with all the press and couldn't have been more charming.

She was drinking quite a bit in those days—Russian vodka so you couldn't smell it—but she never was out of hand. At least not in public. Whether she was at home, I don't know. I too, have gotten drunk at home—by myself—but never in public.

Several months later when I was in New York again, I called Joan and asked if we could meet for lunch or dinner. She didn't want to go out.

"How are you feeling?" I asked, concerned.

"I'm fine," she said, "just tired."

"Then why don't I come over and visit you?" I suggested.

"Oh, thank you, Debbie, but I'm not seeing anybody. We can talk on the phone." Like Mary Pickford on the speaker box. She didn't like the way she looked. Her hair was thinning and she'd lost weight. She was moving to a smaller apartment and giving her clothes away.

"But, Joan," I said, "why would you give up your beautiful apartment?" She always had a huge home, never a little house. Huge rooms all white. Guests could never wear their shoes, we had to take them off. Everything had to be clean, clean, clean. She was a maniac about clean. She and Howard Hughes would have made quite a pair.

"I just don't need very much anymore," she said quietly.

Three weeks later, Joan died in her sleep. The papers said it was a heart attack. I never bought that story. There were too many coincidental events leading up to it. Joan loved her two dogs more than anything in the world. Yet, shortly before her death, she gave them to friends.

I just feel she found some way to exit this life before she looked too bad, before she had to suffer the ravages of time. Decay, as Miss Hepburn says. Unlike Miss Hepburn, however, but like so many of us, Joan couldn't face it anymore.

After *Star Wars* Carrie now had a life quite apart from her mother and Debbie Reynolds. Her career took her all over the world, introducing her to many successful new people.

After a number of successful films, Carrie wrote a novel, her first book, loosely based on some of her own experiences. Titled *Postcards from the Edge*, it was on the national best-seller lists for fifteen weeks in 1987–88. She is a gifted writer and I was thrilled by and proud of her literary success.

Todd and I were never not close. Fortunately for all of us, he and his sister have always been close too. He once said to her, years after our problems had been patched up, "How come you had such a different childhood than me? We lived in the same house; went through the same things." "Because you weren't aware of anything," was her answer.

Of course that was true. Carrie was told about Harry and told not to tell Todd. Todd found out after I went to New York to do *Irene*. Then Harry would bring the women right into the house. Not just the masseuses and the pedicurists anymore. Young girls, not much older than Carrie and Tina, including, as Tina learned years later, a friend of hers.

Todd, who was then only fourteen, was shocked that Harry was so open about it. He also was concerned about keeping it from me. He didn't know that I knew. When I did finally tell him a few years later, he was relieved that he didn't have to keep the secret from me any longer.

Carrie's career gave us something in common. A couple of years after *Star Wars*, she was doing a film on location and having a problem with the director, which no one else was aware of. But the man was in the habit of verbally coming on with her. I had never had that problem on my films, but it's not unheard of.

Carrie called me about it one night. She found it very difficult to handle and it was affecting her work. She didn't ask me, but I decided to visit her. I spent five days. She didn't need any help with her part; she had that down. I looked after the trailer and picked up her clothes—anything, just to be around. The problem was the director's way of relating to her. It was subtle but very disturbing for her, besides being rude and disrespectful. It made it harder for her to get into the role and concentrate.

He and I had dinner one night. He behaved similarly with me—little suggestive hints. Debbie Reynolds was his girlfriend when he was growing up, he told me. And now he was directing Carrie, he added, suggesting that it would be even nicer if we all could be closer.

"What is it you want to do," I asked, "sleep with Tammy and her daughter?"

He thought that was a terrific idea; great fun.

I told him I thought he was a very fine director, and that's what he should do. He should concentrate on his wife and family and leave mine alone. I don't think I cured it. But my simply being there made him back off.

The cinematographer was an older man, who had done one of my films. I didn't tell him what was happening, but I did say that Carrie felt very much alone and that maybe he could look after her. Some of the men in the crew whom I had known started looking after her too. She felt the presence of other men more, and not just the director coming at her. And he did ease up. I saw that before I left.

Carrie finished the film within a week or so of my forty-sixth birthday. Bob Fallon, Lillian, Mother, Todd, and a few others celebrated it quietly at Bob's house. Mary cooked dinner. Carrie came after dinner. She asked me to come outside because she wanted to talk to me. In front of the house, she handed me some keys.

She was walking toward the driveway. "Just get in," she said. "It's my car, my new car."

"But you have a car," I said, referring to her Mercedes.

"Well, this is another one," she said. "Do you like it?"

It was a green Cadillac Seville.

"It's gorgeous," I said. "But green? You don't like green."

"No, Mother, but you do," she said opening the door for me. "Happy birthday."

It was more than thanking me.

"I love you, Mother."

To this day we have never talked about how difficult those times were when I felt I had lost my daughter.

CHAPTER 63

WHEN TODD TURNED NINETEEN, I sold the property in Palm Springs, got out from under that mortgage, and with the money left from it, I bought him a house in Benedict Canyon. Carrie had already bought a house for herself. I still owned the house at the beach although it was usually rented to pay the big mortgage. With everyone off on their own, I gave up the house in Beverly Hills. I couldn't really afford to keep the beach house, but I didn't want to sell it until I absolutely had to because prices in Malibu were beginning to skyrocket and I felt I could use that money in the future. A good chunk of my income was still paying off debt, but the day would come when I would be finished—if it didn't finish me first—and then I would get a place of my own.

The trouble with living in Malibu—when the house wasn't leased out—was that it was an hour and a half back and forth to town. Nights that I was seeing Bob, of course, I stayed with him. Mary would come up and prepare our dinner.

It was a very nice way to spend a quiet evening. After dinner we'd have coffee and drinks in the living room overlooking the city lights.

We had been going together more than four years when on one of those nights, the phone rang. Bob answered it.

Sitting within ten feet of him, I couldn't help but listen. His conversation was normal but yet like a sketch.

"Oh yes, well . . . no, that can't be. . . . Well, no, that, uh . . . I will . . . yes . . . well no, yes, yes . . . Uh-huh."

I could absolutely hear the other half of the conversation. "Oh, is Debbie there?"

"Well, yes." (No, I can't see you tonight.) "Well, no, uh, but that'll be fine. Yes, tomorrow I can manage."

I knew because it was so dumbly handled.

When he hung up, I looked at him.

"Business?" I asked.

"Oh, yes, yes. Business."

I thought about it for the next four days. That weekend he came down to the beach.

We were sitting out on the patio overlooking the ocean. I still hadn't been able to get that phone call out of my mind. It was time.

"I want you to answer a question," I started out carefully. "And if you lie, I'll know it and I'll never speak to you again. As long as I live. If you answer it honestly, we will remain friends."

He sat there looking at me, curiosity in his eyes.

"Wasn't that a girl who called the other night when we were having dinner at your house?"

He paused for a very long time. Finally he took a deep breath. "Yes," he said.

I paused too. I knew it and I didn't want to know it. That meant it was the end; and I didn't want it to be.

"Is she your lover?" I asked, adding, "If you lie, I'll find out, Bob."

He nodded. "Well, yes."

So. I was right; and I lose. "I see. All right. Well then, our arrangement is off," I said. "I will not be with you again."

"Well, that's not necessary, Debbie," he said. "I don't love her."

"I know. But you've been with her. You asked me not date others, and to just be with you. And said that you cared for me only. Now obviously you don't."

"But, Debbie," he interrupted.

"No, no. I don't like that feeling, Bob. I've had that before. I'm fine by myself. What I would really like to know is, where did I go wrong?"

"It has nothing to do with you," he said. "It's just my craving. If you want, I'll marry you tomorrow to prove to you that I do love you."

"No, I don't want you to feel you have to marry me. That won't make me feel better because that doesn't mean you will be faithful. I don't need that. It's best we finish it now."

And we did. That was the end for us. I never dated him again after that day, nor do I see him anymore. It's too bad lovers can't stay friends.

When he walked away that afternoon, I was sitting there staring out at the sun setting on the Pacific horizon. Down at the water's edge, a man and a woman, both gleaming with golden tans, their hair tousled by the wind, galloped along the beach, riding bareback on Palominos. So romantic. For somebody.

I felt like the horse that broke its leg. They put me out to pasture and just didn't shoot me. There was no way I was going to make any relationship work, it seemed.

The best thing, Debbie, I told myself, is you should forget about it.

I was loving to him and giving to him and he was to me. But obviously, again, I wasn't enough. So what was wrong with me? That was the question in the front of my face.

What is wrong with you, Debbie?

Obviously you haven't got enough. You're not enough woman for any man.

An inadequate woman? Are you?

What is wrong with you? What is the matter?

There must be someone somewhere.

As much as other people in my life might have disliked him, Bob was really very good for me. When I discovered how to be a good lover, I believed that would be enough for him. It was foolish of me to think that.

Had I been able to continue going with Bob, knowing he was involved with other women, we'd probably still be together. I'm a one-man woman. He was a man of many women. I had long before heard the rumors, and ignored them.

Bob came into my life at a very lonely time and was a good friend for many years. I had just wanted companionship. It's probably an impossible quest—you really want to meet a man who's going to love just you, as my father loved only my mother.

The worst part, after the breakup, was coming home from being on the road. Or rather, coming home to no home. Whenever I returned to Los Angeles, if the beach house was leased, I was left with no base. My things were in storage or with various friends.

I could have stayed with Todd or Carrie, I suppose. But I didn't want to. They had their own lives now, away from Mother. They were grown-up. Soon Todd would be married.

I could get a hotel room and sometimes I did—which was like coming home and being on the road at the same time. In my lowest moments, I felt that it was what I deserved: Nothing.

It came down to nights when I'd leave a restaurant, or a cocktail party, and have no place to go.

I was extremely angry and had incredible rage that after all the years of work and effort and caring, my life had come to this cold, empty place, where I felt as if I had been stripped of everything.

When I was really upset, I'd get in my car and just drive. I'd always done that when I had to get away. I'd drive through Beverly Hills or

Holmby or Bel Air or the Palisades or the Valley and look at the houses. Sometimes I'd even drive down Greenway, where the house had been completely remodeled twice over and surrounded by a high wall, so that really it no longer existed.

There was a very big, pink, two-story Mediterranean house on the street. I'd first met the owner when her housekeeper came down and introduced herself many years before.

"My lady is lonely," she said, "and your house seems so busy and happy. I just wondered if you could invite us down sometime."

I was very touched by the woman's compassion for her employer. In those days we always ran movies on the weekend. So I invited them. For two years they came almost every weekend.

One day, driving by the house—twelve or fifteen years must have passed—I decided to stop and pay a call.

All the shades were drawn over the windows. I knocked at the door. Another housekeeper answered it.

I went into the huge dark house, full of antiques, full of money; everything untouched.

"We keep all the shades down now," the housekeeper said. "You see, it's the end of our lives and we're just living them out," obviously referring to her employer.

In the solarium, a magnificent room surrounded by ferns and orchids and other exotic plants, the old woman sat in a rocking chair. She was now in her nineties. Next to her, in a wheelchair, sat her old housekeeper, a shawl covering her lap. Both legs had been amputated. They spent their days there, watching religious programs on television.

She was very happy to have a guest. She hadn't seen her two adopted children in more than five years. "Well, you know, I have millions," she said. "And it doesn't seem to be very much in the end."

Her life had turned to just waiting. When she asked me how I'd been, it was easy to say "Not too good." We were all lost souls at that moment.

I stayed the night in the guest bedroom. When my hostess learned that I really had no place to stay, she offered the apartment over her garage. I should have accepted it but I was too proud.

I was more comfortable alone; by myself and in my car. Sometimes I just parked on a quiet street and curled up in the backseat. I told no one, and when friends learned years later that I'd slept in my car, they were surprised. "But, Debbie, how could you?!" But it was easy. It felt so right for a woman who'd lost it all. It expressed most clearly the state of my life: desolate.

Everything felt impossible. I related to the women who live on the street with their shopping carts. I was making good money but it was still all going to the banks. Some nights I'd actually go to the house of friends—Bob and Margie Peterson—and knock on the door. Can I stay the night? I wouldn't do that with everybody. Just certain people I was sure wouldn't turn me down. The Petersons understood my pain.

It was like dying, but I wasn't a suicide case.

CHAPTER 64

I DID HAVE ONE MAINSTAY—a great one—through all this, and that was Bob O'Connell. Bob O'Connell was in wardrobe during *Irene* on Broadway. A huge man, six three, hands right for basketball; blue eyes; he looked like he could be a really rough guy. One day, backstage, I saw him going by with some clothes and I asked somebody who he was. He looked like a cop.

"That's O'Connell. He's wardrobe."

Most costumers don't look like ex-basketball jocks. But if you met O'Connell in a dark alley, he would have scared you.

However, he was a costumer, and a good one. He ironed and sewed, and adored show business. He dressed Nureyev and, it turned out, even sewed the ballet slippers.

When I took *Irene* on the road, and Janie Powell took over the role, he was dismissed from the company for some reason. He was stricken that he'd lost his job, so I hired him to go on the road with me. It was a lucky move for me. He became invaluable. He was like my right hand, and one of the most giving, loving people I'd ever known.

After my breakup with Bob Fallon, O'Connell was my savior, the light in my life. He was a homosexual, an enchantment; so wonderful, so devoted to me that I could see us in old age, in our wheelchairs together. He was the only reason my life wasn't completely lonely.

Being in his company was stabilizing for me. "It's okay," I could say to myself, "that it doesn't work out to date men. I will simply be creative and I have my dear friend. We'll go out together."

And we did. He loved the theater, the ballet, the movies. I wouldn't have a lonely life. I would have O'Connell. And he would have me.

We had great times together; and we were always together on the road. He would eat ice cream and pickled pigs' feet and I had my tacos. He had a little apartment in North Hollywood. He had a few friends, but I was his life.

He was an angel in my life. Ours was unlike a heterosexual relationship, of course. But, in a sense, I thought O'Connell's love was better. He was loyal. He was true. He was honest. He was real and he was my friend. I just adored him.

By the late 1970s, for the first time in almost ten years, I was beginning to put some money aside for my future. It wasn't *all* going out. I'd reached an age where I had to think of what I could do if I couldn't get show-business work. I knew I might always have to go out and earn an income.

The only thing I'd ever been educated and trained for was entertaining. I could teach; I could pass on what I had learned. The most sensible path to the future, therefore, would be a school. I looked for a building. The more I looked, the more I saw the possibilities of my project. A good building with clean facilities and professional space could double as rehearsal studios and classrooms for other teachers. One day I was taken to the Valley to the old North Hollywood post-office building. One story, built like a fortress with solid walls and floors and large spaces and a parking lot for forty cars, it was ideal. I bought it. DR Studios was in business, with my loyal pal Margie Duncan at the helm.

Rehearsal studios for dancers and actors are notoriously filthy and run-down operations. The one we used to rehearse *Irene* in New York was an eyesore; cold and shabby, with one dirty little bathroom to change in. It's degrading, and I wanted my studios to be different. A year later, DR Studios opened, completely renovated with beautiful bathrooms and shower stalls, large freshly painted and partitioned rehearsal studios, offices, as well as storage space for my memorabilia.

Now it was time for me to seriously look for a new home. I needed a base and I'd been without one for years. It had to be near the school.

There was a dream house right on Toluca Lake. It had first taken my fancy when I was fourteen, selling Girl Scout cookies on my bicycle. Since that time I'd driven by that house at least a thousand times, just to look at it.

It's an English house, designed by Paul Williams, one of Los Angeles's foremost residential architects; a large house, with room for all my antiques and collections as well as a pool and tennis courts. The price was almost a million. I went to look at it several times. My beach house, in the current market, was now also worth a million, which was why I was able to have two mortgages on it. But the truth was, there was no way I could afford the Toluca Lake house.

I was hungering for a place of my own. Better I should have a little house and money in the bank. Then I could also have some security.

I was driving around everywhere in the area—Studio City, Sherman Oaks, North Hollywood. I couldn't afford Beverly Hills, or Encino. I couldn't afford Toluca Lake. I started looking in areas below $200,000. A real-estate agent told me about a small two-bedroom house in a quiet neighborhood in North Hollywood.

Sitting on a corner lot, a one-story, brick, English-style bungalow with casement windows and gable roofs, it was charming. It was also tiny and dark and old. The bedrooms were minuscule, but I could make them into one. There was a fireplace in the living room and a lovely fenced-in backyard full of trees. There was a two-car garage and room to add a dressing room and guest room. It would need a lot of renovation to make room for me. But the price was right, and I bought it.

Despite the pressures and difficulties of remodeling a house while I was out of town working for weeks, I was energized by the prospect of having my own little place.

A few months later, when I was playing Spark's Golden Nugget in Reno, I went out one day antiquing, and bought some pieces for the new house. O'Connell went out and got a truck to pick up the furniture.

When he was loading the stuff into the truck, he hit his shoulder on a large armoire. When he got home he had a terrible ache. Instead of getting better with each day, it got worse. By the time we got to the Desert Inn in Las Vegas, the pain was so great that he had to sleep on the floor.

When I came back to Los Angeles, my pal Jerry Wunderlich, who was on location with a picture, let me stay at his house, which happened to be right near my studio in North Hollywood. O'Connell came to stay with me too. I sent him to my orthopedic doctor. They thought he had bursitis or arthritis and did all kind of testing for the next two weeks.

One day, a week after the tests were completed, O'Connell went off one morning to see the doctor for the results.

A couple hours later, the phone rang. It was the doctor.

"I have some very bad news about your friend O'Connell," he said. "He has cancer. Lung cancer. And he maybe has six months."

I sat down on the edge of my bed; the phone dropped out of my hand, I was so incredulous.

"Did you tell him?" I asked.

"Yes."

"What did he do?"

"He just stared at me."

"I can't believe you told him," I said.

"Well, he asked me. I believe in telling my patients the truth."

I thanked the doctor and hung up.

A few minutes later I heard a key in the front door. I went, and standing there, his big blue eyes just staring at me, wearing a blue sling around his arm, was O'Connell.

"I'm going to die," he said.

I'll never forget the sight of him in the doorway. It was so awful. And so, I said, "Well, at least you know."

"Why me?" he asked, his voice quaking. "Just when life is so beautiful."

We went into the living room where he sat in my lap; this enormous man, this huge boy; and we sobbed for hours.

He wanted to take chemotherapy. I begged him not to, but he had to try. He would comb his hair after a shower, and it would come out in big gobs. He'd look at me with those pained and innocent blue eyes.

"Well, you look so cute, Yul Brynner has nothing on you," I cracked, and O'Connell laughed.

Jerry came home from location and when I told him about O'Connell, he moved out of his house to a motel so that we could continue to stay there. We told O'Connell that Jerry had to go away again.

O'Connell's body began to deteriorate very quickly, getting weaker and weaker. I slept in the next room from him. At night he would moan in pain. I would go in and pour the morphine down his throat and rub his back until he could slip off a bit into some painless moment.

He couldn't go on the road, so I had to find a replacement for him. I knew he was in such pain, yet he never complained.

One day not long after he'd found out, I said to him, "O'Connell, do you want to go home?"

"Oh," he said, "no, no, I want to stay with you."

"Fine," I said, "then I will take care of you until you die."

"That is too hard for you, Debbie."

"No. You've been so wonderful. We'll just get through this. We will manage."

It was very hard. He could eat only oatmeal. Occasionally, I would be off for two or three weeks to work. We'd call each other every day.

When I came home, he'd have the bottle of wine chilled—although he couldn't drink anything—and we'd sit and talk about what happened. I'd have to tell him everything that went on—who did what, who missed their cue; who sang this; how the show went.

We went to the doctor in a van with O'Connell on a mattress. He would shuffle down, take his terrible chemotherapy, and then we'd go home where he'd throw up for hours. Then I'd give him his medicine so that he could sleep some more.

I had to go to Hawaii for several weeks to do a show for my dear Jimmy Nabors. I told O'Connell he was going too. The doctor said no, he couldn't.

"What do you care where he goes?" I said to the doctor. "He wants to go with me. And I'm not going to leave him."

We went on the plane. We carried him on a gurney and placed him in two seats. I had rented a home right on the water where I could nurse and watch over him.

He was having very high, raging temperatures. I would pour alcohol all over him and massage him lightly. By then he was becoming delirious, going in and out. Now he weighed about 115 pounds; 110, 105. The only thing that never got small were his feet.

Every morning, with his long, emaciated body leaning on me, I would shuffle him out to the deck so he could look at the water. My dream was that he would succumb looking at this wonderful view— from a private home with the waves rushing up to the beach.

A young boy named Frankie, who had been a very special friend but who became like his son, came just in the nick of time, having managed to scrape up enough money for his air fare. When I went to the theater, he would baby-sit until I came home. Frankie stayed with us the whole time. He never left.

O'Connell was from an Irish Catholic family in the Bronx. His father died when he was a young boy. He was very sensitive and never really felt comfortable with anyone who didn't understand his style of living. Of course, I did. Most show people do. That's part of our life. His older brother, Buddy, who looked like his twin, was a cop. I sent for him and their sister to come out for a week. By then I could use the help because it was becoming twenty-four-hour nursing. He was so sick, yet he just wanted to live so much. His will kept him alive—too long actually.

When the Nabors show was over, we got O'Connell back on the plane somehow and got home. Jerry moved out again. But death was closing in and neither the house nor I was equipped for it.

Finally I said, "O'Connell, we have to go to the hospital. Your body is so weakened now that you are going to pass on in a few days."

"All right, I'll go," he said.

We put him in the van and took him to Cedars. They put him on pain killers every three hours. Despite his terminal condition, they kept testing him. Finally I was outraged.

"You can't test him anymore. You can't move him anymore. That's it. You know he's dying; why do you have to keep giving him tests?"

"We don't want to kill his will to get better," one of them said.

"If he's going to die, that's what he has to know," I said, "to make his peace."

I was supposed to do a *Love Boat* episode around that time. I was getting ready to cancel because his death was lingering. The doctor suggested putting him on a morphine drip because the pain was so intense.

He couldn't speak anymore. It was very difficult just breathing. I would talk to him and sing songs from *Irene*. Tears would well up in his eyes, but he'd never close them. I had to close them. Frankie and I would take turns staying with him for two hours at a time.

O'Connell knew I was supposed to be leaving on a Thursday morning to do the *Love Boat*. He didn't know I had already alerted them about canceling. On the Wednesday night, he died. It was as if he'd decided it was time. The show must go on.

He wanted to be buried at sea so a friend rented a small plane for Frankie and me. We flew out toward Catalina and over a spot where the sunlight seemed to make a cross on the water, we emptied O'Connell's ashes into the wind. He was forty-eight years old.

His life was looking after people. Nothing gave him more pleasure than taking care of others. And he loved Show Business, especially the theater; oh, he loved the theater more than anything. He is never far from my thoughts, and his spirit, I believe, like Agnes's, is always around me.

CHAPTER 65

MY LITTLE HOUSE in North Hollywood took almost a year and a half to renovate. Jerry Wunderlich advised me in redesigning the entire place. I turned the two small bedrooms into a master, with walls covered in an antique chintz, and with a banquette for the king-size bed of white eyelet lace. On one wall I hung a large Georgian gilt-framed mirror over an eighteenth-century writing table, on which sits a large photograph (inscribed of course) of the heavenly Cary Grant in an antique silver frame. On the other side sits a wide shelf of photographs of all of us: Todd, Carrie, Mother, Daddy, Bill, the Karl children, the spouses and nephews and nieces, and me. I wanted it to be comfortable and yet elegant, with room for all the mementos of my life and my loves. The bedroom is also the office. The bed inevitably is the desk; that's the way I am.

Off the bedroom I added a large one-and-a-half-story closet/dressing/makeup room with three walls of double-level closets, a wall for my shoes, and an island counter with lots of storage space for small items like jewelry, scarves, stockings, makeup, and wigs.

We raised the ceiling in the living room and I built a family room, or second living room. We added a large alcove of eight small panels of leaded stained-glass windows, to hold the ornate cherrywood Steinway grand, one of the rare player grand pianos built by Mr. Steinway especially for Harold Lloyd.

It was the first house that I could actually call home in almost ten years. I had walls on which to hang the dozens of photographs inscribed to me by movie legends I've had the privilege to know.

And it was mine, all mine, this house with no mortgage; and big enough for me and me alone, if that was how things were going to be for the rest of my life.

No more would I leave a restaurant or a theater or someone's house at night with the gnawing feeling that I had no place to go. Now I could be alone, under my own roof, curled up in front of my own fireplace.

There were many nights like that after the loss of O'Connell, when I'd come back from the road wanting to be alone. Many a night I would sit up for hours in my living room with my bottle of wine, having removed my wig and my makeup, wrapped in a warm wool or terry-cloth jumpsuit, and amuse myself. Sometimes I'd clown—and *always* get laughs; sometimes I'd put on records and sing—or dance to them. Ooh, there were some wonderful routines. Sometimes I'd tell myself the sad stories that brought forth floods of tears. The dreams that Debbie never dreamed that didn't come true. I could sit there by myself on the floor of my own little house, and talk or laugh or sob for hours, or until I'd fall asleep—waking up in the morning not remembering how I'd ended up there. Many a night, a lonely night, I hoisted that bottle and tipped the wine into the crystal goblet and sipped it until there was no night left.

Harry often came to mind. I hadn't had a conversation with him in years. The last few times I'd seen him I'd always been purposefully calm. I'd never said to him, I hate you I'm angry I'll never forgive you. I never said any of that to his face. I said it to Lillian and other friends. Carrie and Todd heard it. Maybe my mother heard it. But never Harry.

What I mean is, it didn't go away. I was still racked by all of the unexpressed rage. Years had gone by, the debts were finally paid off and the fury was still there. I heard about him from time to time. His health was bad. He was in and out of the hospital a couple of times. I really didn't care. I just felt sorry for him. Pity is more like it. I hated him.

One night, sitting there, thinking about him, I decided it was time to call and make an appointment. To tell him.

He didn't sound surprised to hear from me, or happy or sad. Maybe he was drunk. I still couldn't tell.

We met at Trader Vic's, where, in the good times long ago, he and I would take the children for an early Sunday dinner. As I pulled into the restaurant driveway, I noticed a beige and maroon Rolls with the California license plate HK-1 parked in the number-one spot and protected by a velvet rope, definitely not the kind they use for hanging.

When the valet parking attendant took my car, I couldn't resist asking him if the man with the Rolls had tipped him.

"Oh, yes, ma'am," he said with enthusiasm.

"And let me guess," I said, as if I were fascinated, "how much. I'd guess . . . a twenty. . . ."

The parking attendant grinned broadly, his eyes sparkling, shaking his head.

"More?!"

"Uh-huh!" he nodded happily.

"Fifty?"

Without his answering, I knew.

A *fifty*! I thought to myself. A leased Rolls-Royce and a fifty-dollar tip! A man without a dime to his name.

Harry was waiting inside, impeccably dressed, of course. He had aged and his eyes seemed glazed and almost squinty behind his thick glasses. But he looked as if he had taken a lot of time to prepare for this meeting. I'm sure the barber had been there.

It was still the Harry who took it all and blew it all away. I don't remember how I started in. Once I'd decided I was going to do it, I had too many things I wanted to say.

I remember telling myself beforehand to look him straight in the face. I had to be able to tell him finally how much I hated him; how much I resented what he had done; how angry I was and how I would never forgive him.

I told him all that. And I wasn't calm. When I felt like it, I yelled at him.

I hate you; do you understand?!

"Do you understand how you really hurt my life? How I can't get over it? Why did you do that?"

He sat across the table and calmly looked at me.

"How you could allow it?!"

Very quietly, with no expression, he spoke. "I didn't mean it to happen," he said. "It was all out of my control."

"But *why*?! I want to know. I have to know why!"

"I don't have any answers why. I didn't do it on purpose. After all," he added, "it destroyed my life too."

"No, I got it—really got it!"

He very quietly changed the subject. He told me that he still loved me, and that I *loved him*!

"You're completely insane!"

"No, you're coming back to me, Debbie," he said. "I know we can still be happy. You're going to marry me again."

"Marry you?! I don't even like you. I don't respect you. I feel tremendous anger toward you."

"Well, you shouldn't feel that way. It will all pass."

"No. When I married you, I trusted you. I trusted my life and my children to you and you tried to destroy me. And in a way you have because I don't trust anybody anymore."

It was true, and to some degree, still is. I distrust. I'm always testing the water. I don't trust life in general. I always trusted Eddie until it ended. I always trusted Harry until I learned I couldn't. Now when it's looking good, I get very nervous. Because maybe there is an ending coming. Isn't that awful? It's also sad.

Again Harry mumbled, "Just come back to me. We'll be happy."

I looked at him, speechless. I realized there was no one home; no one really there to talk to.

When I left Trader Vic's that night, I didn't feel any better having told him off. I may have been even more frustrated, knowing that Harry didn't even know why or how any of it happened. I found myself wondering if it was his gambling that had affected our life; if perhaps he'd felt so guilty about using my money that he was unable to perform with me. It will always be a mystery to me.

So I was left with the same feelings. My heart was broken.

It was like a excruciating headache or a back pain that lingered for life. I could still work but once the show was over, it was back there again.

One night in Vegas, I went over to another hotel to visit an old friend who was performing there. This was a woman I'd known since the days I was married to Eddie; a star, and still a very successful one. She was eating strawberries and I was having a glass of wine.

I can't remember what I was saying, but she stopped and said to me, "You're so angry, Debbie," as if there were something wrong with that.

"Yes, I am."

"You've gone through all these problems and yes, maybe they were terrible for you, but it's over; it's past. And yet you still have all that anger."

"Yes, you're right," I said. I stood up. "I am angry. So angry that I'm going to leave now because I don't want to disturb your strawberries." And I left.

She was right. I was angry and full of hostility. Since the two of us been working our asses off every night, and since we'd known each other forever, I felt I could go back and say hello. I hadn't known, when I walked in, that I was going to be judged.

I went back to my apartment that night feeling even more alienated by the realization that even an old friend didn't want to talk to me.

I remembered the night in Chasen's years and years before, in the powder room, when she was throwing up because she was pregnant and had just realized it. She didn't want to have the child; she didn't want it to interfere with her life. We talked for quite a while about it. I told her how wonderful it would be for her; how much joy the children had brought to my life. She had the baby, and went on with her life.

I admired her and still admire her. I admired the fact that she'd survived, and her tenacity. I admired the fact that she hadn't remarried a zillion times; that she could walk in and walk out of relationships. I'd look at her and wonder how she did it, since I never could.

The only thing I knew how to do was work. In 1983 I went back to Broadway to replace Raquel Welch in the musical *Woman of the Year*. Again Lillian worked with me on the role, and Rudy Render, who'd retired from the business ten years before, came to New York to coach me with the songs. The night I opened, the New York newspapers went on strike for only the second or third time in their history. That closed the school. One of the highlights of being in New York with the show, however, was the fact that Carrie was also appearing on Broadway in *Agnes of God*, and was brilliant in her role.

Later that same year I went to Reno to tape a television special called *Classic Cars and Classic Stars*, featuring the world's largest antique-car collection. The evening was sponsored by Chrysler and was a tribute to Mr. Bill Harrah of Harrah's Hotels. Bill Cosby and I were the emcees. The stars included Sammy Davis, Suzanne Somers, Jimmy Nabors, and many others.

We started rehearsals at eight in the morning and by the time we finished shooting the show it was midnight. That same night, after the show, there was a big cocktail party. Everyone was going to be there including the governor of Nevada and the heads of Time-Life and Chrysler. I was so tired at the end of the taping that I decided to go back to my suite. But Rip Taylor and Bob Peterson, who is president of *Hot Rod* Magazine, insisted I join them. So I put myself together, and swollen ankles and all, I did.

As soon as we walked into the party we were asked to pose for photographers with the various dignitaries. A good-looking man with beautiful blue eyes asked if he could take a picture of me with his friends. Naturally I obliged and when he was finished, I walked on to our table. My feet were killing me!

Rip ordered some wine and our table was soon filled with friends. A few minutes later I heard my name and a request to dance. I turned around with "no" on my lips and saw that it was "the beautiful blue eyes" who had taken my picture. He also had a handsome face and gray hair. All favorites of mine. So the no turned into a yes.

We had our dance and then he joined our table, where everyone sat and talked into the early-morning hours. At the end of the evening, we exchanged phone numbers, and we parted. Back in my room, I looked at his card. "What was his name?" Richard Hamlett. "Like Shakespeare," I remembered him saying.

Our lives parted. I went back to Los Angeles and he went back to his home in Roanoke, Virginia, where he was a real-estate developer, and I forgot about the moment. There had been too many of those moments that didn't work out, so, as a rule, I don't think about what I can't have.

About three months later, the phone rang at home one day and a southern man's voice asked if Debbie was there. Richard Hamlett calling. At first I couldn't remember. Then the blue eyes and gray hair came into my mind's focus. Something about hearing from him make me feel good. We talked and made a date in Las Vegas, where I would be going to a physical-fitness convention to publicize my exercise video, *Do It Debbie's Way.*

I'd rarely dated a man I didn't know, a stranger really, so I was nervous. What would he really be like? Still the same old worry?

We arranged to meet at the Desert Inn in the front lobby and then go on to dinner. I was on time that night—which is unusual for me. I waited by the bell desk where I knew the head man. It was a busy night. Many women and men were meeting there. I noticed that Mike, the head bellman, kept shaking his head and looking my way, as he spoke to various men. Fifteen minutes later, I saw Richard pass through the lobby and go right into the bar. A minute later, he came out of the bar, looking around. Then he saw me and came over to the desk.

"Why are you standing here?" he asked before he said hello.

"Why not?" I answered.

"Well, for one thing, this is where all the hookers stand for their nightly pickups."

Now I knew why Mike had kept shaking his head. Just think of the money he could have made. A night with Tammy.

Richard and I had a laugh about that and went in to dinner. From the start, it was very comfortable. He was very entertaining and seemed to like me. I didn't feel, as I often have with a new man, that I had to carry on all the conversation.

Then, over dessert, he asked me to marry him! I was astounded. I liked him, but I hardly knew him.

"Why do you want to marry me? You don't even know me."

"Yes, I do," he replied. "You see, Debbie, I have an advantage over you. I've known all about you all my life through the press and the movies. I have loved you since *Tammy*. I just never thought I'd get a chance to meet you. But now that I have, I want to marry you."

I had heard everything. Now I knew I'd met a full-blown nut. Marriage?! First date?! After all my problems with me, marriage was the last thing I wanted to hear about.

I told him to forget about it. I said we could see other and maybe grow as friends, travel, be companions.

He said, "No!" He wasn't "that kind of man." He was a "country boy"! I thought, oh, brother.

We made a date for the next night. It worked again. We had a lovely time. "Maybe this one is different," I remember thinking. "Bull! Don't ever believe that," another voice said. "Oh, go ahead, Debbie, try," said Peter Pan.

So I did try. And I fell in love with a southern boy from Virginia.

We dated for three months after that, and talked on the phone almost every day. He kept asking me to marry him. Finally one day, I called him and said: "Yes."

"Yes what?" he asked dumbly. He'd forgotten!

"Yes, I'll marry you," I said.

"Oh, my God, that!" Richard shouted over the phone.

"Yes, that."

"Well, you bet." Yes. Sure. Okay. Yeah. I had shocked the hell out of him.

It was silly for me to think that I was destined to be alone the rest of my life. If you don't take a chance, you won't have much of one. But if I didn't overcome my fear of trusting, that's what I was facing.

Once we'd decided to marry, there were a lot of decisions to make. He lived on one side of the continent, and I on the other. Fortunately, I traveled so much, we figured in the beginning we could balance our time between the East Coast and the West Coast. Richard had always wanted to live in Los Angeles. Now he had a reason to make that move.

I was scheduled to perform on a Caribbean cruise in early May of 1984. Richard and I decided that was when we should be married. My friends Nancy and Joe Kanter gave us a small wedding at their lovely home in Florida. The minister performed the ceremony outside on the patio overlooking the water. Todd gave me away and Kelly Muldoon was my maid of honor. My mother and brother flew in for the ceremony as well as my friend Sandy Avchen.

So again, i thought, breathe deeply. Let life in. Don't be afraid! He loves you! I felt like the train going up the hill in the children's story: "I think I can, I think I can, I think I can; I *know* I can!"

Richard and I survived the ceremony. We are now happily married and the best of friends. Of course we have not been without our share of problems. For one thing, Richard, at forty-seven, when many people are settling in, dramatically changed his life by marrying me. He'd been married once before but had never been a father. Suddenly he was married to this woman who lives on the other side of the continent, who is working on the road ten months out of the year, and who has grown children. He joined the Marines when he married Tammy. But he's earned his stripes and I'm proud of him. He is brave, loyal, and loving. We are so much alike in so many ways that it is as if we had been brother and sister in another life.

CHAPTER **66**

CARRIE GOT MARRIED that same year to Paul Simon. They had known each other for years, so it didn't surprise me when Paul very nicely—out of respect for my sense of tradition—asked me for her hand in marriage. I was pleased. I knew they loved each other and wanted to be together. I suppose one should always have doubts about the potential of a marriage of two performers. But it was none of my business. I could see how much they loved each other.

The amazing coincidence that Carrie was marrying a good Jewish boy who was also one of the most popular recording stars in America didn't escape my notice. However, I felt the similarities between Paul and Carrie's father began and ended there.

Daddy also got sick that year. It came on gradually. He was getting on in years—he was seventy-eight—and his body was giving out at times.

Although I have not often mentioned them during much of this story, my mother and father, and my brother and I, have never been far from each other, at least in our thoughts. The close-knit family that we were in Burbank has survived despite the extravagant life I never intended to live. My children grew up, much of their time, in the company of Gramma, Grandpa, and Uncle Bill. The family has been a profound stabilizing force for Carrie and Todd. Perhaps because of that, Todd and Carrie are and have always been very close. Todd is very much like his grandfather. His interests in life, his love of all things mechanical, of working with his hands, comes from my father. Carrie inherited a lot of her strength from her grandmother. And Uncle Bill was always there, especially when we needed him.

After he retired from the railroad, Daddy worked for Harry for a number of years, supervising the construction and maintenance of the shoe stores. Finally he and Mother sold the house in Burbank and retired to Palm Springs.

Both Mother and Daddy were always supportive but they had their own life. I rarely ever had a personal conversation with my father. He was never one to just talk, like his daughter, Sis. So I was surprised when I called them one day and my father said, "It's over; nothing matters anymore."

I was taken aback. "What do you mean, Daddy?"

"It's over," he said. "My life is over."

It was so unlike him to put anything in such emotional terms. It was the closest he could get to distraught, and it upset me very much because I knew a lot was going wrong. He'd started to lose his memory. It was difficult for him to follow the baseball and football games. It was impossible for him to play his game of solitaire. He couldn't read his Louis L'Amour novels. Daddy had little patience for the whole distressing aging experience, and for the first time in his life, he was absolutely helpless and humiliated too.

He had never been ill. He'd lived a simple, uncomplicated life. To his way of thinking, he was happy.

He never had to run the ship. Mother did that. She was his captain. She wrote the checks and did the worrying. Daddy didn't like problems. He didn't like arguments. He didn't want them, so he ignored them. He never wanted to be rich. He had no lofty goals or big aims. He never wanted to accomplish anything materialistic except to take care of his family as best he could.

Bill's very much like my father—shy, reclusive, charming—yet stubborn like me, and a sweet man. I love him!

Because I became successful and Bill also became accomplished in his work, Daddy was exposed to a different life. He went with me on trips to England, to Acapulco, and traveled around the world. He was proud of my work but rarely saw it. To him, watching me perform was all the same thing. It was just Sis doing what she always did.

My father had an easier life because of my mother. Mother has much more ambition, much more drive. All of the women in our family are stronger than the men, in that sense. When I'm angry, I try to back off and think a little, like my father. My nature is to finish the argument right then and there. Yet I think it's far better to wait and let everybody cool off, then reapproach the problem. I try very hard to do that.

Mother and I got along better before I married because I did whatever she told me to do. I had no problem with that. As my life became more complicated—marriage, children, career, having to listen to others with more experience with complex situations—I think Mother felt left out at times. She had been the decision maker at home and then the role was suddenly taken away from her. It must have been a little like losing a part of herself.

Mother's manner is direct. She can be outspoken. So can I, however, and my daughter has the same difficulty with my being outspoken as I do with Mother's. We say, "Oh, my goodness, you've cut your hair," rather than saying something nice about the haircut first. I've often wondered why I've done that as a mother. Sometimes I think it's because I had no control over the decision. It's partly never wanting to let go. It's hard for a mother to loosen her arms.

By 1986, my father's condition had deteriorated to the point that he needed around-the-clock care. Everything had broken down, including his spirit. Mother couldn't take care of him anymore. She wasn't well herself. She decided to put him in a nursing home. I wanted to bring him up to Los Angeles, turn my family room into a bedroom for him, and bring the nurses in to take care of him. No. Mother didn't want to come to Los Angeles. She was still captain of the ship. She wanted to put Daddy into a nursing home. It was a difficult decision for her.

In April, just a few weeks after my fifty-fourth birthday, Daddy died.

I don't like funerals and I don't go. But naturally I went for my father. Instead of a religious service, we played the sounds of a major-league baseball game on a cassette tape; batter up, you're out! At the burial, we stood around the grave and Carrie read a poem she had written for eulogy.

Recipe for Ray

take one small stubborn Texan
preferably lean
add a big busted gal from
       thereabouts
that answers to Maxene
fold in some railroad work,
       a depression
two kids and a move to L.A.
beat in a bunch of baseball
(and) you've begun your recipe
       for Ray

take your small stubborn
       Texan
and gently remove all his
       hair

build him a shop
outside any house he's got
and stick a radio there
sift in some well chosen
            words
a kind heart beneath
            leathery skin
stir in some peanuts and
            coke
a tendency to smoke
sprinkle in some "Dear Lord
            Help us jump in." [Daddy's version of Grace]
add a dash of the sweetest
            smile
some Palm Springs and a
            little Ouray
fold in a favorite chair
the funny walk that gets him there
add "and the farmer hauled
            another load of hay": [Daddy's phrase for B.S.]

This recipe for Ray
can be cooked up anytime
it simmers in our hearts
it fills us up real fine.

The loss was greatest for Mother because they shared sixty years of her life. It wasn't long before she couldn't bear to be alone in the house in Palm Springs. Last year she moved into a house right across the street from mine, where both my brother and I are easily accessible.

My mother has given me great lessons in strength. She's never down, even when she's been ill and very near death. She believes in life, hangs on to it, and fights her way through.

CHAPTER 67

LIFE TODAY, compared to ten years ago, is better for me.
I know I have a ways to go. But I have a husband who is also a friend,
and I love him. Marriage does make my life more complicated because
for years now, my work has commanded all my time. But after work, I
used to be lonely. Now I have someone to share my visions and plans
with.

There are many days when I like to be totally alone and quiet. Brash
and forward and off-the-wall as I can be in public, I can be equally
subdued at home. Richard is the same. We can have deep lapses of
conversation for hours and not even know we haven't talked. I'm certain
that either I was his sister, or he was mine, or I was his brother, or he
was mine, in another incarnation. Because we're much more comfortable with each other than two people usually are who've lived two distinct kind of lives and have known each other only a few years. It's like
we've known each other forever.

I still have bad moments when I think of Harry Karl, although they
don't come as frequently as they did ten years ago. Harry died in 1985.
The last time I saw him was when Todd got married in 1981. Harry was
upset that he wasn't seated at the bride and groom's table, because he
considered himself Todd's "real" father. It was true enough, in that
Todd did love Harry and mourned him when he died. He still visits his
grave and leaves a couple of golfballs instead of flowers.

Tina had many years of struggling with her life. She was so devastated by her father's death, she had to be hospitalized. Now she truly
had lost him. I was her only connection to a family. However, after all
of her pain and struggle to find recognition and love, a few years ago
Tina met and married a fine man. He is also a man with a great sense
of humor, which has helped Tina see more of the light side of exis-
tence. With him, she has finally achieved a lovely life. I shall always
remain an anchor and adviser to her, but she has won the battle against

herself, and I am proud of her growth. She is a caring and loving wife with a marvelous, understanding husband.

No one ever told me that raising children was going to be easy. But then no one ever said that sometimes it was going to be impossible either. As a young person I was simply not prepared for the emotional turmoil that seems to be inherent in assisting our babies' growth. I nurtured, pampered, spoiled, adored, and made mistakes. I love my children more than life itself. During their early years, after I divorced Eddie and married Harry, we had the perfect happy life. When the calm turned to chaos, Carrie took a direct hit and fell to her knees emotionally. But for the past ten years, with professional help, she has struggled to make peace in her mind, so that her heart could heal. I wasn't as wise. She has grown intellectually and emotionally and today she is a wise, giving, deeply loving daughter and friend. The chasm that existed between us is now, thankfully, a meadowland of conversation and love.

Todd is our guardian angel, always there for those he loves. It was very difficult for Todd to lose the father he loved, Harry, and not to have pride in the one who's living. Like his sister, he too suffered through the failed marriage and the loss of our home. Yet his shining love fills everyone who meets him. He is a special spirit and a special man. When I look at him, my heart lifts and I can't help but smile and feel good. I know he will always be there for his sister Carrie because he certainly loves and understands her. He now also has a special love in his life, Rene, a wonderful, beautiful woman, who has brightened all our lives by her presence.

I can't say I didn't learn something from Harry Karl. I never sign anything without reading it twice. Our marriage taught me how to take charge of my business and my professional life. I learned how to produce and keep myself working. I learned how to book myself and negotiate deals.

My life is, essentially, activity. I like having many projects going on at all times. Three is manageable, five is chaos, but I love to work. I love being around creative, funny people and I would never want to give that up.

There are certain people who've remained very much in my life for the past thirty or forty years, despite all the changes and moving around. More than friends, they're like family. Jerry Wunderlich is one. Margie Duncan is another. Margie's divorce was as traumatic as mine was from Eddie. When she was on her own again, with children to support, she moved back to California and came to work for me, first as a stand-in, then as an assistant, now as the woman who manages my studio and the logistics of my professional life. Rudy Render retired from show business about fifteen years ago, and now teaches. I still consult him for musical guidance and we still spend every Christmas Eve together. Phyllis Berkett has been a steady friend since we met in Florida in 1957. Sandy Avchen and I met at our daughters' Girl Scout meeting. She and her husband, Tex, are my closest friends.

There's also Mary Douglas French, my housekeeper, who's looked after my house, my children, and my well-being for almost thirty years while raising her own family and grandchildren, and running her own house. There's the gang from the Thalians: such as Bob and Margie Peterson; Jack Haley, Jr., and Ruta Lee, who has even more energy than I have and keeps the Thalians working.

Clearly, I am a lucky woman to have had so many to care and be cared about. I am also a lucky woman to have been able to keep myself in business all these years. Besides my regular stints in Tahoe, Reno, Vegas, Atlantic City, I've toured the United States playing clubs, concerts, and state fairs.

In the summer of 1987, I played a night at the Universal Amphitheatre here in Los Angeles. The biggest pop and rock stars from Sinatra to Sting play the Amphitheatre during the summer season. For a performer, it's always a big thing to come back home. I'd done *Annie Get Your Gun* and *Irene*, but I hadn't done an act or a concert appearance in Los Angeles since the mid-1960s. It was a chance and a challenge.

It was a fantastic night for me as a performer. In the past thirty-five years, I've played to great audiences throughout America and halfway across the world, from England to Australia. But at the Amphitheatre, less than half a mile from where Mary Frances began her career on the Warners lot, I'd come full circle and the audience opened its arms to me. I was in the right place, doing what I should be doing, and I loved being there. I loved that audience as much as I loved it the first time Grandpa Harman laughed when I did a pratfall on the front porch of the house in El Paso. Katharine Hepburn has said that as performer, you sell it as long as the world buys it. I am the same. No matter what, I want to go on as long as the people want me. That is my life.

INDEX